The Rejuvenation of Political Economy

T0313141

This book provides the basic knowledge of Japanese contributions in political economy and the ongoing research agenda, such as the pursuit of theoretical consistency in Marxian economics by Uno School; the concept of 'civil society' as a criterion of existing socio-economic structure; a mathematical reconstruction of Marxian theory; and an analysis of environmental pollution. The new generation of Japanese political economists in collaboration with their overseas counterparts have produced new insights into political economy and into the newly emerging structure of the world economy.

The book provides useful insights into international capitalism and how past patterns of uneven development are now changing; the role of international finance in affecting both national and international growth and employment patterns; an analysis of recent growth patterns in Asia; and the specific issue emerging within the Asian region and the implications for economics, social change and geopolitics.

Nobuharu Yokokawa is Professor of Economics at Musashi University, Tokyo, Japan. He was educated at Shiga University (BA), the University of Tokyo (MSc) and Cambridge University (PhD). He co-edited *Capitalism in Evolution* (2001) and *Crises of Global Economies and the Future of Capitalism: Reviving Marxian Crisis Theory* (2012). Since 2007, he has been editor of the *Uno Theory Newsletter*. He is Chairman of the Japan Society of Political Economy (JSPE) Committee for International Communication and Exchange.

Kiichiro Yagi is President of Setsunan University, Osaka, Japan. He was educated at the University of Tokyo and Nagoya University. He received his PhD from Kyoto University. He taught political economy and history of economics at Kyoto University for a quarter of a century. Since the mid-1990s, he has tried to integrate the ideas of evolutionary and institutional economics with classical political economy, including Marxian economics. He is Chief Representative of the JSPE.

Hiroyasu Uemura is Professor of Economics at Yokohama National University, Japan. He was educated at Hitotsubashi University. He is a contributor to Japanese *régulation* theory. He has published numerous books and articles in the field of institutional economics and macroeconomic analysis.

Richard Westra is Designated Professor in the Graduate School of Law at Nagoya University, Japan. He received his PhD from Queen's University, Canada. He has authored and edited thirteen books. His work has been published in numerous international peer-reviewed academic journals.

Routledge Frontiers of Political Economy

For a complete list of titles in this series please visit www.routledge.com/books/series/SE0345

The Rejuvenation of Political Economy

Edited by Nobuharu Yokokawa, Kiichiro Yagi, Hiroyasu Uemura and Richard Westra

Routledge
Taylor & Francis Group

LONDON AND NEW YORK

First published 2016 by Routledge

2 Park Square, Milton Park, Abingdon, Oxfordshire OX14 4RN
711 Third Avenue, New York, NY 10017

Routledge is an imprint of the Taylor & Francis Group, an informa business

First issued in paperback 2018

British Library Cataloguing in Publication Data
A catalogue record for this book is available from the British Library

Library of Congress Cataloging-in-Publication Data
Names: Yokokawa, Nobuharu, 1950– editor.
Title: The rejuvenation of political economy / edited by Nobuharu Yokokawa, Kiichiro Yagi, Hiroyasu Uemura and Richard Westra.
Description: Abingdon, Oxon ; New York, NY : Routledge, 2016. | Series: Routledge frontiers of political economy ; 207
Identifiers: LCCN 2015044134 | ISBN 9781138832626 (hardback) | ISBN 9781315621920 (ebook)
Subjects: LCSH: Economics—Japan—History. | Economics—Political aspects—Japan—History.
Classification: LCC HB126.J3 R45 2016 | DDC 330.952—dc23
LC record available at http://lccn.loc.gov/2015044134

ISBN: 978-1-138-83262-6 (hbk)
ISBN: 978-1-138-31798-7 (pbk)

Typeset in Galliard
by Apex CoVantage, LLC

Contents

Figures

Tables

Contributors

Robert Boyer is a Fellow at the Institut des Amériques, Paris. His website is http://robertboyer.org. He is one of the editors of *Revue de la Régulation*.

Jayati Ghosh is Professor of Economics at the Centre for Economic Studies and Planning, School of Social Sciences, Jawaharlal Nehru University, New Delhi. She received the NordSud Prize for Social Sciences 2010 from the Fondazione Pescarabruzzo, Italy, and was awarded the ILO Decent Work Research Prize for 2010.

Kenichi Haga is Specially Appointed Professor at Saitama Gakuen University, Japan, and Professor Emeritus at Niigata University, Japan.

Yuji Harada is Associate Professor at Fukuyama City University, Hiroshima, Japan.

Jan Kregel is Director of Research at the Levy Institute and head of its Monetary Policy and Financial Structure program. He also holds the position of professor of development finance at Tallinn University of Technology. In 2010, he was awarded the prestigious Veblen-Commons Award by the Association for Evolutionary Economics for his many contributions to the economics field.

Seiichi Nagashima is Emeritus Professor, Tokyo Keizai University, Japan. He is one of the leaders of the Society for Research of Monopoly in Japan.

Michiaki Obata is Professor of Economics at University of Tokyo, Japan.

Hiroshi Onishi is Professor of Economics at Keio University, Tokyo, Japan. He is vice-chairman of the World Association for Political Economy.

Robert Rowthorn is Emeritus Professor of Economics and Fellow of King's College, Cambridge. He has been a consultant on these topics for a variety of bodies, including the International Monetary Fund, the UN Commission on Trade and Development, the International Labour Organisation and the British government.

Yoshikazu Sato is Professor of Economics at Hosei University, Japan. He taught political economy based on Okishian Economics for more than thirty years at

Toyama University and Hosei University. He is a member of the executive board of the JSPE.

Yoshinori Shiozawa is Emeritus Professor of Osaka City University. He is one of the founding members of the Japan Association for Evolutionary Economics and its second president.

Hiroyasu Uemura is Professor of Economics at Yokohama National University, Japan. He is a contributor to Japanese *régulation* theory. He has published numerous books and articles in the field of institutional economics and macroeconomic analysis.

Richard Westra is Designated Professor in the Graduate School of Law at Nagoya University, Japan. He received his PhD from Queen's University, Canada. He has authored and edited 13 books. His work has been published in numerous international peer-reviewed academic journals.

Kiichiro Yagi is President of Setsunan University, Osaka, Japan. He was educated at the University of Tokyo and Nagoya University. He received his PhD from Kyoto University. He taught political economy and history of economics at Kyoto University for a quarter of a century. Since the mid-1990s, he has tried to integrate the ideas of evolutionary and institutional economics with classical political economy, including Marxian economics. He is Chief Representative of the JSPE.

Toshio Yamada is Emeritus Professor at Nagoya University, Japan.

Nobuharu Yokokawa is Professor of Economics at Musashi University, Tokyo, Japan. He was educated at Shiga University (BA), the University of Tokyo (MSc) and Cambridge University (PhD). He co-edited *Capitalism in Evolution* (2001) and *Crises of Global Economies and the Future of Capitalism: Reviving Marxian Crisis Theory* (2012). Since 2007, he has been editor of the *Uno Theory Newsletter*. He is Chairman of the JSPE Committee for International Communication and Exchange.

Fumikazu Yoshida is a Professor of Economics at Aichi Gakuin University, Nagoya, Japan, and Emeritus Professor of Hokkaido University, Sapporo, Japan.

Introduction

Kiichiro Yagi and Nobuharu Yokokawa

Brief history of Japanese political economy

Since the early years of the last century, Japan has nourished a rich tradition of political economy, in which Marxian economics occupies the central position. The Japan Society of Political Economy (JSPE), as the recognized forum for heterodox economics researchers, has made its mission the rejuvenation of critical economic thinking in Japan. Such thinking is necessary to respond to the radically altered economic situation in Japan and the world over.

The first part of this volume introduces contributions from Japan to this tradition in the post 1945 period.

The second part of the volume extends the politico-economic perspective to the transformations of contemporary global economy.

In Japan the translation of Marx's *Capital* was completed as early as 1924. By the end of the 1920s, Hilferding's *Finance Capital*, Luxemburg's *Accumulation of Capital*, and Lenin's *Imperialism* were all made available in Japanese. Together with classical political economy literature by Adam Smith, David Ricardo, and J. S. Mill, all the foregoing were in the list of the "must reads" of ardent economics students at the time. Marxian economists, divided in the two camps of *Koza-ha* and *Rono-ha*, continued a major debate on the nature of Japanese capitalism up to years when the military regime banned Marxism. From that point, critical study of Japanese capitalism became impossible. Germaine A. Hoston dedicated a whole book (*Marxism and the Crisis of Development on Prewar Japan*, Princeton University Press, 1987) to this debate. The debate is now regarded as a pioneering contribution to the understanding of capitalism in late industrialized nations.

In the postwar democratization, Marxian economics revived after a decade of suppression. The controversy over Japanese capitalism was resumed in the new circumstances. The democratization of Japanese society was performed on the orders of the General Headquarters of the allied forces, partially against the will of conservative interests. The nature and the limit of democratization, and the land reform in particular, were intensely discussed among Marxian economists. By the mid-1950s, after the waning of the once dominant view that stressed the survival of semi-feudal remnants in the country, Marxian economic theory in Japan confronted the beginning of rapid industrialization in which surplus labor in rural villages functioned as a reservoir of labor power for urban industrial growth. The postwar rapid industrialization occurred under the framework of Japan's subordination to the United States (US) hegemonic strategy over the Asia-Pacific hemisphere. Whether postwar Japanese capitalism would develop into an independent imperialism or remain a subordinate capitalism under the U.S. hegemony was the issue that divided Marxian economists in Japan in the 1950s and 1960s.

In the early 1970s, Japan was accepted as a leading nation of the capitalist world system. Japanese firms extended their production and trade networks across the globe. The competitive strength of Japanese manufacturing exports caused successive trade conflicts with the US. When the Japanese economy overcame two oil shocks by the collaborative efforts of capital and labor, it reached the peak of its prosperity. Japanese postwar prosperity was particularly remarkable because it continued into the 1980s even as growth slowed in the United States and Western Europe. When the Japanese economy entered into stagnation after the burst of its asset bubble in 1991, the economic system that had supported the high growth of the Japanese economy revealed its vulnerability in the new environment of globalization and the IT revolution. Japanese economists have since been divided between neoliberal supporters of deregulation policies and those who seek to emplace a new coordination that guarantees welfare and decent work for the population. In the light of such an impressive and interesting historical development of Japanese capitalism, researchers of critical political economy and heterodox economists in Japan are re-examining their views and their approaches incessantly.

Rejuvenation of political economy

The first part of the book shows that the tradition of political economy in Japan has never been, nor is currently, monolithic. In both the past and the present, the tradition of critical political economy in Japan has been packed with exciting controversy and efforts at renewal. Over the last few decades, neoclassical hegemony in academia has become dominant all over the world. Today to rebuild critical political economics is the most important agenda for all non-neoclassical economics, including radical economics, structural macroeconomics, French *régulation* theory, Minskian financial analysis, analytical Marxism, and evolutionary economics. In Japan, Marxian economists have a long academic tradition of productive discussion with left Keynesians and post-Keynesians. The emergence of neo-Ricardian economics made them realize the common interests in the broad streams of classical political economy. This volume contributes to the rejuvenation of political economy in Japan and the world by building on the pluralism that enables creative collaboration across these different streams.

The second part of the volume focuses on the contemporary transformation of national economies and their global interdependence. Chapters in that part of the book consider not only the fate of Japanese capitalism but also emerging

Asian capitalisms and the world economic consequences of the rise of the Asian region. In addition to contributions by the Japanese members of the JSPE who have dealt with politico-economic analysis of financial instability and the sway of the mode of *régulation* of Japanese capitalism as well as the shifts of industrial structure in an international perspective, some international scholars also provide fresh views on this global transformation. The continuing relevance of the analytical perspectives outlined in the first part of the book is therefore reaffirmed through the more contemporary analyses in the second part.

Part I: Japanese contribution to political economy

The first three chapters of Part I deal with the trend of Marxian economics grounded on such a historical experience.

Chapter One: Kiichiro Yagi, "Marxian economics in Japan after 1945: between heritage and innovation"

This chapter offers an overview of the historical trend of politico-economic investigations of Marxian economists in Japan. The heated disputes on the nature of the land reform and other postwar democratizations as well as on the resurgence/subordination of Japanese imperialism are now far remote from the memories of present-day researchers. However, these early debates are relevant to today's researchers because they are now living through the historical process set in motion by postwar developments. Yagi also describes the widening of the perspective in theory as well as in academic international communications after the 1970s.

Chapter Two: Michiiaki Obata, "The Uno theory and Marx"

Obata discusses the basic view of capitalism of the Uno School that emerged from the methodological reflection of the prewar controversy on Japanese capitalism and its transformation under the present globalized economy. The founder, Kozo Uno, conceived his distinction between pure theory and the stage theory of capitalism in the context of the switch of historical tendency from convergence to divergence in the age of imperialism. Obata, however, advocates the inclusion of noneconomic factors as well as global geographical limitations into the theoretical system of Uno economics.

Chapter Three: Hiroshi Ohnishi, "Non-Western Marxist traditions in Northeast Asia"

Ohnishi is enthusiastically engaged in conversation with Korean and Chinese leftist circles of economists. He identifies similarities between the views of Korean and Chinese researchers and those of Japanese scholars with regard to controversy and strategy, in particular with those of the Koza-ha. This chapter contains the author's personal remarks and provocative views. Yet his proposal to set

Marxian economics in Japan in the wider perspective of East Asia is valuable and even his rather unique views are worthy of consideration.

The following five chapters deal with theoretical contributions that are beyond the narrow distinction between Marxian economics and non-Marxian economics.

Chapter Four: Fumikazu Yoshida, "Japanese contribution to environmental economics: fighting against pollution problems and Fukushima nuclear disaster"

Yoshida describes the peculiar characteristics of environmental economics in Japan. Appreciating contributions of two explorers (Kenichi Miyamoto and Shigeto Tsuru) in politico-economic investigations into pollution problems, he describes the lessons from some serious pollution issues and analyzes the ongoing Fukushima nuclear disaster. It is noteworthy that Yoshida starts his argument with Marx's view of the "metabolic interrelationship" between human beings and nature and combines it with Amartya Sen's capability approach.

Chapter Five: Seiichi Nagashima, "Business cycles of contemporary monopoly capitalism"

Nagashima presents a model of business cycles that consists of the monopoly sector that adopts quantity adjustment and the non-monopoly sector with a price adjustment strategy. In his view, the construction of the theory of business cycles of monopoly capitalism is the base on which the financial and fiscal interventions of the economic superstructure of state monopoly capitalism have modifying effects.

Chapter Six: Yoshikazu Sato, "Okishio's contribution to political economy"

Sato introduces Nobuo Okishio's theory of growth and capital accumulation. Although Okishio's name is associated worldwide with Marx's fundamental theorem and the Shibata-Okisho theorem, his main works in Japanese are out of the reach of overseas researchers given language barriers. Sato summarizes the centrality of conflict, capital accumulation as an independent variable and technical change as a constraint upon capitalist development as the three essential points of Okishio's accumulation theory. In his view, Okishio's theory is still viable in the politico-economical investigations to explore the instability of capitalist market economy.

Chapter Seven: Hiroyasu Uemura, Toshio Yamada and Yuji Harada, "Régulation approach to Japanese and Asian capitalisms: understanding varieties of capitalism and structural dynamics"

Uemura, Yamada and Harada investigate the specific characteristics of the Japanese version of the *régulation* theory that has developed since the mid-1980s: the original understanding of the varieties of capitalism and the different patterns of "civil society" formation between the West and the East; a structural analysis of hierarchical industrial sectors and firms in non-Western economies, especially the Japanese economy; and the contribution of the analysis of Asian capitalisms to the "varieties of capitalism" approach and the *régulation* theory.

Chapter Eight: Yoshinori Shiozawa, "The revival of the classical theory of values"

Shiozawa contends that the true criticism of mainstream neoclassical economics should be based on the revival of the classical value theory. In this chapter he summarizes his efforts for the modern reconstruction of classical theory. Classical value theory here conceived is, in fact, Ricardian production cost theory as it is reformulated by Piero Sraffa. Combining this value theory with the pricing behavior of modern firms, the author argues that the determination of the production quantity along the lines of the Keynesian concept of "effective demand" is well fitted to the modern classical framework.

Part II. Cataclysm of global economy and future of capitalism: political economy of global interdependence

The new generation of Japanese political economists, working both inside and outside of the JSPE, has developed their research in collaboration with their overseas counterparts. Their research has produced new insights in theory and in the newly emerging structure of world economy. The themes include: the broader tendencies in international capitalism and how past patterns of uneven development are now changing; the role of international finance in affecting both national and international growth and employment patterns; analysis of recent growth patterns in Asia; and the specific issue emerging within the Asian region and the implications for economics, social change and geopolitics.

Chapter Nine: Nobuharu Yokokawa, "Dynamic comparative advantage and the new flying geese theory of capitalist development"

Yokokawa emphasizes the importance of dynamic industries and the role of government intervention and rebuilds Akamatsu's flying geese theory, incorporating dynamic comparative advantage theory and the financial instability hypothesis. He analyzes long waves and super long waves and the flying geese pattern of industrialization and the re-emergence of Asia after World War II. Then he answers three questions: (1) why a structural crisis occurred in East Asia in the 1990s; (2) whether an open modular architecture of global value chain (GVC) with core chipsets is a new dynamic industry; and (3) is the world financial crisis since 2007 a systemic crisis of the present capitalist world system?

Chapter Ten: Robert Rowthorn, "The emergence of China and India as great powers"

Rowthorn discusses long-term implications of the emergence of China and India as great powers. As China moves up the value chain, it will focus on more "knowledge-intensive" products, creating new competition for established makers of knowledge-intensive products in advanced economies as well as new demand for labor-intensive products from the poorer countries. He goes on to consider the impact of China and India on the economies of sub-Saharan Africa. Outward investment by Chinese and Indian firms is growing rapidly, but it will be a long time before their overseas operations compare in scale to those of their established rivals from more advanced economies. This is followed by a discussion of the changing balance of power in the world. This includes a discussion of the military balance. He concludes that, despite its GDP and its newly acquired status, China is still a partial power.

Chapter Eleven: Robert Boyer, "Asia: renewal of the diversity of capitalisms, the sudden turn in international relations"

Boyer studies the circumstances and processes that have allowed Japan, then Asian dragons, and finally China, to build their original forms of capitalism from the point of view of the *régulation* theory. He identifies the factors shaping the transformation of each type of capitalism and the renewal of their collective diversity. Then, in the second section, the analytical framework of the *régulation* theory is extended to geopolitical analysis, emphasizing complementary relations in the economic sphere and rivalry in the political sphere that lead to a largely original configuration of international relations. He then examines the following questions: is there any regionalization trend of the international division of labor in Asia; does the concentration of both manufacturing production capacity and reserve currency in Asia give a new configuration for the international system; and is China the future hegemonic power, or is the current multipolar world already anticipating the international system of the 21st century?

Chapter Twelve: Jan Kregel, "Minsky's financial instability analysis: financial flows and international imbalances"

Kregel argues that Minsky's financial instability hypothesis is not limited to closed economies, that it is easy to extend his analysis to international economic instability and that it is particularly useful in the analysis of financial crises that have become endemic in developing economies since they have adopted policies to open their economies. He argues that these financial flows cannot be made stable and will always be speculative and thus subject to transforming into Ponzi finance. After the Asian financial crisis of 1997, the Asian policy of hedge finance provided the potential for higher growth than that of Latin America. However, while it is possible to formulate the conditions of hedge finance for a national economy, there is no such thing as a perfect hedge in an interdependent international trading and financial system. Therefore, the provision of global liquidity requires a global institution based on symmetrical adjustment through automatic provision of liquidity, such as what is proposed in Keynes's International Clearing Union.

Chapter Thirteen: Kenichi Haga, "Malfunction of capital accumulation regime in present-day Japan"

Haga analyses the malfunctioning of the capital accumulation regime in Japan since the late 1990s. After the financial crisis of 1998, Japanese firms shifted their business strategy from market share to profits, suppressing wages. The reduction of labor costs was introduced in the dual labor market with regular and non-regular workers, such as part-time, temporary and day-workers. At the same time, unit–labor costs were reduced with productivity growth. Corporations' low-wage strategy adversely affected the demand regime and caused deflation. He argues that to solve the malfunction in the capital accumulation regime requires the conversion of non-regular employees into regular ones and a policy of wage increases in line with increased labor productivity.

Chapter Fourteen: Jayati Ghosh, "Indian capitalism in the global context"

Ghosh emphasizes that it is a mistake to club together China and India – they are very different economies. China has followed what could be described as the classic industrialisation pattern, moving from primary to manufacturing activities in the past 25 years, with associated expansion of services. In India, by contrast, the move has been mainly from agriculture to services in share of output, with no substantial increase in manufacturing. Greater economic openness is the primary cause of the growing divergence between output and employment growth. She argues that the unbalanced and fragile nature of Indian capitalism is due to the inability of the state to control the capitalist class and direct its investments in ways that are beneficial for society. Despite these limitations, there are still possibilities for more sustainable and equitable economic growth to emerge, and the vibrant but chaotic democracy may become an important means of generating more sustainable economic growth based primarily on the home market and on the generation of decent work. This makes the nature of Indian economic interaction with global capitalism different; in particular, internal changes will necessarily have wider impact on the world economy given the size of India's population and its economy.

Chapter Fifteen: Richard Westra, "China in the crash lane"

Westra argues that the meteoric rise in the global economy of East Asia in general, and China in particular, cannot be grasped in terms of a largely endogenous process of social change, such as market-friendly economic policies nor "statist-institutionalist" policies. The Japanese "miracle" story begins with vehement US anticommunist policy projections at the onset of the Cold War. First, the Korean War, then, shortly afterwards, Vietnam, provided a bonanza of wealth, prosperity, growth and development for East Asia's anticommunist soon-to-be miracles. He then argues that China represents something radically different from so-called catch-up industrial development and predicts that it will *never* taste capitalist wealth effects enjoyed historically by advanced states and the anticommunist third world showcases that climbed the economic development ladder. He concludes that what is hastening China's maneuver into the crash lane is the seething discontent throughout the vast expanse of the country.

This volume contributes to the rejuvenation of political economy by building on the pluralism that enables creative collaboration across different streams. It is hoped that its more textured approach will contribute to a broader revival and rejuvenation of political economy not only in Japan but across the world.

Part I

Japanese contribution to political economy

1 Marxian economics in Japan after 1945

Between heritage and innovation

Kiichiro Yagi

Three essential elements of the post-1945 situation

Since its influx nearly a century ago, Marxism has remained one of the most influential elements in the intellectual life of the Japanese (Morris-Suzuki 1989 and Barshay 2004). Nevertheless, in the past century the influence of Marxism has fluctuated widely; for instance, the publication catalogue of the National Diet Library shows three waves that had significant impact. The first emerged in the mid-1920s and ceased after a decade because of harsh political suppression. The second flourished during the democratic revolution following the collapse of the militarist regime in 1945. The third occurred from the late 1960s to the late 1970s and was related to the student revolution and the Marx renaissance in the Western countries.[1]

Each of these three waves brought about academic outcomes to the wider field of economic research as well. Although this section does not delve into the details of the three waves, it does offer three essential elements in understanding the situation of Marxian economists (hereafter MEs) during the first stage of the postwar years, which is from the second wave to the advent of the third wave, or the late 1960s.

The first is on the division of MEs between two main schools: the "Koza-ha" and the "Rono-ha." This division emerged when a *Series* on the *Historical Development of Japanese Capitalism* (*Nihon Shihonshugi Hattatsushi Koza*) was published by Iwanami Shoten during 1932–1933. The contributing scholars shared a vision of Japanese capitalism which was deeply rooted in semifeudal and military order and the concentrated power of absolute monarchy (Tenno system). Moritaro Yamada (1897–1980) provided a representative analysis in his monumental work *Analysis of Japanese Capitalism* (*Nihon Shihonshugi Bunseki* 1934). He saw the vast agricultural sector, in which a noncapitalist tenant system prevailed, as the base for capitalist industrial sectors and concluded that capitalism in Japan was destined to be in the mold of semifeudal and paramilitary structures. However, this view was challenged by the economists of Rono-ha, whose name came from the journal they published. They argued that Japanese capitalism had reached the matured stage of monopoly capitalism, and regarded the noncapitalist features of agriculture as transient phenomena in the developmental process toward capitalism.

The controversy between the two schools was aggravated to the extent of impacting the choice of revolutionary strategy in Japan. Koza-ha had an affinity with the so-called two-stage strategy, according to which the revolution begins from a bourgeois democratic revolution and is then forcefully driven into a proletarian socialist revolution. In 1932, the Japanese Communist Party (JCP) adopted this strategy under the guidance of the Soviet Comintern. By contrast, the views of Rono-ha were congruent with the one-stage strategy, in which a socialist revolution would emerge in Japan despite the accompanied agenda of the incomplete bourgeois revolution. The views of Rono-ha resonated with those of socialists who led the labor movement and rejected communist intervention. Since the prewar period, and within the spectrum of left politics in Japan, the division of the two schools overlapped in the political lineages of communists and socialists.[2]

This chapter elaborates on the development of Marxian economics after 1945; thus, the works of MEs during the first wave fall outside our scope of consideration. Nevertheless, the division of the two schools with their different political affiliations was revived during the second wave. After 1945, or at least within the following decade or two, most MEs in Japan were aware of the stands their predecessors held before the war. In addition to the reviving of conflict between the two schools, there emerged within each school ambitious challenges against the orthodox views and reflections on the methodology in Marxism. Thus, after 1945, MEs began referencing the works of the two schools and the aggravated controversies between them in their research on postwar capitalism in Japan.

Another essential element of the situation required to understand postwar Marxian economics in Japan in the first two decades after 1945 is the international context of left politics during those years. Along with the resumption of the open propaganda of JCP, an overwhelming influx of Russian Marxism, also known as "Marx-Leninism," dominated the mindsets of a new generation of activists. The terms and criteria that Lenin and Stalin used became the canon of partisan scholars closely affiliated with JCP. Whereas Lenin's distinction of the American and Prussian paths toward capitalism in agriculture (Lenin 1907) was called forth to criticize the standard view of the prewar Koza-ha, Stalin's new "law of maximal profit" stipulated in his 1951 article (Stalin 1951) was widely applied to the pressure of monopoly capitalism on small- and medium-sized enterprises and the people.

On the other hand, criticisms by the Cominform and the Communist Party of China toward the JCP in 1949, Khrushchev's Stalin criticism in 1956, and so on, deeply shocked MEs in Japan. The general crisis of capitalism theory, state monopoly capitalism and structural reform strategy were typical examples imported from international communications. However, due to the paucity of a genuine worldwide academic community of leftist economics in that period, the international scope of Japans ME was extremely biased toward the official theories of Soviet Bloc states and affiliated communist parties in the Western countries such as France and Italy. Further, discussions were often interrupted by politically motivated considerations. It was only after the advent of the Marx renaissance in the late 1960s that this isolation and the eastern bias were mitigated.

The third essential situational element is related to the advancement of MEs in both academia and journalism. In the period when many non-Marxian economists had been discredited for their collaboration with militarist regime, Marxian economics honored for their resistance during the war years represented the people's hope for democratic revolution. The interest of MEs in the real conditions of capitalism allowed them to succeed in academia as well as in journalism.[3]

In Japan's economics departments, Marxists occupied competing positions, if not the majority, in almost all fields of research. Most traditional universities introduced courses on the principles of economics that were concurrently taught by MEs and by non-Marxian economists. Even in the field of management studies, the critical approach of Marxian economics was effective in revealing the hidden motives and related measures of capitalist management.

In the area of journalism, most non-Marxian economists were reluctant to present their views on the Japanese economy or delve into policy matters. Thus, the commercial base for economic journals such as *Keizai Hyoron* and *Ekonomisuto*, which aimed at attracting readers' attention to Japan's economic problems, relied heavily on contributions by MEs.[4]

Meanwhile, non-Marxian economics was rebuilt on the standard theory of the US and the UK. Since it was called "modern economics" (Kindai keizaigaku or Kin-kei), economics journalism described the situation of economics in Japan as a battle between two competing economics, Kin-kei and Maru-kei (Marukusu keizaigaku or Marxian economics). At the beginning, MEs appeared to have an advantage over modern economists in empirical research. However, after the mid-1950s – as was also depicted in the analysis of *Annual White Book on Economy* by government economists – modern economists designed a standard set of analytical tools to evaluate Japan's current economic conditions. While modernists utilized advanced theories and analytical tools, most MEs were satisfied with the barren criticisms against Kin-kei and learned little from them.

Of course, there are few exceptions. Economic researchers closely following Shigeto Tsuru (1912–2006), who was well versed in Marxian and modern economics, aimed at creating a new political economy by synthesizing both.[5] Nobuo Okishio (1927–2003), who began his academic career as a mathematical economist, undertook efforts to reformulate Marxian economics in mathematical economics using the criticisms of representative modern theories.

Postwar reforms

Despite a decade of suppression, the appreciation that prewar Marxism heritage received did not wane. Prominent MEs, such as Hyoe Ouchi (1888–1980), Hiromi Arisawa (1896–1988) and Moritaro Yamada, were invited to join a special committee, launched by the Ministry of Foreign Affairs (then the Ministry of Great East Asia) immediately after the surrender, to discuss the fundamental direction of the reconstruction of the Japanese economy. They were in accord with bureaucrat experts and non-MEs who were not involved with the fanatic militarism during the war period to prepare the report[6] that emphasized the democratization of Japanese economic systems. Ouchi and Arisawa were requested by conservative Prime Minister Shigeru Yoshida to dispense advice on the reconstruction of public finances and industry domains. Yamada was invited by the Ministry of Agriculture to monitor the land reform. Thus, in the first stage of postwar reform, a consensus on the democratic reconstruction of the Japanese economy was reached beyond the borders of MEs and non-MEs.

At first, the Allied Forces, almost exclusively the United States, expected the support of socialists and communists in oppressing the sabotage of the conservatives, who endeavored to maintain their hegemonic position. The socialists and communists regarded the Allied Forces as the protectors of the democratic revolution. However, this harmony was first threatened in early 1947, when General MacArthur banned the general strikes planned by unionists. The discord became even more salient when the land reform, dissolutions of *zaibatsu* (financial cliques) and labor reforms were fulfilled. Under the growing tension with Soviet Russia, the GHQ (General Headquarter of the Allied Forces) illegalized the JCP and switched the target of purge from war supporters to communists. With this so-called "reverse course," the previously achieved consensus was lost.

While Marxian professors who had been forced to leave academia returned to their interrupted research, the younger generation was heavily influenced by the overwhelming influx of Marx-Leninism. Even in the camp of Marxian scholars, who stood by the JCP, perspectives challenging the standard view of the Koza-ha under the influence of Lenin and Stalin emerged.

Debate on agricultural issues

The first prominent economic debates of this period were related to the evaluation of the land reform, which emerged as the urgent agenda in 1946 and was executed in 1947.[7] Rejecting the first moderate plan drafted by the Ministry of Agriculture, the GHQ ordered the Japanese government to impose a radical reform that would abolish absentee landowners and restrict the remaining land lease to a limit of 1 *chobu* (about 0.99 ha).

While socialists had high expectations that farmers' cooperatives would modernization agriculture, communists were eager to propel the anti-landowner campaign in the countryside. At first, a group of activists, including the JCP's chief of agriculture Ritsu Itoh (1913–1989), applied Lenin's two paths theory of bourgeois agricultural development to the land reform. They judged that land reform implemented by the government was destined to be incomplete and proposed to push the farmer-oriented agricultural revolution forward by mobilizing tenant farmers to prevent the landowner type of bourgeois development. However, in relation to the direct application of Lenin's theory (Lenin 1907) to Japan's agricultural situation, criticisms arose from another group of theoreticians who denied the prospect of the bourgeois type of upward agricultural development in postwar Japan.

Thus, moving away from the support of land acquisition by tenant farmers, JCP adopted the nationalization of land in its agricultural program and, as a provisional measure and a step toward collective farming, it introduced the control of released tenant land by a farmers' committee. However, farmers who acquired land did not proceed toward collective farming, and the JCP's demands in the countryside only created confusion. Theoretically, the characterization of small farmers who owned land, yet had no prospect to develop into capitalist farmers, was still unclear. One of the researchers who made a valuable contribution to addressing this problem was Hyakujyu Kurihara (1910–1955), who reflected on the application of Marx's concept of small-holding peasants (Parzellenbauern).[8]

Even after the execution of the land reform, the investigation of ruling semi-feudal landowners by JCP-affiliated researchers continued; they revealed owner-ship and use of forests and fields, control of irrigation and traditional customs of rural society as the foundation of semifeudal powers over farmers. JCP's adoption of the new 1951 party program, which aimed at Japan's national democratic revolution, strengthened this adhesion because it corresponded to China's anti-imperialism and anti-feudalism revolution as a colonized or subor-dinate nation. According to JCP, the semifeudal rule of parasitic landowners must exist to support the subordinate situation in the countryside.

Although this was a revival of the standard view of Koza-ha during the prewar, Moritaro Yamada, protagonist of this view, did not approve such a caricature. As the supervisor of land reform records, he admitted that this reform abolished the semifeudal relations in the countryside (*Nouchi Kaikaku Kiroku Iinkai* 1951). Since the progress of the agricultural revolution toward collectivism ceased, a new research agenda emerged that addressed the productivity of the remnant small-scale farmers and aimed at grasping the repetition of primitive accumulation under these conditions.

Here, it is noteworthy to mention that a group of social policy researchers supporting the view of Kazuo Okouchi (1905–1984) applied the concept of "migrant worker" to explain low wages and backwardness in labor relations. Although Okouchi never considering himself a Marxist, the original version of his explanation lays in the double determination of low industrial wages and living standards in the semifeudal agricultural sector, as stipulated by the Koza-ha. The noncapitalist agricultural sector supplied low-wage laborers to rapidly growing industries. It was around the early 1960s, when the reservoir function of the agricultural sector was lost in the last stage of rapid economic growth, that working class wages substantially increased and the mass consumption of electrical appliances and Western-style diets commenced.[9]

The recognition of such linkages in dual-structured sectors became a topic of interest for MEs and pro-MEs doing empirical research. The term "dual structure" was coined by Arisawa and indicates an economy characterized by low productivity from small- and medium-sized firms and high productivity by large-scale businesses. Yoshihiro Takasuka (1932–1991) applied a similar dual sector adjustment to explain the mild but sustained inflation that was conspicu-ous in consumer goods and services (Takasuka 1972).

From dependency-autonomy debates to structural reform[10]

Debates on postwar Japanese capitalism focused on whether Japanese capitalism could recover its autonomy to develop into an independent imperialism, or whether it was destined to remain a dependent economy subordinated by US hegemony.

When the dream of peaceful revolution under occupation was broken by the reality as well as by the criticism from Beijing and Moscow, the JCP switched its strategy to national democratic revolution, making American imperialism the primary enemy. In 1951, the JCP adopted a new party program that regarded Japan as a colonially subordinated nation and called for a national liberation front to attain independence. According to the JCP, the peace treaty signed in September 1951 did not change the situation: the US–Japan security treaty guaranteed the preservation of US bases in Japan and assigned the US with a privileged status to use Japanese resources for military operations in the eastern Pacific region.

Scholars who were loyal to the JCP edited 11 volumes of the *Series on Japanese Capitalism* (*Nihon Shihonshugi Koza*) that were published by Iwanami Shoten (1953–1955). The aim of this new series was to vindicate the 1951 party program and reveal the dependency of Japanese monopoly capital on US imperialism. As mentioned before, the series also focused on revealing the duration rule for semifeudal landlords. Economists who contributed to this new series were called Shin Koza-ha (New Koza school) to distinguish them from those who were part of the prewar series. However, because of the ambiguity in political strategies and dependent analyses of contributions, this new series was unsuccessful in gaining prestige. It was soon forgotten as an unhappy experience of the MEs in relation to politics.

The Shin Koza-ha's views on postwar capitalism in Japan resemble many aspects of the standard view of old Koza-ha. First, both emphasized the semifeudal relations in the countryside. Second, they believed that capitalism in Japan was in a critical situation due to the shrinking market. Third, they regarded military power and its configuration as key elements in defining the nation's ruling power. Replacing the key role of semifeudal militaristic apparatus in the standard view of Koza-ha with that of the US–Japan military nexus under US hegemony appears similar to the image of Japanese capitalism, which is trapped in political constraints and immobile structures. As for the first point, the argument for the duration of semifeudal landlords after the land reform was far from the truth. Second, the crisis thesis from the viewpoint of market shrinkage during the postwar period was not supported by facts. Such a situation existed only in Stalin's speculation, which he discussed in his much-admired 1951 article (Stalin 1951). By contrast, whether Japan's dependency on the US for security was sufficient to be defined as an essential feature of Japanese capitalism remains an open question.

In 1955, after a change in JCP leadership, the discussion to renew the program continued until 1961. The 1961 program described Japan as "a highly developed capitalist country," but regarded it as a "virtually subordinate nation half occupied by US Imperialism." The new leader, Kenji Miyamoto (1908–2007), did not deny the possibility of Japanese capitalism recovering autonomy, but regarded "US imperialism and its inferior partner, monopoly capital of Japan" as "two enemies" and stressed the struggle against both. Thus, the subordination view of Japanese capitalism survived as the orthodoxy of communists and influenced their anti-US struggle.

The open challenge against this dependency view emerged in 1956–1957 with the application of Lenin's criteria for the definition of imperialism (Lenin 1916). Jokichi Uchida (1912–2002) and Yoshihiko Ono (1914–1990) argued that since postwar Japanese capitalism concentrated on production and capital accumulation (first criterion) and the system of financial oligarchy (second criterion), the development toward imperialism was inevitable (Uchida 1961 and Ono 1963). Noboru Sato (1916–1993), who later emerged as a leading theoretician of the strategy of structural reform, contributed to this criticism and maintained that Japanese capitalism had already regained its autonomy as independent imperialism (Sato 1961). Despite most US bases being retained under the revised US–Japan security treaty of 1960, given that large-scale businesses in Japan began to build overseas networks, and the growing trade conflicts between the US and Japan, this view of resurrecting Japanese imperialism gradually penetrated into the left.

State monopoly capitalism

A drawback of the subordination view is its approach to determine the nature of Japanese capitalism using political factors. After the attempt to divide capitalists between the nation and foreign agents failed, the theory of state monopoly capitalism appealed to economists who had been seeking an appropriate theory to grasp contemporary capitalism.

At first, state monopoly capitalism was not conceived as a category distinct from that of monopoly capitalism. The pioneering work of Harumaru Inoue (1908–1973) and Seiichiro Usami (1915–1997) regarded it as a partial component (*uklad*), which was an outcome of the need for monopoly capitalism that faced critical conditions necessitating involvement of state powers (Inoue and Usami 1951).

Then, the view that state monopoly capitalism represented a new stage of production relations within capitalism appeared. Citing Kurt Zieschang's 1957 article, Takuichi Ikumi (1901–1995) argued that state monopoly capitalism emerged and inherently developed from the contradiction between the social nature of production and the private appropriation of its result (Ikumi 1958). It implied that the state's intervention in the economic process was not necessarily determined by the interest of monopoly capital alone.

Thus, the new view of state monopoly capitalism paved the way for a discussion on whether the working class could utilize state intervention for their interests. Impressed by the advancement of Italian communists in their central and local governments, theoreticians who looked for a new concept of revolution in advanced nations considered a combined structural reform strategy with state monopoly capitalism to build new production relations.

Since this group was open to progressive thoughts from Western countries, they spearheaded the emergence of a new stream of Marxist scholars widely influencing academia and journalism. This stream was called the Kozo Kaikaku school (school of structural reform), after its policy. The journal *Gendai no Riron* (1959, 1964–1989) functioned as its central outlet.

However, this group was unsuccessful in affecting strategy discussions held in the JCP, which stuck to the 1961 program's anti-US imperialism and anti-monopoly strategy. And they were unsuccessful in changing the views of scholars who were close to the JCP. Incidentally, these scholars who stood loyal to the position of the JCP would later be called the orthodox school (Seito-ha).

Interestingly enough, a fraction of the Social Democratic Party of Japan (SDPJ) led by Saburo Eda (1907–1977) showed sympathy to the strategy of structural reform. Thus far, the left wing of Japanese socialists maintained their orientation by the doctrine of the orthodox Rono-ha, which regarded monopoly capital as the primary enemy of the working class and compelled long-term resistance to offensive capitalists. The most highlighted class battle was the 1960 strike by the Miike Miners, whose union leaders were disciples of the patriarch economist of the Rono-ha Marxism, Itsuro Sakisaka (1897–1985).

Despite Eda's popularity outside the party, this group failed to redefine the strategy of the SDPJ. However, the practical approach for reform politics, advocated by the supporters of structural reform, significantly contributed to bringing forth a wide range of activists, experts, and local politicians in support of progressive municipalities in the 1960s and 1970s.

Formation of academic Marxism

The preceding two sections discussed the MEs' debates and research interests in Japan, focusing on their relationship with revolutionary strategies of the JCP. It was only natural that most of the mentioned scholars were closely associated with the JCP or belonged to Koza-ha in its wider sense.

However, this does not mean that economists of Rono-ha, here and in a broader context, did not contribute to the discussion. Sakisaka often criticized JCP program discussion from the viewpoint of antimonopoly socialist revolution. However, because the Rono-ha took upon themselves the task of democratizing reform and not revolution, they tended more toward modernization or rationalization than their Koza-ha colleagues. Arisawa, who exemplified these characteristics, invented the "priority production system" for the reconstruction of the Japanese industry and continued to influence industrial policy, particularly energy policy, until his death.

Emergence of Uno-economics

The most influential step within Rono-ha was the emergence of the Uno school. Kozo Uno (1897–1977), who in 1946 assumed the chair at the newly established Institute of Social Science at the University of Tokyo, looked for logical consistency in the theory of Marxian economics and established a system that comprised three levels of research: basic theory of pure capitalism, stage theory and real economies analysis.

This three-level approach emanated from his reflection on prewar debates on Japanese capitalism. As Uno saw it, the failure of both the Koza and Rono schools can be attributed to their approach, which is to explain real economic phenomena using a direct application of the basic capitalism theory without an intervening apparatus. With such a hasty approach, economists of the Koza school called forth noneconomical feudal coercion to explain the anomalistic features of Japanese capitalism, whereas those of the Rono school dissolved them into transient features of global development. The appropriate way was to grasp the manifestation of the general essence of capitalism that was modified by the typical conditions of the stage in which the capitalism under consideration was located. The persistence of noncapitalist features in Japan's agricultural sector had to be explained based upon the weak absorption of labor power, which was due to exigencies of the accumulation of capital as it entered the stage of imperialism (Uno 1947a).

Uno's unique reconstruction of Marx's capital system aroused ME discussions in almost all parts of Uno's *Principles of Political Economy*.[11] In the value theory, he disclaimed Marx's reduction of value into labor substance and stressed the primacy of value form, which appeared at the circulation of commodities (Uno 1947b). This criticism against the prevailing view of substantial labor value theory was brave. Some of Uno's disciples succeeded this criticism and developed it into an interactive theory within the circulation process of capitalist economy (Yamaguchi 1985).

In addition, Uno's theory of economic crisis (Uno 1953) evoked animated discussions. Since Uno believed that a consistent theory of capitalism must explain the operation of capitalist economy using pure economic logic, he expelled from the theory of capitalism the elements that could possibly block this normal rotation. Even the economic crisis should not be seen as a catastrophe of capitalism but as a phenomenon of normal cyclical mechanisms that guarantee the viability of capitalism. He rejected the underconsumption theory of crisis and adopted an excess capital theory, according to which the capital consolidation during the economic crisis regulates the labor market within the tolerable barriers of capitalism. Since this version of crisis theory involved money and credit and the labor market theory, Uno's disciples developed these elements further (Itoh 1973).

Uno interpreted Lenin's *Imperialism* and Hilferding's *Finance Capital* as the precursors of his stage theory that stated the conditions and mechanisms under which the theory of capitalism should be utilized. As the stage theory included the world markets, types of representative capital, credit and finance, public finance, economic policies, labor markets, agricultural problems and conditions for industries, it served as a base for specialized research as well as intervening theory to analyze the current economic situation.

Uno's three-level approach functioned as a full-fledged research program, so that Imre Lakatos demanded the emergence of its own school of science (Lakatos

1978). It is for good reason that Uno Economics is the name that has been heard up to this day. Despite mountains of criticism against his theory, Uno succeeded in founding his school, which occupied considerable chairs of Marxian economists in academia. Further, the fact that Uno was aloof from the infamous authority of Stalin improved his reputation, attracting the attention of the new left activists who advocated anti-Stalinism.[12]

Civil society school

Another notable trend of Marxian economics in academia is the emergence of the so-called "civil society" school of Marxism. Compared with the Uno school, which had distinctive theory and methodology features, this school represented a similar tendency to place Marx and Marxism in the development of theories for modern civil society. The origin of this school could be sought in Zen'ya Takashima's (1904–1990) investigation of Adam Smith's economic thought during the war period. Although the schools of Hisao Otsuka (1907–1996) in economic history and Masao Maruyama (1914–1996) in political science were often thought to share this tendency, the emergence of this school has been generally attributed to Yoshihiko Uchida's (1913–1989) study on Adam Smith (Uchida 1953).

The implicit criticism against the prevailing concept of socialism held by this school became apparent after a decade, when Kiyoaki Hirata (1922–1995) accused orthodox Marxism of neglecting the basic categories of modern civil society (Hirata 1969). It was in that year that the troops of the Warsaw Pact crushed the Prague Spring. He maintained that the conclusion of Marx's *Capital* was based not on nationalizing the ownership of production means but on rehabilitating the individual ownership of workers in social production, which ignited a fierce dispute that continued for several years.

Okishio's mathematical Marxian economics

Nobuo Okishio's mathematical formularization during this period is noteworthy. He applied simultaneous equations to determine value and price prior to the publication of Sraffa's *Production of Commodities by Means of Commodities* in 1960 (Okishio 1957) and formulated Marx's fundamental theorem on the need to exploit for profits. Further, he appreciated Kei Shibata's (1902–1986) critical examination of the fall in the profit rate in the third volume of Marx's *Capital* (Shibata-Okishio theorem) and presented a theory of capital accumulation during the third wave of Marxism. Although sporadic attempts have been made to use mathematics in the reproduction scheme, its multisectoral version, the solution of the transformation problem, or a discussion of the balanced accumulation path in the MEs camp of Japan, Okishio was the first mathematical economist who systematically approached Marxian economic theory. However, since he was originally from the circle of mathematical economists, he was not well known to most MEs in Japan. It was only with the trend of applying mathematics in Marxian theory, which was ignited by the emergence of the Sraffian approach in the 1960s and the appearance of Michio Morishima's (1923–2004) *Marx* (Morishima 1973), that the significance of his works was widely appreciated.[13]

Keizai Riron Gakkai

The academic association of MEs, the Japan Society of Political Economy (JSPE; Keizai Riron Gakkai) was founded in May 1959. It was a unified association that involved all groups of MEs, and not only renowned economists of all schools but also young researchers gathered at the foundation meeting. Some opposed the name of the society and maintained "Society of Marxian Economics" as the alternative. Nevertheless, the choice of the majority proved to be right because the present JSPE functions as one of Japan's most active forums of heterodox economists, who are all critical of mainstream modern economics. Yet this does not affect the position of Marxian economics as its main pillar of research and related activities.

The following are the topics that were discussed at its plenary sessions before the advent of the third wave:

> 1960 spring: "Problems of the Theory of Wages and on the Law of Tendential Fall of the Profit Rate"
> 1960 fall: "Basic Structure of System of Crisis Theory and Nature of Business Cycles in Postwar Years"
> 1961 spring: "Marxian Economics and Modern Economics"
> 1961 fall: "Problems on Monopolies"
> 1962 spring: "Theory of World Market"
> 1962 fall: "On the General Law of Capitalist Accumulation"
> 1963 spring: "Business Cycles under State Monopoly Capitalism"
> 1963 fall: "Modern Capitalism and the Problem of Commodity Prices"
> 1964 spring: "Hike in Commodity Prices"
> 1964 fall: "Theory of National Incomes"
> 1965 spring: "Theory of Socialist Economy"
> 1965 fall: "Structure of Modern Capitalism"
> 1966: "Credit and Crisis"
> 1967: "Problems of the State in Economics"
> 1968: "Problems of Socialist Economies"

As the list indicates, the interest of MEs transcended the peculiarity of Japanese capitalism and gravitated toward the general problems of modern capitalism. In addition to the analysis of monopoly capital, the path of economic growth and business cycles also became popular topics of Japanese MEs.[14]

After the third wave

The surrounding conditions of the third wave of Marxist literature in Japan differed from those of preceding waves in that the Japanese economy was not in a crisis but growing rapidly. The wave occurred under the impact of the worldwide youth rebellion that emerged in 1968. It included Japan's youth who were piqued by the role of the conservative government in the US Vietnam War and their tightening of societal control. Youth resistance was visible both on the street and on university campuses. They had to develop ideas that could vindicate their resistance, and generational predecessors who supported the angry youth would answer them with the most advanced ideas in the world, including those of the emerging Marx renaissance in Western countries.

The flourishing Japanese economy evoked demands not for revolution strategies or detailed economic analysis, but rather for key ideas to understand the current repressive conditions. Thus, the young researchers included those who aspired to study Marxian economics and Marx's basic ideas, such as "alienation" or "reification," texts, intellectual backgrounds and the existing methodological problems of Marxian economics, as well as those who were interested in analyzing the real economic situation. It was not a pure coincidence that Marxist philosophers, notably Louis Althusser and, particularly in Japan, Wataru Hiromatsu (1931–1994), attracted the youth in the West and Japan.

With respect to its impact on the history of Marxian economics in Japan, the third wave widened the scope for MEs to receive innovative ideas, which were previously being regarded as deviation or heresy. Many Western Marxists who opposed the tyranny of Marx-Leninism were brought back to the discussion. However, and more importantly, the conjuncture saw the opening of channels of collaboration with various heterodox economic streams that were outside the ambit of Marxian economics.

Impulses from outside

There were several impulses that encouraged the new generation of MEs. First was the emergence of radical economists in the US. Their egalitarianism and anti-authoritarian stance appealed to the Japanese youth. Second was the communication between Sraffaians and neo-Keynesians. Both the reconstruction of classical value theory and the focus on distribution problems were well within the scope of Marxian economics. Later, the revival of the Kaleckian scheme and the progress in Keynesian monetary aspects by H. P. Minsky strengthened the sympathy of young MEs. Third was the introduction of works of the so-called "dependency school," such as those of Andre G. Frank, Samir Amin and Immanuel Wallerstein. For the young MEs who began studying world economy when Japanese capitalists began expanding overseas, the idea of the "development of subordination" brought forth fresh insight.

Obstacles in the direct communication with overseas economists or those studying abroad were mitigated. Some Japanese MEs, notably Itoh Makoto (1936–), initiated international activity, and several other young researchers began studying under overseas scholars, who were not always Marxists but were working in the broad direction of political economy.

Regulationists in Japan

Despite these impulses, the outcomes from the third wave were delayed. It was only after a decade that serious debates emerged among Japanese MEs. It was the newly born regulationist school – the Japanese version of the French regulationist school – that ignited the debate. The first step was the debate on Fordism. This school described Fordism as an accumulation regime, in which the profitable capital growth and income increase of the working class were compatible based on productivity growth. The regulationists were criticized for their harmonic vision, the applicability of which to the Japanese economy was doubted. The second step was the debate on Toyota. Benjamin Coriat, a French regulationist, praised the production system of Toyota as a candidate model of post-Fordism, in which the initiative and capability of workers had priority over mechanical automatization (Coriat 1991). Along with reactions by critics, MEs' attention was now directed to production systems in Japanese firms.

The regulation approach was born under the impact of the May 1968 events in Paris and was introduced to Japan in the mid-1980s. Because this approach comprised elements of macro growth theory, monetary regime, norm-oriented coordination, and wage–labor relations, it offered potential for a research program that could combine empirical research with discussions for future development. Thus, it attracted many new-generation MEs who were keen on international collaboration. In 2000, this group published their summary view on the Japanese economy, in which they proposed the implicit barter of company loyalties and guarantee of long-term employment between firms and employees as the key functions in industrial relations. Toshio Yamada (1942–) called this "company-ism" (Kaisha shugi) (Yamada 2000).

From their point of view, the stagnation of the Japanese economy since the 1990s could be attributed to the existing dysfunctional regime under the altered condition. The existing capitalist regime in Japan did not satisfy the domestic demand for economic growth. It is noteworthy that this view resembled the orthodox Koza-ha view – for example, Kiyoko Imura's (1930–) view that the reproduction of the existing economic regime had entered into disarray (Imura 2000). Imura maintained that although Japan was developing its heavy and chemical industries until 1990, the condition for their further development was lost and their dependency on US capital became more apparent. While Imura stressed dependency on the US from the viewpoint of reproduction, regulationists focused on industrial relations and retained their hope to overcome the crisis with a wage-led growth regime.

Modifications in Uno economics

Even after Uno's death, his school thrived by recruiting many young researchers. However, the tendencies of diversification and modification became apparent. The most controversial was the stage theory. Originally, Uno conceived the stage theory as comprising mercantilism, liberalism and imperialism, taking Britain as his reference. According to him, the normal stage of imperialism ended with the emergence of Soviet Russia, after which trends were to be studied as the objects of contemporary analysis. Thereafter, over half a century, this argument became untenable. Hiroji Baba (1933–2012) proposed the switch from a Britain-centered view to a US-centered one, regarding the third stage to contain the historical process of the 20th century (Baba 2011). The proposal of the fourth stage of "consumerism" by Robert Albritton (1991), a Canadian follower of Uno economics, also attracted attention.

On the other hand, the need to include institutional and historical elements in the basic theory of capitalism was felt. Michiaki Obata (1949–), the leader of the new generation of Uno school economists in Japan, called his approach to the basic theory of capitalism the "modification approach" (Obata 2003).

Some other directions

Apart from the division between Marxian economics and other heterodoxies in modern economics, the move toward evolutionary and institutional economics has currently been gaining influence. Some economists working in this direction have maintained that the true significance of Marxian ideas could be revived by the absorption of advances in evolutionary sciences.[15] On the other hand, stimulated by the advances of analytical Marxism in the US, the recent years have seen rigorous mathematical examinations of exploitation (Yoshihara 2008) and normative discussions of Marxian ideas (Matsui 2012).

The archival study of Marx and Marxism survived and joined the network of collaboration that sustained the continued publication of the *Complete Works of Marx and Engels* (MEGA). Several working teams were organized in Japan to participate in the editorial work for each planned volume. The contributions to the parts dedicated to *Capital* are particularly noteworthy. In 2008, Teinosuke Otani (1934–) completed volume 11 as its responsible supervisor. Izumi Omura (1948–) and his team in Sendai completed volumes 12 and 13 in collaboration with German experts. Recently, this group provided a digital version of *German Ideology*, which vividly reproduces the detailed collaborative process of two authors. At present, several Japanese teams are working on notes and excerpts. Marxology in Japan has matured to the extent that it can begin "repaying its debt" through participation in this grand publication project.

In retrospect

Nearly four decades have passed since the third wave. However, despite the outcomes mentioned in the preceding sections, and other valuable works during these years, the third wave has not thrived up to the present. In contrast with the first and second waves, in which the consciousness of crisis and revolutionary change supported the reception of Marxian ideologies, the third wave was no more than a counter wave to the prevailing attitude under the flourishing of capitalism. After the short-lived enthusiasm in the age of cultural rebellion around

1968–1970, the mechanisms of adaptation and selection within capitalism as well as in academic institutions were resumed. At present, whereas the members of the society of mainstream economists, the Japanese Economic Association, number nearly 4,000, those of the JSPE, which maintains Marxian economics as one of its main pillars, remains at approximately 900. Thus, as a minority in the academy, MEs face the pressure of fierce competition and marginalization. Whether they can conquer the pressure rests on their capability to produce valuable knowledge over the truly essential agenda of present society.

The author of this chapter began his academic career by experiencing the third wave of Marxism. Most of his mentors grew up in the years of democratic revolution (the second wave). His generation was thus influenced directly by the third wave and indirectly by the second. However, even in the second wave, the themes of the first wave were still relevant and most of its eminent leaders were alive. The works that his mentors' generation produced can be interpreted as the result of the problems passed down by the first generation. Thus, the author wishes to connect the ambitions of the three generations of MEs rather than merely comparing their works.

The newer generations are experiencing more freedom than the author's liberation from the domestic heritage of Marxian economics in Japan; indeed, sticking to one's heritage is not a recommendable attitude. However, the author believes that understanding the past efforts of predecessors is also a source of innovation.

Notes

1 The number of hits, along with the corresponding year of publication, for the books that contained "Marx" in their title from the National Diet Library Catalogue are 252 (1926–1930), 180 (1931–1935), 241 (1946–1950), 165 (1951–1955), 312 (1966–1970), and 373 (1971–1975). Their shares of the total publication for the relevant years are provided in per mill as follows: 3.61, 2.05, 0.96, 0.91, 1.26, and 1.27, respectively, whereas their share in total items is 0.47 (retrieved from https://iss.ndl.go.jp/?Ar=4e1&locale=en on September 4, 2014).
2 The debate gained so much momentum across various areas that several referential guides were published on it. Koyama and Yamazaki (1953) catalogued over 2,000 works of debate-related literature in its appendix. Also, see Hoston (1987) for an interesting take on the debate. Yasuba (1975), a non-Marxist development economist, provides valuable insight that helps understand the socioeconomic conditions of a densely populated nation with a developing economy.
3 See Yagi (2000) for information on the situation of economists in academia after 1945.
4 See *Ekonomisuto* Henshubu ed. (1958). The results of the competition between Kin-kei and Maru-kei were reviewed after a decade in *Ekonomisuto* Henshubu ed. (1970).
5 Tsuru's English writings were compiled in Tsuru (1976). See chapter 4 of this book to learn his lasting influence on the political economy of environmental problems.
6 This report is included in Nakamura (1990).
7 See the first volume of Ueda (1957–1958) and Uehara (1971) for more details on this debate.

8 See the works of Kurihara (1974–1988) and Marx (1852).
9 Cliometrician Ryoshin Minami (1970) assumed the Lewis turning point of labor supply in Japan to be around the early 1960s.
10 Much of the analysis in this section is owed to Ueda (1956, 1957), Furukawa (1970), Kawanabe (1971), Masamura (1971) and Takauchi (1973). Among them, Takauch (1973) is particularly recommended for a detailed understanding of the topics discussed.
11 The first version of Uno's basic theory was published in two volumes during 1950–1952 (Uno 1950-1952). The direction of his argument became more apparent in the new concise 1964 version (Uno 1964), which was translated into English later (Uno 1980)).
12 One of the interesting episodes occurred when Masahiko Aoki (1938–2015), before his turn toward modern economics, published under a pseudonym (Himeoka 1960) his view of state monopoly capitalism in Japan, which was essentially based on the works of the Uno school. His book represented a standard view of leftist groups at the time.
13 His English papers are available in Okishio (1993), although his works in Japanese are far more insightful.
14 As the MEs' attention shifted to the organization and behavior of big business, the use of "state monopoly capitalism" was gradually replaced by a more neutral term, "contemporary capitalism" (Gendai Shihonshugi). After the 1990s, the term "global capitalism" prevailed.
15 An academic association of heterodox economists was born in 1997 under the name of Japan Association for Evolutionary Economics, which nearly a hundred members of JSPE, including the author of this chapter, joined.

References

Albritton, R. (1991) *A Japanese Approach to Stages of Capitalist Development*. Macmillan: London.
Baba, H. (2011) *Uno Riron to America Shihonshugi (Uno Theory and American Capitalism)*. Ochanomizu Shobo: Tokyo.
Barshay, A. E. (2004) *The Social Sciences in Modern Japan: The Marxian and Modernist Tradition*. University of California Press: Berkeley.
Coriat, B. (1991) *Penser a l'envers: travail et organisation dans l'enterprise Japonaise (Thinking in Reverse: Labor and Organization in Japanese Firms)*. Christian Bourgois: Paris.
Ekonomisuto Henshubu (Editors of the Economist) ed. (1958) *Taiketsu-suru Futatsu no Keizaigaku: Kindai Keizaigaku ka Marukusu Keizaigaku ka (Two Economics in Confrontation: Modern Economics vs. Marxian Economics)*. Mainichi Shimbunsha: Tokyo.
——— ed. (1970) *Sengo Nihon Keizai Kenkyu no Seika to Tenbou (Outcomes and Perspectives of the Research on Postwar Japanese Economy)*, 2 volumes (vol.1, Part of Modern Economics, vol.2, Part of Marxian Economics). Mainichi Shimbunsha: Tokyo.
Furukawa, T. (1970) "Sengo Nihon Shihonshugi Bunseki no Shukaku (Outcomes of the Analysis of Postwar Japanese Capitalism)," in Ekonomisuto Henshubu ed. (1970), pp. 8–44.
Himeoka, R. [Aoki, M.] (1960) *Nihon Kokka Dokusen Shihonshugi no Seiritsu (Emergence of State Monopoly Capitalism in Japan)*. Gendai Shicho-sha: Tokyo.

Hirata, K. (1969) *Shimin Shakai to Shakai-shugi (Civil Society and Socialism)*. Iwanami Shoten: Tokyo.

Hoston, G. A. (1987) *Marxism and the Crisis of Development in Prewar Japan*. Princeton Legacy Library: Princeton.

Ikumi, T. (1958) *Kokka Dokusen Shihonshugi-ron (On State Monopoly Capitalism)*. Otsuki Shoten: Tokyo.

Imura, K. (2000) *Gendai Nihon Keizai Ron, Shinban (On Contemporary Japanese Economy, New Version)*. Yuhikaku: Tokyo.

Inoue, H. and Usami, S. (1951) *Kiki ni okeru Nihon shihonshugi no Kozo (Structure of Japanese Capitalism in Crisis)*. Iwanami Shoten: Tokyo.

Itoh, M. (1973) *Shin'you to Kyoukou (Credit and Crisis)*. Tokyo Daigaku Shuppankai: Tokyo.

Kawanabe, M. (1971) "Nihon Teikokushugi no Jyuzoku Fukkatsu Ronsou (Debates on Autonomy of Japanese Imperialism vs. Subordination)," in Cho, Y. and Sumiya, K. eds. *Kindai Nihon Keizai Shiso-shi, II (History of Modern Japanese Economic Thought, part II)*. Yuhikaku: Tokyo, 1971, pp.357–398.

Koyama, H. and Yamazaki, R. (1953) *Nihon Shihonshugi Ronso-shi (History of the Debate on Japanese Capitalism)*. Aoki Shoten: Tokyo.

Kurihara, H. (1974–1988) *Kurihara Hyakujyu Chosaku-shu (Works of Hyakujyu Kurihara)*, vol. 10. Azekura Shobo: Tokyo.

Lakatos, I. (1978) *The Methodology of Scientific Research Program*. Cambridge University Press: Cambridge.

Lenin, V. I. (1907) *The Agrarian Programme of the Social-Democracy after First Russian Revolution, 1905–1907*. In Lenin's *Collected Works*, vol. 13, pp.217–429. Progress Publisher: Moscow, 1972.

Lenin, V. I. (1916) *Imperialism, the Highest Stage of Capitalism*. In Lenin's *Collected Works*, vol. 22, pp. 187–304. Progress Publisher: Moscow, 1964.

Marx, K. (1852) *Der achzehnte Brumaire des Louis Bonaparte*, in Marx/Engels *Werke*, Bd.8. Dietz: Berlin. S. 111-207, 1960. (English translation available from https://www.marxorg/archive/marx/works/1852/18th-brumaire accessed on 17/01/2015)

Masamura, K. (1971) "Marukusushugi no Jiko Kakushin (Self-Innovation of Marxism)," in Cho, Y. and Sumiya, K. eds. (1971) *Kindai Nihon Keizai Shiso-shi, II (History of Modern Japanese Economic Thought, part II)*. Yuhikaku: Tokyo. 1971, pp.415–431.

Matsui, S. (2012) *Jiyushugi to Shakaishugi no Kihan Riron: Kachi rinen no Marukusu teki Bunseki (Normative Theory of Liberalism and Socialism: Marxian Analysis of Their Value Concept)*. Otsuki Shoten: Tokyo.

Minami, R. (1970) *Nihon Keizai no Tenkan-ten: Rodo no Kajou kara Fusoku he (Turning Point of Japanese Economy: From Excess to Deficit of Labor Supply)*. Sobun-sha: Tokyo.

Morishima, M. (1973) *Marx's Economics: A Dual Theory of Value and Growth*. Cambridge University Press: Cambridge.

Morris-Suzuki, T. I. (1989) *A History of Japanese Economic Thought*. Routledge: Cambridge, MA.

Nakamura, T. ed. (1990) *Shiryou Sengo Nihon no Keizai Seisaku Kousou (Concepts of Economic Policy of Postwar Japan: Materials)*, vol. 1. Tokyo Daigaku Shuppankai: Tokyo.

Nouchi Kaikaku Kiroku Iinkai (Registrarial Committee of Land Reform) ed. (1951) *Nouchi Kaikaku Tenmatsu Gaiyou (Summary of the Historical Outcomes of the Reform)*. Nousei Chousakai: Tokyo.

Obata, M. (2003) "Shihonshugi no Tayousei to Genriron no Ippansei (Variety of Capitalism and Generality of the Basic Theory)," in SGCIME ed. *Shihonshugi Genri-zou no Saikouchiku (Reconstruction of the Basic Image of Capitalism). Marukusu Keizaigaku no Gendaiteki Kadai (Series: Contemporary Agenda of Marxian Economics)*, vol. II-1. Ochanomizu Shobou: Tokyo, pp.23–43.

Okishio, N. (1957) *Saiseisan no Riron (Theory of Reproduction)*. Sobun-sha: Tokyo.

——— (1993) *Essays on Political Economy: Collected Papers*. Ed. By Flaschel, P. and Krüger, M. Peter Lang: Frankfurt A.M., Berlin, and Bern.

Ono, Y. (1963) *Sengo Nihon Shihonshugiron-Jyuzoku Keizairon Hihan (On Postwar Japanese Capitalism: Criticism against Subordination Theory)*. Aoki Shoten: Tokyo.

Sato, N. (1961) *Gendai Teikokushugi to Kouzou Kaikaku (Contemporary Capitalism and Structural Reform)*. Aoki Shoten: Tokyo.

Sraffa, P. (1960) *Production of Commodities by Means of Commodities: Prelude to a Critique of Economic Theory*. Cambridge University Press: Cambridge.

Stalin, J. (1951) "Economic Problems of Socialism in the USS" (Available from https://www.marxists.org/reference/archive/stalin/works/1951/economic-problems accessed 17/01/2015).

Takasuka, Y. (1972) *Gendai Nihon no Bukka Mondai (Contemporary Problem of Prices)*. Shin Hyoron: Tokyo.

Takauchi, S. (1973) *Gendai Nihon Shihonshugi Ronso (Debates on Contemporary Japanese Capitalism)*. San'ichi Shobo: Tokyo.

Tsuru, S. (1976) *Towards a New Political Economy*. Kodan-sha: Tokyo.

Uchida, J. (1961) *Sengo Nihon Dokusen Shihonshugi Shiron (On the History of Postwar Monopoly Capitalism of Japan)*. Nihon Hyoron Shinsha: Tokyo.

Uchida, Y. (1953) *Keizaigaku no Seitan (Birth of Political Economy)*. Mirai-sha: Tokyo.

Ueda, K. (1956–1957) *Sengo Kakumei Ronso-shi (History of the Debate on Revolution in Postwar Years)*, 2 volumes. Otsuki Shoten: Tokyo.

Uehara, N. (1971) "Sengo Nihon Shihonshugi no Futatsu no Michi (Two Paths of Postwar Japanese Capitalism)," in Cho, Y. and Sumiya, K. eds. (1971), pp. 253–278.

Uno, K. (1947a) *Nogyo Mondai Joron (Introduction to Agricultural Problem)*. Kaizo-sha: Tokyo.

——— (1947b) *Kachi-ron (Value Theory)*. Aoki Shoten: Tokyo.

——— (1950–1952) *Keizai Genron (Principles of Political Economy)*, 2 volumes. Iwanami Shoten: Tokyo.

——— (1953) *Kyokou-ron (Theory of Crisis)*. Iwanami Shoten: Tokyo.

——— (1964) *Keizai Genron (Principles of Political Economy)*. Iwanami Zensho: Tokyo.

——— (1980) *Principles of Political Economy: Theory of a Purely Capitalist Society*. Translated from Japanese by Thomas T. Sekine. Harvester Press: Sussex.

Yagi, K. (2000) "Economics in the academic institutions after 1945," in Ikeo, A. ed., *Japanese Economics and Economists since 1945*. Routledge: London and New York, pp.50–92.

Yamada, M. (1934) *Nihon Shihonshugi Bunseki: Nihon Shihonshugi ni okeru Saiseisan Katei Haaku (Analysis of Japanese Capitalism: Grasping Its Reproduction Process)*. Iwanami Shoten: Tokyo.

Yamada, T. (2000) "Japanese capitalism and the companyist compromise," in Boyer, R. and Yamada, T. eds., *Japanese Capitalism in Crisis: A Regulationist Interpretation*. Routledge: London and New York, pp.19–31.

Yamaguchi, S. (1985) *Keizai Genron Kogi (Lectures of Principles of Political Economy)*. Tokyo Daigaku Shuppankai: Tokyo.

Yasuba, Y. (1975) "Anatomy of the Debate on Japanese Capitalism," *Journal of Japanese Studies* 2(1), August 1975.

Yoshihara, N. (2008) *Roudo Sakushu no Kousei Riron Josetsu (Prolegomena to the Welfare Theory of Labor Exploitation)*. Iwanami Shoten: Tokyo.

Zieschang, K. (1957) "Zu einigen theoretischen Problemen des staatsmonopolistischen Kapitalismus in Westdeutschland (On Some Problems of the State Monopoly Capitalism in West Germany)." *Probleme der politischen Ökonomie*, Instituts für Wirtschaftswissenschaften: Berlin.

2 The Uno theory and Marx

Michiaki Obata (translated by Kei Ehara)

Introduction

The Japanese have arguably been some of the most ardent readers of Karl Marx's *Capital* in the world. Nevertheless, the large volume of its text includes few parts about Japan. Even after the publication of *Capital*, Marx seems to have had little interest in the small island country in the Far East until his death in 1883, whilst he paid much more attention to India and China. Though, Marx did devote a few lines to Japan: "Japan, with its purely feudal organization of landed property and its developed small-scale agriculture, gives a much truer picture of the European Middle Ages than all our history books" (Marx 1992a p.878). And "[i]f the foreign trade imposed on Japan by Europe brings with it the transformation of rents in kind into money rents, then the exemplary agriculture of that country [Japan] will be done for" (1992a p.239).

This prediction proved wrong. The Convention of Peace and Amity between the United States of America and the Empire of Japan was imposed by the US in 1854. The new Japanese government established by the Meiji Restoration in 1868 (one year after the publication of the first edition of *Capital* Vol. I) carried out the Land Tax Reform in 1873 to consolidate its fiscal basis. The beginning of foreign trade and the transformation of rents in kind into money rents had certainly occurred and their considerable effect on Japanese agriculture cannot be missed. At the same time, however, these two factors promoted the development of the export-oriented light industry, notably represented by the rise in the silk industry, which was followed by full-scale industrialization. But for Marx and Engels, the colonization of Japan must have seemed inevitable, as the neighboring enormous empire, China, had already been semicolonized by the European great powers. "Since the world is round, the colonisation of California and Australia and the opening up of China and Japan would seem to have completed this process" (Marx 1975 p.347) Marx and Engelsenvisaged. The rising locale of indigenous capitalism in the Far East resisted this kind of European expansion of market. During half a century up to the First World War, Japan had rapidly fostered industrialism and militarism, which led to the invasion and colonization of the Korean Peninsula, Taiwan and China and its growth into the imperialistic capitalism that ranked it among the European great imperialist powers.

European social science was introduced and spread in Japan in the beginning of the 20th century. Young scholars who studied in Germany played a particularly important role in introducing the latest Marxism around the end of WWI, and all volumes of *Capital* had already been translated into Japanese before the outbreak of the Great Depression in 1929. Marxian political economy in Japan developed rapidly, focusing on the historical development of capitalism from the viewpoint of *Capital* in order to understand the political and economic features of Japan, the nation chasing Germany along the capitalist path. The issues discussed were both academic and practical: had Japan already grown into the completed capitalism described in *Capital*? What did the dual structure mean, where the conflict between the capitalists and the workers intensified while a large number of the poor farmers and small producers remained in the countryside? These discussions cultivated the unique Marxian political economy in Japan.

As Japan strengthened militarism and plunged into World War II (WWII), the study of Marxian political economy was restrained and finally prohibited. Consequently, the following defeat in WWII especially benefited Marxism, allowing Marxian political economy to bloom spectacularly in Japanese academia.

Nevertheless, the mainstream Marxism revived in Japan was then strongly influenced by Stalinism. The criticism of Stalinism began in 1956 but it could not overcome the official line of the Communist Party of the Soviet Union. It argued that Japan was subordinate to the US under the Cold War regime. Yet it consequently failed to take account of the significant capitalist development of Japan after WWII. On the contrary, what Japanese Marxist economist Kozo Uno did was not only to reject Stalin's view but also to reconstruct political economy originally on the basis of *Capital*, which made it possible to grasp the rise and fall of high economic growth that Japan had experienced from a Marxian perspective. Hence Uno's approach gradually won popularity among young scholars and formed one of the leading schools of Marxian political economy in Japan.

This article intends to introduce the features of Uno theory with its historical uniqueness in Marxian political economy in Japan. Further, it attempts to show problems the Uno school faces today, together with possible solutions to them. That, then, will lead to renewed development of the school. In order to understand Uno's approach, we need first to summarize the theoretical image of capitalism observed in *Capital* and the transformation of this view into Marxism-Leninism in the 20th century. The Uno Theory was built up on the criticism of these generally accepted theories of Marxism.

Capitalism for Marx

Though *Capital* was written in German and it presupposed a German reader initially, what was mainly analyzed in the book is capitalism in Britain where Marx had sought asylum since 1849. He refers to this gap between the reader and the subject as follows:

> What I have to examine in this work is the capitalist mode of production, and the relations of production and forms of intercourse that correspond

to it. Until now, their locus classicus has been England. This is the reason why England is used as the main illustration of the theoretical developments I make. If, however, the German reader pharisaically shrugs his shoulders at the condition of the English industrial and agricultural workers, or optimistically comforts himself with the thought that in Germany things are not nearly so bad, I must plainly tell him: De te fabula narratur! [The tale is told of you]

(Marx 1992a p.90)

And "[t]he country that is more developed industrially only shows, to the less developed, the image of its own future" (Marx 1992a p.91), Marx maintained, insisting that the study on British capitalism was useful in understanding the future of Germany. In so far as we read *Capital* Vol. I, which was published and revised by Marx himself, Marx seems to have considered that wherever capitalism grew it would evolve in the same way. German capitalism was thought to be following British capitalism with the class struggle getting more and more violent. This idea of the universal converging tendency of capitalism can be found in other parts of *Capital* Vol. I:

No period of modern society is so favorable for the study of capitalist accumulation as the period of the last twenty years. . . . But of all countries England again provides the classical example, because it holds the foremost place in the world market, because capitalist production is fully developed only in England, . . . We have already sufficiently indicated the titanic progress of production in Part IV; in fact, in the latter half of the twenty-year period under discussion it has gone far beyond its progress in the former half.

(Marx 1992a p.802)

Here, too, England is supposed to be running as the top of capitalist development and be marching toward "the classical example".

The end of the convergence is, in a word, the internal collapse. What *Capital* Vol. I is about can be largely divided into two parts: the former half elucidates the formation of surplus value, assuming that a labor-power commodity is sold at its value just like other commodities in general; the latter half discusses the accumulation of surplus value along with the fast mechanization of production, the result of which is the progressive production of the industrial reserve army. According to volume one of *Capital*, capitalist development is heading toward an extreme society which would have a handful of huge capitalists on the one side and an enormous number of unemployed proletarians on the other. To put it simply, the converging tendency and the internal collapse are at the core of *Capital* Vol. I. When the class struggle reached its limit, the political revolution would inevitably replace capitalism. The transition to socialism was, therefore, expected to happen in the most developed capitalist country as revolution.

However, a sign of change in Marx's view of revolution can be traced during the period when *Capital* was prepared, i.e. from the latter half of the 1850s to the 1860s. The January Uprising in Poland began in 1863, leading to the formation of the First International. Meanwhile, the movement for Irish independence peaked in 1867, when *Capital* Vol. I was published, and Marx was inclined to conceive Irish workers as a promising revolutionary vanguard, gradually estranged from English workers in the First International. This was one of the causes that changed his straightforward view of revolution into a multitracked path[1].

As a result, *Capital* Vol. III includes a view which cannot be reduced to the converging tendency or the internal collapse perspective of Vol. I.

> On the basis of capitalist production, however, extended operations of long duration require greater advances of money capital for a longer time. Production in these branches is therefore dependent on the extent of the money capital which the individual capitalist has at his disposal. This limit is overcome by the credit system and the forms of association related to it, e.g. joint-stock companies.
>
> (Marx 1992b p.433)

It is here maintained that large-scale production that cannot be launched by an individual capital is subsumed under the motion of capital in the form of a "joint-stock company". In these sentences, we can catch a glimpse of the idea of the expansion of the capitalist mode of production into new branches such that capitalism historically transforms itself at the same time.

In addition, it is stated that the expansion of the capitalist mode of production at its center destroys the forms of production at the periphery.

> [T]he same circumstance that produces the basic condition for capitalist production, the existence of a class of wage-laborers, encourages the transition of all commodity production to capitalist commodity production. To the extent that the latter develops, it has a destroying and dissolving effect on all earlier forms of production, which, being pre-eminently aimed at satisfying the direct needs of the producers, only transform their excess products into commodities. It makes the sale of the product the main interest, at first without apparently attacking the mode of production itself; this was for example the first effect of capitalist world trade on such peoples as the Chinese, Indians, Arabs, etc. Once it has taken root, however, it destroys all forms of commodity production that are based either on the producers' own labour, or simply on the sale of the excess product as a commodity.
>
> (Marx 1992b pp.119, 120)

We can observe in this text the thought that western capitalism does not develop on its own and does dissolve the former forms of production around the world, carrying out both the formal and real subsumption. This notion of exterior infiltration, together with the idea of interior expansion mentioned above, reflects the beginnings of the stage of imperialism, which are characterized by the rise of the latecomers to capitalism.

Capitalism in Marxism-Leninism

Marx's view on capitalism was reinterpreted after his death, with capitalism transforming itself drastically. As Marx's plain grave in Highgate cemetery was relocated hundreds of yards away and was rebuilt into a giant monument, Marx's image of capitalism formed in the 19th century was converted into that of Marxism–Leninism in the 20th century.

This conversion was fuelled by the rise of new capitalist countries such as Germany and the resultant worldwide redivision of colonies that brought about the opposing upsurge of independence and revolutionary movements. In the super long term, the center of the swirl of revolution began to move away from the Western developed capitalist countries at the beginning of the 20th century. It is true that the German revolution might have been possible and the Euro-communism could have sprouted at that time, but the countries that had materialized "socialism" emerged and spread in the areas where capitalism had not yet developed "maturely". Since *Capital* does not refer to these regions, "Marxism" there had to be mediated by Lenin's works, e.g. *Imperialism*. "Marxism" turned into "Marxism-Leninism", thus permeating into noncapitalist areas. This "popular edition" of Marxism is much easier to read than Marx's works, but what it discusses is actually as complicated as Marx's thought. Here we try to classify the difficulty in terms of two sides: on the "outside" it is about a so-called two-stage revolution, the idea of aiming at two revolutions, i.e. the bourgeois revolution and socialist revolution separated accordingly as historical stages of development of respective regions; the "inside" is insisting on a universal revolution, conceiving the two revolutions as inseparable in the age of imperialism.

The two-stage revolution is considered an extension of the converging tendency of capitalism. If latecomers to capitalism such as Germany were chasing England on the straight road of capitalist development, still later countries would have to start the race at any rate. This starting point is so-called "primitive accumulation" in *Capital*, but the 20th century Marxists were first engaged in activities to overthrow feudalism. They thought the typical example of the bourgeois revolution was the Great French Revolution, even though the Puritan Revolution and the Glorious Revolution in England preceded it and primitive accumulation in France was not complete. Orthodox Marxism–Leninism argued that the capitalist class, who had seized power through bourgeois revolution, would be defeated by the workers and that this proletarian revolution would achieve the transition to socialism.

Indeed, with the benefit of hindsight, all revolutions are composed of democracy, socialism and nationalism, as was the French Revolution.[2] They are always nothing but a civil revolution in a broad sense. The Russian Revolution was copied from Commune de Paris. The method was applied to various kinds of struggles for emancipation against colonialism, which were followed by the democratization movements like the overthrow of the Marcos Government in the Philippines, the Arab Spring being the recent case. The modern history of socialism was that of the movements of political revolution seeking freedom and equality, making it natural to think socialism and revolution were inseparable. Experiencing the collapse of socialism created by the revolution, today we cannot find the specific reason why the revolution is indispensable for the transition to postcapitalism. The historical context in the 20th century allowed Marxism-Leninism to spread, supporting the argument of the two-stage revolution that was based on the view of converging capitalism and the following straight-line process toward socialism. Japan was no exception in this regard.

However, the inner side of Marxism-Leninism is rather different. Lenin proposed the conversion of imperialist wars into civil wars. The country that would be defeated in this scenario of "revolutionary defeatism" was supposed to be the imperialist state. On the contrary, the actual result of the imperialist war was the upsurge for independence and emancipation in the colonial and semi-colonial regions. After the First World War, the national self-determinism escalated among the peripheries of the imperialist great powers. This difference between the theory and the reality reflects the complicated issues at that time: while the solidarity between the class struggle at the suzerain and the emancipation movement at the colonies should be achieved, socialism had little social influence without the support of nationalism. Being "international" on the basis of the national self-determinism was just an ideal. So the socialists under the "revolutionary defeatism" in the imperialist states were confronted with a serious disease of xenophobia arising from nationalism. The peripheral regions had no trouble of this kind as anti-imperialism and nationalism were successfully compatible there. Hence the periphery was far more prone to revolutionary pressure than the center of capitalism.

As the interpretation of Marx's *Capital* was changed accordingly as the changes occurred at the end of the 19th century, that of Lenin's *Imperialism* was also subject to the realities of the Cold War structure. The image of the universal revolution itself had transformed: it would first be considered to be triggered at the periphery which was deemed to be "the weakest chain-link of the imperialism", but later Marxism-Leninism-Maoism regarded it as the besiegement of cities by rural movement, thus propagating itself into the Third World. If the imperialism suppressed the periphery in particular, no area in the world could avoid the effect of imperialism, the highest stage of capitalism; hence all anti-imperialism movements would be part of the socialist revolution. Marxism in the 20th century thus aroused socialist states in the regions that were far away from the content of *Capital* and they were organized accordingly to the advantage of the Soviet Union under the world regime of the Cold War, forming the East camp against the West.

Capitalism for Kozo Uno

Kozo Uno went back to Marx's *Capital* abandoning the political economy in Marxism-Leninism. The Uno theory now holds renewed meaning in watching the globalism dominant in the post–Cold War world, which Uno himself did not foresee. This unintended consequence will be discussed later; here we are going to see what Uno intended.

The essence of Uno's argument is, in a word, the reversal of the recognition of conversing tendency of capitalism in *Capital*. Uno considered the convergence depicted by Marx as the process in which capitalism purified itself by removing noneconomic factors and letting market doctrine control everything. Uno insisted that this tendency of purification slowed down or reversed at the end of the 19th century, and he distinguished "the stage of imperialism" from "the stage of liberalism". The core of the Uno theory is the stages theory, which clarified "the stage of imperialism" as one of the stages of capitalism (Uno 1962).

What follows this basic historical view is the claim that the principles of political economy should be established as the "pure capitalism" that the tendency of purification hypothetically reaches in the end. We have no space in this article to explain the world of Uno's principles of political economy in detail. To sum up, it is the society that consists of only the three main classes – capitalists, workers and landlords – where capitalists manage social production competitively on the basis of the complete labor market, accompanied by periodic business cycles (Uno 1977). The content of *Capital* was purified, and consequently molded into the single image of capitalism where the logic of capital maximizing profit was exclusively dominant. Uno discarded several topics in *Capital*, such as the immiseration of workers in capitalist accumulation and the historical development of the capitalist mode of production as inexplicable in the principles of political economy. The theoretical subject of these was to be considered only within the operation of economic laws, including business cycles.

The establishment of Uno's theory of principles impacted upon the structure of the stages theory. It is expanded to cover three stages of capitalism, which respectively correspond to the generation, development and downfall of capitalism. Purification and its reverse explain only the separation of two stages. The theoretical capitalism that shows how the same situation of accumulation is repeated enables us to assume that the stage in question maintains the similar situation. Hence, the tendency of purification was divided into two stages, i.e. the stage which experienced the process and the stage which saw the maintained state. The former is the stage of generation of capitalism or the stage of mercantilism, and the latter the developed stage of capitalism, namely the stage of liberalism. The third stage, the stage of imperialism, saw the tendency of purification reversed, which was regarded as indicating the downfall of capitalism. The other reason for the additional division of the purification into two stages was the necessity to explain the historical shift in the economic policies. Actually, this three-stage configuration originally derives from the lecture on economic policies Uno gave when he was young Uno (1971). The big change in economic policies naturally suggests certain historical distinction in the underlying economic situations (we do not owe this to Marx's historical materialism).

There is, however, a problem with this "popular edition" of the stages theory arranged as the three-stage structure. As I have discussed elsewhere (Obata 2014 Ch.7), labeling the stage of generation as "mercantilism" had biased the understanding of the origin of capitalism. Though Uno himself did not adequately discuss the distinction between the generation and the origin of capitalism, it virtually meant the generation of capitalism in England was considered as the single origin of capitalism. It is true that the transition from the putting-out system in the wool industry to the large-scale mechanical production in the cotton industry marks the difference between the stage of generation and that of development. We must, however, pay attention to the preceding rise of the wool industry on the European continent. If this relation were ignored, we would miss the originality in the rise of Germany in the end of the 19th century, which was grounded in the expansion of heavy industry. The origin determines the future. The view of the England-based single origin is certainly an obstacle to the analysis in today's globalism, as we will argue soon: the rise of emerging countries is regarded as the effect of capital exports mainly from the US and their indigenous origins are dismissed, hence the stage of "imperialism" is just prolonged and the three-stage configuration is also fixed.

Capitalism after Uno

The main target of Uno's own stage theory was the period of classical imperialism up to WWI. The supporters of Uno extended his framework in order to grasp the world after WWII. The extension has two directions.

The one direction focuses on the enlargement of noneconomic factors in general. What Uno himself argued in the stage of imperialism where the noneconomic factors had gained momentum was the inevitability of war. Since there remained a large number of the peasantry and the small producers in the capitalist nations such as Germany that achieved rapid growth centered on heavy industry, the internal market was too small to consume the products, forcing the capitalists to go abroad. This movement conflicted with the developed capitalist nations such as England, hence the military clash occurred. The clash of WWI was not, however, the death knell of capitalism, even though it gave birth to the Soviet Union. Capitalism entered again the high-growth period under the US regime fighting the Cold War after the WWII. The Uno Theory spread in this very period.

The stage of imperialism had to be redetermined accordingly. If the stage of liberalism is characterized by the tendency of purification that excludes state intervention and lets a competitive market thrive, its reversal can be interpreted as the enlargement of noneconomic factors in general, not specially restricted to the forceful colonialism and militarism. The menace of socialism in the time of the Cold War cannot be imagined today. It was taken for granted that capitalism had to avoid a severe crisis and economic depression and to reinforce the system alleviating the conflict between management and unions. The renewal of "the stage of imperialism" was conducted so as to capture the new realities: very unique "state monopoly capitalism" was formulated to characterize the managed currency system as the policy that tried to evade crisis by causing mild inflation, mitigating the profit squeeze by the rise in wages; the analysis of finances emphasized the role of the welfare state to balance the economy by means of fiscal and financial policies in general. "The pure capitalism" that was illustrated in the principles of political economy in which only market forces dominate social reproduction definitely helped grasp and contextualize the enlargement of the noneconomic factors.

With the Cold War suppressing the breakout of imperialist war, the "decay of capitalism" in Lenin's *Imperialism* was reinterpreted (Ouchi 1970) and stated differently, as in "over-enrichment" or "companyism" (Baba 1986), and mingled with "creeping socialism" (Shibagaki 1997). All these kinds of extensions shared the same recognition: the capitalism in the golden age would gradually self-destruct by way of strengthening the system of the welfare state. Their extension meant getting out of capitalism without revolution.

The second direction of extension redefined the downfall of capitalism as the geographical limit of capitalist development (Iwata 2006). The rise of new capitalist nations such as Germany suggested the beginning of the age of imperialism when the great powers literally divided the whole world and ruled others as colonies and dependencies. The colonial and dependent regions could have no chance at capitalist development for a long time. The reversal of purification tendency could be regarded not only as the enlargement of the noneconomic factors inside the imperialist countries but also as the worldwide fixation of the noncapitalist countries. The downfall of capitalism indicated the partiality of capitalism, which was the result of the decline of a wave of industrialization originated in England; hence capitalism was supposed to be unable to sweep the Earth entirely.

The partiality of capitalism that arose in the stage of imperialism remained consistently throughout the so-called long 20th century. The high growth in the developed countries after WWII was achieved while oppressing the economic development in the postcolonial areas. Political independence did not lead to economic independence and the disparity grew between the developed countries and the rest of the world, referred to as the North–South problem. The growth in the developed capitalist countries was possible on the condition of crushing other "origins" of capitalism in the rest of the world.

The Third World which had been banned from capitalist development had to seek another way. Advocating socialism was one of the choices. The emergence of socialist countries among the Third World led to the conviction that world history had entered the transitional period from capitalism to socialism (Takumi 1980, p.310). Uno also suggested socialism would be launched from the peripheries of the developed capitalist states, mentioning that capitalism had started not at the place where feudalism had advanced most, namely France, but at the peripheries of feudalism, i.e. England. At least it is certain that Uno had no doubt that the Soviet Union at his time was a socialist nation, and no one had foreseen the collapse of the USSR. We cannot use the benefit of hindsight after the Soviet collapse to support Uno's ideas (Uno 1971, p.268).

But the Uno Theory held a possibility of challenging the orthodoxy of Marxism effectively in the ideological context of the 1960s. The USSR in the Cold War had controlled the Third World to its own advantage while supporting both economically and militarily the national emancipation movement and the socialist countries at the periphery. The strategy of the USSR was formed in the twisted course of history but was fundamentally based on the concept of socialism in one country and of the two-stage revolution, both of which had originated from the view of the converging tendency of capitalism. The limits of this socialist oppression began to be revealed in the 1960s, as shown in "the Prague Spring" in 1968. In addition, the Vietnam War sparked the national emancipation movement in the Third World and the corresponding antiwar and dissident movement in the developed countries. The Uno theory that implied the partiality of capitalism was attractive for the universal revolutionists because it could be shared between the two movements. While Uno began his criticism of Stalinism soon after WWII ended, the Uno Theory based on the criticism of the converging view of capitalism had the possibility of developing the unique understanding of the Cold War regime. This possibility might be beyond the scope of Uno's work, but surely was the reason why the young generation acceded to the Uno Theory in the 1960s, when the high growth in Japan began to fade away.

Globalism

The environment described above changed drastically in the 1980s. The cataclysm of the global economy on a scale as great as that which once made Uno oppose Marxism-Leninism, is named globalism. As is the case with imperialism, the word "globalism" also contains diversified and often contradictory phenomena. It is of no use to stick to the meaning or the origin of this kind of label. It is necessary to conceptualize and elucidate the complicated phenomena hidden under the label.

Globalism can be interpreted largely in two ways. The one interpretation explains that the system and custom of the US form the global standards, under which international trade and finance expand and the movement of labor forces is accelerated (Baba 1986). Globalism is in fact Americanization, according to this interpretation, and the industrialization in the Third World is regarded as the result of the foreign investments from the developed countries after all. This view also considers globalism as inseparable from neoliberalism, which originated in the Anglo-American countries and swept the developed countries after the 1980s.

By contrast, another view emphasizes the momentum in the Third World (Obata 2012). The fundamentals of globalism are supposed to be found in the gradual industrialization scattered in the Third World from the 1970s. This source grew into newly industrializing countries (NICs) and newly industrializing economies (NIEs), following which the countries with massive populations swallowed them and now are leading the development of the emerging countries. From this point of view, the rise of the emerging countries has forced neoliberalism and "financialization" on the developed countries. Indeed, the foreign investment from the developed countries and the indigenous energy of the developing countries are interrelated and cannot be simply separated. The globalism that continued after the failure of neoliberalism, however, suggested to me that the momentum innate in the emerging countries should be taken as the core of globalism in the long run.

With all these interpretations, the reality of globalism forced the Uno Theory to retransform itself, not just to extend itself. Indeed, the first direction of the extension of the Uno Theory described above, which had expected the gradual evolution toward socialism without revolution, quickly lost validity when the developed countries were faced with the rise of globalism and began to resort to neoliberalism all together. The continued increase of wages could not be observed anymore, income disparity has enlarged with recurrent bubbles and long-term recession and, finally, the immiseration thesis in *Capital*, which had long been discarded as a relic of the past, attracts public attention now. Actually, we need to pay more attention to the fact that the widening wealth disparity within the developed countries is accompanied by the narrowing gap between the developed countries and the developing countries due to the development of the emerging countries. In other words, the welfare states in the developed countries could find their class struggle alleviated only on the condition that industrialization in the Third World was prevented. Though we must make sure not to oversimplify the discussion of the gap between the developed and the developing worlds, the developed world should not be investigated separately. The issue of neoliberalism must be studied from the globalized point of view concerning the rise of emerging capitalism as the foundation.

This contemporary situation leads to a more general problem: mature capitalism will not change itself spontaneously into socialism and rather reveals social conflict between commercialism and welfare. In order to analyze this problem, we need a new theory focusing on the dynamics of capital which dissolve and subsume the noncommercialized areas. The principles of political economy based on the assumption of "pure capitalism" have not analyzed these processes of transformations while the stages theory based on the principles has just enumerated various noneconomic factors, failing to observe the qualitative historical development.

The second direction of the extension of the Uno Theory was also seriously damaged by the phenomenon of globalism. The partiality of capitalism that did not welcome new industrialization had characterized the downfall of capitalism: "the downfall of capitalism with newly emerging capitalism" makes no sense. We cannot simply install the fourth stage into the Uno stages theory: the two-stage configuration was explained by the purification tendency and its reverse;

the expansion into the three-stage configuration was barely accomplished by the theoretical establishment of the principles of political economy describing the repeating laws of capitalism. The additional stage without any critical reconsideration would end up with mere classification of facts that do not elucidate any historical development. Labeling the current situation as a "spiral reversal" to the past has no chance of grasping the new origins of capitalism, which cannot be reduced to the past.

What is necessary is not a mere rearrangement of the partition of stages but a reconsideration of the method of composing stages itself. We must go into the principles of political economy and criticize the assumption of "pure capitalism" which is the basis of the stages theory, thereby constructing a completely new theory. I myself have been working on this task, trying to reorganize the theory of the principles of political economy in order to investigate the newly globalized capitalism (Obata 2012; 2013 and 2014). Though I am not confident yet about my own solutions, the problems surely exist, requiring the critical investigation into Uno's view of capitalism as much as the then contemporary issues of imperialism demanded Uno to criticize Marx's view of capitalism.

Capitalism in future

This article has discussed how Marx and Uno envisaged the future of capitalism. I would like to mention my current view on this issue as the closing remarks. When the partiality of capitalism that was supposed to be the limit of imperialism has been lost, the future of capitalism should be considered with regard to the developed countries again. The developed countries have no right to meddle in the development of the emerging countries. The capitalist development will bring about various bad effects in emerging countries, but they should be dealt with by the self-government of the people in the emerging countries.

Meanwhile, it will be increasingly difficult for the developed countries to compete with the emerging countries which are developing more and more rapidly. Indeed, we can observe the change in the profit-making business in the developed countries: the motion of capital is now penetrating into and reconstructing diverse spheres of consumption including education, medical services, nursing care, childcare, academia, art, culture, sports, entertainment, etc. The situation is grotesque, with ends and means reversed. Cost-effectiveness, which was formerly confined to the sphere of physical production, is now being pursued everywhere in human life. The social conflict will soon increase to be fatal, consequently compelling us to abandon the profit-making business in those spheres.

Though we cannot deduce the concrete image of the future, the reconstruction of the theory of the principles of political economy based on the historical development of capitalism up to today suggests the deliverance from capitalism in its mature state. If the power promoting this deliverance is drawn back from the continuous penetration of capital into the spheres other than production, the complete abandonment of the market will not be necessary in the transition. The physical production can be reasonably managed by the profit-making enterprises, since the input-output relation is technically obvious so that efficiency can be measured objectively there. Also, if the various kinds of consumption work regarding people's lives will be undertaken increasingly socially, it will not be necessary to forcibly abolish the social evaluation by wage payment. What is needed is to establish a style of work suited for the sphere of social life which is different from the production sphere and to create a new method of the distribution of social surplus.

Here we presuppose that all workers will be guaranteed to get a job for wages. In order to achieve this, it is not necessary to enlarge the scale of social production. We often take it for granted that enlarging employment opportunities needs growth. Yet enlarging physical production is not in principle necessary to secure employment. What we need is not only the reduction of working hours per capita or simple work-sharing: we need to reconsider the style of work in a broad sense. When I earn wages by teaching something while spending the wages to learn something else, national income is certainly increased, but this is very different from the growth by the expansion of physical production.

The most difficult matter in this change in the developed countries would be the issue of immigrants. If the style of work and the evaluation of it were determined by the social agreement, the local self-government must replace the national level government, while immigration should be strictly controlled. Cross-border friendship and trade should be freely promoted. Investing in the region of high capitalist development would be allowed so long as it would abide by the local rules. However, the movement of the labor force should be restricted, since toil and trouble must be highly evaluated and be undertaken by the people inside the community. This localism regarding labor-power does not mean xenophobia. When we are trapped in the dogma that maintaining growth and depending on low-paid immigrants are inevitable to ensure employment, xenophobia overcomes us. It is necessary, therefore, for us to recognize the difficulty of analyzing the parallel dynamics of capitalism and postcapitalism when considering the future of capitalism.

Notes

1 See Anderson (2010), Ch. 4.
2 Historians summarize the French Revolution as follows.

> Between 1789 and 1794 France changed from a country with many different outlooks and even languages to a single nation. France had created nationalism. The nation could override tradition and history. Moreover France, as the Great Nation, could override the national claims of others. Here were the three themes that revolutionary France launched into the world and that have continued to haunt the world ever since. They developed in many different ways. Nevertheless the three revolutionary causes – democracy, nationalism, socialism – all sprang from the fall of the Bastille on 14 July 1789.
>
> *(Talor 2014)*

References

(Titles in brackets are translated from Japanese.)

Anderson, K. B. (2010) *Marx at the Margins: On Nationalism, Ethnicity, and Non-Western Societies,* Chicago: University of Chicago Press.
Baba, H. (1986) *(Over-enrichment and Finance Capital),* Kyoto: Minerva–Shobo.
Iwata, H. (2006) *(World Capitalism I),* Tokyo: Hihyosha.
Marx, K. (1975) *Karl Marx, Frederick Engels: Collected Works,* vol. 40, New York: International Publishers.
Marx, K. (1992a) *Capital,* Vol. I, London: Penguin Classics.
Marx, K. (1992b) *Capital,* Vol. II, London: Penguin Classics.
Obata, M. (2012) *(Critical Studies on the Marxian Methodology of Political Economy),* Tokyo: Ochanomizu–Shobo.
Obata, M. (2013) *(Critical Studies on the Marxian Theory of Value),* Tokyo: Kobundo.
Obata, M. (2014) *(Critical Studies on the Marxian Theory of Crisis),* Tokyo: University of Tokyo Press.
Ouchi, T. (1970) *(State Monopoly Capitalism),* Tokyo: University of Tokyo Press.
Shibagaki, K. (1997) *(The Logic of Modern Capitalism),* Shibuya: Nihon–Keizai–Hyoronsha..
Takumi, M. (1980) *(World Capitalism),* Tokyo: Nihon-Hyoronsha.
Taylor, A. J. P. (2014) *Revolutions and Revolutionaries,* London: Endeavour Press.
Uno, K. (1962) *(Methodology of Political Economy),* Tokyo: University of Tokyo Press.
Uno, K. (1971) *(Theory of Economic Policy),* Tokyo: Kobundo.
Uno, K. (1977) *Principles of Political Economy,* London: Harvester.

3 Non-Western Marxist traditions in Northeast Asia

Hiroshi Onishi

Globally, Marxism has multiple origins and traditions, some of which are distinctly non-Western. For example, certain schools of Japanese Marxism, Maoism, and Stalinism[1] have evolved differently from Western anti-neoliberalism. Although Stalinism is not considered Asian Marxism, it differs from the Western Marxist tradition in highly advanced capitalist countries. To this effect, it can be classified as non-Western Marxism. In present-day China, at least, Stalinism coexists with Maoism and Western-oriented leftism. Japanese Marxists developed various original forms of Marxism, some of which resonated with other forms of Asian Marxism. This resonance may have been formed by the essentially similar socio-political situation created by the backwardness of their countries. In this chapter, I will discuss the originalities of Asian Marxism and its international influences, especially in Northeast Asia.

South Korean Marxism and leftism after the democratization movement

Because Marxists around the world have different interests regarding global reformation, their selection of theoretical approaches is also based on practical usefulness. For example, Vietnamese Marxists needed a theory that had practical implications for the anti-imperialist struggle during the Vietnam War, whereas Indian Marxists needed one to overcome the religious conflicts between Muslims and Hindus. This was a very natural evolution and explains the changes in the theoretical landscape of South Korean leftism.

The Korean capitalism debates

For many years, South Korea had functioned under a dictatorial rule, where, before 1987, Marxist documents were prohibited from being published under the National Security Act. Although they were prohibited, many young students were eager to read them and utilized them as a theoretical basis for their political movements. There was a wide array of Marxist or leftist documents to choose from. At first, the South Korean leftists selected Frank-Amin's dependency theory in their fight against the world capitalist system. At the time, they asserted that capitalism was incorporated in the periphery of underdeveloped states in South Korea, a situation similar to Latin American countries, and therefore, its government exerted authoritarian rule over the people. Using this framework, they explained the reality of the high dependency on US imperialism and formulated the *peripheral capitalism theory*. However, another group that was strongly inclined toward traditional Marxism claimed that a dependency theory of this nature could not explain the development of Korean capitalism or analyze the class relations within South Korea. They believed that state monopoly capitalism prevailed in South Korea and that capitalism had expanded beyond the expectations of the peripheral capitalism theory. This new standpoint gave birth to a new theory, the *state monopoly capitalism theory*. These two theories sparked much controversy and were the subject of the *Korean capitalism debates*. However, just before the controversy, a Japanese professor, Kajimura Hideki,[2] published a book (Kajimura 1977) in Japan that clearly analyzed Korean capitalism according to Yun (2000); at least one theoretician of the peripheral capitalism theory was strongly influenced by the book. This could be considered a form of Asian theoretical interaction.

National liberation group vs. people's democracy group

However, after democratization by President No Tae-woo in 1987, the situation changed. After democratization, the above-mentioned groups reviewed their own theories, particularly their analyses of class relations in South Korea, and introduced a new perspective within the traditional theories of peripheral capitalism and state monopoly capitalism. South Korea was defined as a colonial semifeudalist (capitalist) economy by the former, and as a neocolonial state monopoly capitalist economy by the latter. The former was named the national liberation (NL) group and the latter the people's democracy (PD) group. They fervently fought against each other, which led to the next big controversy of the late 1980s, the *social formation debates*.

These two theories are of particular interest from the viewpoint of Asian theoretical interactions. The NL focuses on national interests, giving priority to national reunification. This school of thought suggested that North Korea was already liberated from the imperialists and, therefore, its extension to the South would liberate the entire peninsula. Here, it is worth noting that this framework is similar to Mao Zedong's revolutionary base theory, which highlighted the building of regional bases and expanding them to liberate the whole country. Kim Il-Sung's intentions at the time of the Korean War were similar to Mao's theory in that he wanted to liberate South Korean peasants from semifeudalism and win their support for the North Korean army; however, his intentions were not realized.

The PD theory at the social formation debates was strongly influenced by external Marxist ideologies. Although it also conceded that postwar US policy placed South Korea in a neocolonial position, it made a strong point regarding the already developed monopoly capital. Thus, their theory can be regarded as a revolutionary strategy against both imperialism and monopolistic capitalism,[3] which is identical to the Japanese *Koza-ha* theory after World War II.[4]

As the Koza-ha theory and its counterpart, Rono-ha,[5] are discussed in the debates on Japanese capitalism in the first chapter of this book, we need not delve into the details of this theory. The Koza-ha theory was established circa 1930 and became the Japanese Marxist orthodoxy in analyzing Japan's social structure before World War II. It maintained that prewar Japanese society was based on absolutism, which represented two social classes – monopoly capital and semifeudal landowners – and therefore, called for an anti-semifeudalist and antimonopoly revolution. After the fundamental social change that occurred in 1945, the school identified two new ruling classes in Japan, monopoly capitalism and US imperialism, and thus called for an anti-imperialist and antimonopolistic revolution, which is considered the postwar *Koza-ha* theory. Given that the social structures of Japan and South Korea were similar, the characteristics of the *Koza-ha* theory and PD theory in South Korea were identical. In summary, similar materialistic bases produce similar theories. In both pre- and postwar Japan, the Japanese Communist Party has been guided by the *Koza-ha* theory and is therefore called the Marxist orthodoxy in Japan.

Crucial to understanding the influence of Japanese Marxism on this controversy is a remark in Shin Gi-Wook (2002):

> . . . at the "social formation debates" . . . The intellectual discourse articulated the goals, meanings, targets, tactics, and strategies of the 1980s anti-American, nationalist democratic movements in a fashion reminiscent of the *Koza-ha–Rono-ha* debates among Japanese Marxists in the 1920s and 1930s and the 1930s debates on Chinese capitalism. Like their counterparts in Japan and China, Korean Marxists and dissident intellectuals believed a proper specification of the nature of Korean economic and political development was necessary to guide their movements.
>
> (pp. 360–361)

This explanation is exceptionally honest in admitting the influence of their East Asian precursors. It also mentions that the accurate theorization of society is needed for a progressive movement[6] and discusses the influences of the Chinese Marxist controversy. All of these points are of much importance to this chapter.

However, the strength of South Korean leftists was soon affected by the collapse of Eastern Europe and the Soviet Union, and thus, needed to build or seek a defensive theory. This held true for Marxists and leftists around the world.[7]

After the collapse of the dictatorship

Over the years, the practical interests of South Korea have changed. The primary issue is no longer the anti-dictatorship movement, and the US military presence has been reduced. The more recent social problems are, for example, the 1997

Asian financial crisis and the end of the "Miracle on the Han River". Therefore, their interests have shifted to that crisis, along with declining profit rates and share of labor income, and surplus value. All of these issues have been addressed by Marxist mathematicians, such as Rieu (2008; 2009), Kang and Rieu (2009), and others. In addition, the Okishio theorem has also been discussed by many researchers, not only in the context of its Japanese or Asian origin but also in relation to the law of declining profit rates.

As an open economy, South Korea had strong interests in its international economic relations with the US and others as well as in understanding export-oriented growth strategies.[8] Its mainstream economists believed that exports were the only possible strategy to foster growth in South Korea; however, leftist or Marxist economists were against this strategy and called for a wage-oriented growth strategy. This struggle is closely related to that between South Korea's strong export industries and other weak ones. In reality, South Korea's export industries have achieved significant success owing to the export-oriented growth strategy, whereas its weak industries, such as agriculture and fishing, are deteriorating. In other words, the success of export industries has been realized by victimizing the weak ones. The choice of growth strategy has been widely discussed in academia that focuses on the struggle between export industries and others.

Thus, many South Korean leftist scholars are now engaging in research on growth patterns of the Korean economy based on French regulation theory and US Social Structures of Accumulation (SSA) theory.[9] This competitive situation regarding the choice of strategy is the same as that in Japan and encourages many academic exchanges between Japan and South Korea in this field.

Asian two-stage revolution theories: dividing enemies

To understand individual societies, it is important to know who the ruler is and who is being ruled – this was the fundamental viewpoint of Mao Zedong (1940). In the first two lines of the first of seven volumes of his collected works, he stated, "Who is the enemy and who is the friend is the fundamental problem of the revolutions". With this thought, he divided landowners into big and small landowners, capitalists into big and small ones, and the national party into the patriot wing and betrayers. In addition to the abovementioned revolutionary theory, this class theory was a strategy to maximize friends and minimize enemies and, in fact, led to the victory of the Communist Party in China; this Chinese strategy was even proclaimed in Mao's (1940) book, titled *On New Democracy*. This draft was written soon after the Nationalist and the Communist Parties established their second alliance, which was symbolic of the victory against Japan's invasion of China and the maintenance and expansion of communist power after the victory.

Mao identified two basic enemies, big landowners and Japanese imperialism, and stated that the coming revolution should be an antifeudalist and anti-imperialist one. Mao said that this revolution should be led by the proletariat but would not be a socialist revolution. The socialist revolution would and should take place in the distant future.

This is the well-known two-stage revolution theory formulated by Lenin. Lenin supported the anti-absolutist revolution in the spring of 1917, and then joined the socialist revolution in late 1917. Nevertheless, the point remains that there was backwardness in the social structure, and the two-stage revolution strategy was applied particularly to backward countries including Japan.

The Japanese communists established their own two-stage strategy of revolution that was based on the *Koza-ha* theory or the then Japanese Marxist orthodoxy.[10] This theoretical determination is elucidated in the following words by Noro Eitaro (1935), a prominent theoretician on the *Koza-ha* faction and a top leader in the Japanese Communist Party:

> When I read *Thesis on Japan* [i.e., *1927 Thesis*] by the executive committee of the Comintern, I know that my analysis is consistent with that of the Comintern in general and has no serious mistakes (to cause strategic conflicts) in the details.
>
> (p. 4)

The *Thesis on Japan* written by the Comintern was virtually the party program in itself. At the time, each national communist party was merely a branch of the Comintern and each of their programs was given or sanctioned by the Comintern's headquarters in Moscow. At this point, it is important to know that the two-stage revolution strategy was established under the influence of Russia's experience of an actual two-stage revolution. Also noteworthy is that this thesis was written by reading Japanese Marxists' theoretical achievements, and that the most important achievement was the *History of the Development of Japanese Capitalism*, written by Noro just before the thesis. After writing the book, from 1932 to 1933, he edited seven volumes of the *Series on the Historical Development of Japanese Capitalism (Nihon Shihonshugi Hattatsushi Koza)* with the help of his fellow theoreticians. This is regarded as one of the principal achievements of the *Koza-ha* Marxists in the prewar period, which also influenced the next political program given by the Comintern in 1932. Adhering to the two-stage revolution theory,[11] the *1932 Thesis* focused its attention on the nature of the emperor system and stressed the strategic significance of the anti-imperialist struggle of the working class in Japan.

The most important characteristic of Japan's two-stage theory of revolution was its class analysis: which classes were ruling and which classes were ruled. In this case, Japanese society was defined by the emperor's despotism under which people were oppressed by two ruling classes, monopoly capitalists and semifeudal landowners. Here, even if the existence of monopoly capitalists is proof that capitalism was well developed, that of semifeudalist landowners was evidence of backwardness. On the other hand, China's backwardness was demonstrated by the rule of not only feudalists but also imperialists. Both countries were plagued by such backwardness and ruled by the two ruling classes.

Marxism in both China and Japan share similar characteristics; this is connected to Nosaka Sanzo's stay in Yan'an during 1940–1946. Nosaka succeeded
Noro after his demise in 1932 and became the then Japanese representative of
the Comintern. After his return to Japan in 1946, he became one of the top
leaders of the Japanese Communist Party. Nosaka was a key person in international interactions. He graduated from Keio University and was junior to Noro.
Nosaka was strongly influenced by the *Koza-ha* theory.[12] The strength of Nosaka's
personal connection with Mao remains unclear. However, when Nosaka moved
to Yan'an from Moscow in 1940, he spent much of his time with Zhou Enlai
during his journey,[13] and at the time, Zhou was a strong supporter of Mao.[14]
Araki (1993) provides two additional facts that show Mao's theoretical influence
on Nosaka. First is that Nosaka's six years in Yan'an coincided with the period
when Mao strongly took to theoretical leadership and is just short of Mao's
campaign of the two-stage revolution theory. Second, soon after Nosaka's return
to Japan in 1946, Mao's *On New Democracy* was listed as an academic book
for Communist Party members in Japan.[15]

It is important to explore the influence of the theory of democratic revolution of Palmiro Togliatti on Nosaka. This influence has been evidenced and
identified in Araki (1993)[16] and in Nosaka's (1989) autobiography. Although
Togliatti was not Asian, it is of significance that his theory differed from that
of the core doctrine of the Comintern. In 1935, when Georgi Dimitrov was
elected as the general secretary of the Comintern, Togliatti was his junior
partner as a member of its Secretariat. According to Yamazaki (1975), Togliatti's concept of a united front was different from that of Dimitrov. For
example, while Dimitrov's main report to the seventh congress of the Comintern in 1935 asserted that building a new democratic republic was not a revolution in itself but simply a process, Togliatti argued that the antifascist
democratic movement of the united front, which developed inevitably to the
point of taking power, creates supporting blocs for the socialist revolution.
While Dimitrov's concept of a united front remained as a tactic at the political
level, Togliatti's view of a united front was a strategy based on the in-depth
analyses of class structures.

In my view, the most important difference between them was that Dimitrov
regarded fascism as a phenomenon occurring at the most developed stage of
capitalism, which is represented by the power of financial capital, while Togliatti
thought that the task of the united front in Spain was not confined to defeating
the capitalist system alone but included conquering the entire politico-economic
system, including the semifeudalistic land system. Therefore, a frequently asked
question in the debate was whether a united front was suited to advanced countries or less developed countries. Because Nosaka was interested in revolution of
the country of late-developed capitalism, he naturally followed Togliatti. Admitting that Nosaka was influenced by Togliatti, a Western Marxist in the present
view, his choice was a deliberate one based on a deep analysis of Japanese society
that had been accumulated by his party since the debates on Japanese capitalism
in the 1930s.

It is possible that the same conditions applied in the case of Mao Zedong since the Chinese revolution in 1949 was declared as a democratic revolution.

The strategy of two-stage revolution has been often criticized as a deviation from the idea of a socialist revolution. Today, however, very few Japanese Marxists believe that a socialist revolution could occur in the near future. They expect at most a democratic revolution. Furthermore, as mentioned, the Japanese Communist Party and Japanese Marxist orthodoxy continue to assert that the Japanese people have two enemies: monopoly capitalism and US imperialism. Therefore, the present task of the people should be an antimonopoly and anti-imperialist revolution at the first stage. Most Japanese Marxists believe that a far more realistic objective is comprised of everyday struggles, such as the anti-TPP,[17] anti-US base, anti–nuke plant,[18] and anti–mass taxation struggles. All of these can be understood as antimonopoly and anti-imperialist struggles.

In conclusion, I make the following two comments as a supporter of this type of two-stage revolution theory in Japan. The first is based on the small difference between actual rulers and monopoly capitalism under Abenomics. Japan's state power mainly represents the interests of the major parts of monopoly capitals, which sometimes differ from those of minor parts of monopoly capitals. However, sometimes, the interests of the state apparatus differ from those of monopoly capitalism and US imperialism. Marxists have recognized this as the problem of relative autonomy of the superstructure, which has intensified under the Abe administration because it wants to justify Japan's invasion of Asia before 1945 and its current preparation for another war against China. These phenomena have created conflicts with the US government and the export industries whose major customer is China.[19]

My second comment draws on socialism. For a long time, leftists have lost sight of the larger socialist revolution, especially since the collapse of Eastern Europe and the Soviet Union, and because daily struggles against rulers do not require them to question the fundamental social system. As mentioned, the crucial difference between socialists and social democrats is the ultimate aim or the final decision on whether we must proceed toward socialism. In fact, many Japanese Marxists have lost their confidence in this matter and have become pure and simple leftists.

However, mentions of socialism alone do not make one a Marxist. Our task is to envision a more realistic socialist revolution. As in my earlier research on understanding 20th-century socialism, I continue to propose a much more realistic style of socialism. In my understanding, a market system with a small government and shareholding companies can be called a socialist order if state monopoly is broken down and national independence is secured, and more importantly, if society has changed its priority from capital accumulation to enriching human lives. After the Industrial Revolution, we prioritized capital accumulation because of its role in economic development, and therefore, all sociopolitical institutions and ideologies served this purpose. This is capitalism. If we pass this stage, we can progress to the next stage, which should be socialism.[20] If we must discuss revolution, we must do so in the context and with an understanding of socialism.[21]

Three types of present-day Chinese leftism

We now turn to present-day China, a country with an ideological disruption between the left and right. Although the official term for China's socialist market economy is "market socialism" or "socialism with Chinese characteristics," many social scientists including a certain number of Chinese economists believe that the economy has capitalist features. Therefore, neoclassical economics has already occupied the mainstream, placing Marxist and leftist ideologies under pressure.

Of course, this situation differs from, and is better than, that in capitalist countries. For example, current human development economics lectures are being delivered in universities under the leadership of Marxian economists. I explain this new trend in the following section. Even today, Chinese Marxian or leftist economics have a strong influence and broad scopes of application. According to Chinese leftist political scientist Yang Fan (2013),[22] there are three types of leftism: Stalinism (old left), Maoism (Cultural Revolution), and the Western-oriented new left.

Stalinism

According to Yang, Stalinism is an ideology adopted by bureaucrats, a major ruling social class in so-called socialist countries. Nevertheless, with deregulation and privatization, their interests are being threatened and they are gradually losing power. However, different stages in history need different social systems, or more precisely, governments of different sizes. This is historical materialism. To this effect, Stalinism identified the period in which a big government was needed. In my understanding, the size of government inevitably shrinks and so does their power. However, in the case of rapid deregulation and privatization, it is important for this ideology to resist conservatism. A majority of present-day Chinese Marxists belong to this wing. They believe that the present deregulation and privatization process is happening faster than what was historically anticipated; if so, they must play a crucial role in adjusting the process.

Maoism

On the other hand, Maoism has goals that are contrary to those of Stalinism because of its tendency to attack the bureaucracy.[23] In fact, in the 1960s and 1970s, many anti-Stalinist students supported Maoism on university campuses in Japan with antibureaucratic intentions. This was the reason why Maoism created a god of Mao. Under the rule of Mao, China wanted to overthrow the social classes between the people and their rulers; in fact, during the early phases of the Cultural Revolution, the sizes of the governments, both central and local, decreased. Thus, Maoism, which is the same as neoliberalism, sought small governments. Of course, there were those who disagreed, such as professor Yang Fan, who claimed that a bureaucracy was necessary and that discarding it was impractical. However, the optimum size of a government varies by stage, and if the bureaucracy generates problems such as corruption, restricting their free hand is very important. Thus, China once made Bo Xilai the secretary of the Communist Party's Chongqing branch, and many people supported him. In this sense, now Maoism still has a historical role as well.

The Western-oriented new left

The recent Chinese leftist tradition has very different objectives. Because it sprung from Western ideologies, it does not support Stalinism since it is a form of liberal democracy. For example, the Chinese philosopher Li Zhongshang differentiated Western Marxism from Soviet Marxism and the communist principles of Leninists (Li 2011).[24] In addition, it cannot support Maoism because Western Marxism is a supporter of big governments. The most important characteristic of Western leftism is its resistance to neoliberalism. Yang (2013) insists that the Chinese leftists should import moderate type of Western leftism; social democracy, which is fighting for the oppressed in advanced countries by deregulation and privatization. Today, this is the fundamental contradiction between the ruling and ruled classes in advanced countries. However, leftists were not always against small governments. Before 1945, the Japanese people suffered under an absolute monarchy; therefore, anarchism significantly influenced Japanese leftism. Germany and Russia faced a similar situation before 1945 and 1917 respectively. In the early stage of capitalism, leftists were against big governments because of the state dictatorship, while in the latter stage, leftists turned against small governments because the new ruling system followed the principles of market fundamentalism. The present-day influence of this tradition on Chinese Marxism shows that China's society has already adopted the characteristics of the present type of capitalism.

Global extension

Under these conditions, Chinese Marxists have been actively promoting global academic exchanges with other Marxists and leftists around the world,[25] possibly because they want to keep up with the globalization of mainstream economics, even though they are fairly against this idea. China's mainstream economists believe that economics should also be globalized like the economy, and non-internationalized economics should be excluded from universities. Therefore, Chinese Marxists and leftists have been trying to gain international recognition and find counterparts and have successfully done so in advanced countries, including Japan and South Korea. This process requires large-scale funding, for example, to bring in famous foreign professors, to send young Marxist students to other countries, and to translate several foreign books.

Another important element in these academic activities is the slogan "Against the foreign power," which implicitly means to be against US hegemony. As a rapidly growing power, China has begun to oppose US pressure, and therefore, this slogan has been accepted by its government and people. This slogan also appears in Yang (2012a; b) and is being repeatedly used by Xi Jinping. There-fore, even when the above-mentioned third tradition imports Western leftism, they do not make it clear that their theoretical positions are imported.[26] While Chinese Marxists are against neoclassical mainstream economics in foreign countries, they import foreign leftist ideologies. In this way, the structure of the academic struggle in advanced countries has been wholly imported into China. This is because the present social structure and resulting social struggle have become the same as those in advanced countries.

In view of these international exchanges, the Institute of Marxism at the Chinese Academy of Social Science initiated two activities: the establishment of the World Association for Political Economy[27] and the publication since 2011 of the journal *International Critical Thought*. The Institute of Marxism at the Chinese Academy of Social Science is the center of Marxism in China, and these two initiatives can be said to represent the activities of Chinese Marxists. How-ever, it is noteworthy that they also used three types of connections prior to these activities: with international communist parties; with young Chinese Marxist economists, who graduated from or were educated in Western universities; and with Japanese Marxist economists (an international exchange strongly advocated by Chinese Marxists) whose situation was similar to Marxists in China. Among these, the second represented the influence of Western leftists. However, as discussed, traditions of Chinese Marxists also resonated with those of Japanese Marxism, such as *Koza-ha*'s two-stage revolution theory. Thus, it is important to explore theoretical interactions between Marxists from Asia and those from outside of Asia.

Marxism with Chinese characteristics that differ from Western Marxism

Beijing Consensus

The key message of this chapter is that ideologies are determined by material reality. As discussed, irrespective of whether a country is under invasion or independent, or whether an economy is underdeveloped or developed, the definition of revolution and, thus, applied theories, differs on the basis of reality. Materialism is observed not only at a national level but also at the class or personal level. For example, ruling and opposing parties have a different materialistic basis for politics. A majority of the ruling communist parties are based in Asia, and Asian Marxism has been influenced by materialism. The Chinese and Vietnamese communist parties have very similar policies, even if they do not share a good relationship. However, this characteristic explains why Chinese Marxists are not welcomed by Marxists living and fighting in capitalist countries.

Therefore, Japanese and Chinese Marxists tend to have different objectives. For example, Japanese Marxists oppose government intervention in ideologies, as do other Marxists in capitalist countries. By contrast, Chinese Marxists look for the control of ideologies with the help of the government. Japanese Marxists focus on redistribution, whereas Chinese Marxists prioritize economic growth. These differences have also led to ideological struggles among Japanese Marxists, particularly regarding the understanding of the present Chinese social system. What Western countries refer to as "state capitalism," China calls the "Beijing Consensus," which is widely criticized by Western and Japanese Marxists. However, those critics do not concern themselves with how national economies are managed.

"Class society" can be defined as that notion that what is good for some may not always be good enough for all. For an entire economy to be successful, it is important that some members are made to endure adverse conditions or make sacrifices. For example, in a capitalist society, without exploitation – private or public – there is no capital accumulation and, therefore, no economic growth. In a feudalistic craft system, without craftsmen's personal dependency on their masters, there is no way to improve the scale and skill of craftsmen and, thus, no development in the sector. In the field of transportation, because of technological developments in railways or airways, small-scale entrepreneurs lose their business opportunities to more active and established ones. In general, without loss there is no progress, and in particular, without someone taking a risk, there is no progress in class society.[28] These conditions are merely inevitable in class society, and thus, some become promoters, while others are protesters. In China, Marxists who belong to the ruling party act as promoters, which is the underlying reason for the introduction of the Beijing Consensus.

However, state capitalism or the Beijing Consensus has certain advantages over the Western viewpoint – one of them being the political system. In China, citizens cannot elect national-level senators and the president directly. They can elect prefecture-level and village-level representatives. However, the direct election system can cause unnecessary political conflicts. For example, imagine a country that has two groups with competing interests. If these two groups nominate a presidential candidate and one of the candidates wins, the winner will implement policies that are favorable to his group, creating irreconcilable conflicts with the other group. We have already seen such conflicts in Iraq and Ukraine, and introducing such direct elections in ethnic minority areas in China will have unimaginable repercussions.[29] Thus, it is important for us to understand that the Western type of democracy is not flawless.

In such a situation, a consensus among the groups is more important than a competition for votes. Of course, in typical capitalism, where people struggle under the dictatorship of a small number of rulers, Western democracy is a useful tool for the majority to overthrow the rule of a minority. For example, Shias and Sunnis in Iraq, Ukrainians and Russians in Ukraine, and Han Chinese and Uygurs in the Xinjiang Uygur Autonomous Region must coexist without a ruler in either side's favor. In China, such kind of power balancing is institutionalized as the Chinese People's Political Consultative Conference.

Although this system was launched as a united front during the new democratic revolution in 1949, it originated in the Soviet system, which comprised a representative group of workers, farmers, soldiers, intellectuals, and others against their national rulers. However, it was an alliance not of all social classes, but of a select few. Among these selected social classes, there was no discrimination and the number of representatives from each social class did not matter. The conference was a platform to negotiate different interests among each social class, for example, farmers and workers. While farmers wanted a higher price for agricultural products, workers did not. In addition, it also facilitated negotiations between various religious and ethnic interests.

Stages of development of Chinese socialism

We must remember that China is a communist country led by Marxism, a major factor that distinguishes it from Western countries. However, as I mentioned in the previous section, the present social structure in China has changed and is now similar to that in the Western countries. For example, social struggles between neoliberalism and anti-neoliberalism exist both in China and Western countries. Thus, present-day China should be regarded as a capitalist economy under the leadership of a communist party.[30]

More precisely, before 1978, China had a state capitalist system[31] but since 1978, it has a market capitalist economy, even though in the political sense, it has been able to gain recognition as a socialist country. Of course, this understanding differs from that of Chinese authorities, and Chinese Marxists cannot politically oppose the authorities. Thus, even though Chinese Marxists cannot influence overall policy-making processes, they are far more critical and powerful in matters of socialism and capitalism, or any other issue in the Marxian textbook.[32] Chinese Marxists continuously discuss socialism, sometimes even with Japanese Marxists. For example, the Japanese and Chinese communist parties have engaged in several discussions on the matter.[33] In addition, academic exchanges feature a continuous series of joint conferences between the Nanjing Normal University–led Marxist group and the Japan Society for Socialism Theory. The main topics of these conferences have been the definition of socialism and ways it can be reformed.

An important fact underpinning these topics of discussion is that many Chinese Marxists are aware that Chinese socialism should be reformed. However, a reformation could reduce the gap between socialism and ordinary capitalism. In fact, the history of China's socialism is defined using the official definition and redefinition of socialism:

- **Before 1978**: planning economy, public ownership, and communist leadership in politics
- **After 1978**: public ownership and communist leadership in politics
- **After the ownership reformation**: public ownership with over 51 percent stockholdings in leading companies by the public sector, and communist leadership in politics
- **After the further ownership reformation**: public ownership with the top stakeholders of leading companies in the public sectors, and communist leadership in politics

If this type of redefinitions will be continued in the future, there will be a much weaker political redefinitions of socialism, for example, just as public land ownership and communist leadership. I believe that many Chinese Marxists know this problem and therefore need a strong theoretical base to justify the new definition. However, a basic misconception is that Marxists must always establish a socialist society. As I mentioned, the Asian two-stage revolution theory justifies the continuation of the capitalist society under a given condition, and if this is the case, the next question should be, "What is this condition?" According to Marxian theory, the criterion should address whether the present system can increase productivity, and, undoubtedly, present-day Chinese capitalism continues to satisfy this criterion. Thus, as long as Chinese capitalism increases productivity, it should be maintained. This should be the primary task of the Communist Party, and in this sense, there can be capitalism under the leadership of communist parties. In other words, Chinese capitalism under the leadership of the Communist Party can be justified by the fundamental Marxist theory.

In addition, there are several theoretical exchanges which are characteristic of Marxism between Chinese and Japanese Marxists on the core problem.[34]

Without Asia, we cannot imagine a future for Marxism.[35]

Notes

1 Although Stalin declared that his ideology was Marxist–Leninist, Japanese Marxist orthodoxy identified Leninism as being different from Stalinism. One of the reasons for this identification is Lenin's desire to include non-state economic sectors under the *new economic policy* after *wartime communism.*

2 In this chapter, names of East Asians are written in the East Asian style, that is, family name before the given name. When only one name is used, it refers to the family name.

3 It was common knowledge that the former was regarded as an anti-imperialist and anti-feudalist revolution (see Yun 2000, p. 19).

4 See Lee (2005) and Yun (2000). Although chapter one of the latter which provides an overview of the controversy on formation of society in South Korea does not mention the influences of Maoism and the Koza-ha theory, it does not mean that there were no Chinese or Japanese influences, even though foreign influences were not welcomed in Korea, both socially and politically. Even if there had been no direct influence, it is important to know that similar conditions create similar ideologies, which is the Marxian way of understanding ideologies.

5 In the prewar period, Japanese Marxists created another school called Rono-ha, which became the basic framework for the Japanese socialist party. It believed that Japanese society was ruled by monopoly capitalism, and therefore, sought a socialist revolution.

6 In other words, a revolutionary theory should have its own deep understanding of the concerned objective society. This characteristic is clearly expressed by Benjamin Schwartz (1954) in the context of the Chinese revolution: "Theory here does not mean simply a well-thought out political strategy. It means nothing more or less than a thorough sociological analysis of the society in which the revolution is to take place" (p. 144). Shin (2002) pointed out a similar necessity with respect to revolution theories.

7 In 1992, I published a book in Japan titled *'Socialism' as Pre-capitalism and Socialism as Post-capitalism*. Since the dichotomy as is represented in its title fits the interests of Koreans living in a divided country, it was translated and published in Seoul in 1999. This book was also translated and published in Russia in 1994 and China in 2002.

8 However, one of the growth strategies widely criticized by South Korean leftists was a finance-led one. For example, see Kim (2010).

9 This new trend is critically examined in Lee (2005).

10 The first section in Sugiyama (2002) is a brief introduction to the *Koza-ha* faction's theoretical framework, printed in the English language.

11 Between the two theses, a group in the Comintern and Japanese Communist Party attempted to set a different program, called the *Thesis of Politics (draft)*, which declared the next revolution as a socialist one. However, a Japanese representative of the Comintern deemed the draft unofficial and rejected it.

12 When a US delegation visited Yan'an in 1944, Nosaka discussed with them his three-stage theory of revolution. However, the first and second stages were in fact two phases of the democratic revolution (see Araki 1993, pp. 107–108).

13 This fact was revealed in Nosaka (1989).

14 Not only Zhou Enlai but also other Chinese communist leaders were well acquainted with Nosaka and trusted him. Nosaka's house in Yan'an was next to General Zhu De in the headquarters of the military base (see Stein 1945).

15 Wada (1996) provides evidence to support this influence. For example, his lectures to captured Japanese soldiers in Yan'an were strongly influenced by Mao's style of thinking and practice.

16 See Araki (1993, pp. 70–71).

17 TPP stands for the Trans-Pacific Strategic Economic Partnership Agreement led by the United States.

18 This struggle became especially well known after the accident at the Fukushima Daiichi nuclear power plant in 2011. The Japanese people recognized that the Tokyo Electric Power Company is a product of a state monopoly and shares common interests and personal relationships with the state.

19 In all honesty, in questioning the present Japanese government's underlying motives regarding such a dangerous war, which is independent of the interests of monopoly capitalism and the United States, we must mention the peoples' nationalism against China. With the support of its people and their sheer enthusiasm, the government can gain independence from the ruling classes, a situation very similar to Japan's absolutism before 1945. The prewar Koza-ha theory postulated that the powers of the two ruling classes were overridden by the superior powers of the Japanese emperor. This problem is closely related to that of the people's nationalism and populism (see Onishi 2014). Thus, we must rediscover the distinct characteristics of the prewar Koza-ha theory.

20 Onishi (2011) presents a basic understanding of capitalism and socialism.

21 Another problem is imagining "socialist agriculture." That is, should small individual farmers be cast aside at this stage of socialism? Some Japanese Marxist economists believe that such small farmers will survive forever by the technological advantage, for example, diminishing returns to scale (see Nakamura 1977).

22 Yang Fan is an internationally acclaimed political scientist at the Chinese University of Politics and Law and has engaged in many intensive academic exchanges with Japanese Marxists.

23 Maoism has another definition that contains different characteristics – that is, the strategy to set up revolutionary bases in rural areas and besiege cities. This strategy was adopted by Nepali Maoists, Latin American communist guerrillas, and Kim Il-sung.

24 Li also defined Western Marxism as "non-materialistic Marxism." However, because materialism is the core focus of Marxism, it cannot be regarded as its inherent feature. This is a point of view that clearly separates leftists and Marxists.

25 These international theoretical exchanges are also being conducted among political parties. An example is the series of talks between China and Japan's communist parties. The Chinese Communist Party is engaged in theoretical exchanges with not only the Japanese Communist Party but also other global communist and leftist parties.

26 Although a similar phenomenon is seen in Yang (2012a), Yang (2012c) criticizes Chinese theoreticians who simply follow and import trendy overseas theories.

27 The influence of the association and its members has spread worldwide, including to Latin America, India, Russia and Africa. The association organizes forums every year in May.

28 In such difficult situations, some want to help those who struggle, whereas others choose to neglect such social hazards. The former type belongs to the "left" and the latter to the "right."

29 Onishi (2012) discusses some key characteristics of the Chinese political system from this viewpoint.

30 This is the essence of Onishi (1992).

31 According to Yang (2012a), the age of "primitive accumulation for the Chinese industrialization has been already accomplished in the period of planning economy" (p. 2).

32 However, at the same time, some of them simply support or justify definitions by Chinese rulers. This situation is entirely the same with mainstream economists in Japan.

33 The Japanese Communist Party has also engaged in a series of discussions with the Vietnamese Communist Party.

34 In addition to the mentioned core problems, academic exchanges between the Chinese and the Japanese Marxists address many other issues and are probably among the longest continuous exchanges between the Institute for Fundamental Political Economy in Japan and a group at the Nanjing Normal University in China. In addition, there have been numerous theoretical China–Japan academic exchanges among, for example, the Central Compilation and Translation Bureau of Central Committee of Communist Party of China, the members of Marx–Engels Researchers' Association of Japan, and the methodological Marxists who focus on the methodology of *Capital*. The former exchange addressed topics such as market mechanisms, the Asian economy, and market socialism, while the latter exchange translated one of the greatest books on Japanese Marxism – *Methodology of Capital* – into Chinese. The original book was written by Mita (1963), and the Chinese version was published twice, in 2007 and 2012.

35 To assess the effect of Asian Marxism, the North Korean situation is noteworthy. North Korea's official Juche ideology (*Juche* means subjectivity) acknowledged its origin in Marxism; however, Marxists are against subjectivism, and thus deemed it a non-Marxist ideology. Therefore, they formed their own international association named the "Institute of Juche Idea" and do not want to form any link with the international Marxist networks such as the World Association for Political Economy.

References

Araki, Yoshinobu (1993), *Senryo-ki ni okeru Kyousanshugi-Undou (Communist Movement under the US Occupation)*, Ashi Shobo, Tokyo, in Japanese.

Kajimura, Hideki (1977), *Chosen niokeru Shihonshugi no Keisei to Tenkai (Form and Development of Korean Capitalism)*, Ryukei Shosya, Tokyo, in Japanese.

Kang, Namhoon and Dong-Min, Rieu (2009), "The Case for Reformulating Marx's Theory of the Falling Rate of Profit," *Political Economy Quarterly, Japan Society of Political Economy,* vol. 46, no. 3, 53–60.

Kim, Hyungkee (2010), "Capitalism after the Great Recession: Agenda for a New Progressive Development Model," *World Review of Political Economy,* vol. 1, no. 2, 335–343.

Lee, Kangkook (2005), "Political Economy Research in Korea: Economic Development, Democratization and Crisis," *Political Economy Quarterly,* Japan Society of Political Economy, vol. 41, no. 4.

Li, Zhongshang (2011), *"Xin Makesi Zguyi" Lun (Neo Marxism and the Chinese Way)*, China Renmin University Press, Beijing, in Chinese.

Mao, Zedong (1940), *On New Democracy*, Foreign Language Press, Beijing.

Mita, Sekisuke (1963), *Shihonron no Houhou (Methodology of Capital)*, Kobundo, Tokyo, in Japanese.

Nakamura, Satoru (1977), *Doreisei to Noudosei no Riron (Theory of Slavery and Serfdom System)*, University of Tokyo Press, Tokyo, in Japanese.

Noro, Eitaro (1935), *Nihon Shihonshugi Hattatsu Shi (History of the Development of Japanese Capitalism)*, Iwanami Shoten, Tokyo, in Japanese.

Nosaka, Sanzo (1989), *Fusetsu no Ayumi (My Windy and Snowy Life) (Fusetsu No Ayumi)*, vol. 8, Sin'nihon Shuppan, Tokyo, in Japanese.

Onishi, Hiroshi (1992), *Shihonshugi Izen no Shakaishugi to Shihonshugi Go no Shakaishugi ('Socialism' as Pre-capitalism and Socialism as Post-capitalism)*, Otsuki Shoten, Tokyo, in Japanese.

——— (2011), "Marxian Optimal Growth Model: Reproduction Scheme and General Law of Capitalist Accumulation," *World Review of Political Economy,* vol. 2, no. 4.

——— (2012), *Chuugoku ni Shuchou Subekiwa Nani Ka (What should we insist on China?)*, Kamogawa Shuppan, Kyoto, in Japanese.

——— (2014), "Zero Seicho Keizai Ka no Seikenkotai to Ukeika" ("Political Instability and Turn to Right under Zero-growth Economy"), in Usui, T. and Onishi, H. eds. *Seichou Kokka kara Seijuku Shakai e (Growth State to Matured Society)*, Kadensya, Tokyo, in Japanese.

Rieu, Dong-Min (2008), "Estimating Sectoral Rates of Surplus Value: Methodological Issues," *Metroeconomica,* vol. 59, no. 4.

——— (2009), "Has the Okishio Theorem Been Refuted?" *Metroeconomica,* vol. 60, no. 1.

Schwartz, Benjamin (1954), "A Marxist Controversy on China," *Far Eastern Quarterly,* vol. 13, no. 2.

Shin, Gi-Wook (2002), "Marxism, Anti-Americanism, and Democracy in South Korea: An Examination of Nationalist Intellectual Discourse," in Tani, E. Barlow ed. *New Asian Marxisms,* Duke University Press, Durham and London.

Stein, Gunther (1945), *The Challenge of Red China*, Whittlesey House, New York.

Sugiyama, Mitsunobu (2002), "The World Conception of Japanese Social Science: The Kōza Faction, the Ōtsuka School, and the Uno School of Economics," in Tani, E. Barlow ed. *New Asian Marxisms,* Duke University Press, Durham and London.

Wada, Haruki (1996), *Rekishi toshiteno Nosaka Sanzo (Sanzo Nosaka as a History)*, Hebon-sha, in Japanese.

Yamazaki, Isao (1975), "Kaisetsu (Comment)," in Togliatti, P. ed. *Touitsu Sensen no Shomondai Hoka (Problems of United Front, et. al.)*, Otsuki Shoten Publishers, Tokyo, in Japanese.

Yang, Fan (2013), "Gendai Chuugoku no Shakaishicho nitsuite" ("On the Present Chinese Social Ideal Trends"), *Letters of Economic Science*, Institute for Fundamental Political Economy, vol. 132, in Japanese.

Yang, Fan (2012a), "Lun Xin Gaige Kaifang Guan" ("A Perception on a New Reform and Opening Policy"), in Fan, Y. ed. *Feizhuliu Jingji Xuejia Wenxuan (Selected Papers of Non-mainstream Economists)*, China Economic Publishing House, Beijing, in Chinese.

Yang, Fan (2012b), "Quanqiuhua Yu Shichang Jingji Tiaojian Xia De Guojia Anquan" ("Globalization and National Security under the Condition of the Market Economy"), in Fan, Y. ed. *Feizhuliu Jingji Xuejia Wenxuan (Selected Papers of Non-mainstream Economists)*, China Economic Publishing House, Beijing, in Chinese.

Yang, Fan (2012c), "Zhongguo Zhishi Fenzi Ying You Lishi Dandang" ("Historical Task of the Chinese Intellectuals"), in Fan, Y. ed. *Feizhuliu Jingji Xuejia Wenxuan (Selected Papers of Non-mainstream Economists)*, China Economic Publishing House, Beijing, in Chinese.

Yun, Kencha (2000), *Gendai Kankoku no Shisou 1980–1990 Nendai (Thought in Modern Korea 1980–1990s)*, Iwanami Shoten, Tokyo, in Japanese.

4 Japanese contribution to environmental economics

Fighting against pollution problems and Fukushima nuclear disaster

Fumikazu Yoshida

Introduction

In modern economics, where neoclassical economics still occupies the commanding heights, those theories that criticize it insist on asking what kind of significance it can have in the field of environmental economics. In Japan, pioneer work such as that of Kenichi Miyamoto (1967; 1989; 2007) and Shigeto Tsuru (1972; 2000) looked at the issue from a historical perspective as a practical/theoretical battle with the problems of pollution, and their findings established a basis for further work. Confronted by the reality of the serious pollution problems that Japan was by then facing, they amalgamated Marx's theory of capital and William Kapp's (1950) theory of social costs, and in this task they were truly world pioneers. In light of their studies, the present author attempted a theoretical elucidation of Japan's pollution problems, based on "a theory of the metabolic inter-relationships that exist between human beings and nature" and on his reading of Marx's *Capital* (Yoshida 1980).

We must first consider what we shall be able to contribute to a historical analysis of the character of capitalistic forms of production on which we base our understanding. Serious environmental problems erupted during the Industrial Revolution, were exacerbated by the creation of monopolies, and intensified hereafter by both World Wars and what followed. With regard to global environmental problems it is particularly important to look carefully at historic social analyses of mass production, mass consumption and mass disposal. Such a point of view can also be applied to an analysis of environmental damage done under the aegis of "the socialist system".

Second, we must also consider the contribution made to the analysis of environmental problems from "the theory of the metabolic inter-relationships that exist between human beings and nature". Such perspectives, based as they are on the history of the earth and the place of human beings on that earth, command a wide perspective, one that looks beyond the individual human being as having mere economic existence to a broader and deeper view of nascent problems, from garbage accumulation to global warming. From such a vantage point, we can recognize the problems that have so often been dismissed by the neoclassical theory as "outside (the concerns of) the market". It can help us to see how we may be able to reach a solution that will realize sustainable development by severing the "vicious circle of the environment and poverty".

This approach can, in the third place, provide an overall framework for economic and social analyses that are capable of covering policy processes, distribution patterns, expense burdens, and so on. It is able to focus upon the role played by persons and agencies concerned with policy: politicians, the political system itself, the industrial structure and international relations, and the very nature of democracy. We should follow the lead of such pioneer studies as "Intermediate System Theory" (Miyamoto 1989; 2007), "Capacity Building for Environmental Policy" and "The Theory of Environmental Governance" (Jänicke 1995; 2002).

Finally, one tradition of radical economics has consistently questioned the problem of "externality", the external or collateral effects – that is, which economic activity produces – and has focused instead on the rights and claims for justice of the socially vulnerable, in contrast to the neoclassical or mainstream line of modern economics, which has focused on an analysis of utility and efficiency. In *A Theory of Justice* (1971), the American political scientist and philosopher John Rawls argued for what he called "the difference principle" to improve the lot of persons in the most disadvantageous positions. While critical of some aspects of Rawls's thinking, Amartya Sen developed Rawls's views in economics and for his work was awarded the Nobel Prize in economic science (1998). Japanese pollution studies, triggered by Japan's own pollution problems, are firmly tied to the views of these two notable thinkers. By its very nature, Sen's "capability approach" cannot avoid examination of the basic problem of what equality is and what it is for, and the argument has now been broadened to include discussions of sustainable development as scholars discuss how to "increase the well-being of the least advantaged people in societies today, while at the same time ensuring that the prospects of future generations are not seriously impaired (intra-generational and intergenerational equity objectives)" (Turner et al. 1994, p. 33).

Political economy of environmental problems

Political economists hold the view that the origins, conditions and policies that give rise to environmental problems are governed by the state of the political economy. We need to view these relationships in terms of (1) economic change, (2) the environment and its amenities, and (3) environmental policy (Miyamoto 2007, Chapter 1).

Let us look at how the origins, conditions and effects of environmental problems on policy decisions are prescribed, or governed, by the state of political economy. For example, in the early history of Japanese capitalism, the mining industry (coal and metals) played an important role not only as a supplier of solid-fuel domestic energy but also as an early exporter of its products. At the same time, however, mining activities also caused air pollution and the pollution of such essentials as water, thus damaging crop production, at all times a key activity; and so, from the very beginning of Japan's own industrial revolution, pollution came to be known as "mine pollution" (*Kogai* in Japanese, which has the same pronunciation as "pollution *Kogai*"). It was a difficult problem and the Meiji government was hard pressed for a solution. Those affected by it made their own views felt, too: one of the most significant social movements of the Meiji period was initiated and led by Shozo Tanaka in response to the pollution caused by the mining company Furukawa Zaibatsu, a disaster that was known subsequently as the Ashio mining pollution incident where many downstream peasants were forced to evacuate to other areas. Subsequent incidents of air pollution reveal the significance of the mining industry's support for Japan's early industrial efforts. We may note the case of air pollution caused by smoke emitted by the Besshi copper mine run by Sumitomo Zaibatsu, air pollution from smoke emitted by the Hitachi copper mine, and pollution caused by the Kamioka lead and zinc mine owned by Mitsui Zaibatsu, from whose roots grew the industrial giants Mitsui, Mitsubishi, Sumitomo and Furukawa, as well as the corporate group Hitachi. Furukawa produced copper wire, and Furukawa Electric later became Fuji Electric, a joint company with Siemens of Germany. From these beginnings grew Fujitsu, a company that manufactured telephones; later, this in turn gave birth to a company that now makes computers and another that makes robots. These developments chart the changes in 100 years of Japanese capitalism.

As for the country's environmental policy, the government at first approached water pollution and pollution-abatement measures as separate issues. During the late 1960s, however, a rash of environmental problems led to the enactment in 1970 of 14 environment-related laws in a session of the Japanese parliament that came to be known as the "Pollution Diet", and, in 1971, to the foundation of the Environment Agency. All this helps us to see immediately how intimately the outbreak of environmental problems has played its part in the development of the Japan's political economy.

Although economic analyses of environmental problems have tended to focus on "pollution control", we have already noted that, in addition to environmental pollution, the rates of deforestation, overgrazing, natural disasters and ecocide have also been accelerating, and that we should therefore widen the object of our analysis to cover both "amenities" and "the conservation of nature".

We must also note the importance of the difference between economic growth and economic development as a difference that is basic to the political economy approach to the environment. The concept of economic growth stands for a scale increase in the physical dimension of the economy, and is calculated by a quantitative index of money (GNP, GDP). On the other hand, the range of economic development includes such qualitative improvements as are needed in the structure of physical stock, in designs and their constitution, and in the quality of their contents (as well as general considerations such as life expectancy, the rate of literacy and income, the quality of life, liberty, and so forth) (Daly 1991, Chapter 12).

On the other hand, the neoclassical view regards such features of the environment as water and air as having no market value: they are therefore free goods. Consequently, we tend to waste them and pricing becomes necessary, which, in turn, requires the setting of proprietary rights. It has been said that the problem of pollution conflicts with the "complete property rights" because all the benefits or costs must accrue to the agent holding the property right for good or bad (negative goods) (Kolstad 1999, p. 62). Yet the neighbors of a factory that emits soot cannot help but be themselves the "owners" of soot (negative goods). The difficulty lies in setting proprietary rights for the air, and this has provoked the criticism that the root of environmental destruction is not a "market failure" resulting from a vacuum in pricing or property rights, but is a consequence of the economic activities undertaken for the development of the market system that is a feature of capitalism itself (Tsuru 1972, pp. 98, 130). It has often been pointed out that environmental destruction occurs, in economic terms, when (1) what is destroyed are free goods that are not priced, (2) the victims are socially/biologically vulnerable, or are future generations who will not be able to reverse the damage, and (3) there is lack or asymmetry of available information, thus causing uncontrollability (Ueta 1996, pp. 19–20).

We should be able to deal with (1) by using market mechanisms such as pricing, (2) by overhauling the global social system, and (3) by improving such social infrastructures as information disclosure or by correcting the information asymmetry. Yet while market mechanisms may solve problem (1), they will not be able to tackle the problems of the vulnerable (2) or of insufficient information (3). It will therefore be necessary to construct social systems that will provide a base upon which to build the means to solve them. That will be difficult and take time, but we must not give up the struggle.

Regional revival through environmental restoration

The environmental restoration of polluted areas

During the 1960s and 1970s, Japan experienced serious problems as a result of industrial pollution, and it was in those years, therefore, that the country began to take action to restore the polluted areas to environmental health. At least three issues needed to be solved before this goal could be contemplated, let alone achieved (Isono and Yokemoto 2006, pp. 7–8). In the first place, a full-scale solution had to be found to eliminate the damage caused by environmental pollution; the victims had to be relieved and they had be compensated for the disease that they had suffered. Such a commitment must be the starting point for any kind of environmental restoration. The victims must be helped to recover their functions and they must receive compensation for their lost capability, quite apart from pecuniary compensation for the income that they lost as a result of damage to their health and the costs of medical care. At the same time, steps must be taken to revive the region itself so that it will be able to provide the victims with improved "quality of life".

The second issue is to reduce levels of pollution to a threshold below which contaminated matter can no longer damage the environment, while simultaneously purifying the areas where the contaminated matter has accumulated. Such areas include not only the natural environment but also such historical and man-made environments as, let us say, a row of houses along a city street. Specifically, the problems that require clarification here are not only those that have to do with cleaning the polluted soil but also with the restoration of defiled nature and the spoiled cityscape.

The third issue concerns the restoration of damaged social relationships when the problems that were caused by pollution have led to conflict between the local inhabitants and those enterprises that have been the source of the pollution: the opposing parties must be reconciled and a collaborative relationship must be forged whose aim must be regional revival. The whole community must collaborate in mending the fractured social structure that was broken by the pollution.

We thus see that the three keywords of this article – "sustainability", "capability" and "governance" – relate to each of these three issues. The issue of the reduction of pollution is closely linked to the restoration of a sustainable environment, while we need a theory of sustainability and a theory of governance to cope with the abatement of any current pollution and with the purification of the previously polluted areas, with a view to establishing a system that will provide for and support a sustainable environment.

At the same time, the reconstruction of social relations needs both the capabilities approach and the theory of governance, with a view to establishing a system built upon the participation of the citizens in forging renewed and healthy social relationships.

When we consider Japan's experience of environmental pollution, we may say that the nation's response to the Itai-itai disease (caused by heavy metal pollution of the soil) accomplished a great deal, thanks to concerted efforts by many people to reduce the pollution dramatically and recover its nature meanwhile, in the case of the Yokkaichi atmospheric pollution, long-lasting results were achieved by proper analysis of the damage and through compensation for the victims.

While major problems of compensation and a thorough analysis of the damage that followed the outbreak of the Minamata disease (caused by the mercury contamination generated by a chemical factory) still remain unresolved, notable results have already been accomplished in the restructuring of social relations.

The Minamata disease: an examination of the damage done and of the inadequate steps taken to relieve the victims

We must thus question why it is that in the case of the Minamata disease, over 60,000 people are still asking for recognition of their victim status. The reason that they still need to ask is that throughout the long history of the recognition of environmental damage caused by pollution, the Japanese system has confined

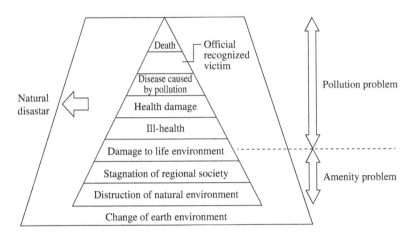

Figure 4.1 Pyramidal damage structure

compensation relief to the top of the pyramidal social structure, and many of the victims are at the bottom of the social hierarchy.

In the case of the Minamata disease, the legal action for damages that the victims first sued for in 1969 was not decided in their favor until 1973, when their damage claim was at last admitted. As a result of negotiations for compensation between the patients and Chisso Corporation (the source of the pollution), the patients' application for recognition as sufferers from the Minamata disease based on the "Law Concerning Pollution-Related Health Damage Compensation and other Measures" (1970) was accepted by the prefectural governor, and after the compensation agreement had been reached, they received compensation for damages from the Chisso Corporation.

Consequently, this arrangement set a precedent for the institution of pollution recognition (administrative recognition), whether applicable to the Minamata disease or not. Yet four problems still bedevil this system of pollution recognition.

First, the protocol of administrative recognition set up by the Law Concerning Pollution-Related Health Damage Compensation and other Measures has limited the category of victims almost entirely to the cases of Itai-itai disease, Minamata disease and other cases. As in the case of recognition of radiation sickness caused by the atomic bomb, so here, too, the bureaucracy's occasional policy measures and budget constraints have restricted recognition only to the victims directly affected. As a result, frequent cases of litigation have been brought to court to recognize those suffering from the pollution who had not been officially authorized as victims; and many sufferers have been accredited as genuine victims only after such judicial proceedings rather than as a result of any formal recognition within the institutional framework.

Second, because institutions follow the judgment of the Certification Council, which is composed solely of expert witnesses, the institutional qualification requires a double or threefold procedure; and so, rather than being allowed to represent themselves, the suffering victims must wait for their case to be presented by officials and doctors.

Third, because the recognition system decides which patients are affected by the Minamata disease, those patients whose condition may be ambiguous have been left unattended; and no compensatory relief system corresponding to degrees of damage has yet been established.

Fourth, since the actual survey of damage has only been conditional, no clear picture of the damage has emerged and little progress has been made to clean up polluted areas, while the Japanese government and prefectures have neglected to elucidate the damage realistically. In 2004, however, after a decision of the Supreme Court had emphasized the responsibility of the Japanese government and the administrative responsibility of the prefectures, the number of patients who applied for accreditation increased remarkably, as did those who were willing to take their cases to court. This was because the Supreme Court's decision made governmental responsibility clear and thus reduced people's fear of the discrimination that would follow should they admit to being sufferers of the Minamata disease. Yet, since such victims are growing older, the situation does not allow us to come to any premature conclusions.

After 1975, the management of Chisso was deeply troubled when the fear that they would not be able to pay compensation became publically known. Therefore, from 1975 to 2000, Kumamoto prefecture issued a public loan and supported Chisso financially (a loan amounting to approximately 260 billion JPY). Since Chisso found it hard to pay back the loan, however, the prefecture took the drastic step of remitting repayment from February 2000.

In the meantime, the Japanese Government began to pay yearly compensation in Chisso's place. The Japanese government supports Chisso since it recognizes that should Chisso go out of business, bankrupted by "the polluter pays principle", it would have a most serious impact on the Minamata area.

Policies to protect the people and the environment from generated pollution: the Itai-itai disease

Ever since the Itai-itai disease Court Case (one of the four major pollution tribunals presided over by the Japanese judiciary), its judgments regarding "the reduction of contamination and the cleaning up of the environment" as well as "the active participation of citizens" have come to represent long-term goals as means to protect the public from generated pollution. The implementation of such a policy naturally requires close cooperation between the enterprises concerned, scientists with specialist knowledge and the legal authorities.

The main purpose of the Itai-itai disease tribunal was to ensure that polluted rice would not go on sale and that any damage caused by pollution had to be rectified. Since countermeasures were deemed necessary, both to clean up polluted soil (which might mean having to discard polluted rice) and to check the source of pollution, and since it was considered that this would require a continuous on-site inspection of the Kamioka lead and zinc mine, a pollution control agreement was concluded the day after the appellate judgment on the Itai-itai disease was passed down (August 10ʳ, 1972).

The content of the agreement was epoch-making: never before had a company accepted on-site inspection of its plant by the local residents and a scientific expert, who was empowered to submit research data at the company's expense. The participation of an attorney and the scientist was particularly important. For nearly 40 years, this on-site inspection by local residents has continued, and the quantity of cadmium drained from the mine has been reduced to one 15th of what it had been at its worst, while the water quality of the Jinzu River has almost returned to its natural condition, proof that it is practically possible for such an industry to be nonpolluting if it tries. As of 2009, the action to reduce environmental pollution at the Kamioka mine was determined, including separating clean water and polluted water at the headwaters (since mixing conditions make it difficult to collect metals from waste water).

We can now extend our analysis to embrace the ideals of "sustainability" and "governance". As a consequence of the ruling laid down in the Itai-itai suit with the aim of defending the public from generated pollution, farmers living in Toyama, the affected area, studied the technology and pollution control of the Kamioka mine. Each participant (the enterprise, an attorney and a scientific researcher, for example) cooperated and pledged to create a relationship that combined "trust with effort". Such cooperative efforts are closely related to the reduction of pollution and the relief of the environment.

People's confidence that "We can eradicate pollution" has been borne out by adhering to the principles of "scrutiny by the victims", "corporate efforts" and "the wisdom of the scientist".

Settlement of Yokkaichi's air pollution through total volume control

Thanks to technical settlements designed to reduce contamination the Japanese effort to combat air pollution has achieved notable results. As a consequence in particular of the judgment handed down in the Yokkaichi pollution tribunal, the attitude of the Japanese people towards pollution changed, and the notion of total volume control, which would ideally resolve the problem, at last became feasible. In order to achieve total volume control, the first need was to reduce both the capacity of an enterprise to emit poisonous substances and the effects on the environment of various kinds of damaging emissions. A comprehensive control system was also needed to maintain an environment reference standard and thus ensure that there would be no epidemiological impact on human health anywhere in the Yokkaichi region (SO_2 annual average 0.017 ppm). Since such flexibility is attained through detailed research data on the sources of every discharge and on local weather conditions, we need the best possible model to obtain an acceptable concentration of discharge by constructing a base system to simulate atmospheric conditions, and by making factories subject to regulation to optimize desulfurization.

Since the reduction rate of SO_2 necessary for a satisfactory result is around 80 percent, and since the countermeasures that the company would have to take would be exceptionally costly, many people were apprehensive that the company might refuse to accept or implement the scheme. Yet the aim was accomplished within three years.

This was because the company believed that it would be unable to continue operating unless total volume control was achieved; consequently, it poured all its energy and immense amounts of money into technical development to improve its facilities and to regulate its working practices (Yoshida 2002, pp. 157–208).

Since engineers in the field doubted whether they would be able to continue operating in Yokkaichi without substantial developments in desulfurization technology and fuel conversion, they struggled to improve the production system so that it could also collect chemical substances from the production process in the most thorough and efficient manner. While the original aim was pollution control and the initial investment was huge, before long an industrial plant of high productive efficiency had been completed and the company was even able to export its technologies, proof that antipollution measures are compatible with sound economic management. The methods and technology capable of total volume control can thus become the most effective measures for the reduction of greenhouse gases and air pollution in such countries as China.

Even so, we must not forget that 30 years after they contracted the disease, more than 500 victims of Yokkaichi pollution are still suffering from it, while, at the same time, action to restore the environment itself remains weak. The environmental NGO the Japan Environmental Council has therefore proposed as targets for Yokkaichi's revival that it should focus on (1) a safe city, (2) the replenishing of the city's water, (3) an industrial policy based on inner spontaneous development, and (4) autonomous participation by local residents (Miyamoto 2008).

Lessons of environmental restoration

It is imperative that we build an unbreakable framework strong enough to ensure proper compensation and the very best free medical treatment and aftercare for the afflicted patients. As the Supreme Court has pointed out, the government bears heavy responsibility in this matter, while the subsequent "Minamata Disease Special Measures Law" (2009) adds to the weight that the government is obliged to bear in providing for patients who have already applied for compensatory treatment and patients who are still waiting for the opportunity to apply.

As for the second point, the reduction and clean-up of environmental pollution, the long-term countermeasures proposed to deal with the source of the pollution responsible for the Itai-itai disease have certainly attracted wide attention. When we review the issue of capability we recognize that both the on-site inspection involving the participation of the local residents and taking of appropriate steps to improve the ability of the plant to clean up its own mess are considerations of especial importance. The international community has responded favorably to Itai-itai example of successful environmental governance and it has applauded the reduction of the environmental load that has resulted from the building of confidential relationships between companies, local residents, legal consultants, and scientific advisers.

The case of Minamata has also attracted attention for its emphasis on the third point we raise: the rebuilding of social relationships and a healthy community. The key to the lessons of the Minamata affair with regard to "environmental restoration for regional revival" are the enhanced capability of citizens as actors and effective strategies of environmental governance. We may generalize "environmental restoration for regional revival" as follows. Since "environmental restoration" does not simply mean cleaning up the polluted environment, we must, to begin with, seek to restore the social environment and social relationships to their original state. And in addition to recognizing that environmental pollution degenerates and damages human capability, we must view as necessary the effective building up of the citizens' capability as actors who think, participate and act as responsible members of the public (Yoshida 2012).

Fukushima: a political economic analysis of a nuclear disaster

The perspective afforded by the theory of the problems of pollution

As a scholar who for many years has been devoted to the study of Japan's pollution and environmental problems from the standpoint of environmental economics, I want first to discuss core concepts that are relevant to understanding the nuclear disaster based on lessons learned from earlier pollution problems.

(1) The purpose of analyzing pollution and the environmental problems that follow in its train is to determine the situation confronting people and the environment and the actual scope of damage. Only then is it possible to suggest how we may counteract the effect of the damage to the greatest extent possible. Yet since research into and countermeasures against the Fukushima nuclear disaster have been delayed, knowledge concerning the scope and degree of the radioactive damage caused by Fukushima's damaged reactor is still seriously insufficient. Indeed, tardy disclosure of information and improper instructions for evacuation are everywhere manifest.

(2) The investigations to date have identified the electric company's "saving on safety measures" and the "site location mistake" as overlapping causes of this nuclear disaster and the pollution that it has caused. These are measures that ought to have been avoided. The Investigation Committee on the Accident at the Fukushima Nuclear Power Stations needs to shed light not only on the evacuation support that has been provided to affected

communities since the accident, but also on problems existing before the accident, such as the lack of adequate preventive measures.

It also must focus attention on future steps and measures needed to correct flaws in the national safety regulations and standards. The committee's conclusions should be used during the overhaul of all nuclear power plants across the country.

(3) While the provision of relief to the victims has been delayed, a system to protect and relieve the victimizer (in this case, Tokyo Electric Power Company [TEPCO]) has been set up. When the Nuclear Damage Liability Facilitation Fund Law designed to bail out TEPCO was passed, the reason given was to avoid bankrupting the victimizer so as to ensure that indemnities would be paid out. The logic of this reasoning is clearly similar to that which led to the breakup of the Chisso Corporation after the outbreak of Minamata disease: despite the enormous number of victims, the political and economic domination of the victimizer entails an asymmetric relationship between the victimizer and victims.

(4) The issue of insufficient compensation to residents for "voluntary evacuation" is a question for the administrative authorities. During the Minamata disease, the authorities advocated "self-regulation" of seafood consumption as a method to lessen their liability for indemnities and therefore reduce the total amount. The Nuclear Safety Commission has initially tolerated the dumping of radioactive contaminated water in the sea since they claim that it will be diluted. But even if diluted in seawater, contaminants can be concentrated thousands of times throughout the food chain. Such elementary knowledge concerning the environmental consequences of pollution, one of the main lessons of Minamata disease, is now apparently being forgotten.

(5) We must also recognize that another consequence of contamination is the problem of discrimination and what has been called "reputational damage". The outbreak of Minamata disease meant that people would no longer buy products labeled as being from Minamata, and locals could not reveal their identities for fear of facing discrimination. That Fukushima Prefecture and neighboring areas are likely to face the same problems of discrimination is an issue of grave concern. Of course, the polluter is responsible, and sufficient compensation ought to be obligatory.

(6) We anticipate long-term pollution and the enormous costs of decontamination, while analysis concerning the social costs due to the nuclear disaster will be a major challenge for environmental economics, a matter that we shall discuss in detail later. The problems experienced during earlier outbreaks of Japanese pollution and the course these problems followed are now being repeated. Indeed, it might be better to say that the phenomenon is a symptom of a regular and recurring characteristic of Japanese society. Different from earlier industrial pollution problems, the nuclear disaster is in addition characterized by radioactive contamination. This puts it on a scale that reaches far beyond the scope of traditional environmental issues.

Rather than simply being a local problem, it has been from the beginning a nationwide and potentially international issue (some say that it has the potential to affect the whole of the northern hemisphere).

If we consider the nature of the devastation and the number of victims (about 130,000 people subject to evacuation and about 1 million people located in relatively high-level radiation zones) as well as the extent of the affected areas (the evacuation area alone is 800km², equivalent to Tokyo's 23 wards and the city of Hachioji combined, and the contaminated area extends up to a 200km radius, from the whole of the Kanto region to Iwate and Yamagata), then we understand that the Fukushima Dai-ichi Nuclear Power Plant accident has been the cause of injury to human society and the natural environment on a scale that is unprecedented in its scope and the life-threatening nature of its effects.

The theoretical concept of the causes of pollution as applied to the nuclear disaster

The events that followed the tsunami that hit Japan were so severe that Masao Yoshida, the director of the TEPCO Fukushima Dai-ichi Nuclear Power Plant, confessed at a press conference on November 12, 2011, that "During the week after March 11th, I thought many times that I would die". According to the testimony of Mr. Yoshida, his images of that accident could bring "the total destroy of Eastern Part of Japan" (August 8, 2011, testimony to Government Investigation Committee). At the height of the immediate crisis, the prime minister even examined the possibility of evacuating 30 million people from the Tokyo metropolitan area. As for the causes of the accident, many questions have been asked, yet we wonder how many of them have been answered in the Investigation Committee on the Accident at the Fukushima Nuclear Power Stations' report. We can thus understand that what we may call the theoretical concept of "the causes of pollution" is at the root of the concept of nuclear pollution.

There are several questions that the report does not really address:

- Why in an earthquake-prone region like Japan have 54 nuclear power plants been built?
- Why when the Onagawa Nuclear Power Plant managed by the Tohoku Electric Power Company was closer to the epicenter and also hit by the tsunami was it able to prevent a total loss of power, while the Fukushima Power Plant was not?
- Why have measures against severe accidents been left to the voluntary initiatives of the operator?
- Why had no adequate measures been taken against a total loss of power?

The interim report of the Investigation Committee on the Accident at the Fukushima Nuclear Power Stations focuses on the official response after the earthquake and tsunami, and draws attention to certain failures that have, in various ways, been widely reported: poor communication between TEPCO and the government, a lack of cooperation within the cabinet over measures to cope with the crisis, and the fact that even TEPCO itself did not really grasp the full implications of the developing situation nor notice the dysfunction of the emergency condenser in Unit 1.

We may cite for comparison the tsunami countermeasures undertaken by Tohoku Electric Power Company, whose Onagawa Nuclear Power Plant was built 15m above sea level, and as an earthquake countermeasure, its earthquake-resistance strength was three times that required by the Building Standards Act. Consequently, although closer to the epicenter of the earthquake, it was somehow able to secure its power supply. TEPCO's Fukushima Nuclear Power Plant, on the other hand, had taken neither of these measures.

The Fukushima Nuclear Power Plant, built originally by the United States(US) General Electric Company (GE), was not designed to withstand either large earthquakes or tsunamis, and though over the last 40 years, earthquake resistance standards have certainly become more stringent, no drastic measures to strengthen the plant's defenses were carried out. It is no exaggeration to say that at the time of the disaster, the Fukushima Nuclear Power Plant was a defective plant.

We can postulate the following as likely causes for TEPCO's total loss of power: (1) the immediate collapse of power transmission lines due to the earthquake, (2) the breakdown due to the tsunami in the operations of the emergency diesel power supplies placed beside the sea, and (3) an inadequate supply of batteries in the control room so that the reactors became inoperable.

At the same time, during the process leading to core meltdown, deficiencies in the vent and filter system (which are required in the European Union but were not required in Japan) became apparent. We can therefore point to TEPCO's efforts to cut costs by making "savings in safety measures" a primary cause of the accidents.

According to the interim report, TEPCO ran a trial calculation in 2008 on the effects of a tsunami based on expert opinions and the views of the national Earthquake Headquarters. The result indicated the need for a seawall of at least 15.7m in height. Current estimates suggest that the installation of such a seawall would cost tens of billions of JPY and that it would take about four years to build. In fact and ironically, only on March 7, 2011, four days before the earthquake, did the Nuclear and Industrial Safety Agency (NISA) learn of the 15.7m estimate, but the agency did not specifically request that this countermeasure should (at once or at any time) be undertaken. It goes without saying that TEPCO bears responsibility because unacceptable tradeoffs were made. Out of its desire to contain cost increases that would be incurred by installing a higher seawall, the issue was ignored. Yet responsibility also lies with the state given its loose application of regulations that were themselves already too loose.

During their interviews, the TEPCO executives are all reported to have affirmed, "We never thought that a natural disaster would exceed the design criteria, nor that it would be necessary to deal with it." Nobody has clearly explained why they believed this, but some testimonies hint at reasons: "There would be no end if we were to start making hypotheses about likely catastrophes" or "Since the Kashiwazaki-Kariwa Nuclear Power Plant was able to deal with the situation, we judged that the design was correct" (Mr. Yoshida, director at the time). These responses indicate the company lacked any proper awareness of possible dangers (Schreurs and Yoshida 2013).

The theoretical principle of "social cost" as applied to the nuclear disaster

- ### *Cost range of nuclear power*

Until now the main reasons given for the promotion of nuclear power have been that nuclear power is cheap, safe and the trump card in the battle against global warming. Now, the nuclear-power-is-safe myth is no longer viable. Nor, when we consider the many trillion yens' worth of damage that the accident has caused, does the nuclear-power-is-cheap argument hold anymore. Even if the costs occasioned by the accident are not taken into account, some studies, such as Takeshi Murota's *Economics of Nuclear Power* (1981) or Ken-ichi Oshima's *Political Economy of Renewable Energy* (2010) have shown that nuclear power was not cheap even in the first place.

According to Oshima, nuclear power involves four types of costs: (1) the direct cost of power generation, (2) the back-end cost (fuel reprocessing, reactor decommissioning and disposal of radioactive wastes), (3) the public investments (development and location costs), and (4) the cost generated by an accident and its compensation. On the basis of data listed in the annual securities report of the nine power companies, the sum of costs (1), (2) and (3) from 1970 to 2007 are as follows: The cost for 1kWh has risen to 10.68 JPY for nuclear power, 9.90 JPY for thermal power, 7.26 JPY for hydraulic power, 3.98 JPY for general hydraulic power, 53.14 JPY for pumped-storage hydraulic power, and 12.23 JPY for the combination of nuclear and pumped-storage hydraulic power. It is clear that nuclear power is not cheap. Moreover, the back-end cost (2) has not adequately been calculated or accounted.

- ### *The social cost of nuclear power*

The nuclear disaster at the Fukushima Dai-ichi nuclear power plant is a "multiple disaster" of a kind never before experienced in human history, composed of one part that can be evaluated in monetary terms and one part that cannot. While, as we see below, there are common points and differences with traditional pollution cases, the present disaster is also characterized by a high degree of uncertainty; and though huge future costs are expected as inevitable, their actual extent is quite beyond our power to foresee. This is linked to the problem of trying to give an economic measurement to the social costs of a nuclear disaster. The social costs of nuclear power include but are not limited to:

- "Invisible pollution" with "no direct fatalities"
- Health hazards (radioactive contamination of residents and workers, social stress)
- Income loss due to suspension of business in offices, agriculture and fishery
- Soil pollution with a halt to all planting and marine pollution caused by radioactivity
- Expenditures and opportunity loss caused by evacuation
- "Reputational damage" (farm and marine products, land assets, tourism)
- Reduction of tax revenues (halt of power plant operations, the closedown of factories, evacuation of residents)
- Reduction in numbers of students enrolled in educational institutions, and consequent loss of educational opportunities

A number of important empirical and theoretical studies clarify the characteristics of the nuclear seismic disaster that has generated the wide-ranging multitude of issues listed above. They support policy proposals that will contribute to the relief of victims, as well as providing tools to study the social cost of nuclear power more deeply, and more objectively.

After the accident, the government carried out a review of the cost of nuclear power. According to the estimates (December 2011) of the Cost Verification Committee, which included accident costs and social costs such as CO_2 emissions, the generation cost of nuclear power is at least 8.9 JPY per kWh.

This is about 1.5 times the price previously published by the power companies and the government. If we add the cost of the removal of radioactive material, the decommissioning of the reactors and consequent compensations, the cost will rise further. And since coal-fired and liquid natural gas (LNG)–fired thermal power generation cost around 10 JPY per kWh, the cost advantage of nuclear power generation basically disappears. Under favorable conditions, wind and geothermal power can compete with nuclear power. In 20 years' time, solar power is likely to be cheaper than nuclear energy.

We do not therefore need to include the accident cost in our calculations to conclude that nuclear power is not (and never has been) cheap. If we add the cost of the accident to the calculation, it is even more evident that nuclear power is actually the most expensive form of power generation. Yet despite it is not being viable economically, Japanese electricity policy uses nuclear power as the base-load source of electricity production.

Given that nuclear fuel itself is cheaper than the fuel used for thermal power, restarting the already-built nuclear power plants will, in fact be a way for power companies to save on (1) the direct cost of power generation, although this does not take into account (2) the backend cost, (3) the public investments, and (4) the cost generated by the accident. So if we calculate the loss of shutting down nuclear power plants at several hundred million

JPY per day, management will use this argument to support a decision for restarting them; and, indeed, by doing so, even if each power company has to pay tens of billions of JPY for earthquake and tsunami countermeasures, nuclear power generation would still be a profitable business for them. However, rushing to restart nuclear power plants in a seismically active zone like the Japanese archipelago means risking a second nuclear disaster. This is an unacceptable risk because of the enormous costs of damage (as stated in number 4 above). There is no doubt that were such a worst-case scenario to reoccur, Japan would not be able to recover and would suffer social and economic collapse.

Conclusion

The basic factors when dealing with pollution cases are (1) the elucidation of the cause of pollution and its source, (2) countermeasures to the source of the pollution emission, and finally (3) a study of damage and the relief of victims.

On each of these matters, the investigation of the Fukushima disaster is still in its early stages.

(1) As for elucidation of the cause of pollution and its source as applied to the nuclear disaster, the results of the investigation headed by the Investigation Committee on the Accident at the Fukushima Nuclear Power Stations of Tokyo Electric Power Company must challenge not only the adequacy of the safety regulations and countermeasures at the Fukushima Dai-ichi Nuclear Power Plant but also how these apply to all the nuclear power plants across the country. The new Nuclear Regulation Committee introduced new standards but they are not valid or adequate because the new regulations are not based on fully investigated causes of the Fukushima accident and its recommended safety measures.

(2) Furthermore, measures to counter the source of pollution emissions are problematic, too. We are still quite ignorant of many important features of the contamination of underground water or seawater that is being brought about by the radioactive pollution emitted by the Fukushima Dai-ichi Nuclear Power Plant; and since, as Chairman of the former Nuclear Safety Committee, Mr. Madarame admits, it is not possible to go on-site or discover the actual situation within the reactor, we cannot predict how the state of the plant will evolve. Yet the release of contaminated water into the ocean is still permitted.

(3) Even if we consider only the damage caused by the nuclear pollution and the compensation that must be given to victims, we recognize that further huge efforts are needed. The current state of study of radioactive contamination is insufficient and many residents in the vicinity have great anxiety because of the abnormally high levels of radiation in their regions. Even among those living about 60km away from the plant, anxiety about high levels of radiation persists. While it is necessary to give priority to evacuation

and decontamination, it should be done carefully so as to avoid spreading pollution over a wider area.

Although, as we see, none of the three basic conditions for dealing with cases of pollution has, at this stage, been met, the authorities have declared a cold shutdown condition and have claimed that the accident has been contained. The timing of these statements raises suspicions. Rather than quick statements of reassurance, we require measures that address the true reality of the Fukushima disaster and that attempt to grasp what is really going on at the plant. Yuko Endo, mayor of Kawauchimura, a village that has been forced to evacuate everyone to Kouriyama City, stated that the accident can only be considered contained "when the removal of fuel, the decommissioning of the reactor and the process of residents return has been completed". If we consider this nuclear disaster to be the world's largest and worst case of pollution, then we should be prepared for its resolution to take time as well as huge efforts and costs. If we are over-eager to announce that the crisis is passed, the damage in the long run could be even greater.

References

Cost Verification Committee, Report, December 19th, 2011. (https://www.npu.go.jp/policy/policy09/pdf/20111221/hokoku.pdf)

Daly H (1977, 1991) *Steady-State Economics*, Washington DC: Island Press.

The interim report of the Investigation Committee on the Accident at the Fukushima Nuclear Power Station, published on December 26, 2011.

Isono Y and Yokemoto S (2006) *Chiiki to Kankyo Seisaku* [Region and Environmental Policy], Tokyo: Keiso Shobo.

Jänicke M (1995) "The Political System's Capacity for Environmental Policy," in Weidner H and Jänicke M eds., (2002) *Capacity Building in National Environmental Policy*, Berlin: Springer Verlag.

Kapp W (1950) *The Social Cost of Private Enterprise*, Cambridge: Harvard University Press.

Kolstad C (1999) *Environmental Economics*, Oxford: Oxford University Press.

Miyamoto K (1967) *Shakai Shihon ron* [Social Overhead Cost], Tokyo: Yuhikaku.

Miyamoto K (1989, 2007) *Kankyo Keizaigaku* [Environmental Economics], Tokyo: Iwanami Shoten.

Miyamoto K ed. (2008) *Kankyo Saisei no Machizukuri* [Community Creation for Environmental Restoration], Kyoto: Minerva Shobo.

Murota T (1981) *Economics of Nuclear Power*, Tokyo: Nihon Hyoronsha.

Ohshima K (2010) *Political Economy of Renewable Energy*, Tokyo: Toyo Keizai Shimposha.

Rawls J (1971) *A Theory of Justice*, Cambridge: The Belknap Press of Harvard University Press.

Schreurs M and Yoshida F eds. (2013) *FUKUSHIMA A Political Economic Analysis of a Nuclear Disaster*, Sapporo: Hokkaido University Press.

Tsuru S (1972) *Kogai no SeijiKeizaigaku* [Political Economy of Pollution], Tokyo: Iwanami Shoten.

Tsuru S (2000) *Political Economy of the Environment: The Case of Japan,* London: Athlone Press.

Turner K et al. (1994) *Environmental Economics, An Elementary Introduction,* Coleshill: Harvester Wheatsheaf.

Ueta K (1996) *Kankyo Keizaigaku* [Environmental Economics], Tokyo: Iwanami Shoten.

Yoshida F (1980) *Kankyo to Gijyutu no Keizagaku* [Economics of Environment and Technology], Tokyo: Aoki Shoten.

Yoshida F (2012) *Lecture on Environmental Economics,* (Sapporo, Hokkaido University Press).

Yoshida K (2002) *Yokkaichi Kogai* [Yokkaiichi Air Pollution], Tokyo: Kashiwa Shobo.

5 Business cycles of contemporary monopoly capitalism

Seiichi Nagashima

Introduction

Since Marx's death in 1883 up to the present, capitalism has experienced a multi-layered transformation. First, around the turn of the 20th century, a concentration of capital brought about economic change, in which free competition was suppressed and monopolistic control over prices prevailed. Thus, capitalism entered the stage of monopoly capitalism. This change affected business cycles – that is cyclical patterns of capital accumulation. After World War II, most governments of advanced capitalistic states began to assume active roles in the circulation of capital. They intervened in the process of the valorization movement of monopoly capital. This relationship that was known as state monopoly capitalism modified the movement of business cycles, since states adopted fiscal and financial policies to mitigate economic fluctuations. However, since the end of the last century, globalization of the world economy – that is the global accumulation of multinational companies – undermined states' ability to control business cycles. As a result, the recent world economy has repeatedly experienced bubble cycles led by global financial capitals, causing a global financial crisis such as that which occurred in 2008.

Our interest resides in analyzing these changes of business cycles under capitalism from the viewpoint of Marx's *Capital*, which criticized capitalism fundamentally. However, as Marx could not complete his business cycle theory, the elaboration of a Marxian business cycle theory (or theory of economic crisis) that is applicable to contemporary capitalism constitutes our present task.

To accomplish this task, we need first to construct a general theory of business cycles, and then move to the stage theory of business cycles under monopoly capitalism, and finally, proceed to the modification of business cycles under contemporary capitalism.[1]

As far as the general theory of the business cycle is concerned, we can detect two streams, underconsumption theory and overinvestment theory, which cover modern business cycle theory. As Howard Sherman classified them, the former is characterized as demand-side theory, the latter as supply-side theory (Sherman 1991). Sherman who judged both one-sided partial theories proposed "the integrated or synthesized model", a direction we would support. After Marx, Rudolf Hilferding (1910), Michal Kalecki (1939; 1954), Paul M. Sweezy (1942) and Howard Sherman (1991) provided significant contributions to the theory of business cycles. However, they also did not complete this theory of the business cycle, in particular as it applies to the condition of monopoly capitalism.

Marx considered the circuit of capital (or value valorization movement of capital) which consisted of production-process (vol. 1 of *Capital*) and circulation-process (vol. 2 of *Capital*). In the former, surplus value is produced. It is then realized in the latter. Further, he tried to explain the total process of capital in vol. 3 of *Capital*. In our view underconsumption theory focuses on the circulation-process of capital, while overinvestment theory on its production-process.

Among Marxian economists in Japan, Kozo Uno (1953) elaborated on his theory of economic crisis that focused on production-process, especially on the difficulty of the integration of the supply of the commodity of labor-power into the movement of capital accumulation. On the other hand, the "orthodox" Marxians focused their attention on the circulation-process (realization of value).[2] However, we must point out that a third stream has emerged, as Sherman suggested in the US, which covers both processes to provide a unified theory of the business cycle.[3] Our position is that Marxian economists in Japan are surely in the third stream. Further, a theory of business cycles under monopoly capitalism has to distinguish quantity-adjustment and price-adjustment in the behavior of capital. The model we construct as a system of nonlinear differential equations is introduced in the second section.

In our model, social reproduction consists of three fundamental departments: means of labor (fixed capital), objects of labor (raw materials namely circulating constant capital), and means of consumption (consumer goods).[4] Under monopoly capitalism, monopoly capital exerts the power of price control and adjusts the quantity of products in response to the oscillation in the market. We can regard this quantity adjustment as the price maintenance policy of monopoly capital.[5] On the other hand, those who possess non-monopoly capital adjust product prices while trying to maintain the quantities of products. In other words, the policy of non-monopoly capital is that of quantity maintenance by way of price adjustment.[6] This policy of monopoly capital that manifests itself in the behavior of price and investment changes the process of the business cycle considerably, particularly the way overproduction manifests itself.

Under state monopoly capitalism after World War II, interventions of government fiscal and financial policies introduced new changes in the processes of business cycle which was modified considerably due to the policies of monopoly capital. This chapter concentrates on these changes of the business cycle. We must admit that the analysis of recent bubble cycles and the worldwide financial crises remains our next task.

Business cycle model of price-adjustment and quantity-adjustment

Before entering into the business cycle of monopoly capitalism, we build formal business cycle models with the features of price-adjustment and quantity-adjustment. Under monopoly capitalism, the former works in the sector of non-monopoly capitals and the latter in the sector of monopoly capitals.

Let us use the following symbols: D1 is department 1 that produces means of labor; D2 is department 2 that produces the object of labor; and D3 is department 3 that produces means of consumption). X_i: output. F_i: Means of labor to use. R_i: Object of labor to use. L_i: the number of employed labor power. N: labor population. θ: employment rate (L/N). n: natural growth rate of labor population. θ_s: standard employment rate. w: money wage rate. w_s: standard money wage rate. P: market price. P_e: expected price. u: planned utilization rate. u_s: standard utilization rate. z_i: realization rate. π_i: realized profit rate. $1/\alpha_i$: capital coefficient (F_i/X_i). $1/\beta_i$: technical composition of capital (F_i/L_i). δ_i: means of labour to object of labour ratio (F_i/R_i). M_f: demand for means of labor. M_r: demand for object of labor, π_{ei}: expected profit rate. ε: depreciation rate.

Accumulation model with price-adjustment

(1) Quantity of term-end output is determined by means of labor, object of labor and labor power at the beginning of t period.

$$X_i^t = \alpha_i F_i^t \quad \alpha_i = \text{constant} \tag{1a}$$

(2) Demand for means of labor consists of replacement investment and new investment.

Let us suppose that the desired expansion rate of means of labor in the next period is dependent on the expected profit rate at term-end (π_e^t). Firms are supposed to expect the prices with which to obtain means of labor. Also, suppose that replacement rate is equal to depreciation rate (ε).

$$M_{fi}^t = P_{ei}^t F_i^t \left(\varepsilon + \rho\pi_{ei}^t\right) \quad \rho \text{ is reaction-coefficient} (>0) \tag{2a}$$

(3) As quantity of output of means of labor and money demand for them is given by (1a), market price of means of labor is determined. We suppose that all output is realized (sold) by "market-clearing price".

$$P_1^t = \Sigma M_{fi}^t / X_1^t \tag{3a}$$

(4) Means of labor of the next period are existing means of labor (not replaced) plus its addition.

$$F_i^{t+1} = \Sigma M_{fi}^t / P_1^t + F_i^t(1 - \varepsilon) \tag{4a}$$

(5) Object of labor and labor power of the next period are determined as follows.

$$M_{ri}^{t+1} = F_i^{t+1}/\delta_i, \quad L_i^{t+1} = \beta_i F_i^{t+1} \quad \delta_i \text{ and } \beta_i \text{ are constant} \tag{5a}$$

(6) Demand for object of labor is determined by the expected price.

$$M_{ri}^t = P_{e2}^t R_i^{t+1} \tag{6a}$$

(7) As quantities of output of object of labor and money demand for them are now given, price of object of labor is determined.

$$P_2^t = \Sigma M_{ri}^{t+1}/X_2^t \tag{7a}$$

(8) As labor power of next period is given by (5a), money wage rate is determined in the labor market. Let us suppose that money wage (w) rises if employment rate (θ) rises over standard employment rate (θ_s).

$$w^t = w_s + \iota\left\{\Sigma L_i^{t+1}/Nt - \theta_s\right\} \quad \iota \text{ is reaction coefficient} (>0) \tag{8a}$$

(9) Let us suppose a Kalecki-type economy where all means of consumption are purchased by laborers. As quantity of output of means of consumption and money demand for them are given, the price of means of consumption is determined.

$$P_3^t = w^t \Sigma L_i^{t+1}/X_3^t \tag{9a}$$

(10) As prices of means of labor, object of labor and labor power (P_1^t, P_2^t, w^t) are now determined, we know the realized profit rate (π_i^t).

$$\pi_i^t = \left(\alpha_i P_i^t - P_1^t\varepsilon - P_2^t/\delta_i - w^t\beta_i\right)/\left(P_1^t + P_2^t/\delta_i + w^t\beta_i\right) \tag{10a}$$

In order to complete the model, let us fill the expected variables by the realized value of the preceding period (expected profit rate = π_i^{t-1}, expected price = P_1^{t-1} and P_2^{t-1}). When initial values, technical coefficient and reaction coefficient, are given, then we can get economic variables of the first period. As means of labor, object of labor and labor power to be used in the second period and realized profit rate of the first period already known, the production-reproduction in the second period proceeds in the same manner once again. This price-adjustment accumulation works in the non-monopoly sector of monopoly capitalism.[7]

Accumulation model with quantity-adjustment

In the quantity-adjustment model, as firms fix prices, they know prices before the purchase. At the beginning of the first period, capitalists decide the utilization rate (planned utilization rate), and at the end of production they know the realized utilization (realization rate or unplanned utilization rate).[8] If they cannot sell the whole output, the unsold rest are kept in the storehouse. Accumulation proceeds as following.

(1) Planned utilization rate

$$u_i^t = z_i^{t-1} \tag{1b}$$

(2) Output at the end of production

$$X_i = u_i{}^t \alpha_i F_i^t$$

(2b)

(3) Money demand for means of labor

$$M_{fi}{}^t = P_1 F_i^t \left(\epsilon + \rho \pi_{ci}{}^t \right)$$

(3b)

(4) Realization rate (unplanned utilization rate) in the department of means of labor

$$z_1{}^t = \Sigma M_{fi}{}^t / \left(X_1{}^t P_1 \right)$$

(4b)

(5) Means of labor in the next period

$$F_i^{t+1} = \Sigma M_{fi}{}^t / P_1 + F_i^t \left(1 - \epsilon \right)$$

(5b)

(6) Object of labor and labor powers in the next period (same as [5a])

$$R_{ri}{}^{t+1} = F_i^{t+1} / \delta_i, \ L_i{}^{t+1} = \beta_i F_i^{t+1}$$

(6b)

(7) Money demand for object of labor

$$M_{ri}{}^t = P_2 R_i{}^{t+1}$$

(7b)

(8) Realization rate (unplanned utilization rate) in the department of object of labor

$$z_2{}^t = \Sigma M_{ri}{}^t / \left(X_2{}^t P_2 \right)$$

(8b)

(9) Money wage (same with [8a])

$$w^t = w_s + \iota \left\{ Li^{t+1} / N^t - \theta_s \right\}$$

(9b)

(10) Realization rate (unplanned utilization rate) of means of consumption

$$z_3{}^t = w^t \Sigma L_i{}^{t+1} / \left(X_3{}^t P_3 \right)$$

(10b)

(11) Realized profit rate

$$\pi_i{}^t = \left(\alpha_i P_i z_i{}^t - P_1 \epsilon - P_2 / \delta_i - w^t \beta_i \right) / \left(P_1 + P_2 / \delta_i + w^t \beta_i \right)$$

(11b)

Production-reproduction in the second period proceeds in the same manner as that of price-adjustment accumulation. This quantity-adjustment accumulation works in the monopoly sector of monopoly capitalism.

Accumulation under monopoly capitalism

Changes from the free competition capitalism

After Marx and Engels, Hilferding (1910) and Lenin (1917) analyzed important changes in the capitalist economy. Hilferding analyzed the effects of monopoly capital (in the form of cartel) on business cycles and pointed to interesting modifications of economic crisis.

In Japan, among various attempts to analyze the modifications of business cycles, Tsutomu Ouchi (Ouchi 1970) was outstanding in dealing with the business cycle under state monopoly capitalism theoretically. However, as a work in the tradition of the Uno school, Ouchi's theory also partiality ignores the realization process of surplus-value in the demand side. Further, Ouchi did not analyze the price and investment policy of monopoly capital. As is shown in this chapter, our theory of business cycles differs from Ouchi's in this respect.

Different policies in pricing and investment of monopoly and non-monopoly capital

Under monopoly capitalism, barriers for new entry and free competition among owners of capital grow considerably. As capital accumulation advances, the necessary size of capital to adopt new technology and to utilize the economy of scale increases, small capital (non-monopoly capital) cannot compete against large capital under the same conditions. At the same time, as the production capacity of individual firms in comparison with the market attains a significant size, this functions as a barrier to prevent new entries from other industries. Thus, free competition of capital on both intra- and inter-industry levels is limited.[9] The profit rate of capital is not equalized, unlike under free competition capitalism, where production prices are determined by market forces. Decisions in pricing and investment differ between monopoly capital and non-monopoly capital.

Owners of monopoly capital are supposed to follow the "full-cost principle" in their pricing. That is, price is set to cover standard cost (prime cost + fixed cost) with target margins. In order to avoid the losses from severe competition, monopoly capital firms tend to avoid price competition and maintain monopoly price by adjusting quantities of production to the demand of the market.[10] But as the competition to introduce new technology continues, the fall in cost and value of the product occurs in spite of maintained prices. In contrast, non-monopoly capital with no control over price cannot but adjust the price to the oscillation of the demand in the market. Prices of non-monopoly sectors fluctuate similarly under free competition capitalism. Thus, with the trend of technological progress, total prices under monopoly capitalism tend to surpass the total values due to the price maintenance policy of monopoly capital.

Also, investment decisions differ between monopoly capital and non-monopoly capital. Non-monopoly capital decides to invest if the expected profit rate is higher than the market interest rate. Monopoly capital tends to refrain from new investment due to the risk of the loss in previously invested capital by the fall in prices or utilization rate. Monopoly capital evaluates investment by calculating marginal profit as P. M. Sweezy (1942, pp. 275ff.) explained. We assume that monopoly capital decides to invest if the expected marginal profit rate is higher than the target (or required) profit rate which monopoly capital insists on obtaining.

Reproduction process under monopoly capitalism

Production and reproduction of capital proceeds as follows:

(1) As noted above, the essential elements are means of labor, object of labor and labor power (laborers). At the beginning of production, they are divided into three departments. Monopoly capital decides the utilization rate of means of labor (planned utilization rate). We assume that monopoly capital decides the planned utilization rate according to the realization rate of the previous period ([1b] detailed in the second section above). Non-monopoly capital utilizes its production capacity fully in the period of expansion of a business cycle, so the quantity of production is decided by technological coefficients at the beginning of production (1a).

(2) Monopoly capital decides to invest at the end of this period if the expected marginal profit rate meets or exceeds the target profit rate. Non-monopoly capital decides to invest if the expected profit rate exceeds the market interest rate. Both the expected marginal profit rate and the expected profit rate are dependent on the realized profit rate of the previous period.

(3) The amount of investment for means of labor produced by non-monopoly capital is determined as follows: the quantity of means of labor required in the next period multiplied by its expected price (2a). The amount of investment for means of labor produced by monopoly capital is determined as follows: the quantity of means of labor required in the next period multiplied by the fixed monopoly price (already known) (3b).

(4) Since the quantity of production (supply) and the amount of investment (demand) have been decided, the market price of non-monopoly capital is determined as follows: investment demand divided by quantity of production (supply) (3a). Since monopoly capital maintains monopoly prices to avoid cutthroat competition in the contraction period, the realization rate (unplanned utilization rate) is determined as investment demand divided by the total amount of price (quantity of production multiplied by monopoly price) (4b). As positive excess-demand continues during the

expansion period of the business cycle, the realization rate is always 1. During the contraction period, it falls below 1 and unsold products are kept in the storehouse (inventory). A decline of the realization rate or increase of inventory reduces the realized profit rate for this period, and planned utilization rate of the next period.

(5) Since the amount of investment and market prices of non-monopoly capital have been decided (monopoly prices are fixed and known), so means of labor available in the next period is likewise determined ([4a] and [5b]).

(6) Since means of labor have been determined, needed objects of labor and labor powers in that period are determined automatically ([5a] and [6b]).

(7) The amount of investment for the objects of labor produced by non-monopoly capital is determined by anticipating their market prices. As monopoly prices are fixed and already known, so firms need not anticipate their prices ([6a] and [7b]).

(8) As production of objects of labor (supply) and demand for them are determined, market prices of the objects of labor produced by non-monopoly capital and realization rates of objects of labor produced by monopoly capital are determined ([7a] and [8b]).

(9) Under monopoly capitalism, labor markets are divided into the non-monopolistic labor market and the monopolistic labor market; and wages in the two markets are decided differently. In a non-monopolistic labor market, the money wage rate is decided according to the employment rate as under free competition capitalism (8a). In a monopolistic labor market, labor unions tend to maintain or raise the real wage rate, so the money wage rate is decided by estimating the price of consumer goods.

(10) As the money wage rate and labor power to be employed in the next period have been decided, the demand for consumer goods is determined (supposing that laborers do not save and capitalists do not consume). Production of consumer goods (supply) and demand for them have been decided, so the market price of consumer goods produced by non-monopoly and the realization rate of monopoly capital are determined ([9a] and [10b]).

(11) As the prices of means of labor, objects of labor, consumer goods and labor power (wage rate) are decided, we can obtain the realized profit rate of each of them. The amount of capital stock equals fixed capital (means of labor) plus circulating constant capital (object of labor) plus variable capital, and the profit equals the amount sold minus depreciation cost minus objects of labor (raw material) cost minus wage cost. Realized profit rate is determined as profit divided by capital stock ([10a] and [11b]).

As means of labor, objects of labor and labor powers to be used in the next period and the realized profit rate of this period are decided above, production and reproduction in the next period continues in the same manner once again.

Business cycle policies of government under state monopoly capitalism

We define the capitalism after World War II as state monopoly capitalism, where the state aims to control society in total through social, economic, educational and ideological policies. In the economic sphere the state intervenes in all processes of capital circuit, and supports the value valorization movement of capital.[1] Before the advent of the dominance of neo-liberalism, Keynesian policy was widely applied to reduce unemployment and to support public education and social welfare with the vision of the "welfare state".

As mentioned above, under monopoly capitalism total prices exceed total value. In consequence, the gold standard system does not work well. Historically, it was suspended during World War I and during the Great Depression of the 1930s. After World War II, the gold standard system was replaced by the administered monetary system (IMF system). At first, this new system was based on a combination of the gold standard and the "dollar standard"; in 1973 the gold standard was abandoned completely for the floating exchange rate system.

Governments aim to control the business cycle by means of fiscal and financial policy. During periods of economic expansion, governments are on the alert for signs of "overheating of prosperity", such as growing a deficit in the balance of international payments, runaway inflation and a rapid rise in wages. To prevent a severe economic crisis governments react quickly at the first sign of trouble by tightening credit and decreasing fiscal expenditure. Conversely, in periods of economic contraction, governments ease credit in order to stimulate the economy and avoid the deepening of depression. In this way, state monopoly capitalism endeavors to conquer the autonomous movement of the business cycle. But in reality, government's policies to control business cycles are not always successful.

The business cycle under monopoly capitalism

In view of the above considerations, we describe the process of the contemporary business cycle.

Expansion process – prosperity

Let us start with the prosperity stage of the cycle. Even late in prosperity, firms continue to produce near their top capacities, on the confidence that the excess demand in the phase of prosperity will continue. The market price of the product of non-monopoly capital and the utilization rate of monopoly capital both rise because excess-demand continues during prosperity. As the production costs are reduced both in the production of monopoly capital and non-monopoly capital, by the introduction of new technology by way of the replacement investment, realized profit rates in all industries rise and, in turn, make the estimates of future profit rates also rise. Consequently, investments increase, increasing further excess-demand. Thus, realized (and expected) profit rates and accumulation (investments) together create an upward spiral, and accelerated accumulation gives birth to continuous prosperity.

a)   Uneven development of the three departments

The expansion rates of departments vary because the realized as well as the expected profit rates are different. It brings about uneven developments of sectors and elements of the economy.

The replacement investment of fixed capital with new technology increases the demand for D1 and D2 first. At the same time, new technologies result in temporary unemployment and suppress the rise of money wages. So the demand for D3 lags behind the demand for D1 and D2. This leads to higher profit rates for D1 and D2 and a lower profit rate for D3. As a result, more investments move to D1 and D2 and less to D3. Thus, the accumulation rates and the growth rates of D1 and D2 exceed those of D3. Normally, D1 and D2 expand unevenly relative to D3. But after World War II, government expenditure and pent up demand for consumer goods caused D3 to develop as rapidly as D1 and D2.

As the uneven developments of D1 and D2 continue, the employment of labor power begins to increase rapidly, particularly spurred on by new investment of fixed capital. As the cumulative increase of production of means and objects weakens excess-demand for them, neither the market price of non-monopoly products nor the utilization rate of monopoly rises as rapidly as before. On the other hand, the increase in employment and rise of wage rates promote the rapid increase of total demand for consumer goods, though the supply of consumer goods tends to lag due to the uneven development of departments. Consequently the market price of consumer goods and the utilization rates of D3 rise more rapidly. Eventually, they rise more than those of D1 and D2 and the profit rates of D3 become higher than those of D1 and D2. Then, uneven development of D3 begins.

When D3 leads the way to prosperity as in the boom of durable consumer goods following World War II, especially after the end of the worldwide high growth, prosperity begins with the uneven development of D3.

We define real wage as total consumer goods divided by the number of employed labor power. This definition supposes that consumer goods multiplied by its price equals the money wage multiplied by the number of employed labor powers; that is, the total supply of consumer goods is equal to its total demand (9a). When D1 and D2 develop unevenly, the numbers of employed labor increase more than consumer goods, so real wages fall.[12] Conversely, during uneven development of D3, the supply of consumer goods increases more than the number of employed labor power, so real wages rise.[13] If real wages do not move to equilibrate the supply and demand, overproduction or underproduction occurs. In the model we posit, real wage rates adjust so as to equilibrate supply and demand, and so prosperity continues.

b)   Acceleration of expansion by monopoly policy and credit

Having planned excess-capacity, monopoly capital can adjust to excess demand rapidly, and the adjustment of the market is accelerated. This promotes increased prosperity. Furthermore, monopoly capital tends to maintain monopoly prices to avoid cutthroat competition during the construction period and enlarge market-share in the prosperity period. This too promotes prosperity.

At times of excess-demand in the phase of expansion, goods are sold easily and the interest rate of commercial and bank credit is stable. This stability accelerates accumulation. If an easy-money policy in the recovery period continues during prosperity, low stable interest rates would accelerate accumulation. Under state monopoly capitalism, the credit creation of banks is dependent on the financial policy of the central bank. But during this period, money is supplied endogenously to meet the desired accumulation of real economy.

Under monopoly capitalism as well as under free competition capitalism, the final phase of the prosperity is characterized by widespread speculation. Historically, the destruction of speculation triggered economic crises. Since the late 20th century, the bubble of financial assets has appeared repeatedly.

Economic crisis

When real wages do not equilibrate demand and supply, there arises the possibility of overproduction. In the *Capital*, Marx mentions two possibilities of economic crisis: first, "the abstract possibility of crisis" caused by the separation of sale and purchase; then in his analysis of reproduction schemes, "the developed possibility or substantially defined possibility of crisis". However, these are nothing but possibilities,[14] and we must now inquire into the factors which ultimately change "the possibility to the actuality of economic crisis".[15]

a)   From the opposite movements of real wage and profit
  rate to the exhaustion of industrial reserve army

As defined above, real wage is the amount of consumer goods divided by the number of employed labor powers, and the total price of consumer goods equals money wage multiplied by the number of employed laborers. Thus, in case consumer goods increase more than employed labor power or wages rise above consumer goods prices, the real wage rises.[16] During the last phase of prosperity, as the industrial reserve army shrinks, firms tend to employ unskilled laborers and reactivate old machines and facilities to expand production; consequently labor productivity falls. This rise of the real wage and fall of productivity result in a fall of the profit rate. The falling profit rate decreases the expected profit rate and thus the accumulation rate falls.[17] This sudden and rapid decrease of investment leads to an overproduction crisis.[18] In reality, profit rates of non-monopoly capital are lower than those of monopoly capital, and the lone interest rate for the former is distinctively higher than that of the latter. As a result non-monopoly capital is more susceptible to economic crisis.

Regardless of the movement of the real wage, accelerated accumulation runs counter to the supply of labor power, and the industrial reserve army is exhausted at the end. Then capital cannot expand production and increase the surplus value or profit, which are dependent on surplus production means, surplus production objects and surplus living means. This is "the absolute overproduction of capital" as Marx described in Chapter 15 of the third volume of the *Capital*. So with little warning, absolute overproduction precipitates a rapid decline in profit rate, producing an overproduction crisis.

b)   *Wage and credit*

When D1 and D2 develop unevenly, real wages fall in order to equilibrate consumer goods supply and demand. However, there is a natural limit below which the real wage cannot fall.[19] When capital offers wages under this limit, laborers have no incentive to work; instead they remain home or engage in demonstrations and strikes. When workers withhold their labor, it has the same effect on the economy as when the industrial reserve army has been exhausted. In a monopolistic labor market, trade unions often are able to maintain the real wage, but in a non-monopolistic labor market the wage easily falls to the lower limit.

At times of crisis, the business cycle shows inevitable results of the three factors that cause overproduction: (1) the uneven rise of real wages alongside the fall of profits brought about by the uneven development of D3 relative to D1 and D2; (2) the exhaustion of the industrial reserve army, brought about by the uneven development of all departments relative to the supply of labor power; and (3) the fall of wages to the lower limit, brought about by the uneven development of D1 and D2.

When overproduction is revealed, interest rates rise abruptly. As a result, markets become unstable and unpredictable, leading to widespread fear and mistrust. Historically, seeking a safe haven, capital flees from paper money to gold money, again weakening the credit system and further exacerbating the overproduction crisis.

However, in history the restriction of credit often happened before overproduction, and this led to the overproduction of goods. For example, when the outflow of gold from England due to increases in imports or the domestic outflow of gold because of increased wages occurred, the Bank of England restricted credit. Speculation occurred during the last phase of prosperity. Inevitably, speculators rushed to banks to acquire speculation money and to raise interest rates unintentionally.

The steep rise in interest rates soon exceeds profit rates, thus leading to the revelation of the overproduction. Under state monopoly capitalism, the central bank responds to the speculation by restricting the money supply, but is still forced to bail out financial institutions in a critical situation in order to avoid financial panic.

When there are signs of the "overheating of prosperity", such as the deterioration of the balance of payments, galloping inflation, the rapid rise of wages and so on, governments adopt tight-money policies in order to avoid a full-scale economic crisis. In these situations, the overproduction crisis is mitigated artificially and prosperity changes into a mild economic crisis.

Contraction process – depression

Economic crisis as the explosion of the inner contradictions of capitalism means the inevitable emergence of the inner equilibrium mechanism of capitalism. The crisis suddenly and rapidly begins to equilibrate the various disequilibria produced during expansion. When the price-mechanism fails, extended reproduction turns forcibly into reduced reproduction. When the price-mechanism works, the turn is gradual and smooth.

a) Stagnant accumulation

During the contraction phase of the business cycle, excess-supply brings forth the fall in the market price as well as the utilization rate of production capacity. Monopoly capital lowers the utilization rates, maintaining monopoly prices, to avoid cutthroat price competition. Non-monopoly capital lowers both the market prices and utilization rates. In both cases, the realized and expected profit rates fall, and if they fall below the interest rate, new investments of fixed capital stop completely. But even during contraction, leading or rapidly growing industries invest with a view towards long-term growth of demand, and firms still invest in new machinery and equipment to replace the old machinery and equipment that are worn, broken or outdated.[20] Thus there is still demand for means of labor in D1, and D1 demands objects of labor (D2) and labor power, and accordingly, production-reproduction proceeds on a reduced scale.

In contrast with the prosperity stage, the economy enters a downward spiral during the contraction phase: from the declines in prices and utilization rates to the fall of realized profit rate, then to the fall of expected profit rates, and further to the decrease of accumulation. The accumulation rate declines successively, and reduced reproduction continues. In the stage of contraction, monopoly prices are maintained, prolonging depression. Since World War II, governments have increased expenditures in the stage of economic contraction in order to mitigate economic stagnation.

b) Uneven contraction

Just as departments expand unevenly in the prosperity (expansion) stage, they shrink unevenly during the contraction stage. When D1 continues to develop unevenly in the prosperity stage and enters economic crisis first, then D1 contracts more deeply than D3. Unemployment increases in all departments, but the greater contraction of D1 produces the greater increase of unemployment in D1, so the laborers employed in D1 decrease more than consumer goods (D3). Since the real wage is equal to the per capita consumer goods of laborers, this relative rise in real wage prolongs depression.

While D3 tends to expand unevenly and enters into economic crisis first, D3 may contract more than D1 and D2. This means that the output of consumer goods (D3) decreases more than the number of employed labor, and real wage rates fall, allowing substantial profit rate recovery.

However, since World War II, governments have adopted fiscal policies to mitigate the uneven contraction in order to soften the severity of economic crisis and shorten its duration. Furthermore, public safety nets such as unemployment benefits and welfare programs mitigate the decrease in the demand of consumer goods. Monopoly capital continues to make long-term investments with the anticipation of economic recovery based on the policies of public expenditure. While discretionary constraint in consumers' spending emerges sharply during the contraction stage, they still have to replace essential goods that attain the expiration of their usage. These factors work to lessen the severity of recession and prevent depression.

c)   *Easing credit and destruction of capital*

During a severe economic crisis and continued depression, firms go bankrupt, and credits-debts are written down mercilessly. As money-capital is accumulated in financial institutions, banks compete for lending by reducing interest rates. This promotes profit rate recovery, leading to general economic recovery. The easy-money policy of government supports banks in reducing the loan rate.

In the non-monopoly capital sectors, market prices fall in depression. If prices fall below costs, firms must abandon the value of machinery and equipment that has still remnant value in order to replace them with more efficient or less expensive ones. In the monopoly sections the utilization rate and realization rate fall and inventories increase. If cost exceeds monopoly price, monopoly capital too has to scrap machinery and equipment and replace them with the latest technology. This destruction and replacement of fixed capital boosts profit rate towards recovery. And here again, increased government spending mitigates the contraction, breaking the fall of market prices and the utilization rate. Thus the destruction of capital is weakened under state monopoly capitalism.

Recovery

Even under monopoly capitalism, depression does not become chronic.[21] The conditions for recovery occur autonomously and endogenously during depression.

a)   *Decline of real wage and interest rate and recovery of profit rate*

As explained above, the policies of contemporary states cushion the destruction of capital. During contraction, excess capital is depleted slowly, expecting the recovery of profit rates. When D3 contracts unevenly, real wage rates must fall. At the same time, as explained before, during the recovery stage interest rates fall and governments adopt easy-money policy; the simultaneous trends of falling profit rates and rising interest rates found in the final stage of prosperity are now reversed. These factors engender autonomous recovery.

b)   Increase of unemployment and formation
of industrial reserve army

Uneven contraction of D3 brings about the fall of the real wage. This fall expedites the recovery of the profit rate. When falling real wages do not raise the profit rate and the real wage rate reaches the lowest limit,[22] then workers have to draw on their savings and rely on borrowing. If this should happen on a large scale, it may be the nadir of the recession/depression.

Under state monopoly capitalism, sooner or later, the increased expenditures by way of fiscal policies mitigate the depth of economic crisis and reduce the uneven contraction of D3 and the cumulative increase of the reserve army. Then, the falling of real wages is counteracted. In case trade unions succeed in maintaining the wage in the sector of monopoly capitals, the fall in wages may be prevented. However, from the 1980s up to the present, under the dominance of neoliberalism and neoconservatism, the preference of governments switched to the prevention of inflation, from achieving full employment. As a result, economies emerge from economic crisis extremely slowly. As the current world financial crisis, which began in 2007–2008, has brought increased unemployment and a lowered real wage rate, there is the possibility that depression will turn into long-term stagnation.

c)   Replacement investment begins

Destruction of capital under monopoly capitalism still forces businesses to replace worn and outdated machinery and equipment with more advanced ones. The final means with which to win the battle of "to be or not to be" is the efficiency of production. This is the same under monopoly capitalism as under free competition capitalism. In case a new technology emerges in an industry, firms are forced to choose whether to replace equipment that is not fully depreciated with new machinery. Thus, the consolidation of capital may start the replacement boom of machinery and other productive equipment. It brings about the extra demand for fixed capital, thus spurring the expansion of D1. This replacement investment is a fundamental factor in the stage of economic recovery.

However, under state monopoly capitalism, the pressure for the destruction of capital is mitigated considerably and monopoly capital tends to disperse investment throughout the business cycle. Accordingly, replacement investment of fixed capital is not so much concentrated in the last phase of depression and its significance for the recovery is weakened.

Changes of economic crises and the business cycle

Under contemporary capitalism, the business cycle and economic crises still exist, but in moderated form.[23]

Changes of the revelation of economic crisis

During the depression stage, monopoly capital limits production and lowers the utilization rate in order to maintain monopoly prices. The result is the overaccumulation of capital that becomes apparent in the fall of the profit rate. The excess capital produced during prosperity manifests as the excess capacity of unused productive equipment (unplanned excess capacity) not as unsold goods in market.

Mitigation of economic crisis and financial crisis

Under state monopoly capitalism, government regulates aggregate demand to avoid a rapid and severe economic crisis, and raises interest rates slowly and steadily to avoid their rapid rise during the last phase of prosperity. When these artificial tight money policies succeed, the end of prosperity is marked not by a sudden explosion, but rather by a smooth and gentle transition into depression. Sometimes governments fabricate artificial economic crises in order to maintain a reserve army (a so-called "stable economic crisis").

Avoidance of financial crisis

Since World War II capitalist economies seem to have avoided severe financial crisis rather successfully. Governments of advanced capitalist nations have controlled interest rates to avoid serious crises of the credit system. Even during severe depression, the banking system has succeeded in maintaining the trust of the depositors. Governments and central banks have been prepared to bail out banks that were endangered through emergency loans. Thus, panic and the destruction of the overall system of money, credit and finance have been avoided.

Suspension of accumulation and maintenance of monopoly profit

As explained above, monopoly capital does not invest if the expected marginal profit rate falls below the target profit rate. Monopoly capital achieves target profits by maintaining monopoly prices. In other words, monopoly capital can exert this control to endure the risk of economic crises.

Shift of the loss of capital value to the other classes

Falling prices force non-monopoly capital to abandon part of their capital, but monopoly capital can usually avoid the loss of capital value by adjusting monopoly profits. This means that monopoly capital shifts the burden of economic crisis to non-monopoly capital and other social classes and retard the process of recovery.

Tendency to shorten the business cycle

As discussed in this chapter, the following mechanisms are currently working to mitigate business cycles: (1) The profit rate of non-monopoly capital is lower than that of monopoly capital, and the interest rate of their loans is higher than that of monopoly capital. If their profit rates fall and, concurrently, interest rates of their loans rise, non-monopoly capital enters a critical situation sooner than monopoly capital. This means the shortening of prosperity. (2) Periods of prosperity and depression are both shortened by fiscal and financial policies of the states. (3) The employment policies of the governments produce the rapid exhaustion of the industrial reserve army and shorten the prosperity. (4) Worldwide resource nationalism raises the resource price early and rapidly. (5) Planned excess capacity of monopoly capital shortens the adjustment period of supply and demand. Thus under state monopoly capitalism, the length of the business cycle has been shortened considerably.

Concluding remarks

So far we have sketched the modifications of business cycles of capitalism under contemporary monopoly capitalism. This is not the full description, but we tried to develop a united theory of business cycles. The analysis of the most recent changes after the world financial crisis of 2007–2008 remains open. However, it is sufficient to make clear my position that the investigation into the elements that bring the abstract possibility of crisis to its actuality is important. Our effort toward a united theory of business cycles is dedicated to this purpose.

Notes

1 The author of this chapter elaborated the theory of business cycles under free competition capitalism, monopoly capitalism and state monopoly capitalism in chapters 1, 2 and 3 of Nagashima (2006). Here, due to page constraints, we confine ourselves to sketching main features of business cycles under monopoly capitalism on which modifications by policy interventions under state monopoly capitalism occur.
2 See Imura (1973) as a representative of the "orthodoxy".
3 The third stream contains Nagashima (1994; 2006), Okishio (1967; 1988) and Tomizuka (1975).
4 When the three are subsumed in the production process of capital, the former two consist of "constant capital" while the third is "variable capital" in Marxian terms.
5 According to Yoshinori Shiozawa, economists such as Adam Smith and David Ricardo, John Maynard Keynes and Piero Sraffa are in the group of quantity-adjustment (Shiozawa 2014a; 2014b). Further, we can count the business cycle theories of Kalecki, Harrod and Okishio in this group of quantity-adjustment theory.
6 Generally neoclassical economics is confined in the world of price-adjustment and supposes that price-adjustment can attain the equilibrium of supply and demand. In business cycles, however, price-mechanism intensifies cumulative disequilibrium.

As a result, the process of equating supply and demand must occur violently in the form of an economic crisis. In this respect a fundamental contrast exists between Marxian economics and neoclassical economics.

7 Various patterns of cyclical movements and long-term growth cycles, which are caused mainly by the relation of reaction coefficient (ρ) to natural growth rate of labor population (n) are shown in Nagashima (2006), chapter 6, Sec.1.

8 The distinction between planned excess-capacity and unplanned excess-capacity was discussed in Steindl (1952). But he did not develop business cycle theory and deduced stagnation tendency directly from the structure of monopoly capitalism without analyzing the movements of monopoly capitalism.

9 See, Bain (1956) and Honma (1974).

10 The contrast in the movement of competitive and monopolistic prices during contraction periods in the United States is shown in Tables 8–5 of Sherman (1976) Chapter 8.

11 Nagashima (2008) Chapter 24 and (1981) Chapter1.

12 When D1 and D2 develop further, real wages turn into rising wages. About this condition, see Nagashima (1994) pp. 95–97 and 143–145.

13 With extreme D3 development, real wage rate falls (Nagashima [1994[, pp. 97–100 and 145–148).

14 The perspective of the underconsumption theory and "the realization theory" in Japan is limited within these possibilities. In order to prove the economic crisis, we must explain "the abrupt decline of profit rate" in the last phase of expansion.

15 Many Marxian economists in Japan attempted to explain "the inevitability of economic crisis", but Marx did not use this term. Samezo Kuruma (Kuruma ed. 1973) explained the conditions that bring the possibility of economic crisis to its actuality. We support Kuruma's view.

16 Uno, Goodwin and other theoreticians of the reserve army focused on the effect of this rise in the real wage.

17 See Mitchell (1913) pp. 475–483.

18 So-called fundamentalists tried to explain economic crisis directly from "Marx's law of falling tendency of profit rate". But this law is for the long term, and furthermore is not proved. In order to prove economic crisis, we must explain overaccumulation in the expansion period and "the abrupt falling of profit rate" in the last phase of expansion.

19 Okisio (1967) explained economic crisis by this limit of the fall of real wage.

20 Hickman (1957), pp. 425–427.

21 Many Marxian economists believed that chronic stagnation continues, but monopoly capitalism does not lose its "endogenous recovery power".

22 Here we won't delve into the possibility of the breakdown of the capitalist system due to an economic crisis.

23 Ouchi (1970) analyzed theoretically the ways economic crises have changed under state monopoly capitalism, and I added some new forms in this chapter.

References

Bain, Joe S. (1956) *Barriers to New Competition*, Cambridge MA: Harvard University Press.

Hickman, Bert G. (1957) "Capacity utilization and the acceleration principle", *Problem of Capital Formation*, Studies in Income and Wealth. Princeton NJ: Princeton University Press.

Hilferding, Rudolf (1910) *Das Finanzkapital (Finance Capital)*, Wien: Verlag der Wiener Volksbuchhandlung, 1927.

Honma, Yoichiro (1974) *Kyoso to Dokusen* (*Competition and Monopoly*), Tokyo: Shinhyoron.

Imura, Kiyoko (1973) *Kyoko Sangyo-Junkan no Riron* (*Theory of Economic Crisis and Industrial Cycle*), Tokyo: Yuhikaku.

Kalecki, Michal (1939) *Essays in the Theory of Economic Fluctuations,* London: Allen and Unwin.

Kalecki, Michal (1954) *Theory of Economic Dynamics,* London: Allen and Unwin.

Kuruma, Samezo ed. (1973) *Marukusu Keizaigaku Rekisikon* (*Guide to Marxian Economics Lexicon*), No.7. Tokyo: Otsuki Shoten.

Lenin, V. I. (В.И. Ленин) (1917) Империаизм *(Imperialism)*, Сочненяния,издание четвертое, том 22, Мосва:1952.(In Lenin's *Selected Works,* pp. 169–267, Moscow: Progress Publishers, 1968.)

Marx, Karl (1867) *Das Kapital (Capital)*, Vol.1, Berlin: Dietz Verlag, 1961.

Marx, Karl (1885) *Das Kapital (Capital)*, Vol.2, Berlin: Dietz Verlag, 1963.

Marx, Karl (1894) *Das Kapital (Capital)*, Vol.3, Berlin: Dietz Verlag, 1964.

Mitchell, Wesley (1913) *Business Cycle,* Berkeley: University of California Press.

Nagashima, Seiichi (1981) *Gendai Shihonshugi no Junkan to Kyoko* (*The Business Cycle and the Economic Crisis of Contemporary Capitalism*), Tokyo: Iwanami Shoten.

Nagashima, Seiichi (1994) *Keiki Junkan Ron* (*Theory of Business Cycle*), Tokyo: Aoki Shoten.

Nagashima, Seiichi (2006) *Gendai no Keiki Junkan-Ron* (*Contemporary Business Cycle Theory*), Tokyo: Sakurai Shoten.

Nagashima, Seiichi (2008) *Gendai Marukusu Keizaigaku* (*Contemporary Marxian Economics*), Tokyo: Sakurai Shoten.

Okishio, Nobuo (1967) *Chikuseki Ron* (*Theory of Accumulation*), Tokyo: Chikuma-Shobo.

Okishio, Nobuo ed. (1988) *Business Cycles,* Bern: Peterlang, 1992.

Ouchi, Tsutomu (1970) *Kokka Dokusen Shiohnshugi* (*State Monopoly Capitalism*), Tokyo: Tokyo University Press.

Sherman, Howard (1976) *Stagflation,* New York: Harper and Row, 1976.

Sherman, Howard (1991) *The Business Cycle,* Princeton NJ: Princeton University Press.

Shiozawa, Yoshinori (2014a) *Rikado Boeki Mondai no Saishu Kaiketsu* (*Final Solution of Ricardo Foreign Trade Problem*), Tokyo: Iwanami Shoten.

Shiozawa, Yoshinori (2014b) "The revival of classical theory of values," in Shiozawa, Yoshinori and Aruka, Yuji eds., *Keizaigaku o Saikensuru* (*Reconstruction of Economics*). Tokyo: Chuo University Press.

Steindl, Joseph (1952) *Maturity and Stagnation in American Capitalism,* London: Basil Blackwell.

Sweezy, Paul M. (1942) *The Theory of Capitalist Development,* Third Edition of Modern Reader Paperback. New York: Monthly Review Press, 1968.

Tomizuka, Ryozo (1975) *Kyoko Ron: Kaitei-Zoho* (*Theory of Economic Crisis,* revised and enlarged edition), Tokyo: Miraisha, 1975.

Uno, Kozo (1953) *Kyoko Ron* (*Economic Crisis Theory*), Tokyo: Iwanami Shoten.

6 Okishio's contribution to political economy

Yoshikazu Sato

Introduction

The main purpose of this chapter is to introduce the theory of growth and accumulation of Nobuo Okishio and to compare it with other theories. In section one, I introduce Okishio. We need some yardstick to evaluate the functioning of a variety of models. In section two, I propose a measure by which I will make such comparisons. The neoclassical model of growth and the neo-Kaldorian model are familiar among analytical political economists in the English-speaking countries, so I contrast Okishio's theory with these models in sections three and four. Finally, I discuss the contemporary significance of Okishio's theoretical approach and that of others in the tradition of political economy and/or heterodox economics in section five. Section six provides some concluding remarks

Who is Nobuo Okishio?

Mathematical Marxian economics

Nobuo Okishio was born in 1927 and passed away on November the 8, 2003. He taught mathematical economics at Kobe University for about forty years, and then at Osaka Keizai University for ten years. Western academic circles have known the name of Okishio as a result of the upsurge in political economy in the 1970s, known as the Marxist Renaissance. In Japan he has been counted as one of the outstanding theoretical Marxian economists. Shigeto Tsuru made the following remarks in his survey article:[1]

> It was before Michio Morishima attempted to solve some of the Marxian theorem mathematically that Nobuo Okishio, as a Marxist economist, applied mathematical techniques to the task of straightening out many of the problems on which Marx's exposition was not clear-cut or did not appear to be consistent. Actually, he was a pioneer in this field in Japan, having started to publish his work in the middle of the 1950s on such problems as the relation of value and price and the rate of profit.

Okishio published 25 books, including co-authored books, and about 250 articles in his lifetime, which covered a wide variety of theoretical topics. His works on the theory of value and price (known as "FMT: the Fundamental Marxian Theorem") and his discussion of the tendency of the rate of profit to fall (known as "the Okishio Theorem") were published in English.[2] There have been many discussions on these topics in the native English-speaking world.

Although Tsuru described Okishio as a Marxian economist, he was not an ordinary member of this school.[3] There are two major economic associations in Japan; Keizai Riron Gakkai, or the Japan Society of Political Economy (JSPE), and Riron Keizai Gakkai (Nihon Keizai Gakkai), or Japanese Economic Association (JEA).[4] If I put these into English literally, the former is "The Society of Economic Theory" and the latter is "The Society of Theoretical Economics". I imagine someone has already noticed the difference in the names. The difference is in the ordering of the words. This may appear very curious to observers. Morishima mentioned this fact in the preface of his book *Marx's Economics* (1973). Roughly speaking, most of the members of the JSPE are influenced by Marxian methodology, while most of the members of JEA are orthodox neo-classical economists. Unfortunately, members of the two associations do not have active communication with each other. Nevertheless, Okishio's work has been very influential in both Marxian economics and mainstream economics in Japan. In this respect, he was an exceptional economist.

Origins of Okishio's economics

The method that Okishio applied could be said to be basically Marxian, in a sense that he thought he could analyze a specific society from two basic relations: productive forces and production relations. However, he was not an ordinary Marxian economist, as I mention above. The theoretical foundation of Okishio's economics is not only from Marx, but also from the works of Hicks, Keynes and Harrod.[5] He learned from Hicks's *Value and Capital* (1946) "the capacity to analyze the interdependence of economic phenomena and to utilize mathematical methods for economic analysis", and was indebted to Keynes's *The General Theory of Employment, Interest and Money* (1936) for realizing the idea of "the importance of investment decisions for macroeconomic behavior". Besides Hicks and Keynes, he learned a very important point from Harrod's *Towards a Dynamic Economics* (1948), this being "the contradictory aspect of a capitalist economy". Harrod gave Okishio "the clue to understanding the relationship between individual investment decisions and economic instability in a capitalist economy".

At first, Okishio regarded Marx's economics (in *Das Kapital*) as "old-fashioned and obsolete". However, he eventually recognized that "its logical foundation is very solid and the basic propositions are capable of being derived by mathematical reasoning". He could here find the argument on the transition of the social system itself that could not be found in the works by Hicks, Keynes and Harrod.

Accordingly, we could argue that Okishio's mission had been to *re-construct* Marx's economics using mathematical methods; at the same time, he introduced some ideas from non-Marxian economics when he judged them useful for his analysis of a capitalist economy. His first paper demonstrating Marx's propositions by using mathematics was published in 1954,[6] which preceded Morishima (1973), mentioned above, by about twenty years. He published his first book entitled *Theory of Reproduction* (in Japanese) in 1957 when he was thirty years old.

Okishio was one of the world's pioneering mathematical Marxian economists, as Tsuru has pointed out.[7] The relationship between Cambridge and Okishio must be mentioned here. To my knowledge he visited Cambridge two times. He wrote: "In 1965 and 1976 I had the chance to study in Cambridge. M. Dobb, J. Robinson, N. Kaldor kindly induced me to write papers and many friends gave me intellectual stimulus".[8]

The paper that he wrote in Cambridge was published in the *Cambridge Journal of Economics* in 1977 with the title "The Technical Progress and Capitalism". His last paper was also published in the *Cambridge Journal of Economics* in 2001. This paper, entitled "Competition and Production Prices", re-examines his own Okishio Theorem.

Comparison: focal points

When we put a variety of models of accumulation and growth to the test, we need a yardstick to judge their performance. Okishio's theory is characterized in contrast, in particular, with a neoclassical growth model and a recent neo-Kaldorian model. In doing so, we focus on the features of the growth path and the institutional configurations that the model assumes.

I would like to focus on the following six points:

(1) Object: Growth, cycles and cyclical growth
(2) Fundamental character of the system: stable vs. unstable
(3) Equilibrium: mechanical stability property, or conditional property
(4) Causation: supply-led or demand-led
(5) Investment demand as an *independent* variable or otherwise
(6) Social institution (conflict, power and so on)

It is not necessary to give explanations for each item, as the meaning of each is straightforward. During the course of the comparison I will add some comments on these issues. However, it might be useful to show the core ideas of Okishio's theory of accumulation in advance. Roughly speaking the overall perspective of his theory can be summarized by three points.

(a) Centrality of conflict
(b) Capital accumulation as an independent variable; and
(c) Technical change as a constraint upon capitalistic development

How should we re-*read* a neoclassical theory of growth?

I will assume that the basic structure of the Solow-type neoclassical model is familiar, so that I may explain my interpretation of the neoclassical model of growth. The point is the manner in which we should read it from the Okishian point of view.

Model

The basic one-sector neoclassical model consists of the following equations:

(1) Equilibrium of goods market:

$$sY = I \text{ (saving} = \text{investment)}$$

where s denotes saving propensity, Y is income, and I represents investment.

(2) Neoclassical production function:
The type of technical progress is assumed to be Harrod-neutral.

$$Y = F(K, e^{\alpha t} N)$$

where K denotes capital equipment, α is the rate of technical change at period t, and N represents employed labor.

(3) Rate of profit:

$$r = \frac{Y - RN}{K}$$

where R denotes real wage rate.

(4) Technical choice:
Capitalists select the technique to maximize the rate of profit. So the real wage rate must be equated to the marginal productivity of labor.

$$R = F_N$$

(5) Supply of labor:
The labor is assumed to grow at a constant rate (n).

$$\hat{N} = n$$

(6) Capital accumulation:

$$\dot{K} = I$$

The model above, which consists of six equations, suffices to determine the behavior of six variables (Y, K, N, I, R and r).

Equilibrium growth path

A reduced form of the model can be easily obtained.[9]

(7) $\hat{z} = \alpha + n - sf(z)$

We can find the equilibrium value $z = z^*$, which satisfies the equation $\hat{z} = 0$. That is,

(8) $sf(z^*) = \alpha + n$

If the initial value of z is equal to the equilibrium, the rate of accumulation is $\alpha + n$. In the case of z is not equal to z^*, it converges to it.

Implications

The assertion of a neoclassical model is that there exists an equilibrium growth path that satisfies three particular conditions and that an economy converges to this path. The three conditions are (i) equilibrium of goods market (eq. (1)), (ii) normal utilization of capital (eq. (2)) and (iii) full employment of labor (eq. (2) and eq. (5)). If we assume there is Harrod-neutral technical change, the growth rates of output, capital and investment are equal to the growth rate of labor supply plus the rate of technical progress (= $\alpha + n$.).

Though a neoclassical model assumes the stability of the equilibrium growth path, this stability is completely different from the so-called stability in the sense of Harrod. In the latter, the problem is whether or not the *dis*-equilibrium, such as excess demand and/or excess supply, can be seen to diminish as time

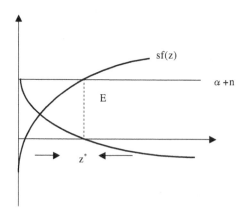

Figure 6.1 Stability of neoclassical model

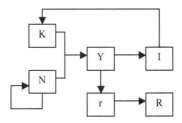

Figure 6.2 Causation of neoclassical model

goes by. However, the path that a neoclassical model follows will always satisfy the equilibrium conditions. The problem in a neoclassical model is whether or not the growth path will generate some inner contradiction that prevents the economy from progressing. The conventional answer is: there will be no inner contradiction as long as the type of technical change is Harrod-neutral.

As Figure 6.2 shows, the level of production is determined so as to satisfy both the normal utilization of capital and full employment of labor. The investment is then adjusted to achieve the equilibrium of the product market (that is, *Say's law*). So we can find no independent behavior of capitalists; they do not exercise their power in the economic scene. In equilibrium the product and capital equipment grow at the same rate; the rate of profit remains constant; and the real wage rate increases at the rate of technical progress, which is altogether a very harmonious state. There emerge no political and/or economic conflicts.

In sum, we have to admit that a neoclassical growth model is a theory of a capitalist economy where capitalists are *absent*. However, someone may assert that a capitalist does choose the production technique so as to maximize the rate of profit subject to the current production function. I think this is not true, the reason being that the production level has to be determined at a full employment level. So there exists no independent behavior in the economy described by a neoclassical model. We can summarize the focal points as follows:

(1) Object: balanced growth
(2) Fundamental character of the system: stable
(3) Equilibrium: no disequilibrium
(4) Causation: supply-led
(5) Investment: no independent investment
(6) Social institution: absence of capitalists, no conflict, no *power*

How can a neo-Kaldorian Model *differ from* a neoclassical?

In this section, I will examine a paper by Setterfield and Cornwall. They extend the traditional Kaldorian model of cumulative causation by introducing institutional considerations. However, they use a basic model with different parameter sets to analyze the different regimes, that is the "Golden Age (GA)", the "Age of Decline (AoD)" and the so-called neoliberal regime of the 1990s. Essentially, the model they apply is the traditional one. So it suffices to examine the difference between a neoclassical model and the traditional Kaldorian model.

Basic model

Setterfield and Cornwall's model consists of four equation, which suffice to determine four unknowns; q (productivity growth), y (the rate of growth of output), x (the rate of growth of export) and p (the rate of inflation).

(9) $q = r + \alpha y$

(10) $p = w - q + \tau$

(11) $x = \beta(p_w - p) + \gamma y_w$

(12) $y = \lambda(w_X x + w_A a)$

where r represents exogenous determinants of productivity growth, α is the elasticity of production with respect to output, β is the price elasticity of demand for export, γ is the income elasticity of demand for export, and λ is an expenditure multiplier, while w_X and w_A represent the share of export and other autonomous expenditures in real income respectively.[10]

Causation

Their model above can be reduced to two equations, which determine the productivity growth and the rate of growth of output. In other words, their Macroeconomic Regime (MR) consists of a Productivity Regime (PR), a Demand Regime (DR) and an Institutional Regime (IR). An IR is "a relatively enduring macro-institutional structure within which economic behavior takes place".[11] It contains such elements as norms of distribution, a social infrastructure necessary to create stability, an institutional structure of international trade and finance.
    Macroeconomic Regime

(a) the Productivity Regime

   PR: $q = r + \alpha y$

(b) the Demand Regime

   DR: $y = \Omega + \lambda w_X \beta q$

   where $\Omega = \lambda(w_A a - w_X \beta r + w_X(\gamma - \alpha_w \beta) y_w)$

(c) Institutional Regime

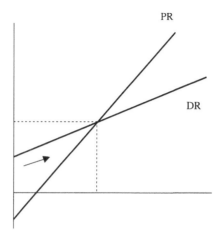

Figure 6.3 Neo-Kaldorian model

Using this framework, they tried to clarify the cause of breakdown of the Golden Age and the viability of the neoliberal regime.

Implications

The point here is to understand the characteristics that differ from a neoclassical model. We first have to notice that their approach rests on the notion that "capitalism is not self-regulating".[12] In addition, the following two points are identified as "fundamentals of a capitalist economy":

(1) "[T]he actual rate of growth is demand determined."
(2) "[T]he division of labor depends on the extent of the market."

The neo-Kaldorian model differentiates from a neoclassical in this sense, that they put stress on the unstable nature of a capitalist economy and its demand-led nature. Nevertheless, the equilibrium, which is defined by two equations mentioned above, is assumed to be stable. However, this stability can only be realized under some specific institutional setting, so it is not mechanical stability in a neoclassical model, but rather a conditional one.

As for the investment behavior that we identify as most important in a capitalist economy, we cannot find any explicit investment function in this model. Setterfield and Cornwall stress the priority of demand in determination of production, though we have to say they fail to understand the "fundamentals" in my sense. On the contrary, for example, Goodwin's famous paper (1967) proposed a Marxian-type model that places stress on class struggle and on the importance of the reserve army of labor, although *Say's law* and the normal utilization of capital are assumed in his paper. Accordingly, his model succeeded in describing one important aspect of a capitalist economy (that is class society),

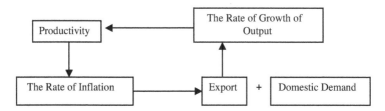

Figure 6.4 Causation of neo-Kaldorian model

but it failed to incorporate the independent role of investment behavior. However, Peter Skott (1989) integrates the Keynesian idea of effective demand with a Marxian stress on class struggle. Though Skott does not examine the fundamental characteristics of a capitalist economy as Okishio did, I think his model is located along similar lines to that of Okishio's argument.

We can therefore summarize the focal points as follows:

(1) Object: [cyclical] growth
(2) Fundamental character of the system: "Capitalism is not self-regulating."
(3) Equilibrium: conditional equilibrium, regime analysis
(4) Causation: demand-led
(5) Investment: no investment function
(6) Social institution: an enduring macro-institutional structure

How can we *catch* the flavor of Okishio's theory of accumulation?

Okishio developed his theory of accumulation and crisis mainly in his book *Chikuseki-ron (Theory of Accumulation)*, which was first published in 1967 and revised in 1976. The following discussion will be based on the revised edition. I will explain the main ideas in a simple setting.

Okishio's basic model

The following is assumed to simplify the argument:

(A1) One-sector model, commodity can be used as both capital goods and consumption goods.
(A2) Capital equipment does not depreciate.
(A3) Capital equipment cannot operate over the rate of utilization $\bar{\delta}$.

(13) Equilibrium of goods market:

$$X_t = R_t N_t + I_t$$

(14) Rate of profit:

$$r_t = \frac{X_t - R_t N_t}{K_t}$$

(15) Production:

$$X_t = \delta_t \sigma K_t$$

(16) Demand for labor:

$$N_t = \tau X_t$$

(17) Rate of accumulation:

$$g_t = \frac{I_t}{K_t}$$

(18) Investment function:

Case 1: $\delta_t < \bar{\delta}$

$$g_{t+1} = g_t + \beta(\delta_t - 1) \quad \beta > 0$$

Case 2: $\delta_t = \bar{\delta}$

$$g_{t+1} = g_t + \gamma(r_t - r^*) \quad \gamma > 0$$

(19) Rate of utilization:

$$\delta_t = \delta(r_t) \quad \delta' > 0, \delta(r^*) = 1$$

(20) Capital accumulation:

$$K_{t+1} = K_t + I_t$$

Unknowns: X_t (output), R_t (real wage), N_t (employment), K_t (capital equipment), I_t (investment), r_t (profit rate), δ_t (rate of utilization), g_t (rate of accumulation)

The model that consists of equations (13)–(20) suffices to determine the actual growth path, that is eight unknowns can be determined in this system. Equation (13) states that the level of production is determined so as to satisfy the demand if the demand is below the production capacity. Equation (14) defines the rate of profit (r_t). Equations (15) and (16) assume that the function describing the influence of production technique is of a fixed coefficient-type. Equation (17) defines the rate of accumulation. Equation (18) is the investment function, which is often called the "Harrod-Okishio type". This investment function shows that "capitalists determine the rate of accumulation at the same rate as the previous period if the capital equipment is normally utilized, at a greater rate if over-utilized and at a smaller rate if under-utilized". The degree of utilization function (19) shows that capitalists require a certain level of the rate of profit in order to carry out production. That is, if the actual level of profit is above (equal or below) the required level (r^*), the degree of the utilization is above (equal or below) the normal level. Clearly the rate of utilization cannot rise unceasingly and so we denote the physical upper limit of δ as $\bar{\delta}$. In this case, as the investment function above cannot operate, we instead postulate that the rate of accumulation depends on the difference between the actual rate of profit and the desired rate of profit. Equation 20 defines the capital accumulation.

Three kinds of growth trajectory

Okishio uses three kinds of growth path in his theory: Harmonious Extended Reproduction Trajectory (HERT), Equilibrium Accumulation Trajectory (EAT) and Actual Accumulation Trajectory (AAT). The definitions of these trajectories are very simple.

(a)   Harmonious Extended Reproduction Trajectory: HERT

First the growth path, which satisfies both the equilibrium conditions of the product market and the normal utilization of capital through time, is called a Harmonious Extended Reproduction Trajectory.

> Condition 1: equilibrium of goods market
> Condition 2: normal utilization of capital (i.e. $\delta = 1$)

In order to move along this path, the following must be satisfied.

(21) $r_t = g_t (= g^* = r^*)$

(22) $R_t = \dfrac{\sigma - g^*}{\tau\sigma} (= R^*)$

(23) $X_t = X_0(1 + g^*)^t$

(24) $N_t = N_0(1 + g^*)^t$

(25) $K_t = K_0(1 + g^*)^t$

(26) $I_t = I_0(1 + g^*)^t$

If the actual economy were to move along HERT, it seems that there would be no problem. Because the capital equipment is utilized normally and then the commodities produced can be completely sold. If there is no technical change, the rate of accumulation is equal to the desired rate of profit.

(b)   Equilibrium Accumulation Trajectory: EAT

There might be no inner contradiction from the viewpoint of the realization of the value of commodities. However, the demand for labor grows at the same rate of accumulation (g^*) when the economy moves along the HERT. Here the supply of labor is assumed to grow at a constant rate (n).

(27) Labor supply: $L_t = L_0(1+n)^t$

We have three cases of possible ways in which the economy will move:

Case1: $g^* > n$

Sooner or later the economy may be restricted by limited labor supply. Once the economy hits this ceiling, it will not be able to move along the HERT.

Case2: $n > g^*$

As time goes by, unemployment will increase cumulatively, so the capitalistic relation of production will not be able to be maintained in the long run.

Case3: $g^* = n$

The rate of unemployment remains constant. The economy can move along the HERT, which is defined as the Equilibrium Accumulation Trajectory.

So we can say an Equilibrium Accumulation Trajectory is a growth path that satisfies three conditions:

(i)   an equilibrium of product market
(ii) a normal utilization of capital through time
(iii) a constant rate of unemployment

The actual accumulation path in a capitalist economy does not always move along EAT. The EAT shows how the actual capital accumulation process can proceed *on average in the long run* while it exhibits the cyclical movement in the short run.

The growth rate of labor supply must be smaller than a specific value. It is necessary to satisfy the following relation for the existence of EAT. The maximum rate of growth can be obtained when the real wage rate is zero. Therefore, EAT cannot exist if the growth rate of labor supply exceeds g_{max}, because the condition $g^* = n$ cannot hold. The rate of unemployment necessarily rises as time goes on.

As the upper limit of the growth rate of demand is $g^*_{max} = \sigma$, n must not exceed σ for the existence of EAT.

(c)   Actual Accumulation Trajectory: AAT

Now we show the necessity of the cumulation of disequilibrium mathematically. From equations (13), (14), (17), (18) and (19), we can obtain the reduced form of the basic model:

$$(28) \quad g_{t+1} = g_t + \beta(\delta(g_t) - 1) \quad \beta > 0$$

If the initial value of the rate of accumulation is equal to g^*, the actual accumulation trajectory can move along HERT. However there is no guarantee that this special case will occur in the actual environment. We must examine the character of the AAT.

The structure of Okishio's theory

The basic components of Okishio's theory are the following:

(a) Viability condition of a capitalist economy
(b) Three kinds of growth trajectory (HERT, EAT, and AAT)
(c) The cumulative process of disequilibrium
(d) Necessity and concrete moments of a turning point
(e) Trade cycles and law of tendency

I would like to explain these points in order. Before undertaking these explanations, I present a diagram of Okishio's model.[13]

(a)   Viability conditions of a capitalist economy

On this point Okishio takes a fundamental Marxist position regarding the viability conditions of a capitalist economy. His starting point is Marx's analysis, which is summarized in the following three propositions:

(1) For any particular mode of production, there is a lower limit of productivity below which it cannot exist and function at all.
(2) Any mode of production, if it can exist and function, contains a mechanism which ensures that its productivity will increase as time goes by.
(3) Any model of production has a certain upper limit to productivity beyond which it cannot continue to maintain itself.

I will not discuss these points further. Okishio's theory is based on these ideas. In Figure 6.5 the two double lines can be seen as displaying the viability condition, which will be discussed later.

(b)   The cumulative process of disequilibrium

One of the most important characteristics of Okishio's theory of accumulation is its emphasis on the distinction between *those causes* that trigger crisis and its

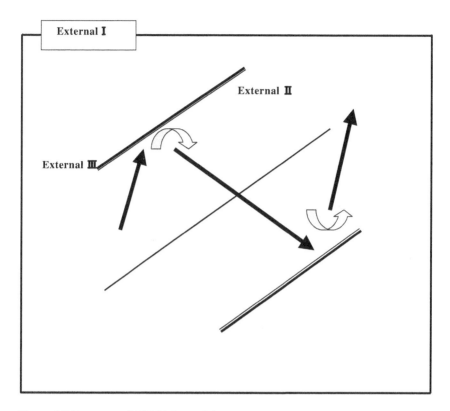

Figure 6.5 Structure of Okishio's model

necessity of this crisis. His demonstration of the necessity of crisis consists of two points. First, he shows that the disequilibrium, once it occurs, spreads cumulatively throughout the capitalist economy, and that is caused by the fundamental contradiction of the capitalist economy. Second, he argues that if this cumulative process of disequilibrium goes on without limit, the conditions for reproduction of the capitalist economy will be destroyed. Accordingly, from these two assertions, we can say that a crisis is inevitable as long as we assume the continued existence of the capitalist economy.

When the economy moves along the path that satisfies both normal utilization of capital and the equilibrium of commodity market (i.e. HERT), the rate of profit must be equal to the required level.

From (13), (14), (17), (18) and (19), we get the difference equation (28), which describes the behavior of the actual rate of accumulation. Equation (28) implies that if the initial value of δ is less than unity – that is the initial value of the rate of accumulation is smaller than the equilibrium level – then g_t becomes smaller as time goes by and vice versa.

Once $g_t (r_t, \delta_t)$ diverges from equilibrium, it cannot return to the equilibrium but diverge more and more.

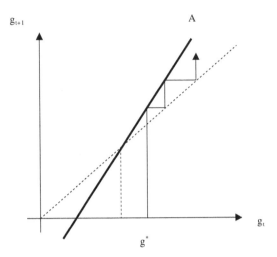

Figure 6.6 Cumulative process of disequilibrium

The slope of the curve A is greater than unity, following from equations (18) and (19).

(29) $\dfrac{dg_{t+1}}{dg_t} = 1 + \beta\delta' > 1$

We know from (13), (14), and (17) that when the rate of accumulation diverges from the equilibrium, so does the rate of profit. The reason why the actual growth path is unstable is that capitalists accumulate according to the "Harrod-Okishio type" of investment function. That capitalists behave as depicted in 18 is rooted in the peculiar manner of capitalist production.

The movement of real wage rate depends on that of the rate of profit.

(30) $R_t = \dfrac{\delta(r_t)\sigma - r_t}{\tau\delta(r_t)\sigma}$

(31) $\dfrac{dR_t}{dr_t} = \dfrac{1}{\tau\sigma\delta}\left(\dfrac{d\delta_t / \delta_t}{dr_t / r_t} - 1 \right)$

If the rate of utilization elasticity of rate of profit is smaller than unity, the real wage rate moves conversely to the rate of profit.

In the upward cumulative process, the investment changes after the rate of utilization hit the physical upper limit. The movement of the real wage rate is governed by:

(32) $R_t = \dfrac{\bar{\delta}\sigma - g_t}{\tau\bar{\delta}\sigma}.$

As the rate of accumulation is rising in the upward cumulative process, the real wage rate necessarily falls.

(c) The origin of the cumulative movement

The reason why the actual movement is so fragile must be explained. It can be summarized graphically as shown in Figure 6.7.

(a) If a capitalist economy were *not a class society*, in which products were produced for exchange purpose, then products would not be commodities, and no problem of realization of commodities could exist. Therefore no disequilibrium of commodity realization would exist.
(b) If the workers were *not exploited and their consumption demand was not limited*, no difficulty of commodity realization would exist and the investment demand by capitalists would not be able to play a critical role in the determination of the aggregate demand.
(c) If the decisions on production were *not determined in pursuit of private profit on limited local information, or there did not exist anarchy of production*, the investment demand could move so as to restore the equilibrium even if the disequilibrium were to emerge.

In sum, the cumulative movement of disequilibrium originates from the basic characteristics of a capitalist economy. This characterization is not found in the neo-Kaldorian model or in the discussion of Harrod's Instability Principle.

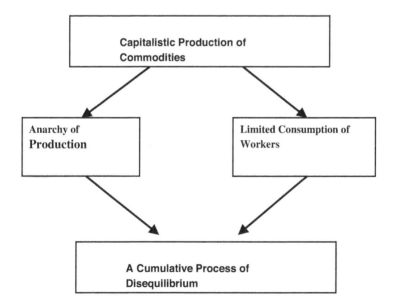

Figure 6.7 The origin of a cumulative process

(d)   Necessity and concrete moments of turning points

Here we examine the behavior of the real wage rate in the cumulative process in detail. The sign of $\frac{dR_t}{dr_t}$ is positive if the rate of utilization elasticity of the rate of profit is larger than unity. Clearly the rate of utilization cannot rise unceasingly. As the upward cumulative process continues, the utilization rate necessarily encounters its upper limit. In this case, the real wage rate necessarily falls. Therefore, it is shown that the real wage rate should fall in the end if the upward cumulative process of disequilibrium were to go on unceasingly. Similarly, the real wage rate should rise in the downward cumulative process of disequilibrium.

As is well known, the most important condition for the reproduction of a capitalist economy is the existence of workers who sell their labor power. This is guaranteed if the real wage rate is limited within a certain range. It must not fall below a minimum level that is determined by physical, cultural and social considerations. At the same time it must not exceed a threshold level that would allow workers to buy the means of production, which would imply that capitalists could not exploit workers. The latter provision means that the surplus condition must be satisfied.

If this upward cumulative process of disequilibrium were to continue unceasingly, the real wage would fall below the minimum level. Then the time would necessarily come when labor power could not be reproduced. Hence, in order for capitalist society to reproduce itself, an influence of some kind must act to reverse this upward cumulative process of disequilibrium.

In sum, two propositions have been demonstrated so far:

(1) Proposition (a): A cumulative process of disequilibrium inevitably proceeds in a capitalist economy.
(2) Proposition (b): The reproduction of a capitalist economy becomes impossible if the cumulative process proceeds unceasingly.

Accordingly, we can say that a capitalist economy is obliged to have a trade cycle.

(e)   Moments of crisis and upturn

In this section, we discuss the causes of crisis and upturn. The characteristic of Okishio's theory of accumulation is that it separates the concrete moments of crisis from its inevitability. He asserts that the direct cause, which reverses the cumulative process, cannot be predetermined *a priori*. He writes: "It is not correct to pick up one specific moment which reverses the cumulative process and then generalize that the cumulative process is necessarily reversed by this moment. We cannot deduce a unique moment of reversal merely from the fundamental characteristics of a capitalist economy".[14]

Okishio then lists the five causes that are most likely to trigger the inevitable crisis. These are as follows:[15]

(1) Over-production in the consumption goods sector
(2) Underproduction in the capitalist goods sector
(3) Labor shortage; full-employment ceiling
(4) Credit restriction
(5) Lower limit of the real wage

Here I will discuss the causal relationship that may trigger the crisis. By way of example, we examine the "labor shortage" case. When capitalists cannot employ workers as they want, this constraint would bring about any shift in their plan to extend production in the subsequent period. This would lead to a fall of investment demand and trigger a downward movement. Facing a shortage of labor, capitalists in the competition goods sector may lose workers due to the competition. This causes an idle capacity of equipment in the consumption sector and a fall of investment demand. In response to this fall in the consumption goods sector, investment demand would also decline in the capital goods sector. This triggers the crisis.

The necessity of the upturn (the upper turning point) can be demonstrated in the same way as the case of a crisis. As causes of upturn, Okishio lists the following five factors:[16]

(1) Prosperity of the consumption goods sector
(2) Dissolution of the bottleneck
(3) Investment demand to introduce a new production technique
(4) Capitalists' consumption demand
(5) Replacement demand of equipment

From the above discussion, we can say that cyclical movements are *endogenous* in the capitalist economy and that this is rooted in the peculiarity of the capitalist manner of production and accumulation.

(f)   Trade cycles and the law of tendency

Now, we explore the behavior of the major economic variables in a cycle. All variables (the rate of accumulation, the rate of profit, the rate of exploitation, the rate of unemployment and the real wage rate) exhibit cyclical movements. Any point of time in the course of the trade cycle cannot satisfy the conditions for harmonious reproduction. The economy is always in the upward or downward cumulative process of disequilibrium. The fact that social reproduction in a capitalist economy is realized through these cyclical movements means that on average some segment of the workforce is always unemployed in the long run.

"Violent equilibrating forces", which could reverse this upward (downward) cumulative process of disequilibrium, must be necessary in order for a capitalist society to reproduce itself. This is why cyclical fluctuations are endogenous in a capitalist society; in other words, crisis and upturn are inevitable. Through the cyclical movements, with recurrent unstable phases of expansion and stagnation, the capitalist economy expands and innovates the existing production techniques. We investigate long-run tendencies that the capitalist economy develops through the trade cycles. The following phenomena, for example, may be observed: a deepening difficulty in finding markets, the tendency towards a falling rate of profit and the rising minimum size of the investment fund necessary in the basic sectors and so on.

As is easily noticed, the line of argument can be characterized as fundamentally Marxian. However, Okishio's theoretical originality lays in the theory of accumulation – in particular, the mathematical analysis of the mechanism of reproduction in a capitalist economy.

Analytics of Okishio's model

The causal relationships among the variables are summarized in Figure 6.8. There are many noticeable features in this macroeconomic process.

(a) The direction of causality runs from the goods market to the labor market. The financial market does not play an active role in this process.
(b) Conditions in the goods market determine the real wage rate and employment. The labor market itself is behind the scenes in this model. Workers' behavior exercises no influence on the determination of the real wage and employment.
(c) Investment demand is decisive in the determination of production.
(d) The major determinant is the profit rate, so it is central to the account of the behavior of the capitalist economy.

If we accept the schematization by Palley (1998), Okishio is a "classical Marxist" in the sense that he emphasizes the centrality of the profit rate for the understanding of a capitalist economy and its relationship to the class relation. However, he is rather Keynesian in his emphasis on the importance of investment demand.

Here we can summarize the focal points of Okishio's model as follows:

(1) Object: cyclical growth
(2) Fundamental character of the system: unstable
(3) Equilibrium: no equilibrium (cumulative process of disequilibrium)
(4) Causation: demand-led
(5) Investment: independent accumulation behavior
(6) Social institution: antagonistic relation between capital and labor

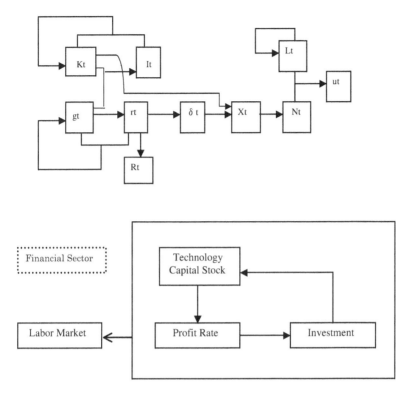

Figure 6.8 Causal relationship of Okishio's model

Concluding remarks: Can the theory *a la* Okishio *survive*? And *how*?

The gist of Okishio's theory of accumulation is to clarify the necessity of cyclical movement in a capitalist economy, using an analysis based on his Harrod-Okishio type of investment function. The realized rate of profit depends on the rate of accumulation, which is based upon decisions, which are private and dispersed. As a result, it generates a cyclical movement of basic economic variables. It can be said that his work is greatly indebted to Marx, Keynes and Harrod. Marx's *Das Kapital* was published in 1867, and Keynes's *The General Theory* in 1936. It is often argued that these works are too old-fashioned and obsolete, and that the same is also true of Okishio's work; and that their analysis cannot contribute to the analysis of the so-called *financialized* global economy in which we now live.[17]

We can summarize the main points of the perspective of Okishio.

(a) Centrality of conflict
(b) Capital accumulation as demand as an independent variable
(c) Technical change as a constraint upon capitalistic development

As for the first point, it is common knowledge that there exists a variety of conflicts in the world. The world is completely different from the picture that neoclassical economics shows. Conflict and/or power issues are absent in the orthodox neoclassical viewpoint. However, it is indispensable for an understanding of contemporary capitalism even if it is globalized.

Second, the accumulation model examined so far abstracts the public sector and foreign sector. When we analyze the economy at a more concrete level, we have to take these factors into consideration. The idea that a capital accumulation as an independent variable is critical can be applied to the analysis of contemporary capitalism. The aggregate demand determines the realized rate of profits. Aggregate demand consists of replacement demand, workers' consumption demand, capitalists' consumption demand, investment demand, government expenditure and export. As is easily shown, the realized rate of profit after taxes is determined by such factors as the rate of accumulation, the rate of government deficit spending, the rate of trade surplus, capitalists' consumption and workers' consumption.[18]

$$(33) \quad s_\pi \frac{\Pi - T_\pi}{K} + s_w \frac{W - T_w}{K} = \frac{I}{K} + \frac{G - T}{K} + \frac{E - F}{K}$$

The rate of accumulation is the most important of these factors. If capitalists cannot maintain a high level of accumulation rate, the realized rate of profit must fall, which induces the rate of accumulation to fall; then the rate of profit will fall and so on; the downward cumulative process proceeds. From the above relation, we can understand how to raise the rate of profit after taxes in the face of a stagnant accumulation by:

(a) Increasing the rate of government deficit spending
(b) Increasing the rate of trade surplus
(c) Decreasing the workers' income distribution
(d) Decreasing the propensity to save

The first two devices can be seen as a strategy of traditional Keynesianism. The mixture of the second and third is what recent neoliberalism pursues. It is apparent that these strategies are not effective in the long run, since government deficit cannot be increased, and all the economies in the world cannot increase their trade surpluses at the same time. Such an expansionist policy will be constrained by environmental issues. Greater inequality in income distribution will heighten social instability. The policy presumes that socio-economic institutions are capitalistic, and *given*. We can, however, discard this presumption, and by doing so, we can pursue an alternative. The perspective that centers on accumulation provides us with a basis for evaluating current policies and the alternative.

We argue that one of the conditions for the existence of an equilibrium accumulation trajectory is that the type of technical change must be such that it keeps the organic composition of capital constant. We know the relation concerning the rate of profit always holds:

(34) the upper limit of actual rate of profit $r = \dfrac{M}{C+V} < \dfrac{V+M}{C} = \dfrac{N}{C}$

where M denotes surplus value, V wages, C constant capital and N living labor. The upper limit on the rate of profit is the ratio of living labor to dead labor, or the organic composition of production. If we rewrite this by our notation, it is expressed as

(35) $\dfrac{N}{C} = \dfrac{\tau X}{aXt} = \dfrac{\tau}{at} = \dfrac{1-a}{a}.$

That is to say, the rate of profit necessarily declines if the coefficient (a) becomes larger, which cannot be solved by a Keynesian policy. It is apparent that this is not a realization problem.[19]

The applicability of a specific theory should not be judged by its superficial resemblance to realities. We need a theoretical apparatus that helps us to understand the mechanism underneath "realities". In this sense the theory of growth and accumulation in the tradition of heterodox macroeconomics is still effective.

About thirty years – the equivalent of one generation – has passed since the Golden Age of advanced capitalist economies ended. However, we are still in the age of long stagnation. In the 1980s and '90s, there was an attempt to privatize and/or deregulate various parts of the economy. Certainly, the US economy improved the macroeconomic performance during the 1990s. Nevertheless, it can be idealized that everything goes well if we emulate the economy that the general equilibrium theory presumes. As is often pointed out, we live in a *financialized* global economy and the instability in the economy has increased. Now we must ask the fundamental question: Where can we find the origin of the instability of the market?

Marx stressed the antagonistic character inherent in a capitalist economy and developed a crisis theory based on the fundamental characteristic of a capitalist economy. Facing the great depression in the 1930s, Keynes showed that a capitalist economy is not a self-regulating system and emphasized the importance of investment demand. Harrod emphasized the knife-edge character of investment in a capitalist economy. Nobuo Okishio (1927–2003) can be placed in this theoretical tradition. However his constructive theory of growth and accumulation, in particular the theory of cumulative process of disequilibrium, has remained totally unknown to Western readers, for it was mainly written in Japanese. No paper that examines Okishio's theory of growth and accumulation has appeared in English as far as I know. I believe that the issue of globalization itself is also necessary in the heterodox economics camp to facilitate the discussion among a wide variety of economics.

Many people still imagine that the market mechanism can work smoothly. This cannot be true. If it is true, why are so many of the world's unemployed unable find jobs? Some may insist that they can get jobs if they accept lower wages. Then equilibrium may be restored; but in what sense does it mean to be in equilibrium? Can people enjoy a stable life in such an equilibrium?

When we re-examine the problem of instability of a capitalist economy in our age, we must not presume that a capitalist economy is the same as the market economy in general. We must not forget the fact that a capitalist economy is a society that is organized by *capital*. Therefore capital accumulation is the core of the working of this system. From this point of view, Okishio's theory might be a good starting point for us to analyze contemporary capitalism even if it is totally financialized. As Okishio applied a mathematical method to develop his theory, it would be easy to bridge his theory and a variety of heterodox macroeconomic approaches in the West.

Finally, I would like to make one last point. I understand that one of the aims of political economy is "opening-up economics", that is "to examine issues and deploying approaches neglected by the current orthodoxy, demonstrating the vitality of heterodox economics and its continued relevance to contemporary social questions".[20]

Notes

1 Tsuru (1984) p. 305.
2 Okishio's paper written in English is available in a collection of his papers edited by Kruger and Flaschel (1993).
3 Itoh (1981) also surveyed "the development of Marxian economics in Japan." From his Uno-ist point of view, he argues somewhat critically: "Nobuo Okishio also employs mathematical methods in his presentation of the quantitative relation between the rate of surplus value and the rate of profit: his discussion of the tendency of the rate of profit to fall also contains some interesting insights. However, Okishio's position seems occasionally to be of a neo-Richardian variant of Marxism although his subjective intent is certainly purely Marxist. This tendency may be the result of the fact he confines his contributions to quantitative, mathematical problems" (p. 30).
4 It was renamed Nihon Keizai Gakkai (Japanese Economic Association) in 1997.
5 Foreword by Okishio in Kruger and Flascel (1993) pp. vii–x.
6 Okishio (1954) formulated the determination of labor value.
7 Arestis and Sawyer's *A Biographical Dictionary of Dissenting Economists* contains Okishio's biography.
8 Kruger and Flascel (1993) p. x)
9 $z = \dfrac{e^{\alpha t}N}{K}$ $y = \dfrac{Y}{K} = \dfrac{F(K, e^{\alpha t}N)}{K} = F(1, z) = f(z)$

$\hat{z} = \alpha + \hat{N} - \hat{K}$

$\qquad = \alpha + n - \dfrac{\dot{K}}{K} = \alpha + n - \dfrac{sF(K, e^{\alpha t}N)}{K}$

$\qquad = \alpha + n - sf(z)$

10 Setterfield and Cornwall (2002) p. 72.
11 op. cit. p. 71
12 op. cit. p. 67.
13 See Sato (2012) p. 54.

14 Okishio (1976) p. 227.

15 op. cit. pp. 228–232.

16 op. cit. pp.242–249.

17 For an analysis of the so-called "finance-led growth regime" from a regulationist approach, see Boyer (2000).

18 *Aggregate Supply = domestic production + import*

(A1) $AS = X + F$

Aggregate Demand = repla[Eqn033093.eps]cement demand + workers' consumption demand + capitalists' consumption demand + investment demand + government expenditure + export

(A2) $AD = Z + c_w(W - T_w) + c_\pi(\Pi - T_\pi) + I + G + E$

The condition of equilibrium:

(A3) $X + F = Z + c_w(W - T_w) + c_\pi(\Pi - T_\pi) + I + G + E$

Considering the following identity,

(A4) $X = Z + W + \Pi$

(A5) $T = T_w + T_\pi$

we can rewrite (A3) as the following:

$(1 - c_\pi)(\Pi - T_\pi) + (1 - c_w)(W - T_w) = I + (G - T) + (E - F)$

If we divide the both side by the aggregate capital K, we obtain,

(A6) $(1 - c_\pi)\dfrac{\Pi - T_\pi}{K} + (1 - c_w)\dfrac{W - T_w}{K} = \dfrac{I}{K} + \dfrac{G - T}{K} + \dfrac{E - F}{K}$

That is,

(A7) $s_\pi\dfrac{\Pi - T_\pi}{K} + s_w\dfrac{W - T_w}{K} = \dfrac{I}{K} + \dfrac{G - T}{K} + \dfrac{E - F}{K}$

19 See Sato (2012).

20 This was the theme of the Annual Conference of Association for Heterodox Economics, which was held in 2004.

References

Arestis, P. and M. Sawyer (eds.) (1992, 2nd 2000). *A Biographical Dictionary of Dissenting Economists*, Cheltenham: Edward Elgar.

Boyer, R. (2000). "Is a Finance-led Growth Regime a Viable Alternative to Fordism? A Preliminary Analysis", *Economy and Society*, vol. 29 (1), pp.111–145.

Goodwin, R. (1967). "A Growth Cycle," in Feinstein, C.H. (ed.) *Socialism, Capitalism and Economic Growth*, Cambridge: Cambridge University Press.

Harrod, R. (1948) *Towards a Dynamic Economics*, London: Macmillan.

Hicks, J.R. (1939, 2nd. 1946) *Value and Capital*, Oxford: Clarendon Press.

Itoh, M. (1981). *Value and Crisis*, Monthly Review Press.

Keynes, J.M. (1936) *The General Theory of Employment, Interest and Money*, London: Macmillan.

Kruger, M. and P. Flaschel (eds.) (1993). *Nobuo Okishio – Essays on Political Economy*, Peter Lang.

Morishima, M. (1973). *Marx's Economics: A Dual Theory of Value and Growth*, Cambridge: Cambridge University Press.

Okishio, N. (1954). *Kokanron ni tsuie (On Theory of Exchange)* (in Japanese), Kokumin Keizai Zasshi.

――― (1957). *Saiseisan no Riron (A Theory of Reproduction)* (in Japanese), Sobunsha.

――― (1961). "Technical Change and the Rate of Profit," *Kobe University Economic Review*.

――― (1963). "A Mathematical Note on Marxian Theorems," *Weltwirtschaftliches Archiv*.

――― (1967, 1976 2nd ed.). *Chikuseki-ron (Theory of Accumulation)* (in Japanese), Chikuma-shobo.

――― (1980). *Gendai-shihonsyugi Bunseki no Kadai (The Problems on Contemporary Capitalism)* (in Japanese), Iwanami-shoten.

――― (1993). *Keizaigaku wa Ima Nani o Kangaeteiruka (What Do Economists Discuss Now?)* (in Japanese), Tokyo: Otsuki-shoten.

――― (2001). "Competition and Production Prices," *Cambridge Journal of Economics*, vol. 25, pp.495–501.

Okishio, N. (ed.) (1992). *Business Cycles: Theories and Numerical Simulation*, Peter Lang.

Palley, T.I. (1998). "Macroeconomics with Conflict and Income Distribution," *Review of Political Economy*, vol. 10 (3), pp.329–342.

Sato, Y. (1985). "Marx-Goodwin Growth Cycles in a Two Sector Economy," *Zeitschrift fur Nationalokonomie*, Vol. 45, No. 1, pp. 21–34.

――― (2004). "Okisho's Theory of Accumulation in the Tradition of Heterodox Economics," *Discussion Paper #04E003*, Institute of Comparative Economic Studies, Hosei University.

――― (2012). "Okisho Theory Revisited in the Light of 'Axiomatic Externality'," *Journal of International Economics Studies*, Institute of Comparative Economic Studies, Hosei University.

Setterfield, M. and J. Cornwall (2002). "A Neo-Kaldorian Perspective on the Rise and Decline of the Golden Age," in Setterfield (ed.) *The Economics of Demand-led Growth: Challenging the Supply-side Vision of the Long Run*, Cheltenham: Edward Elgar, pp.67–86.

Skott, P. (1989) *Conflict and Effective Demand in Economic Growth*, Cambridge: Cambridge University Press.

Solow, R.M. (1956). "A Contribution to the Theory of Economic Growth," *Quarterly Journal of Economics*, vol. 70 Feb., pp.65–94.

Tsuru, S. (1984). "A Survey of Economic Research in Japan: 1960–1983". *The Economic Review*, Hitotsubashi University, Tokyo, Japan.

7 Régulation approach to Japanese and Asian capitalisms

Understanding varieties of capitalism and structural dynamics

Hiroyasu Uemura, Toshio Yamada and Yuji Harada

Introduction

The Japanese *régulation* theory has developed to analyze Japanese capitalism for a quarter of a century, recently extending this study to Asian capitalisms. In particular, *Japanese Capitalism in Crisis: A Regulationist Interpretation* (Boyer and Yamada 2000) and *Diversity and Transformations of Asian Capitalisms* (Boyer, Uemura and Isogai 2012) were published as a result of international collaborative studies on the topic. Following the *régulation* theory originating in Europe, the Japanese *régulation* theory has developed since the mid-1980s, with specific characteristics elaborated through the analysis of historical realities in East Asia.

In this chapter, we investigate the specific characteristics of the Japanese version of the *régulation* theory and its theoretical and empirical academic contribution to political economy and other social sciences. In particular, the Japanese *régulation* theory is an ambitious research project that analyzes the development of Japanese capitalism and the diversity and transformations of capitalisms, including both Western and Asian capitalisms.

Before the *régulation* theory was introduced to Japanese political economy in the early 1980s, Japanese scholars had developed their own theories of "contemporary capitalism" and "civil society". Moreover, post-Keynesian theories were introduced and applied to the analysis of market structures and economic growth of postwar Japanese capitalism. These studies laid the underlying foundations for the introduction of the *régulation* theory and the Social Structures of Accumulation (SSA) theory to Japanese political economy. The Japanese *régulation* theory developed to analyze the "companyist" mode of *régulation* and the transformations of the growth regime after the 1980s. In particular, the export-led growth in the 1980s and the structural crisis in the 1990s were analyzed, based on the study of institutional arrangements and growth regimes of the Japanese economy. Furthermore, the diversity and transformations of Asian capitalisms were analyzed from the perspectives of the *régulation* theory. In this chapter, we thoroughly consider the specific characteristics of the Japanese version of the *régulation* theory: the original understanding of the varieties of capitalism and the different patterns of the "civil society" formation between the West and the East; a structural analysis of hierarchical industrial sectors and firms in non-Western economies; the contribution of the analysis of Asian capitalisms to the "varieties of capitalism" approach and the *régulation* theory.

"Contemporary capitalism"/"civil society" in Japan and the introduction of *régulation* theory

Analysis of contemporary capitalism

Japanese capitalism started exhibiting high economic growth in the mid-1950s. Many political economists recognized the miracle of the Golden Age of postwar capitalism and asked whether capitalism fundamentally changed. Above all, in the late 1950s, Shigeto Tsuru, who studied with Joseph Schumpeter at Harvard University in the 1930s, asked, "Has capitalism changed?" He pointed out the characteristics of contemporary economic institutions such as large-scale innovation, the full employment policy and the increasing importance of oligopolistic firms and trade unions (Tsuru 1959).[1] After his discussion with prominent political economists in the world, he concluded that the "nature" of capitalism has not changed, even showing new institutional characteristics and spectacular economic growth. Therefore, he concluded that capitalism would experience another recession and crisis and asked how we could reform capitalism fundamentally.

In political economy, many Japanese Marxian economists started using the term "state monopoly capitalism" (SMC) as a paradigmatic concept for the analysis of contemporary capitalism. In the original SMC concept, two theoretical compositions are implied: first, that SMC is a product of a "general crisis" of capitalism; second, in an SMC, economic stagnation lasts without a recovery period. However, these theoretical suppositions cannot explain the fact that the Japanese economy realized high economic growth in the 1960s.

In this situation, a new group of political economists began to explain the high economic growth in Japan and in other advanced countries, pointing out that structural change had altered the nature of capitalism in the postwar period. For example, Takuichi Ikumi and other scholars intended to explain SMC not in terms of the general crisis of capitalism but in terms of the "socialization of productive relations", following suggestions by K. Zieschang (1957). In this theory, "the socialization of productive forces" develops in contemporary capitalism, and the production relations must necessarily become socialized. Socialization is reflected by joint-stock companies and monopoly corporations, and SMC is a new phase of capitalist development (Ikumi 1958).

This view is called "the socialization theory of SMC". However, the weakness of this is that its theoretical framework is simply historical materialism, according to which productive relations must develop and socialize themselves, in response to the development of productive forces. Here, the new institutional arrangements of postwar capitalism were not sufficiently analyzed, although postwar capitalism was characterized as a new stage. In this situation, in order to overcome the weakness of the socialization theory, Tsutomu Ouchi developed his own SMC theory based on the crisis theory and the three-stage framework in the Uno theory, emphasizing the important role of the managed currency system for coordinating real wages in business cycles in postwar advanced capitalism (Ouchi 1970).[2] However, Ouchi did not accept the idea that postwar capitalism was a new stage.

At the beginning of the 1970s, many Japanese political economists attempted to theorize contemporary capitalism. Above all, Kazuji Nagasu proposed his hypothesis that postwar capitalism is a new stage of capitalism. He indicated new institutional changes in postwar capitalism, such as innovation and automation leading to the socialization of production, an increased working class and a new middle class; large corporations and an industrial-bureaucratic-military complex; the welfare state; and the managed currency system (Nagasu 1970). Following the new stage hypothesis, Yoshinori Tamagaki finally rejected the concept of SMC itself, as it still implied the exclusive dependence of the state on monopoly capital, and he emphasized the relative autonomy of the democratic state in contemporary capitalism (Tamagaki 1976). In this situation, a systematic theory of contemporary capitalism was needed.

Theory of "civil society" in Japan

The postwar Japanese capitalism had intrinsic socioeconomic dimensions, that is the immaturity of "civil society". In particular, Yoshihiko Uchida's "civil society theory" was influential in Japanese academic society. After the early postwar period, Uchida continuously considered the specificity of economic development in Japan, learning from Hisao Otsuka's historiography. In this context, "civil society" implied an abstract and trans-historical meaning as "a system of equivalent exchange and productive forces" and "a society with freedom and human rights" in democracy. Based on the concept of "civil society", he pointed out the intrinsic problems in Japanese capitalism and the high economic growth in the postwar period (Uchida 1967; 1981). Uchida argued that Japan's economic development was achieved not by the creation of liberated and equal individuals engaged in fair transactions and social policies, but with the coexistence of feudal and pre-modern social elements in the economy and society. Uchida emphasized the distinction between "capitalism" and "civil society" and characterized Japan as "capitalism without civil society".

Moreover, Uchida pointed out the weakness of the civil elements such as human rights and democracy in comparison with the stronger power of capital in Japan. Furthermore, his conception bears a critical perspective on Japan as an "economic power" in the 1970s. Uchida's view became crystallized into a proposition of the "articulation of the pre-modern and super-modern" in Japan, implying "something pre-modern that underlies the Japanese economy and society does not work in the direction to prevent Japan from developing, but to realize excessively high growth or to create the super-modern without the modern" (Uchida 1981, p.11). It is obvious that economic development must not be reduced to mere high economic growth. High economic growth may resolve unemployment and material poverty, but growth was realized without strengthening human rights and civil society in Japan. By emphasizing the concept of "civil society", Uchida proposed an analytical viewpoint for Japan and other non-Western societies in which capitalism has developed in articulation with non-civil society institutions. In this regard, civil society theory originally contended the understanding of the institutional and social varieties of capitalism.

Following Uchida's understanding of "civil society" as universal in human history, Kiyoaki Hirata sensationally argued that socialism must be a society in which full-fledged civil society is realized and "individual property" is re-established, based on the study of *Grundrisse* and the French edition of *Das Kapital* (Hirata 1969). In Hirata's framework, "individual property" means human individuality developing in tandem with community relationships as well as the reestablishment of the identity of labor and property. At that time, his proposition, which asked about the relationship between socialism and civil society, implied a strong critical message against state ownership and the oppressive regime in the USSR. Following Hirata's proposal, social democratic ideas developed widely with the notion of "civil society" and "citizenship" in Japanese society and politics.

Furthermore, as a result of the study of "civil society" in Marx's social thought, Seiji Mochizuki's *The Study of Marx's Theory of History* (Mochizuki 1973) proposed a new understanding of the division of labor, having read *Die Deutsche Ideologie* and *Grundrisse*. In Marx's theory of history, there are two types of universal social relations: "gesellschaftlich" and "gemeinschaftlich". These also correspond to "the social division of labor" and "the in-firm division of labor", respectively, and both promote long-term productivity growth in the economy. Mochizuki's theory can be assessed as a pioneering understanding of the evolutionary dynamics of "market transaction and organization" in economic history, which was fully analyzed by New Institutionalism from a different perspective in the 1970s and 1980s.[3] In the context of the "civil society" theory, he also emphasized that the expansion of "gesellschaftlich" (namely, impersonal and public) relations and "fair" transactions comprise the material basis of civil society formation. Extending Mochizuki's theory of the division of labor, Kiriro Morita explained the development of the capitalist world system from the viewpoint of the international division of labor and interdependence (Morita 1970). From this perspective, he analyzed the internationalization of production which was promoted by multinational corporations in contemporary capitalism. His study predicted the rapid development of international production linkages in East Asia.

The theory of "civil society" is a universal contribution to international academic society. Especially, this social thought focuses on civil society formation in varieties of capitalism, and emphasizes the importance of the social division of labor and fair transactions in the commodity and labor markets toward the promotion of civil society. This understanding of civil society was integrated with the theory of contemporary capitalism to consider the historical dynamics of "capitalism with civil society" and "capitalism without civil society", proposing a much wider perspective that includes the "stages" and "types" of capitalism in world history (Ikumi 1979). In this regard, "stage" and "type" have become key concepts for studying varieties of capitalism in the Japanese political economy (Yamada 2008; 2015).

Development of post-Keynesian and the analytical political economy in Japan

Macroeconomic analysis in Japan was developed by introducing Keynesian theories and applying them to the empirical analysis of the postwar Japanese economy. In particular, John Maynard Keynes's *The General Theory* was translated into Japanese in the prewar period, but the thorough theoretical consideration was conducted by Yoshikazu Miyazaki and Mitsuharu Ito in the late 1950s (Miyazaki and Ito 1961). They interpreted *The General Theory* as a theory of contemporary capitalist society that consists of three classes: managers, workers and rentiers, and they understood its essence as a theoretical analysis of interactions between financial stocks and income flows in the monetary economy.

Miyazaki and Ito also introduced early post-Keynesian theorists such as M. Kalecki, J. Robinson, J. Steindl, R. Harrod and N. Kaldor into Japanese economic studies (Miyazaki 1967). Furthermore, Miyazaki analyzed the dynamic process of postwar high economic growth in Japan from an "institutionalist" Keynesian point of view, mainly focusing on such specific institutions as indirect financing to Japanese company groups through the main bank system and fierce competition among them that led to vigorous investment in the growth process (Miyazaki 1966). Furthermore, the Harrod growth theory was often applied to explain investment-led growth in the high growth period.

A structural analysis of the Japanese economy also developed in the analytical political economy on the basis of the study of Marx and early post-Keynesians. In the high growth period in the 1960s, a specific inflationary process proceeded in the Japanese economy, that is stable wholesale prices and rising consumer prices. In this situation, Yoshihiro Takasuka's "theory of productivity differential inflation" was a remarkable contribution to the structural analysis of the Japanese economy. Based on theoretical traditions of Marx, Kalecki and Sylos-Labini, Takasuka explained the structural dynamics of prices in dualistic industrial sectors in contemporary monopoly capitalism (Takasuka 1965). Especially, in the Japanese economy which consisted of high-productivity-growth sectors (core manufacturing sectors) as well as low-productivity-growth sectors (small and medium-sized firm sectors), inflexible oligopolistic prices in the high-productivity-growth sectors and the wage spillover mechanism over the whole economy pushed up prices in the low-productivity-growth sectors. This theoretical framework of structural dynamics of the price system with productivity growth differentials was an original contribution that was independent of the studies of price dynamics by Balassa, Samuelson and, later, Pasinetti.

Under post-Keynesian tradition in Japan, two remarkable scholars developed theoretical foundations in the 1970s and 1980s. Hirofumi Uzawa, who started his study with the two-sector neoclassical growth model at Chicago University, developed Keynesian macrodynamics, considering inventory changes, in the 1970s (Uzawa 1986). Uzawa also developed the theory of "social common capital" in civil society (Uzawa 2005). Tsuneo Ishikawa formalized different growth patterns of capitalism, extending Stephen Marglin's theoretical framework of growth and income distribution (Ishikawa 1976; 1999). He also developed the efficiency wage model with Herbert Gintis (Gintis and Ishikawa 1987) and analyzed the dual structures of wage determination in the Japanese labor market, pointing out a lack of public qualification systems and worker's autonomy in Japan (Ishikawa 1999).

Post-Keynesians developed theoretical and empirical studies as "institutionalist" Keynesians. Not only did they developed theoretical studies of Keynesian economics, but they also conducted empirical studies closely related to the specific institutional characteristics of the Japanese economy, such as the main bank system, company groups, dualistic economic structures and the high rate of capital accumulation.

Introduction of the régulation *theory and the SSA theory*

Active discussions occurred on postwar capitalism and "civil society" formation, and the post-Keynesian theories were introduced very actively in the 1950s and 1960s. However, the systematic theory of contemporary capitalism was not fully established in the Japanese political economy even in the 1970s.[4] In this situation, the *régulation* theory and the Social Structures of Accumulation (SSA) theory were introduced as theories of contemporary capitalism into Japan in the 1980s. Both theories developed institutional and macroeconomic analyses of postwar capitalism from Kaleckian and post-Keynesian perspectives.

The *régulation* theory was introduced by Toshio Yamada and other Japanese political economists.[5] Furthermore, Michel Aglietta's *Régulation et crises du capitalisme* (Aglietta 1976) and Robert Boyer's *La théorie de la régulation* (Boyer 1986) were translated into Japanese. The analysis of "the intensive regime of accumulation" with high productivity growth and "Fordism" as a new stage of capitalist development attracted many Japanese political economists. Accordingly, Fordism started to be used as a concept for characterizing the postwar capitalism instead of SMC. The framework of *régulation* theory which consists of the mode of *régulation* and the growth regime (or the regime of accumulation) was a promising basis for integrating institutional analysis and macroeconomic analysis (Yamada 1991; 2005).

The SSA theory was also introduced as empirical research by American radical economists into Japan. *Beyond the Waste Land* (Bowles, Gordon and Weisskopf 1983) was translated into Japanese by Tsuyoshi Tsuru and Akinori Isogai. Later, the theory of reserve army effect was applied to the Japanese economy (Tsuru 1992).

Corresponding to the international collaboration in the World Institute for Development Economic Research (WIDER), Japanese political economists conducted a integrative analysis of the *régulation* theory and the SSA theory, and *The Golden Age of Capitalism* (Marglin and Schor 1990) was also translated into Japanese. The *régulation* and SSA theories provided the best catalyst for producing an integrated theory of contemporary capitalism in Japan. In the 1990s, textbooks were published, based on the *régulation* theory, the SSA theory and the post-Keynesian theories, such as Yamada's *The Régulation Approach* (1991), Uemura, Isogai and Ebizuka's *The Institutional Analysis of Socio-economic Systems: Beyond Marx and Keynes* (1998); Uni, Sakaguchi, Tohyama and Nabeshima's *Introduction to Political Economy: Understanding Capitalism* (2004); and Isogai's *Frontiers of the Institutional Economics: Theory, Application and Policies* (2004). Furthermore, Samuel Bowles's textbook, *Microeconomics: Behavior, Institutions, and Evolution* (2004) was translated into Japanese.

Based on these studies, theoretical foundations were constructed as the Japanese version of *régulation* theory. First, socioeconomic varieties of capitalism are recognized from the viewpoint of the "type" and "stage" of capitalism. Second, internal complex structures in each variety of capitalism are analyzed in multisectoral frameworks with various institutional forms. In this context, social rules and institutions in civil society are particularly considered in relation to fair transactions and stable employment in the wage-labor nexus. Third, an institutional analysis of socioeconomic systems, especially firm organization and the labor market, is integrated with the macroeconomic analysis of the "growth regime" (Boyer), focused on growth and distribution (Kalecki), endogenous productivity growth and cumulative causation (Kaldor) and structural economic dynamics (Pasinetti). In the Japanese *régulation* theory, a comparative institutional analysis was developed from the institutionalist Keynesian perspective.

Régulation approach to Japanese capitalism

Companyist régulation *and the hierarchical market-firm nexus*

The *régulation* theory and the SSA theory were applied to the analysis of the Japanese economy in the early 1990s. Considering the Japanese mode of *régulation*, the Japanese *régulation* theory proposed two hypotheses: "companyist *régulation*" and "Hierarchical Market-Firm Nexus". The conceptual frameworks of these hypotheses are depicted in Figure 7.1.

The theory of "companyist" *régulation* as a core institutional arrangement of Japanese capitalism was formalized by Toshio Yamada (1994; 1999; 2000). High economic growth in the 1960s and the export-led growth following the 1970s were coordinated through a specific compromise between managers and workers in large firms. Managers provided job security to workers, and workers devoted themselves to their company. This was reflected by the notion of "lifetime employment". Corresponding to this compromise in the wage-labor nexus, inter-firm relations and company–bank relations were institutionalized to secure

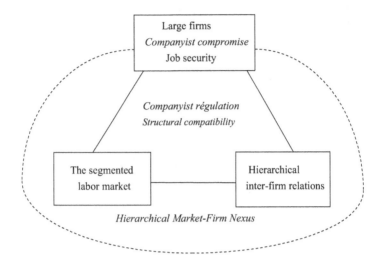

Figure 7.1 Companyist *régulation* and the hierarchical market-firm nexus

the development of firms and banks. In short, the "companyist" *régulation* consists of two main pillars: first, a compromise between the acceptance of unlimited duties and the provision of job security; second, a compromise between preferential treatment for the main banks and security for company managers (Yamada 2000). The large companies have a dominant power in Japanese society, and this often prevents workers' autonomy in the labor market and the full-fledged formation of "civil society". The Japanese economy realized high productivity growth with innovation and skill formation in large firms, coordinated by "companyist" *régulation*. Furthermore, Japanese and French scholars developed researches on the Toyota production system (Shimizu 1999), specific compromise and wage coordination mechanisms (Hirano 1996; Boyer and Juillard 2000) and the social welfare system (Hanada and Hirano 2000).

The "Hierarchical Market-Firm Nexus" (HMFN) was proposed by Akinori Isogai, Hiroyasu Uemura and Akira Ebizuka (Uemura and Ebizuka 1994; Isogai, Ebizuka and Uemura 2000). This theory explains the Japanese economy in terms of three components: (a) firm organization, (b) hierarchically segmented labor market and (c) hierarchical inter-firm relations, which have "structural compatibility". The HMFN theory emphasizes complementary institutional structures with specific coordinating mechanisms surrounding the "companyist" *régulation*, modifying the dualism hypothesis to account for the hierarchical institutional structures which coordinate productivity, wages and employment. In firm organization, there are incentive mechanisms to stimulate work effort with the promotion system, seniority wages and the retirement pay system. Furthermore, the segmented labor market produces the coordinating mechanisms of wages and employment. In particular, seniority wages in combination with their firm-size differentials and downward mobility in the unfair labor market make a mid-career job change expensive and weaken workers' autonomy. The difference between workers' current incomes and the weighted average of income prospects after being fired is called "job-loss costs" in the SSA theory (Bowles and Boyer 1990), which are influenced by the labor market conditions. In the Japanese case, however, the unemployment rate is very low, and the high costs of mid-career job change in terms of lifetime incomes are a functional equivalent to "job-loss costs". Therefore, this is called "institutionalized job-loss costs" as an application of the SSA theory to the Japanese labor market.

Export-led growth and productivity growth differentials among sectors

The Japanese growth regime was also analyzed from the viewpoint of the *régulation* theory. Uemura (2000) developed a long-term economic analysis of the Japanese economy, focusing on structural shifts in growth patterns after the 1960s using the Kaleckian framework of growth and distribution, and conducted an econometric analysis of growth patterns following Bowles and Boyer (1995). The patterns of capital accumulation in the Japanese postwar development can be seen in Figure 7.2 through the accumulation rate and the profit rate.

During the period of high economic growth in the 1960s, the Japanese economy exhibited vigorous "profit-investment-led growth." The high economic growth ended around 1970 because of rising wages and the saturation of domestic demand for consumer durable goods. In the first half of the 1970s, the Japanese economy experienced sharp falls in the profit and accumulation rates, but firm organizations and subcontracting networks were effectively restructured to adjust to new conditions after the first oil shock. Therefore, efficient production systems realized high competitiveness in manufacturing industries, making it possible to increase exports, and the large volume of exports

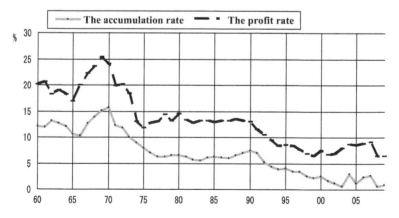

Figure 7.2 Accumulation rate and profit rate in Japan

promoted vigorous investment. The growth pattern turned into "wage-led" growth for domestic demand, but it was weighed down by expanding export demand with a higher profit share, consequently exhibiting "profit-led" growth. In this sense, the growth pattern can be called "export-investment-led growth".

Hiroyuki Uni analyzed the structural dynamics of export-led growth in the Japanese economy after the late 1970s on the theoretical basis of Pasinetti's theory of structural dynamics and Kaldor's theory of cumulative causation (Uni 1998; 2000). Uni pointed out that the Japanese economy showed uneven productivity growth differentials between the investment goods and consumption goods sectors as well as between the tradable and non-tradable goods sectors, using Pasinetti's "vertical integration" approach with the multisectoral framework (Psinetti 1981). In particular, Uni showed very specific structural characteristics of the Japanese economy that the manufacturing sector, especially the investment goods sector, realized very high productivity growth with Kaldorian "cumulative causation" between output growth and productivity growth. In this sense, Uni developed a multisectoral framework for a growth regime analysis originally formalized as an aggregate macroeconomic model by Boyer (1988).

Structural crisis and the transformation of the growth regime

Transformation of the Japanese growth regime in the 1990s

The Japanese economy experienced a "Bubble Boom" in the late 1980s and fell into the long-lasting recession in the 1990s. Uemura (2012) analyzed the transformations of the growth regime after the 1980s. In the first half of the 1980s, heavy investment under an undervalued yen led to the creation of capacity. Then, additional excess capacity was created as "over-accumulation" in the Bubble Boom in the second half of the 1980s. Therefore, the rapid depreciation and scrapping of capital stock after the collapse of the Bubble Boom can be characterized as the adjustment of excess capacity.

In the recession of the 1990s, investment was very stagnant (Uni 2002; 2007a), influenced by excess capital stock and nonperforming loans in the uncertain financial system and the rigid employment system (Boyer and Juillard 2000). After excess capital stock was scrapped and the nonperforming loan problem was resolved, the Japanese economy started to recover in 2002, taking on a new growth pattern. In this process, increasing financial liberalization caused corporate finance to become increasingly dependent on market mechanisms. The employment system also evolved after the mid-1990s. In order to cope with labor hoarding in large firms, non-regular workers increased dramatically, and nominal wage growth was severely depressed. Wage share, which was high owing to labor hoarding in the 1990s, fell very sharply in the early 2000s, and the profit rates of large firms recovered accordingly. Exports returned to play a crucial role in demand formation. Under these conditions, Uni analyzed "productivity-growth-differential deflation" after the 1990s in a multisectoral framework (Uni 2007a; 2007b). International competition with other Asian countries and the increasing foreign direct investment of Japanese multinationals imposed structural constraints on the Japanese economy.

The growth regime shifted before and after the 1990s recession. The transformation is summarized in Table 7.1. Marked features of the growth pattern are the greater heterogeneity of economic structures among various industries and different-sized firms along with the tighter economic integration of the Japanese economy with Asian economies. However, innovation in the

Table 7.1 Transformations of the Japanese growth regime

	The 1980s: Export-led growth regime with structural compatibility	⇒	*The 2000s: Export-led growth regime with heterogeneous structures and regional integration*
Growth rate	About 4%	⇒	About 2%
Export to	US>ASIA>EU	⇒	ASIA>US>EU, increase in intermediate goods trade
Profitability	Relatively high with profitability differentials	⇒	High in large firms in the automobile industry, but very low in small and medium-sized firms in general
Spillover of surplus	The spillover of trade surplus by wage coordination and redistribution through the tax system	⇒	Inter-industry wage differentials and weakening redistribution through the tax system
Industrial structures	Strong manufacturing sector with high productivity growth	⇒	The necessity of promoting innovation in the high-tech industry with the expansion of the service sector, resulting in de-industrialization
International production linkages	Increasing FDI in Asian countries and US	⇒	Stronger international production linkages with Asian countries and de-localisation of production
The mode of *régulation* and structural compatibility	The mode *of régulation* supporting the stable growth regime. Structural compatibility between firm organisation, subcontracting networks and the labor market supporting export-led growth	⇒	The mode of *régulation* has not been reestablished. Weakening structural compatibility and shrinking core socioeconomic structures faced with the international division of labor in East Asia

high-tech industry as a component of an emerging growth regime remains unpredictable, so the new growth pattern has not fully emerged. Furthermore, the "companyist" *régulation* and structural compatibility among institutions has progressively eroded.

Recent empirical study of the Japanese growth regime using a vector autoregression (VAR) analysis and an input-output analysis have been developed in the Japanese *régulation* approach. In particular, Hiroshi Nishi developed a Kaleckian macroeconomic analysis, both theoretically and empirically (Nishi 2011; 2012a; 2012b; 2014). He tried to integrate the *régulation* theory of the growth regime (Boyer 1988) and the post-Keynesian theories of finance and flow-stock dynamics, taking account of "institutional hierarchy" (Amable 2003). He theoretically analyzed the conditions for different growth patterns: profit-led/wage-led growth and debt-led/debt-burden growth (Nishi 2012a). Furthermore, in his sophisticated econometric study with structural VAR, he showed the growth pattern of the Japanese economy after the 1990s was a "profit-led" and "debt-burden" growth, implying that low profit share and accumulated debt led the Japanese economy to a long-lasting recession (Nishi 2012b).[6]

Concerning industrial structural dynamics in the Japanese economy, Shinji Tahara and Hiroyasu Uemura showed the specific structural dynamics of deindustrialization with productivity growth differentials by conducting an input-output analysis (Tahara and Uemura 2014; Uemura and Tahara 2014), following a seminal work by Rowthorn and Wells (1987) and a pioneering input-output analysis of the German economy by Franke and Kalmback (2005). In the Japanese economy, the export core manufacturing industry has realized high growth of output and labor productivity and has caused an uneven pattern of deindustrialization among industrial sectors. Furthermore, the manufacturing industry has externalized business activities and workers to the business-related service industry, which causes an increase in non-regular workers and rising inequality.

Increasing heterogeneity and malfunctioning of the Japanese mode of régulation

During the long-lasting recession in the 1990s, Japanese capitalism experienced institutional changes in its financial system and the wage-labor nexus (Uni, Yamada, Isogai and Uemura 2011). Akinori Isogai analyzed the transformation of the Japanese corporate system, which showed the diversity and hybridization of corporate governance (Isogai 2012). Especially, Isogai called a new hybrid type the "new J-type," which introduced the pay-for-performance system to maintain long-term employment. This transformation, which was promoted by the intentional adaptation by Japanese firms and their stakeholders, also caused a "gradual change" (Thelen) in the Hierarchical Market-Firm Nexus with malfunctioning of some institutional coordinating mechanisms (Isogai 2007; 2012). Sebastien Lechevalier also analyzed the transformation of Japanese capitalism, focusing on the heterogeneity of Japanese firms (Lechevalier 2012; 2014a; 2014b) and pointing out that the "re-segmentation" of the labor market was caused by the heterogeneity of firm organization. He also emphasized the strong impact of neoliberalist policies on the transformation of Japanese capitalism, pointing out the declining of classical forms of coordination.

Following the studies of Isogai and Lechevalier, Yasuro Hirano and Toshio Yamada (2014) analyzed the transformation of "companyist" *régulation* in the Japanese economy after the late 1990s. They thoroughly investigated the malfunctioning of the mode of *régulation*. As explained in the previous section, there were two main pillars of "companyist" *régulation* established in the 1960s: a manager-worker compromise on employment security and a company-bank compromise on management security (securing continuous firm growth). These compromises helped coordinate the export-led growth of the Japanese economy. In the 1990s, however, management security collapsed because of the liberalization of the financial market, and job security was weakened through a rapid increase in non-regular workers.

Concerning the collapse of management security, banking management deteriorated with the weakening of main-banks' function following the bubble collapse. Accordingly, large firms became less dependent on the main bank. Employment security, which was supported by the main bank, also collapsed. The collapse of management security promoted the weakening of employment security, and overall wage depression and increasing non-regular workers caused large inequality and instability in the Japanese employment system, despite the fact that some core workers maintained their job security. Furthermore, the multinationalization of Japanese firms is accelerating the malfunctioning of "companyist" *régulation*. All of these structural changes are creating more fragmentation and unfairness in Japanese society.

Diversity and transformations of Asian capitalisms

After the mid-1990s, the study of Japanese *régulation* theory was extended to East Asian capitalisms, considering their institutional diversity (Inoue 1996; 2000). Boyer, Uemura and Isogai (2012), as well as Uemura, Uni, Isogai and Yamada (2014), were published as a result of the international collaborative studies. In this situation, the "type" and "stage" of capitalism are redefined in the new context of empirical analysis.

Five types of Asian capitalism

In the last two decades, we have seen an increasing number of comparative institutional studies in advanced capitalisms. In particular, studies from the viewpoint of *régulation* theory and the varieties of capitalism (VoC) approach (Amable 2003; Boyer 2015; Hall and Soskice 2001; Tohyama 2010) have argued that an economic system is not entirely characterized by a particular institutional domain, but rather, it consists of a bundle of complementary institutions.

Despite the significant contributions to the understanding of the varieties of capitalism, such studies were likely to focus on advanced countries. However, Asian capitalism has come under the global spotlight (Storz, Amable, Casper and Lechevalier 2013), and some researchers have started to understand Asian economies within the literature on the institutional diversity of capitalisms (Harada and Tohyama 2012; Tohyama and Harada 2013, 2014; Walter and Zhang 2012; Witt and Redding 2013; Zhang and Whitley 2013).

Harada and Tohyama (2012) identified five types of Asian capitalism by applying multivariate analysis methods to institutional datasets covering five different institutional domains. Using a method of multivariate analysis, they identified the determining factors of the diversity of Asian capitalisms: "the degree of liberalization of different markets" and "the contrast between trade dependence and domestic social protection", which are shown in Figure 7.3.

Based on the configurations shown in Figure 4.3 and the results of their collaborative studies, five groups of Asian capitalisms with different institutional characteristics are explained as follows.[7]

Group 1: *Innovation-led capitalism.* Japan, South Korea (hereafter Korea), and Taiwan have common features of higher economic development and some barriers to entry in their product markets. These countries have succeeded in export-oriented industrialization, based on active innovation in the manufacturing industry. The mode of *régulation* of each country is as follows: In Japan, "companyist" *régulation*

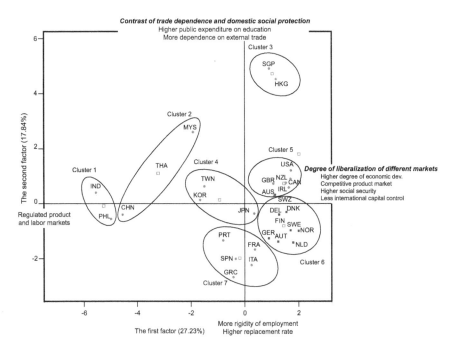

Figure 7.3 Diversity of Asian and advanced capitalisms

has weakened owing to the heterogeneity of firms, but a new mode of *régulation* has not been established. The hierarchical nexus of institutions is eroding because of the reorganization of subcontracting networks and increasing non-regular workers. Civil society formation has been pursued, but it is still insufficient in Japan. In Korea, the mode of *régulation* is characterized as regulatory relations by large companies and the state. Overseas activities have extended rapidly, and the state *régulation* is weakened, causing more dualistic structures in the domestic economy. In Taiwan, the mode of *régulation* is a mixture of market-based coordination and public coordination by the state. Wage growth lags behind productivity growth.

Group 2: *City capitalism*. The following characteristics are shared by Hong Kong and Singapore in this group, as shown in Figure 7.3: a significant *degree of liberalization of different markets*, higher *trade dependence*, lower *domestic social protection*, and high profitability of the banking system. In this group, the mode of *régulation* is based on the liberalization of the markets. Singapore has promoted the development of a market-oriented economy, inviting foreign multinationals. Hong Kong is characterized as "one country, two systems".

Group 3: *Continental mixed capitalism*. China has grown rapidly in the age of modularization and regional integration (Song 2012) and shares many institutional characteristics with Malaysia and Thailand, as shown in Figure 7.3. However, it is different from those two countries in terms of some variables (e.g. the share of private banks in the financial system). Concerning the mode of *régulation*, there exists "local state corporatism" at the provincial and city government level, which promotes capital accumulation (Boyer 2012; 2014), and this is coordinated by the state-level *régulation* (Yan 2011). Civil society and political democracy are still very immature in China.[8]

Group 4: *Trade-led industrializing capitalism*. Malaysia and Thailand have common characteristics similar to those of Group 1 in terms of the degree of liberalization of markets. However, labor market institutions in these countries are more liberalized than in Indonesia and the Philippines, especially in terms of flexibility in employment and working hours. Moreover, this group has relatively higher public expenditure for education, which may lead to the accumulation of human capital and more advanced industrialization. As for the *régulation* mode, in Malaysia, governance based on segregation and cohabitation of multiple races exists, so civil society formation is rather difficult. In Thailand, the informal sector in urban areas has a coordinating function for the labor market.

Group 5: *Insular semi-agrarian capitalism*. This group consists of Indonesia and the Philippines and is characterized by a lower *degree of liberalization of different markets*, as seen in Figure 7.3. Regarding its mode of *régulation*, structural adjustment has been promoted by the endogenous economic crisis and IMF policies. Growth has been recently promoted through an increase in domestic demand. In the Philippines, emigrant workers are a part of this growth strategy.

More detailed characteristics of institutional forms, the mode of *régulation* and the growth regime in each group of Asian capitalism are shown in Table 7.2.

Table 7.2 Modes of *régulation* and growth regimes in East Asia

	Innovation-led capitalism			City capitalism
	Japan	Korea	Taiwan	Singapore, Hong Kong
Forms of competition	The hierarchical nexus between large firms, subcontractors and the segmented labor market had structural compatibility, but this was weakened by the reorganization of subcontracting networks in the 1990s.	Large oligopolistic companies extend their business activities to East Asia, while many small and medium-sized firms exist in the Korean domestic economy.	The networks of competitive small and medium-sized firms develop in the electric machinery industry. The entrepreneurship is strong in the economy.	Inward FDI has been accepted very actively in the process of economic development. In Singapore, the market economy has been developed to promote industrial development.
Monetary / credit regime	The Japanese financial system was influenced by the nonperforming loan problem, the financial big bang, and the subprime crisis. The role of the main bank has been declining, and the stock market is not active.	The Korean financial market was influenced very much by the Asian financial crisis in the late 1990s. Financial liberalization was promoted, and banks became more profit-oriented.	The influence of the Asian financial crisis was not so strong. State-owned banks, private banks and small and medium-sized financial institutions coexist in the financial system.	The capital market has developed with liberalization as an international financial center. Multinational banks and companies realize high profitability.
Wage-labor nexus	The employment security and wage compromise has been weakened. The companyist compromise still exists in large companies, but the companyist regulation appears malfunctioning, faced with increasing non regular workers and the collapse of Shunto. Inequality is rising in Japanese society.	After the Asian financial crisis, the Korean labor market became more flexible and more dualistic. Non-regular workers increased and employment became more unstable. Inequality is rapidly rising in Korean society.	The labor market is flexible, and job hopping is very common. Large companies provide welfare to workers. Foreign workers have been accepted in the economy recently.	The internationalized and flexible labor market has developed. In Singapore, 70% of workers are Chinese. In Hong Kong, the international labor market has developed and the in-flow and out-flow of foreign workers is remarkable.

The state/economy nexus	The public expenditures are complementary to the large company system. However, faced with an aging society, public debt has increased rapidly to sustain even the weak welfare system.	The economic development has been coordinated by the state. The rate of public spending for education is high, while that for social welfare is relatively low.	In Singapore, the development of the market economy has been promoted. The spending for education is high, but that for welfare is low. After Hong Kong was handed over to the PR of China, there exists "one country, two systems".
Insertion into the international economy	Export-led growth has continued since the late 1970s. Foreign direct investment increased for North America in the 1980s and for Asia after the 1990s. Especially, the export of intermediate goods to East Asia increased after the late 1990s.	The flexible exchange rate system was introduced after the Asian financial crisis, and this led to make the Won much cheaper, setting better conditions for exporting companies.	Both entrepot-trade city states have high openness. Singapore has developed with processing trade for external demand. The trade dependence of both countries is very high.
The mode of régulation	Companyist régulation is weakening, faced by the heterogeneity of firms, but the new mode of régulation has not been established. The hierarchical nexus is eroding due to reorganized subcontracting networks and increasing non-regular workers. Civil society formation has been pursued, but it is still weak.	The mode of régulation is characterized as regulatory relations by large companies and the state. The overseas activities have extended very rapidly, and the state regulation is weakened, causing more dualistic structures in the domestic economy.	The mode of régulation is the mixture of the market-based coordination and the public coordination by the state. Low wage growth lags behind productivity growth.	In both Singapore and Hong Kong, the mode of régulation is open, based on the liberalization of the markets. Singapore has developed the market economy, inviting multinationals. Hong Kong is characterized as "one country, two systems".

(*Continued*)

Table 7.2 Continued

	Innovation-led capitalism		City capitalism	
	Japan	*Korea*	*Singapore, Hong Kong*	*Taiwan*
Growth regime	The profit-led and export-led growth regime was established. There are huge productivity growth differentials between the export goods sector and the others. De-industrialization has accelerated since the 1990s.	The economy showed the wage-consumption-led growth in the 1990s, which was transformed to the finance-led (profit-export-led) growth in the 2000s.	The growth regime is an open regime with high trade dependency and a high level of financial liberalization. The economy is prone to be influenced by demand fluctuation in the world market.	The export-oriented industrialization was successful, and the export-led growth is seen. The economy is influenced strongly by demand fluctuation in the world market.

	Mixed Capitalism	Trade-led Industrializing Capitalism	Insular Semi-agrarian Capitalism
	China	*Malaysia, Thailand*	*Indonesia, The Philippines*
Forms of competition	Each provincial government pursues fierce competition to get financial resources from the central government to make investment on infrastructures. There still exists the price control in the product market.	Manufacturing bases have been developed by multinational firms' FDI, and manufactured goods are exported to the world market. In Malaysia, there exist the plantations of natural rubber.	Multinationals control the production and transaction of products in plantations. There are regulations and the high costs of entry and exit in the product market.
Monetary /credit regime	The state-owned banks still exercise credit control effectively. The external openness of the financial market is still very low, so the Chiese financial market was not so influenced by the subprime crisis.	In Malaysia, private banks are still fragile. In Thailand, the bank-centered system has developed, but the finance system depends on foreign banks very much.	The financial system is bank-centered, but is vulnerable to the fluctuations of the international financial market. In Indonesia, the Islamic banking without interest has developed.

Wage-labor nexus	The labor market is determined by the family registration system (urban /rural). The labor market flexibility is different among regions. Trade union, the collactive bargaining, and sufficient unemployment benefit do not exist in China.	Malaysia has accepted foreign workers. In the Malaysian labor market, there are differentials between Malaya people and others. In Thailand, there exists the informal sector absorbing employment. The adjustment of working hours is flexible, and wages are depressed.	Regulations are relatively strong in the labor market, and it is rather difficult to fire workers. There exist excess labor forces in rural areas, which flow into urban areas. Low-wage female workers exist commonly.
The state/ economy nexus	With coordination based on "local state corporatism" consisting of the local government, state-owned firms and private firms, the local governments make public investment, promoting regional growth and getting more tax revenue.	Malaysia is a multi-racial state, so the problems of public finance and income distribution have become serious. In Thailand, the government keeps the balanced budget principle with badly organized taxation system.	In Indonesia, the dictatorship has lasted for long time, and democracy has not developed. In the Philippines, landowners have strong power, and there exists political instability.
Insertion into the international economy	The government controls the exchange rate and FDI and multinationals' activities. The export is promoted with the increase in the import of intermediate goods. Export mitigates macroeconomic imbalance in the domestic economy.	Assembly factories have developed, while accepting foreign multinationals since late 1980s. After the 1990s, multinationals imported intermediate products and assemble them to export final products to the world market. Both economies have the high dependence on foreign trade.	After the Asian financial crisis, neo-liberalist policies were introduced. International capital movement is regulated by taxation, and multinationals come to have dominant power.
The mode of *régulation*	There exists "local state corporatism" in provincial governments and city governments which promotes capital accumulation, and this process is coordinated by the state-level régulation. Civil society is still immature.	In Malaysia, there is a governance based on segregation and cohabitation of multiple races, and civil society formation is difficult. In Thailand, the informal sector in urban areas has a coordinating function for the labor market.	The structural adjustment has been promoted by the endogenous crisis of the economy and IMF policies. Growth has been promoted by the increase in domestic demand recently. In the Philippines, emmigrant workers are the part of the growth strategy.
Growth regime	With decreasing wage share and consumption share, the Chinese economy has shown export-led growth, which depends on export demand and vigorous investment. Growth differentials among regions are a serious problem.	Thiland realized the non-state-led pattern of economic development. Both Malaysia and Thailand has accepted foreign multinationals, and have realized export-led growth, being involved in the East Asian production networks.	The growth regime depends on the export of primary products. Economic growth is supported by income transfer from emigrant workers. There exist growth differentials among islands.

We can also point out the specificity of Asian capitalisms from the viewpoint of civil society. As pointed out by Witt and Redding (2014), "trust", which can be defined as a proxy of social capital, has two types: "interpersonal trust" and "institutionalized trust". Many studies have found that the former develops in Asian societies, in particular, inside the family and among acquaintances. By contrast, the latter varies remarkably among Asian societies. According to Witt and Redding (2014), the extent of "the rule of law" in the Worldwide Governance Indicators is a proxy measure of "institutionalized trust" as an impersonal and public relation. In the mid-2000s, Indonesia had the lowest, level of "institutionalized trust", and Singapore had the highest among Asian countries. Advanced Western countries are situated in higher places than most Asian countries. The order of capitalisms concerning this indicator is almost the same as that of "the degree of liberalization of different markets" in Harada and Tohyama (2012). It implies that the liberalization of markets with proper civil institutions is supposed to be correlated with the development of the impersonal "institutionalized trust", which may provide one of the foundations of civil society in which "fair" transactions are pursued in the market. Furthermore, a more codified "institutionalized trust" plays a crucial role in promoting workers' autonomy in the labor market. In this sense, Asian societies may be situated at an immature stage of civil society and social democracy.

The impersonal "institutionalized trust" and "the role of the state" may have some positive functions in Asian capitalisms.[9] Asian counties have achieved economic development even with an immature civil society. The reason for this attainment can be explained by the fact that Asian economies have conducted "effective" rather than "fair" socioeconomic transactions that promote the high performance of export-led growth (Nishi, Isogai and Uemura 2014). Even with the insufficient "institutionalized trust" and "fair" transactions in civil society, the combination of "interpersonal trust" and state involvement establishes different institutional configurations such as the companyist mode of *régulation* in Japan and the "local state corporatism" and "state *régulation*" in China. In this regards, an analysis of the diversity of institutional configurations in East Asia enables us to understand the complex dynamics of different "types" and "stages" of capitalism (Yamada 2008; 2015).

Evolving interdependence of Asian capitalisms and future research

Asian capitalisms have rapidly developed their international interdependence. As for the development of Asian economies, the "flying-geese" theory of economic development has often been referred to. In this theory, Japan is situated at the lead of the international division of labor in the East Asian region, and other countries follow Japan through industrial upgrading. However, economic development has been showing more complex patterns in East Asia. Standardization and modularization in tandem with FDI mobility have created large production networks and intermediate goods trade.

These have dispersed the specialization of each national economy. Multinationals are organizing this process, and governments do this via industrial and trade policies.

In the 21st century, there are two factors that modify the original "flying-geese" pattern (Boyer, Uemura and Isogai 2012). First, China has rapidly developed to become the second-largest economic power in the world, and Japan became just one of the leading countries in the international division of labor in East Asia. Second, China's industrial development shows "leapfrogging", caused by the development of international production linkages driven by multinational firms. In this situation, more than half of the trade has become intermediate goods trade in the East Asian region. Off-shoring in global value chains has shown more complex patterns of structural dynamics that depend on not only international wage differentials but also on the scale of markets, industrial infrastructures and social capital.

Structural dynamics of the international division of labor has also influenced the coordination of exchange rates among the East Asian economies. Given that international production networks have become wider and deeper, international trade has become strongly determined and steered by intermediate goods transactions in East Asia. In this situation, exchange-rate stability is required for multinational firms to develop their businesses. According to Hiroyuki Uni's structural analysis of labor productivity and unit labor costs in each Asian economy (Uni 2012; 2014), there are two large obstacles to this development. First, there exist large productivity growth differentials among sectors in the East Asian economies. Second, there is a lack of international political consensus for establishing "a collectively managed floating system", the most conceivable monetary system, among East Asian countries.

In this situation, the Japanese *régulation* theory proposes some important subjects for future research. First, economic analysis should be developed at three levels: (a) a comparative institutional analysis of socio-economic systems in each country, (b) an analysis of economic dynamics and industrial structural change in the growth regime of a national economy, and (c) the analysis of international division of labor and interdependence among the economies in the East Asian region. Second, economic analysis and political analysis should be effectively integrated to study the political-economic conflict and compromise among social groups in civil society and the political economy of international governance among Asian countries (Boyer 2015).

Conclusion: toward a comparative analysis of capitalisms from the institutionalist Keynesian perspective

The Japanese *régulation* theory is a macrodynamic theory of comparative institutional and historical analysis from an institutionalist Keynesian perspective. After considering the long history of the Japanese political economy and the Japanese version of *régulation* theory, we can summarize its specific characteristics as the political economy of civil-social democracy as follows.

First, the original understanding of the diversity of capitalisms and the different patterns of "civil society" formation existed in the Japanese political economy as early as the 1950s and 1960s. Japanese political economists studied varieties of capitalism and, in particular, compared Japanese capitalism and Western ones. This tradition has developed fruitfully in the Japanese *régulation* theory in which fair transactions and social policies in the wage-labor nexus are analyzed for the varieties of Asian capitalism.

Second, the Japanese *régulation* theory has been developed through an analysis of complex structural dynamics consisting of heterogeneous industrial sectors and firms in the Japanese economy. Starting from the study of dual economic structures and the co-existence of modern and pre-modern sectors in the high growth period, the study has been developed on the hierarchical nexus of institution, productivity growth differentials among firms and industrial sectors, and uneven development between the export goods manufacturing sector and other sectors in tandem with de-industrialization.

Third, the Japanese *régulation* theory has studied various post-Keynesian theories, such as Kaleckian, Kaldorian, Minskian and Pasinetti's theories, to analyze the long-term growth dynamics of Japanese capitalism and postwar contemporary capitalism. Therefore, the introduction of the *régulation* theory and the SSA theory in the 1980s was the best catalyst for developing the systematic theoretical framework of institutionalist macroeconomics that analyzes the varieties of the "growth regime" based on the study of characteristics of national institutional arrangements in East Asia.

Finally, the Japanese *régulation* theory has been making a remarkable contribution to the varieties of capitalism approach and the *régulation* theory. It analyzes the varieties of Asian capitalism with the complex dynamics of different "types" of socio-economic systems and civil society at different "stages" of development, and explains the rapid growth and evolving interdependence of the Asian economies in the world economic system in the 21st century.

Notes

1 Shigeto Tsuru was a pioneering political economist who studied institutional economics and environmental economics, developing collaborative relations with Paul Sweezy, Paul Samuelson and John K. Galbraith in the postwar period (Tsuru 1993). He also influenced political economists and post-Keynesians in Japan.

2 The Uno theory was a Marxian economic theory that was formalized by Kozo Uno in Japan. This theory has a unique methodology that systematically distinguishes pure theory, stage theory and current state analysis. The Uno theory elaborated the different "stages" of capitalism: "mercantile capitalism", "liberal capitalism" and "imperialist capitalism". However, the Uno theory does not identify postwar capitalism as a new stage.

3 S. Mochizuki explains the evolutionary dynamics of "market transaction and organization" from the viewpoint of the development of the division of labor and productive forces, while New Institutionalism analyzes "market transaction and organization" on the basis of the "transaction costs" theory.

4 As a remarkable exception, we should refer to Shigenobu Kishimoto, who provided a pioneering theory of contemporary capitalism with an analysis of the division of labor in social production, "regulation, coordination and control", the market system, firm organization/ownership structures and capital accumulation. He tried to integrate the "civil society" theory, the ownership theory, and the Sraffian and Kaleckian theories of value, distribution and accumulation (Kishimoto 1975). Above all, Kishimoto's concept of "regulation, coordination and control" is very similar to *régulation* in the French *régulation* theory.

5 Those researchers included Fumitaka Wakamori, Hideharu Saito, Yasuro Hirano, Yasuo Inoue, Masanori Hanada, Akira Ebizuka and Koichi Shimizu who studied French political economy (see e.g. Hanada and Hirano 2000; Hirano 1996; Inoue 1996, 2000).

6 In the similar framework of the *régulation* theory, Okuma (2015) analyzes the effect of environmental policies on economic growth. In particular, he conducted an econometric analysis of the effect of environmental policies on the profit rate and economic growth through channels of "the economy-environment nexus" with different time horizons.

7 In Figure 7.3, we can find seven clusters. Clusters 1 to 4 consist of Asian economies, although they are slightly different from those shown in the figure. Clusters 5 to 7 are referred to as "Advanced liberal capitalism," "Welfare capitalism" and "European mixed capitalism", respectively, by Harada and Tohyama (2012). The groups with detailed description at the bottom are identified by considering the results of plural analyses: that of Asian and advanced economies (Figure 7.3), that of solely Asian economies, the socioeconomic context of each economy and the preceding studies.

8 Aglietta and Bai (2013) analyze the Chinese socioeconomic system from the viewpoint of "civil society." They point out that "sustainable growth involves more participation of civil society in provision of public goods and in social choices" (p.179), but that this condition has not existed in China.

9 As Walter and Zhang (2012), Witt and Redding (2013), and Zhang and Whitley (2013) have suggested, state involvement should be another important factor that promotes development in Asian countries. In order to measure the degree of the role of the state, Witt and Redding (2014) use the following indicators: "voice and accountability", "government effectiveness" and "regulatory quality". Relative positions of Asian economies concerning any of the indicators are similar to those with respect to "the rule of law".

References

Aglietta, M. (1976) *Régulation et crises du capitalisme*, Paris: CalmannLévy.

Aglietta, M. and G. Bai (2013) *China's Development: Capitalism and Empire*, Oxon: Routledge.

Amable, B. (2003) *The Diversity of Modern Capitalism,* Oxford: Oxford University Press.

Bowles, S. (2004) *Microeconomics: Behavior, Institutions, and Evolution*, Princeton: Princeton University Press.

Bowles, S. and Boyer, R. (1990) 'A Wage-led Employment Regimes: Income Distribution, Labour Discipline, and Aggregate Demand in Welfare Capitalism,' in S. Marglin and J. Schor (eds.) (1990).

Bowles, S. and R. Boyer (1995) 'Wages, Aggregate Demand, and Employment in an Open Economy: An Empirical Investigation,' in G. Epstein and H. Gintis (eds.) (1995) *Macroeconomic Policy after the Conservative Era*, Cambridge: Cambridge University Press, pp.143–171.

146   *Hiroyasu Uemura et al.*

Bowles, S., D. Gordon and T. Weisskopf (1983) *Beyond the Waste Land: Democratic Alternative to Economic Decline*, Anchor Press/Doubleday.

Boyer, R. (1986) *La théorie de la régulation: Une analyse critique*, Paris: La Découverte, 2ᵉ éd.

Boyer, R. (1988) 'Formalising Growth Regimes,' in G. Dosi, C. Freeman, G. Silverberg, and L. Soete (eds.) *Technical Change and Economics Theory*, London: Pinter Publisher, pp.608–630.

Boyer, R. (2012) 'The Chinese Growth Regime and the World Economy', in R. Boyer, H. Uemura and A. Isogai (eds.) (2012), pp.184–205.

Boyer, R. (2014) 'Mode of Development in Chinese Economy and Transformation of International System: Focusing on the Post-Crisis in 2008', in H. Uemura, A. Isogai Uni, and T. Yamada (eds.) (2014).

Boyer, R. (2015) *Économie politique des capitalismes: théorie de la régulation et des crises*, Paris: La Découverte.

Boyer, R. and M. Juillard (2000) 'The Wage Labour Nexus Challenged: More the Consequence than the Cause of the Crisis', in R. Boyer and T. Yamada (eds.) (2000), pp.119–137.

Boyer, R., H. Uemura and A. Isogai (eds.) (2012) *Diversity and Transformations of Asian Capitalisms*, Oxon: Routledge.

Boyer, R. and T. Yamada (eds.) (2000) *Japanese Capitalism in Crisis: A Regulationist Interpretation*, London: Routledge.

Franke, R. and P. Kalmbach (2005) 'Structural Change in the Manufacturing Sector and Its Inputs on Business-Related Services: An Input-Output Study for Germany,' *Structural Change and Economic Dynamics*, Vol.16, pp.467–488.

Gintis, H. and T. Ishikawa (1987) 'Wages, Work Discipline, and Unemployment,' *Journal of Japanese and International Economies*, Vol.1, pp.195–228.

Hall, P. and D. Soskice (eds.) (2001) *Varieties of Capitalism: The Institutional Foundations of Comparative Advantage*, Oxford: Oxford University Press.

Hanada, M. and Y. Hirano (2000) '"Industrial Welfare" and "Company-ist" *Régulation*: An Eroding Complementarity', in R. Boyer and T. Yamada (eds.) (2000), pp.87–103.

Harada, Y. and H. Tohyama (2012) 'Asian Capitalisms: Institutional Configurations and Firm Heterogeneity', in R. Boyer, H. Uemura and A. Isogai (eds.) (2012), pp.243–263.

Hirano, Y. (1996) *Japanese Institutions and Economic Growth*, Tokyo: Fujiwara Shoten.

Hirano, Y. and T. Yamada (2014) 'Paralysis on Companyist Coordination and Reform in Social Security,' in H. Uemura, H. Uni, A. Isogai and Y. Yamada (eds.) (2014), pp.369–387.

Hirata, K. (1969) *Civil Society and Socialism*, Tokyo: Iwanami-shoten.

Ikumi, T. (1958) *State Monopoly Capitalism*, Tokyo: Otsuki-shoten.

Ikumi, T. (1979) 'The Historical Structures of Contemporary Capitalism,' in N. Imai and B. Tomiozuka (eds.) *The Contemporary Economy and the State*, Nihon-hyoronsha, pp. 1–62.

Inoue, Y. (1996) *Reading "the Great Transformation fin de siècle": A Challenge by the Régulation Theory*, Tokyo: Yuhikaku.

Inoue, Y. (2000) 'Beyond the East Asian Economic Crisis', in R. Boyer and T. Yamada (eds.)(2000).

Ishikawa, T. (1976) 'Class Conflict, Capital Accumulation and Distribution of Income,' *Harvard University Discussion Paper*, Vol.468.

Ishikawa, T. (1999) *The Economics of Distribution*, Tokyo: University of Tokyo Press.

Isogai, A. (2004) *Frontiers of the Institutional Economics: Theory, Applications and Policies*, Kyoto: Minerva Shobo.

Isogai, A. (2007) 'Towards an Extension of the Hypothesis of ' "Hierarchical Market-Firm Nexus" ', in T. Yamada, H. Uni and N. Nabeshima (eds.) (2007), pp.185–209.

Isogai, A. (2012) 'The Transformation of the Japanese Corporate System and the Hierarchical Nexus of Institutions', in R. Boyer, H. Uemura and A. Isogai (eds.) (2012), 31–55.

Isogai, A., A. Ebizuka and H. Uemura (2000) 'The Hierarchical Marke-Firm Nexus as the Japanese Mode of *Régulation*', in R. Boyer and T. Yamada (eds.) (2000), pp.32–53.

Kishimoto, S. (1975) *The Theory of the Capitalist Economic System*, Tokyo: Nihonhyoronsha.

Lechevalier, S. (2012) 'The Increasing Heterogeneity of Firms in Japanese Capitalism: Facts, Causes, Consequences and Implications', in R. Boyer, H. Uemura and A. Isogai (eds.)(2012), pp.56–71.

Lechevalier, S. (eds.) (2014a) *The Great Transformation of Japanese Capitalism*, Oxon: Routledge.

Lechevalier, S. (2014b) 'Institutional Change and Neoliberal Policies: From a Perspective of International Comparison', in H. Uemura, H. Uni, A. Isogai and Y. Yamada (eds.) (2014), pp.388–415.

Marglin, S. and J. Schor (eds.) (1990) *The Golden Age of Capitalism: Reinterpreting the Postwar Experience*, Oxford: Oxford University Press.

Miyazaki, Y. (1966) *The Economic Organizations of Post-war Japan*, Tokyo: Shinhyoron.

Miyazaki, Y. (1967) *The Historical Development of Modern Economics*, Tokyo: Yuhikaku.

Miyazaki, Y. and M. Ito (1961) *Kommentar: Keynes's The General Theory*, Tokyo: Nihonhoronsha.

Mochizuki, S. (1973) *The Study of Marx's Theory of History*, Tokyo: Iwanami-shoten.

Morita, K. (1970) 'The World System of Capitalism: The Basic Viewpoint,' in K. Nagasu (ed.) *Lecture on Marxism 8: Capitalism*, Tokyo: Nihonhyoronsha, pp.257–324.

Nagasu, K. (1970) 'Contemporary Capitalism and Marxian Economics,' in K. Nagasu (ed.) *Lecture on Marxism 8: Capitalism*, Tokyo: Nihonhyoronsha, pp.1–37.

Nishi, H. (2011) 'A VAR Analysis for the Growth Regime and Demand Formation Patterns of the Japanese Economy', *Revue de la Régulation,* Vol.10.

Nishi, H. (2012a) 'Structural VAR Analysis of Debt, Capital Accumulation, and Income Distribution in the Japanese Economy: A Post-Keynesian Perspective', *Journal of Post Keynesian Economics,* Vol.34, No.4, pp.685–712.

Nishi, H. (2012b) 'The Consequences of Internationalization of Trade and Financial Transactions on Growth: Combining an Institutional Hierarchy Hypothesis with a Keynes-Minsky Approach', in R. Boyer, H. Uemura and A. Isogai (eds.) (2012), pp.264–284.

Nishi, H. (2013) 'On the Short-run Relationship between the Income Distribution- and Debt-Growth Regimes', *International Review of Applied Economics,* Vol.27, No.6, pp.729–49.

Nishi, H. (2014) *Income Distribution, Finance, and Economic Growth: Theoretical and Empirical Analyses of Capitalist Economy*, Tokyo: Nihon Keizai Hyoronsha.

Nishi, H., A. Isogai and H. Uemura (2014) 'Institutional Hierarchy and Varieties of Macrodynamics in East Asian Capitalisms', in H. Uemura, H. Uni, A. Isogai and Y. Yamada (eds.) (2014), pp.98–134

Okuma, K. (2015) *Is Green Growth Possible?: Institutional and Evolutionary Analysis on Economic Growth and Environmental Policy*, Tokyo: Fujiwara-shoten.

Ouchi, T. (1970) *State Monopoly Capitalism*, Tokyo: University of Tokyo Press.

Pasinetti, L. (1981) *Structural Change and Economic Growth*, Cambridge: Cambridge University Press.

Rowthorn, R. and J. Wells (1987) *De-Industrialization and Foreign Trade*, Cambridge: Cambridge University Press.

Shimizu, K. (1999) *Le toyotisme*, Reprères/Editions, Paris: La Décourverte.

Song, L. (2012) 'Development mode and capacity building in the age of modularization and regional integration: Origins of structural adjustment of Chinese economy,' in R. Boyer, H. Uemura and A. Isogai (eds.), pp.131–142.

Storz, C., B. Amable, S. Casper and S. Lechevalier (2013) 'Bringing Asia into the Comparative Capitalism Perspective', *Socio-Economic Review*, Vol.11, No.2.

Tahara, S. and H. Uemura (2014) 'The Growth Regime and De-industrialization in the Japanese Economy,' in H. Uemura, H. Uni, A. Isogai and T. Yamada (2014).

Takasuka, Y. (1965) *Prelude to the Theory of Contemporary Price System*, Tokyo: Iwanami-shoten.

Tamagaki, T. (1976) 'Thoroughgoing Reflection on the Theory of State Monopoly Capitalism', *Contemporary Theories*, Vol.144. pp.59–72

Tohyama, H. (2010) *For Analyzing Varieties of Capitalism: An Interaction between Institutions and Economic Performance*, Kyoto: Nakanishiya.

Tohyama, H. (2014) 'Varieties of Asian Welfare Capitalism and the Influence of Globalization', *Journal of International and Comparative Social Policy*, Vol.31, No.1.

Tohyama, H. and Y. Harada (2013) 'Effect of Institutional Configuration on Innovation Activities in East Asian Firms: A Study of the institutional Diversity of Asian Economies', *International Journal of Asian Business and Information Management*, Vol.4/2, pp.16–34.

Tohyama, H. and Y. Harada (2014) 'The Diversity of Asian Capitalism: Institutional Configuration and Innovative Activities of Firms', in H. Uemura, H. Uni, A. Isogai and T. Yamada (eds.) (2014), pp.58–97.

Tsuru, S. (1959) *Reconsidering Contemporary Capitalism*, Tokyo: Iwanami-shoten.

Tsuru, S. (1993) *Institutional Economics Revisited*, Cambridge: Cambridge University Press.

Tsuru, T. (1992) 'The Social Structure of Accumulation Approach and the Regulation Approach: A US-Japan Comparison of the Reserve Army Effect,' in D. M. Kotz, T. McDonough and M. Reich (eds.) *Social Structures of Accumulation: The Political Economy of Growth and Crisis*, Cambridge: Cambridge University Press, pp.274–291.

Uchida, Y. (1967) *Japanese Capitalism Reflected into the Social Thoughts*, Tokyo: Iwanami-shoten.

Uchida, Y. (1981) *Sakuhin toshiteno Shakai-kagaku (A Social Science for Common People)*, Tokyo: Iwanami-shoten.

Uemura, H. (2000) 'Growth, Distribution and Structural Change in the Post-war Japanese Economy', in R. Boyer and T. Yamada (eds.) (2000), pp.138–161.

Uemura, H. (2012) 'Institutional Changes and the Transformations of the Growth Regime in the Japanese Economy: Facing the Impact of the World Economic

Crisis and Asian Integration', in R. Boyer, H. Uemura and A. Isogai (eds.) (2012), pp.107–121.

Uemura, H. and A. Ebizuka (1994) 'Incentives and Flexibility in the Hierarchical Market-Firm Nexus: A Prelude to the Analysis of Productivity Regimes in Japan', *Japon in extenso*, Vol.31.

Uemura, H., A. Isogai and A. Ebizuka (1998) *Institutional Analysis of Socio-economic Systems: Beyond Marx and Keynes*, New Edition in 2007, Nagoya: Nagoya University Press.

Uemura, H., H. Uni, A. Isogai and Y. Yamada (eds.) (2014) *Asian Capitalisms in Transition*, Tokyo: Fujiwara Shoten.

Uemura, H. and S. Tahara (2014) 'The Transformation of Growth Regime and De-industrialization in Japan', *Revue de la Régulation*, Vol.15.

Uni, H. (1995) 'On Export-led Growth of Japan', *The Bulletin of Japan Society of Political Economy*, Vol.32.

Uni, H. (1998) *Structural Change and Capital Accumulation*, Tokyo: Yuhikaku.

Uni, H. (2000) 'Disproportionate Productivity Growth and Accumulation Regimes', in R. Boyer and T. Yamada (eds.) (2000), pp.24–70.

Uni, H. (2002) 'Causes of the Slow Rate of Economic Growth of Japan: Comparative Analysis of Structural Change in Industry and Employment', *The Bulletin of Japan Society of Political Economy*, Vol.39.

Uni, H. (2007a) 'Growth Regimes in Japan and the United States in the 1990s', *Revue de la Régulation*, Vol.1.

Uni, H. (2007b) 'Export-biased Productivity Increase and Exchange Rate Regimes in East Asia and Europe', *The Kyoto Economic Review*, Vol.76, No.1.

Uni, H. (2011) 'Cumulative Causation and Structural Change: A Growth Model along Kaldor and Pasinetti Lines', *Political Economy Quarterly*, Vol.48, No.1.

Uni, H. (2012) 'Comparative Analysis of Conditions for Monetary Integration: Europe and Asia', in R. Boyer, H. Uemura and A. Isogai (eds.) (2012), pp.287–307.

Uni, H. (2014) 'A Possibility of Cooperative Adjustment in Exchange Rates in Asia: Reflecting the Imbalances of Current Account', in H. Uemura, H. Uni, A. Isogai and Y. Yamada (eds.) (2014), pp.135–162

Uni, H., A. Sakaguchi, H. Tohyama and N. Nabeshima (2004) *An Introduction to Political Economy: Understanding Capitalism*, 2nd edition in 2010, Kyoto: Nakanishiya.

Uni, H., T. Yamada, A. Isogai and H. Uemura (2011) *A Régulation Theory of Financial Crises*, Kyoto: Showado.

Uzawa, H. (1986) *The Theory of Economic Dynamics*, Tokyo: University of Tokyo Press.

Uzawa, H. (2005) *Economic Analysis of Social Common Capital*, Cambridge: Cambridge University Press.

Walter, A. and X. Zhang (eds.) (2012) *East Asian Capitalism: Diversity, Continuity, and Change*, Oxford: Oxford University Press.

Witt, M. and G. Redding (2013) 'Asian Business Systems: Institutional Comparison, Clusters and Implications for Varieties of Capitalism and Business Systems Theory', *Socio-Economic Review*, Vol.11, No.2.

Witt, M. and G. Redding (eds.) (2014) *The Oxford Handbook of Asian Business Systems*, Oxford: Oxford University Press.

Yamada, T. (1991) *The Régulation Approach*, Fujiwarashoten.

Yamada, T. (1994) *The 20th Century's Capitalism: An Analysis by the* Régulation *Approach*, Tokyo: Yuhikaku.

Yamada, T. (1999) 'Japanese Capitalism and the Companyist *Régulation*', in T. Yamada and R. Boyer (eds.) (1999), pp.19–31.

Yamada, T. (2000) 'Japanese Capitalism and the Companyist Compromise', in R. Boyer and T. Yamada (eds.) (2000), pp.21–47.

Yamada, T. (2005) '*Régulation* Approach to the Japanese Capitalism: Comments and Discussions', *Political Economy Quarterly*, Vol.42, No.2, pp.17–27.

Yamada, T. (2008) *Capitalismses: An Comparative Analysis*, Tokyo: Fujiwara Shoten.

Yamada, T. (2015) 'Methodological Reflection on the Comparative Analysis of Capitalism', *The Journal of Comparative Economic Studies*, Vol.10, pp.143–157.

Yamada, T. and R. Boyer (eds.) (1999) *Postwar Japanese Capitalism: Analyses of Its Régulation and Crisis*, Tokyo: Fujiwara Shoten.

Yamada, T. and Y. Hirano (2012) 'How Has the Japanese Mode of "*Régulation*" Changed?: The Whereabouts of Companyism,' in R. Boyer, H. Uemura and A. Isogai (eds.) (2012), pp.15–30.

Yamada, T., H. Uni and N. Nabeshima (eds.) (2007) *A New Perspective to the Contemporary Capitalism: Analyses of Its Diversity and Structural Change*, Kyoto: Showado.

Yan, C. (2011) *Economic Development and Institutional Change in China*, Kyoto: Kyoto University Press.

Zhang, X. and R. Whitley (2013) 'Changing Macro-structural Varieties of Eastern Asian Capitalism', *Socio-Economic Review*, Vol.11, No. 2.

Zieschang, K. (1957) 'Zu einigen theoretichen Problemen ded staatsmonopolistischen Kapitalismus in Westdeutschland,' in *Jahrbuch des Instituts für Wirtshaftwissenschaften: Ploblem der politischen Ökonomie*.

8 The revival of the classical theory of values

Yoshinori Shiozawa

Introduction

Marxian economists generally prefer to talk about economic crises; I will talk here about the crisis of economics. The crisis of economics is much deeper than the crisis of the economy. It is also one of the major causes of the present economic crisis. I am not talking about the lack of efficient economic policies. Bad economics restricts our field of imagination and is confining us to mediocre symptomatic therapies.[1]

How deep is the crisis of economics? One method of measuring it is to estimate for how long economics has "gone wrong". Nicholas Kaldor (1972, p.1240) argues that economic theory went astray in the middle of the fourth chapter of volume 1 of *Wealth of Nations*. Jane Jacobs (1984, Chap.2), my favorite amateur economist and one of the greatest economic thinkers of the 20th century urban design, declared that economics went wrong when Cantillon began to consider nations as units of development. My understanding does not go so far; nevertheless, I contend that economics went wrong when John Stuart Mill (1844) started to consider the present day "terms of trade" problem, which he believed Ricardo had left unsolved. I will explain later why I choose this point.

After the Lehman Brothers bankruptcy and the subsequent economic shock, many economists thought it necessary to return to Keynesian theory. As a necessary step, I would agree with them, but I doubt it is a sufficient condition on its own. Keynes has given us a precious idea, but we should remind ourselves of recent history and study dispassionately why an anti-Keynesian revolution took place in the 1970s. It started with the goodwill of those Keynesians who simply thought that Keynesian economics requires microfoundations (there is no need to explain the details here). Research vis-à-vis a microfoundation led to a revival of ultra-neoclassical economics, starting from rational expectations to recent dynamical statistical general equilibrium theory. Most economists know that these economics provided a theoretical basis for the revival of neoliberal economic thought, and the latter became part of the framework of the present-day globalized economy.

Why did that antirevolution take place so easily and so shortly after Keynes was adored like a cult leader in the 1960s? My understanding is that it occurred because Keynes had adopted a wrong economic framework. Keynes did not distinguish neoclassical from classical economics; he called both of them "classical economics". Therein resides a major problem with Keynes's *General Theory*. What he adopted as the framework of his economics was that of Marshall's; this means that Keynes attempted to build his theory within the neoclassical framework. The methodological core of neoclassical economics is equilibrium. Keynes, in essence, put his new idea in an old wine bag. A typical example is the concept of effective demand. In *General Theory*, effective demand is defined as the intersection value of two functions: one is the aggregate supply function, and the other the aggregate demand function. If this is a definition of "effective demand", it can be called the effective supply at equal capacity. This original misformulation led to a state in which the concept of effective demand was wiped away with the New Keynesian economics.[2]

Many interpretations have been advanced as to why Keynes (1936) adopted an equilibrium framework, rather than his earlier sequential analysis. This is one of the crucial points in the failure of Keynesian economics, but I will not enter in this question here.[3] My fundamental stance is that equilibrium analysis is the major epistemological obstruction to the further development of economics today (Shiozawa 1989). Apart from this crucial methodological framework problem, there is another equally fundamental problem in Keynes's economics. It is the question of value theory. My main contention in this chapter is that Keynes should have adopted the classical theory of value, rather than the neoclassical theory of value.

I am doubtful as to whether Keynes understood well the difference between the two value theories. In opposition to Jevons, Marshall emphasized the continuity from classical economics to neoclassical economics. This explains in part why Keynes did not distinguish neoclassical and classical economics; it also indicates that Keynes did not distinguish the two value theories. In Chapter 21 of *General Theory*, Keynes talks about the "double life" of economists: on one hand, they speak of the theory of value, and on the other hand, they think in terms of the theory of money and prices when they refer to economic fluctuations, *inter alia*. Keynes declares that "[o]ne of the objects of the foregoing chapters has been to escape from this double life and to bring the theory of prices as a whole back to close contact with the theory of value"(Keynes 1936, Chap.21). It is quite doubtful whether Keynes succeeded in bringing about a unified theory. Nowhere in his *General Theory* appears a new theory of value *à la* Keynes. When he spoke of the theory of value, it was the ordinary neoclassical theory of value. He explains that economists are "accustomed to teach[ing] that prices are governed by the conditions of supply and demand" (Keynes 1936): he contests the so-called double life but does not present a new theory of value.

Had Keynes been aware of crucial differences between neoclassical and classical theories of value, he may have adopted a different framework other than the actual framework he adopted. In the first phase of his redaction of *General Theory*, Keynes planned to write a monetary theory of production. As I will argue, neoclassical theory is in its essence the economics of exchange, whereas classical theory is the economics of production. In attempting to write a monetary theory of production, he adopted the framework of the economics of exchange, and this determined the destiny of *General Theory*.

What, then, is the classical theory of value, and why is the classical theory of value an economics of production? These are the themes of this chapter.

Classical economics and its rational core

When we talk about classical economics, we normally include almost all contentions proposed by economists from the days of classical economics. People may disagree as to when classical economics started and when it came to an end, but most people admit that the classical economics canon contains works from Adam Smith to John Stuart Mill. Even if we limit our list only to British writers, it would include Malthus, James Mill, McCullock, Ricardo, Thornton, Torrens, and Senior, to note only the most famous authors. There were many disputes among them, and so it is out of the question to think of classical economics as any consistent, cohesive system.

If classical economics is to be something that gives us hints for reconstructing and further developing economics, we should discard many elements. Many people will agree with me that the list of theories and contentions to be abandoned would include wage fund theory, natural wage rate theory and subsistence wage theory. Many economists except Marxists would agree to abandon the labor theory of value. These theories are what Jevons and other neoclassical fathers vehemently criticized. I abandon these elements of classical economics, not because they are criticized by after-comers, but because they cannot contribute to our challenge of reconstructing and developing further our economics. They all stood on a stage of vague ideas and do not deserve scrutiny in our time.

What is left, then? I do not speak of thoughtful ideas about economic development from classical economists, like those of Adam Smith. They are important, but much time will still be required before we can formalize their ideas and convert them into theories. What I am considering the rational core of classical economics is the theory of value.

The classical theory of value also takes many versions, from the labor theory of value to the subjective theory of value. Lengthy arguments are possible, but please allow me to come to my conclusion. What I consider the essence of the classical value theory is the cost of production theory of value.

This was what Ricardo wanted to formulate and yet could not arrive at. There is some textual evidence that supports this contention. In Section 4, Chapter 1 of his *Principles* (3rd ed.), Ricardo examines how values are affected. He could not bring about a complete formulation of his theory of value, but the core idea is explained clearly. It is not the labor theory of value, in the normal sense of the term. In other words, Ricardo thought that values are not exactly proportional to the embodied content of labor. Marx adopted the amount of labor embodied as a sort of definition of value. Ricardo never did so and tried to discover a more accurate formula. He failed to do so because, as Schumpeter (2006, p.543) correctly puts it, he did not know to use a system of simultaneous equations. However, Schumpeter was mistaken to suppose that systems of simultaneous equations were well known in Ricardo's time. He should be reminded of how Walras struggled with his system of simultaneous equations. A satisfactorily precise formula appeared many years later, when Sraffa (1960) published his small book. The reason for this long delay will be explained later.

Although he could not present a precise formula, Ricardo knew what it was not. Ricardo starts chapter 30 of his *Principles* with this remark:

> It is the cost of production which must ultimately regulate the price of commodities, and not, as has been often said, the proportion between the supply and demand.
>
> (Ricardo 1951, p.382)

It is also important to note that Ricardo included profits in the cost of production. In his footnote at the end of Section 6, Chapter 1, he writes:

> Mr. Malthus appears to think that it is a part of my doctrine, that the cost and value of a thing should be the same: – it is, if he means by cost, 'cost of production' including profits.
>
> (Ricardo 1951, p.47)

It is plausible to rename Ricardo's theory of value as the *cost of production theory of value*, although this term was not employed explicitly by him. This terminology can be attributed to John Stuart Mill (1844; 1848). The concrete formulation of the cost of production theory of value will be given later. Before discussing the formulation, some comments on the value concept itself are necessary.

Substance theory vs. relational theory of value

It is well known that there were within classical theories of value two strands: objective value theories and subjective value theories. The cost of production theory of value apparently belongs to the former strand. For a balanced appraisal of classical economics, however, we should bear in mind that there was a sustained current of subjective theories. O'Brien (2004, pp.114–123) cites, as proponents of subjective theory of value, J. B. Say, N. W. Senior, M. Longfield, and W. E. Lloyd, among others. This undercurrent in classical economics facilitated the resurrection of utility value theory at the time of the neoclassical revolution.

In this section, I want to question objective value theories. Many of them can be classified as substance theory. The labor theory of value is a typical one. This mode of thinking assumes that there is a kind of substance embodied in the commodity. The labor theory of value assumes that the labor embodied in commodities is proportional to their values. A typical argument is given by Marx. Citing the case of measuring rectilinear figures, he contends that "exchange values of commodities must be capable of being expressed in terms of something common to them all, of which thing they represent a greater or less quantity" (Marx 1867, p.27). Marx then argues that "if then we leave out of consideration the use-value of commodities, they have only one common property left, that of being products of labour"; he also concludes that values are measured by the human labor embodied in the commodities (Marx 1867, p.27). There are several logical jumps within these arguments, but I will not enter into the details here. Marx believes that labor is "embodied" as some substance, like the mass or heat of a physical entity.

Although they intend to explain values as things that are determined objectively, substance theories of value have become a major obstacle to the further development of the objective theory of value. When he started to examine the transformation problem, Marx reasoned as if embodied labor were conserved just like mass or energy. Marx derived two propositions on the equality of aggregates: the total sum of profits is equal to the total sum of surplus values, and the total sum of the product prices is equal to the total sum of the produced values. This confusion arose because Marx imagined that embodied labor is a substance that obeys conservation law. Even after it came to be known that there is no transformation process that allows the two propositions to hold simultaneously, except in very special circumstances, many people searched for a possible "means of escape" by which to retain the two propositions, and thus also the labor theory of value. As a matter of fact there is no conservation law for embodied labor, but confusion continues on account of this substance theory of value.

Value is not a substance. Values simply determine the exchange ratios of quantities that are exchanged. One of the reasons why value was often treated as a substance in the time of classical economics lies in the traditional dichotomy between values and prices. It was the custom to think that a value represents a natural price, the latter of which is a mean of an ever-fluctuating market price. Classical economists understood this relationship between natural prices or values and market prices in terms of a parable about gravitation (Kurz and Salvadori 1995, Chap.1). Although the term "gravitation" was not often used, John Stuart Mill and Marx advanced a clear image of it.[4] What, then, is the mechanism or logic that regulates values? One possible but erroneous answer to this question is the analogy of substance. In that interpretation, all commodities contain an essence as a substance, and the value is what this substance represents.

Value is however a social relation and does not necessitate any substance in it. It provides a reference point by which people can assess whether an actual price is high or low. However, as I will show below, the notion of a "center of gravitation" is not essential to an understanding of value. It is sometimes a hindrance to further development in the classical theory of value. The concept of value is defined by a cost of production, and not as the center of gravitation.

Cost of production theory of value (1):
Sraffa's formulation

Although the concepts of "cost" and "cost of production" are crucial to understanding the classical theory of value, these meanings were extremely vague in the time of both classical and neoclassical economics. Ricardo and John Stuart Mill must have had a firm concept of the cost of production, but in the case of Adam Smith, it is doubtful whether he had such a concept. The term "cost of production" does not appear in his *Wealth of Nations* (1776). Smith uses the word "cost" frequently (more than 80 times) in his book, but it is usually used as a verb. The word is used as a noun only nine times: seven times as "prime cost", once as "real cost", and once as "[the] cost". The use of "cost" or "costs" as verbs occurs in various ways, but their objective complements are sometimes monetary expenses, and at other times labor quantities. His "real cost" may stand for an amount of labor and other material consumption. When Smith talks about "prime cost", the term refers to a monetary sum related to the necessities for production. It is remarkable that he comments on this concept in this manner:

> . . . in common language what is called the prime cost of any commodity does not comprehend the profit of the person who is to sell it again, yet if he sells it at a price which does not allow him the ordinary rate of profit in his neighborhood, he is evidently a loser by the trade.
>
> (Smith 1776)

For Smith, the prime cost differs from what Ricardo calls the cost of production, for in Ricardo's case the cost of production includes profits (cited above). In any case, how are profits counted as a part of the cost of production? This was the very point at which Ricardo should have stopped in his tracks.

Ricardo's research agenda was about understanding movements in the profit rate by using values. Present-day knowledge tells us that Ricardo's agenda contained logical difficulties. He wanted to determine the profit rate by using values, but those values depended on the profit rate. To overcome this dilemma, it became necessary to use a two-level system of simultaneous equations. First, we can determine the values through a system of simultaneous equations while assuming that the profit rate and the wage rate are constants. Then, by using the values, we observe what happens to the real wage level when the profit rate varies as a parameter. It took many years from the time of Ricardo for theorists to arrive at this acknowledgement. In fact, it was as late as in 1960, when Sraffa (1960) was published.

Sraffa's system can be written simply, thus:

$$(1 + r)\{w \cdot \mathbf{a}_0 + A\mathbf{p}\} = \mathbf{p}. \tag{1}$$

Here, r is the rate of profit, w the wage rate, $\mathbf{a}_0$ a column vector of labor input coefficients, A a matrix of material input coefficients, and finally $\mathbf{p}$ a price vector. Sraffa preferred to write down a value system when wages were paid *post factum*; here, I have written a form where wages are paid in advance. Note that Sraffa (1960) does not distinguish value from price. In equation (1), the letter **p** can be replaced with **v**, a vector of values.

Suppose w and r are given. Equation (1) shows the circularity inherent in the fact that values are determined through the use of values. In equation (1), labor is assumed to be homogeneous; when there are differences among labor forces, take each class of labor force and assume the wage rates w_j are given. The kth row of equation (1) can be rewritten as

$$(1+r)\{w_1 a_{01} + \ldots + w_J a_{0J} + a_1 p_1 + \ldots + a_K p_K\} = p_k \tag{2}$$

If the wage rate structure (i.e. relative value of wage rates) does not change, we can safely use the simplified form (1).

When matrix A is productive – namely, if there exists a positive vector **y** such that

$$\mathbf{y} - \mathbf{y}A > 0 \tag{3}$$

then matrix $I - A$ is nonnegatively invertible, where I is a unit matrix. In other words, A is productive if and only if $I - A$ is invertible and $(I - A)^{-1}$ is non-negative. If condition (3) holds, matrix $I - (1 + r)A$ is also nonnegatively invertible for a sufficiently small r and equation (1) has a positive solution. The upper bound of such r is denoted as R and called the *maximal rate of profit*, although the rate R does not satisfy equation (1) for any positive vector **p**.[5]

The solution of equation (1) is explicitly written thus:

$$\mathbf{p} = w(1 + r)\left\{I - (1 + r)A\right\}^{-1} \mathbf{a}_0.$$

Note that $(1 / w)\,\mathbf{p}$ is dependent only on r and independent of w, if we assume that the input coefficients are constant. The vector $\mathbf{p}_w(r) = (1/w)\,\mathbf{p}$ indicates the real wage level of the economy; for workers who work for a unit of time and receive wage w, can consume any vector **x**, which satisfies the inequality

$$\langle \mathbf{x}, \mathbf{p} \rangle \leqq w. \tag{4}$$

The brackets <, > indicate the sum of values $x_j \cdot p_j$ for all products. The set of **x** that satisfies inequality (4) gives the set of possible consumptions for a worker who lives on his or her wage. We say "real wage level" instead of "real wage rate", because this cannot be expressed by a single real number. If $\mathbf{p}_w(r)$ is smaller, the real wage level is higher. As $\mathbf{p}_w(r)$ is a vector, there are cases where we cannot compare two such vectors. In spite of this fact, we have the following inequality:[6]

$$\mathbf{p}_w(r_1) < \mathbf{p}_w(r_2) \text{ if } r_1 < r_2 \text{ and } r_1, r_2 < R. \tag{5}$$

Equation (5) shows a tradeoff relation between the profit rate and the real wage level. Sraffa adopted as a measure of the distributional state what is called the "standard commodity". I will not diverge onto this topic, but I wish to note only that measurements that use the standard commodity are not needed to show the tradeoff relations between the profit rate and the real wage level.

Sraffa (1960) provides a formal definition for "values", for which Ricardo searched so long. We now know why Ricardo could not arrive at a correct solution. One reason is, as Schumpeter points out, in the inability of Ricardo and his contemporaries to use simultaneous equations. However, the problem does not stop there. Equation (1) clarifies how the profit rate and the real wage level relate, but it provides no explanation as to how, and in what meaning, the situation expressed by equation (1) relates to actual economy. We cannot stop with Sraffa (1960); we need to go further.

Cost of production theory of value (2): Oxford Economists' Research Group

The key to development beyond Sraffa (1960) lies in the empirical research undertaken by the Oxford Economists' Research Group in the late 1930s. Several reports were published across three issues of *Oxford Economic Papers* (old series) between 1938 and 1940, and a book (Wilson and Andrews 1951) was compiled after World War II.[7] Two notable observations arose from that research:

(1) Irrelevance of interest rate in investment

The interest rate is negligible or irrelevant when managers want to make a decision as to whether or not to invest.

(2) Full-cost principle

Firms obey the full-cost principle when managers set product prices. The general method of pricing involves adding a customarily determined margin to average short-term costs.

Two observations made by the Research Group were extremely important, and yet they were almost ignored or neglected as irrelevant by Cambridge economists, including Keynes and Sraffa. Two issues of *Oxford Economic Papers* were reviewed and criticized by Robinson (1939), and the first shock was absorbed. General attitude vis-à-vis this Group's research was expressed later in Kahn (1952). I will discuss in the next two sections the significance of the doubts presented by Robinson and others. On the whole, there was no drive to learn from the new results. This is one of the "great mysteries" in the history of economics. Some point to a schism between Oxford and Cambridge, but in reality, an appeal to this kind of vulgar sentiment does not help much in clarifying the true reasons for the negligence. We should think about the problem at the theory-structure level.

Attenuating circumstances exist in the case of Keynes. After publishing *General Theory*, Keynes was preoccupied with monetary management problems in Britain and worldwide, and had no time to seriously rethink his economics. *General Theory* relies overly much on the interest rate. The interest rate is considered a main inducement to invest. The Oxford Economic Research Group's first observation implies that Keynes's basic idea on investment was not empirically confirmed. This required a fundamental reorganization of Keynes's system. The same criticism can be addressed against the contemporary New Consensus Macroeconomics. The case of Sraffa is more mysterious, because Sraffa had enough time to incorporate this new knowledge into his economics.

The second observation directly relates to the question posed at the end of the previous section. The margin that is added to costs is calculated by multiplying a customarily determined rate and the total unit cost. This rate is called the *markup rate*. If markup rates are uniform throughout industries, we can write an equation with r replaced with the uniform markup rate m, provided that all production is synchronized in the sense that the processing time from input to output is identical everywhere. In reality, we are not in such a situation, and so a synchronization procedure is necessary. I will not enter into technical details, but this is an important procedure, for production conditions vary widely. This procedure is different from the procedure that becomes necessary with the existence of fixed capital. To treat fixed capital in a formal way, we should deal with joint production. In a case where inputs are consumed in the production process once and for all, it is sufficient to assume a virtual product at the end of each step of the production period. The latter question is not discussed in Sraffa (1960).

Above, we assume that markup rates are uniform. In reality, there is no reason for them to be uniform. In fact, there is a clear reason as to why markup rates differ according to the products that firms produce. Even if they are customarily determined, a markup rate depends on the composition of the circulating capital and the fixed capital. As it is determined as a multiplier of the short-term average unit cost, if the weight of fixed capital is great, the markup rate must be higher than in other cases, so that each industry enjoys a (nearly) uniform rate of profit.[8] There is no fixed relationship between the markup rate and the profit rate, because the profit rate depends on the scale of products sold. I will also discuss this point later (Section 8).

When the markup rates differ, equation (1) should be rewritten as follows:

$$(1 + M) \{w \cdot \mathbf{a}_0 + A\mathbf{p}\} = \mathbf{p}. \tag{6}$$

Matrix M is a diagonal square matrix whose diagonal elements are markup rates.

Equations (1) and (6) are not only different as expressions; they also differ greatly in terms of the meanings they represent. Prices given by equation (1) are not actual prices by which exchanges take place; rather, we often speak of them as long-term prices. They were interpreted as centers of gravitation.

The market price of a good fluctuates around one of these centers. A long-term price may be an average of price fluctuation during a certain period of time. However, the idea of a long-term price contains a weakness, because it does not express the real exchange rate. Prices given by equation (6) have a different meaning. The price of a product determined by the full-cost principle is an actual selling price, if the wage rate and prices other than that of the product itself are actually w and p, respectively. By the universality of the full-cost principle, we can even contend that the prices determined by equation (6) are actual prices, or at least close approximations of actual prices.

This difference of meaning between (1) and (6) is important, in the sense that through the prices given by (6), we can safely reason about what happens in a time of depression or in a time of boom. If we adopt long-term prices, we can analyze a phenomenon that holds only on average throughout a business cycle. To study questions pertaining to involuntary unemployment, it is normally necessary to study a situation where the economy is depressed. This may be one of the reasons why Keynes avoided the use of classical value theory. The full-cost principle gives us a powerful means of analysis vis-à-vis a depressed economy.

We may ask if the full-cost principle was widely employed in the 19th century. The two most prevalent commodities in 19th-century Britain were corn and cotton textiles. Corn is an agricultural product that is harvested once per year in Britain; when the harvest is over, it is difficult to change the national supply volume, unless Britain were to import from abroad. Cotton textiles are industrial products, but their ingredients are agricultural products. Corn and cotton are major commodities quoted in the trade market, and their prices fluctuate daily. The prices of yarn and textiles fluctuate in a similar manner, as their costs fluctuate. We may call these commodities whose prices fluctuate according to market conditions *market-conditioned commodities.*

However, it is not correct to say that the full-cost principle was not employed in the 19th century. Take as an example a small bakery, a coffee shop or a pub house. The shop owners determined the prices of their products or services. We are unsure of whether they knew the exact unit cost of their products and services, but the fact that they determined their own products and services indicates that they had in mind a kind of markup rate. One may argue that they determined their prices without referencing unit costs. This must be true for most shop owners, because many of them merely set their prices to approximate those of their competitors. Prices became sticky, for as long as all shop owners abide by this policy, no shop owners can change their prices. Sooner or later, cost prices change, and they become obliged to change their prices; at that time, some intelligent shop owners will calculate the plausible prices given the cost price conditions.

In the last decade of the 19th century, a big movement of mergers and acquisitions occurred, and giant firms emerged. Those firms had an interest in employing a good pricing policy, and they developed a method of measuring unit cost more precisely. The full-cost principle came to be employed first by those firms, and small and medium-sized firms also had an interest in adopting the same principle if they could afford to do so. We have a deeply entrenched custom of thinking that 19th-century Britain was in a state of nearly perfect competition and prices fluctuated freely and frequently until the turn of the century when imperfect competition intruded in the economy. I doubt that this image is accurate. It is not conceivable that all prices changed every week or so. I believe that the majority of commodities sold in the shops were quite stable in terms of price, although they did fluctuate slowly and sporadically throughout the 19th century.

How are markup rates determined?

The Oxford Economists' Research Group investigation revealed observations that presented an "inconvenient fact" to economics, as the full-cost principle ran counter to both perfect and imperfect competition theories. Perfect competition theory assumed that all firms are price-takers; the Research Group investigation revealed that most firms are price-setters. This fact was interpreted as follows: the firms invited to the inquiry were monopolistic. However, this was not the end of the story. Imperfect competition theory, which barely took form in the 1930s, advanced the thesis that firms fix their prices and production in such a way that the marginal cost is equal to the marginal revenue. The Research Group investigation, however, revealed that firms were not behaving like that. Criticism leveled at the investigation ranged from extenuating arguments to doubts of the validity of the inquiry method itself. Some doubted business people's ability to answer a question posed by economists. Some questioned whether business people had invented a false rationalization for their behavior (Kahn 1952, p.126).

Although it was not a direct reaction, the Research Group investigation also triggered a considerable debate in North America. Based on inquiries posed to factory managers, Lester (1946) submitted to the *American Economic Review* a paper that argued that managers did not know the marginal cost, and that their factories were operating at a point where the average cost was decreasing. Machlup was the acting editor of the *Review* at that time; his first reaction was to reject the paper. Persuaded by Editor Paul T. Homan upon returning from his absence, Machlup agreed to publish Lester's article; he also started to prepare his own paper, which appeared in a subsequent issue (Machlup 1946).[9] This paper marked a breakout of "war" (Machlup 1967, pp.1–2) between antimarginalists and marginalists.[10] The controversy that ensued was called the *marginalist controversy* or the marginalist/antimarginalist controversy, and many papers were published on this matter. Machlup and many American economists took the Research Group investigation and Lester's paper (1946) as an attack on the very core of marginal analysis, and attempted a counter-attack. (I will not enter into the details of this debate, as doing so would require too much space.) The debate was lessening around 1952. Some judged that "Machlup [had] won the battle but Lester won the war" (Machlup 1967, p.2). Lee's book (1998) is an example of one study that pursued a new price theory based on empirical research. The general appraisal among mainstream economists was that it was completely possible to incorporate the general framework of the theory of the firm.[11]

Hall and Hitch (1939), the first proponents of the full-cost principle, were partially responsible for this appraisal. They indicated the idea that demand curves are kinked at the present price (see also Lee 1998, Chap.4). This idea was embraced by Sweezy and many others. In Japan, Takashi Negishi employed this idea when he tried to give a micro-foundation to macroeconomics. A kinked demand curve may explain why a price does not change, but the trouble with it is that the sales volume is fixed for an unknown reason. Full-cost pricing – or, more generally, administered pricing – supposes that firms set prices and sell their products in response to demand. A kinked demand curve does not offer a suitable explanation for firm's behavior. Others assumed an everywhere constant elasticity of demand curve, together with a constant marginal cost. On this assumption, we could induce markup pricing; however, this is too strong an assumption.

Another criticism against the full-cost principle was that it does not reflect demand-side conditions. Some claims were led by misunderstandings. Kahn (1952) highlights firm behavior in a heavily depressed market; in that situation, firms have a tendency to cut their prices. He also points out an inconsistency when the cost is increased or decreased. These matters do not lead to a rejection of the full-cost principle. We should know how markup rates are determined and clarify how demand and competition influence the markups. Markups depend on the competitive conditions of the economy. In normal economic times, the full-cost principle holds with its normal rate but in a heavily depressed time (in the case of Great Depression, for example) the markup rate changes due to the enormous change of the economic situation. Many firms stand at the edge of bankruptcy and the competitive conditions change extremely. In such cases the markup rates or the full-cost principle itself changes accordingly.

The long history of the debate on the full-cost principle teaches us that neoclassical marginal analysis could not advance a theory that explains the phenomenon. What is necessary here is to present a theory that explains why firms behave according to the full-cost principle. I tried it in Shiozawa (1984) and reprinted it as the appendix to Shiozawa (2014a). Here I reproduce only its essence.

The core of my theory is to discard the concept of the demand function. In the neoclassical tradition, we normally assume a demand function at the start of an analysis, but it is quite questionable whether a firm can conceive a demand function all the time. Normally, the argument of the function is the product price, and no other factors are considered. This is completely absurd, because even with a constant product price, the sales volume changes both daily and weekly. Take the example of a convenience store. Around 20–30 takeout lunch boxes are sold every day in an ordinary shop, but if a sports festival were held in a neighborhood primary school, sales of that same lunch box might increase three- to five-fold compared to an ordinary day. Demand fluctuates every day. Knowing the demand function in terms of product price is not only difficult but useless, because prices do not change very often. Shop owners need to foretell demand and its fluctuation, even at a fixed price. What is more important to the shop is the *sales share*. This sales share is defined as the percentage of the shop's sales volume over the total sales volume among the competitors. It remains relatively stable, even if demand changes abruptly, depending on the events that influence total demand within the community.

Shiozawa (1984) examined the case of duopoly. Imagine a town that has two supermarkets, and each supermarket is competing with the other. They set prices for various products. The number of items to be priced exceeds 10,000. It is impossible to assess a demand function for each of the items. They want to determine the correct markup rate, except for bargain goods. Suppose shares are determined by the relative prices of the two competitors. The share function may be influenced by the location of the supermarkets in the town; it may also depend on what kind of loyalty they command from their customers. Suppose we know the share function $\psi(p1/p2)$. Hotelling (1929)–type competition tells us that two competitors come to set their prices at point

$$p = \{\psi'(1)/(\psi'(1) - 1)\} \cdot c, \tag{7}$$

when the share functions are symmetrical between the two competitors and they have the same purchasing cost c. Of course, we should impose some conditions on ψ so that the Hotelling-type competition has a unique absorbing fixed point.

Equation (7) shows the most typical case. Other cases, like the case where purchase costs are different, can be analyzed in a similar way. In the case of equation (7), the markup rate is given as

$$1 + m = \psi'(1)/(\psi'(1) - 1) \tag{8}$$

My theory is superior to the "everywhere constant elasticity" assumptions. It does not contain the defect that the kinked demand curve has, and it explains why managers keep the same markup rates when the cost is cut or, contrarily, when the cost is increased. Upon closer analysis, we see that the markup rate changes if customers become more price-sensitive. Therefore, full-cost pricing reflects well the state of competition. The special behavior of retailers who reduce their markups in a low-income district can be explained by the fact that customers become more price-sensitive as their income decreases. Of course, this does not exclude the fact that suppliers' attitudes change in a deep depression.

The full-cost principle and all other related observations contradict the neoclassical framework, but this fact does not imply that business people behave irrationally. It was the neoclassical economists who clung to marginal analysis who were irrational.

I recommend discarding the demand function containing prices as unique arguments. As for actual everyday use, pricing via the demand function is not practical. On some special occasion, when the stake is large and when they have time, firms may predict a kind of demand function, even if it may be only a very rough one. For example, when an automobile company is planning to launch a new model, it is customary to describe a kind of demand function and examine the possible price line and expected sales volume during the model's lifetime. If the model of a specification is predicted to have such a cost and if it seems difficult to attain a planned sales volume, the specification and the design of the model are changed so as to attain plausible price and sales expectations. This procedure at the beginning of the design process is called *target costing* (or *genka kikaku*), and it is widespread among Japanese manufacturing firms. These practices do not at all contradict the full-cost principle. Once a firm starts to produce and sell cars, the prices are fixed for a certain time span, preferably for the full lifetime of the model.

Price setting and its twinned behavior of firms

I have so far discussed the price or value side of the economy. Neoclassical economists often criticize classical theory of value for lacking demand theory. It is true that demand theory is the most underdeveloped component of the classical theory framework. One can even say it is the lacuna of the economics that stand on the tradition of classical economics. However, the criticism is, in a sense, ill-conceived. The classical theory already has a theory of the firm and on how demand affects production, although it is not widely known. Note that classical value theory does not rely on price adjustment. Firms fix their own prices. Prices do not play an adjustment function when demand fluctuates. Twinned with price-setting behavior, firms adopt a specific mode of quantity adjustment. Firms sell as much as there is a demand for: if they are producers, they produce as much as there is a demand for. This is the principle that was implicitly assumed when Sraffa (1926) discussed the principal factors that limit firms to produce more.

Neoclassical economics, in 1926 and in our own time, explains that a firm determines its production volume in such a way that it maximizes its profits. In a perfectly competitive economy, prices are given. Economists assume a total cost function with production volume as an argument. Let it be $c(x)$. If all products sell, the profit π is given by the formula

$$\pi(x) = p \cdot x - c(x), \tag{9}$$

where p is the product price and x the production volume. If $c(x)$ is an increasing, weak convex function, $c'(x)$ is positive and increasing. Then, if a point

$$p = c'(x^*) \tag{10}$$

exists, and it is unique, *x** gives a maximum profit for the firm. This explanation turns out to be completely baseless, as the marginal cost, if one can ever know it, remains constant or decreases at the point of actual production for almost all firms and all periods, as the marginalist controversy made clear.

In an imperfectly competitive economy, the product price is no longer given. It is a variable that the firm sets. Joan Robinson and other economists assume that firms have a known demand function $f(p)$ with product price p as a unique variable. Then, suppose the product price is fixed. Equation (10) gives a function that gives the production volume for each price p; we write it as $f(p)$. If the product sells as expected, the firm's profit in this time is

$$\pi(p) = p \cdot f(p) - c(f(p)). \tag{11}$$

The expected profit will be maximized at the price p where $\pi'(p) = 0$, or at the point (price or quantity) where the marginal revenue is equal to the marginal cost. Prices can be determined in this way. All right! However, the story does not end here. What happens in the market, and how do firms behave if the prediction included in the demand function is not correct? This is the real problem we should examine.

If the price p is determined, the production volume x is determined by the relation $x = f(p)$. Do firms continue to produce quantity x, irrespective of market demand? What happens when the average demand per unit of time differs from x? No neoclassical economist has discussed or examined this problem, even though these are inevitable and crucial questions. This is the situation Sraffa (1926) discussed, and he concluded that what prevents firms from planning to extend their production is not the increased cost of production, but the limit of demand. A consequence of this observation can be formulated in a principle: firms produce as much as there is a demand for, at least in normal times. I call this principle *Sraffa's principle* (Shiozawa 1978), but it can also be called the *principle of effective demand at the firm level*. In my understanding, this principle – which regulates a firm's production and supply behavior – is twinned with a firm's price-setting behavior.

Equations (1) and (6) determine prices. Once prices are set in this way or another, and as far as firms or shops maintain their prices, they always face problems in adjusting themselves to market conditions. In such a situation, any price adjustment is out of the question, for the price has already been determined. Price theory can only intervene when one considers resetting the price. If the prices do not vary each day, it is necessary to think about quantity adjustment. Neoclassical economics, which are based on the demand function, cannot embark on this question. It is regrettable that Sraffa did not combine his two theories into a unified one. Keynes also had the chance to incorporate Sraffa's principle into his theory of effective demand; he did not, however, and instead presented a halfway neoclassical theory. As I indicated above, this paved the way for the anti-Keynesian revolution in the 1970s.

The Oxford Research Group's economic survey and the subsequent marginalist controversy offered a great opportunity for the revival of classical value theory. However, this chance was not capitalized upon as such, and the marginalist controversy ended around 1952. As Frederic Lee (1984) says in his conclusion, it was a chance to "develop a non-neoclassical theory of price".

As Lee (1984) shows, the marginalist controversy gave birth in North America to a new trend. It centered on the behavioral theory of the firm, and saw the firm as an organization "situated in a complex environment". People in the organization were not assumed to have unlimited rationality. From this starting point, a new science of management arose. The new management science had a strong tendency toward reality, but the lack of a theory connecting new management science and economics led to a wider schism between the two.

In my opinion, classical value theory has lost a precious opportunity. As far as neoclassical theory continues, however, there remains the opportunity to resurrect classical value theory. Of course, the latter should also advance further. State-of-the-art 19th-century theory cannot compete with neoclassical theory. However, we already have a priceless accumulation of theories and observations; if it is reorganized appropriately, the classical theory of value has a great opportunity to become a coherent system of economics by which we can examine all kinds of economic phenomena. It can, in fact, become logically superior to neoclassical economics. The core of this new economics should be the new theory of value, or a new cost of production theory of value.

The new theory of value, like imperfect or monopolistic competition theories, assumes that firms fix their product prices. Classical theory of value, however, does not assume that firms know about demand in advance. Firms may expect an average sales volume, but they know that demand fluctuates greatly and they adjust their production volume to suit the demand that is revealed as time passes. The firms' basic attitude is to sell their products as far as there is demand: if demand is strong, they increase production, and if demand is weak, they reduce production. They adjust their production so as to attain near equality between supply and demand. The difference between supply and demand in a period where the production volume cannot be adjusted will be adjusted by the inventory. In a real operation, adjustment proceeds in the opposite manner: firms observe their inventories and adjust their production accordingly, by determining whether their inventory levels are high or low with respect to normal levels.

These themes were widely studied in the 1950s as a part of activity analysis and as part of inventory theory. We can inherit these results for the new theory of value. Of course, it is still necessary to develop the theory further. John Stuart Mill once wrote in his *Principles* (1848) that "there is nothing in the laws of value which remains for the present or any future writer to clear up; the theory of the subject is complete". We will never arrive at a state like that, and should not expect to. Such recognition must be a major obstacle to the future development of the theory.

Demand growth and profit rate

Although this is an important and productive area for the new value theory, I must be brief on this theme. As I pointed out, profits are not determined solely by prices or markup rates. When a firm fixes the price of one of its products, the profit derived from that product is determined by the sales volume over a period of time – for example, within an accounting period. If the average sales are good, the firm will make a profit that it expected before the period starts. In the opposite case, the opposite results will follow. What determines actual sales volume? It is not the product price. At a given product price, the firm can make a tentative prediction, but there is always a considerable difference between the expectation and the actual result. When the firm behaves according to Sraffa's principle – that is if the firm produces and sells as much as there is a demand for – what determines the sales volume is the demand itself. Because, in a normal case, the effective demand is always satisfied, we can say that the sales volume and the profit are determined by the effective demand. However, this is a satisfactory answer only at the most superficial layer of the problem.

A second and deeper-layer question pertains to what determines or influences the effective demands. An actual firm's actual behavior is very different from what neoclassical economics predicts: if profits grow while the sales volume is larger, firms tend to make efforts to expand their sales volume. This is the reason why firms have in sales department much more personnel than are necessary to execute simple selling operations. In some companies, a major part of the sales division is directed at promoting sales in various ways. However, it is necessary to go further still, into a deeper layer – the third layer of the problem. Let's say that the sales efforts are given; still, there will be great differences of sales volumes depending on the state of the economy. If the economy is depressed, the income of the people decreases and sales volumes will fall, despite increased sales promotion efforts. If the economy is in a boom, the income goes up and the demand will increase beyond what was expected. If the economy is in a steady growth path, the demand will increase constantly, year by year. We should analyze this circular causation of demand and income. It is a theme that directly relates to Keynesian business cycle analysis and post-Keynesian growth analysis. Post-Keynesian economics already has a large arsenal of theories and analysis.

Choice of techniques, and the minimal price theorem

Technology and a variety of commodities are two important factors we should bear in mind. Each of these research topics contains a difficult problem that sometimes transcends our analytical capacities, but in any case of technological development, we must deal with questions pertaining to the choice of technique. Neoclassical economics customarily argue that production theories in the classical tradition lack a theory of input substitutions. They are wrong in the sense that the core problem is already answered, although economists in the classical tradition do not sufficiently recognize this point.

The classical theory of value does not necessitate input substitution. This was the true meaning of the Preface of Sraffa (1960). The neoclassical image of production is horribly disfigured: the concept of the production function, if it is a firm-level concept or a macroeconomic one, lacks any basis in reality. At the firm level, managers decide what and how much they will produce, and they proceed to procure what is necessary for production. The neoclassical production function sees the process in the opposite way: managers see what kind and how many production factors are given, and then they decide upon the optimal product mix. This kind of decision-making never occurs in a real factory or firm. Fixed-coefficient production is much more plausible, if we consider how production takes place. The question that arises from the fixed-coefficient formulation relates to analysis when there are two or more production techniques for a product. Is the classical theory of value in the form of (1) or (6) still valid in the presence of plural production techniques or processes for one product?

The answer to this question is already given, by the so-called Samuelson's non-substitution theorem – or, in more suitable terminology, *minimal price theorem* or *minimal value theorem*. Samuelson found in a two-goods case that the prices remain constant, even if there are several production processes available for a product (Koopmans 1951, Chap.7). This theorem was proved by Koopmans (1951, Chap.8) in a three-goods case and by Arrow in a general N-goods case (Koopmans 1951, Chap.9). This theorem was interpreted as one that gives a certain justification for Leontief input-output analysis, but its true meaning was not really conceived by the developers. The minimal price theorem provides a very good justification for the cost of production theory of value: a set of production techniques (or processes) exists and it gives the minimal price system for a given wage rate. There is no need for prices to change when the demand composition changes. As far as the markup rates of industries remain unchanged, the value formulas (1) and (6) hold true, irrespective of demand.

In explanations of the minimal price theorem, it is said to hold only in the case of simple production, and that it is not applicable to the joint-production case. This is a half-truth: for the most important case of fixed capital, the theorem can be extended if the capital has a fixed lifetime, and its efficiency remains constant during the (possibly infinite) lifetime. Note that this is a sufficiently wide assumption, for this case covers almost all cases that cost accounting assumes.

Tasks that challenge us still

We have now arrived at a provisory conclusion. The classical theory of value, in modernized forms, is much more realistic than the neoclassical theory of prices. The neoclassical theory of prices or values has serious defects in its internal logic and runs counter to observations made in the actual economy.

The classical theory of value is not about long-term analysis, even if it can be used for that purpose. Rather, it provides a theory of prices by which we can analyze actual transactions (i.e., actual exchanges of commodities). It can also produce a micro-foundation for Keynes's idea of effective demand, if it is supplanted by Sraffa's principle at the firm level. As effective demand determines production volume and consequently the demand for labor, it also provides a theory of involuntary unemployment.

There has been another important development in the classical theory of value recently. It is the new theory of international values. Note that the lack of international value theory has been the proverbial "weak link" in the classical value theory chain. Ricardo and Marx knew that the logic of value theory within a country cannot be extended to an international situation without first making a major modification to the theory. Based on the results of Shiozawa (2007), a new theory of international values was developed by Shiozawa (2014a). See Shiozawa (2014b) for a short account of the theory, which is an extension of the classical theory of value. At the same time, it was found that John Stuart Mill's "solution" was a theory pertaining to the almost-nonexistent case where production quantities are determined (Mill 1844). Mill's pseudo-solution led to the establishment of an economics of exchange, thus opening the way to the neoclassical revolution (Shiozawa 2014c).

An important lacuna has been filled. It is now time to develop the classical value theory and make it a superior system of theories and applications that can compete with the neoclassical theory of prices. It may appear to practical people to be a detour of sorts, but I believe that this is the shortest path to redressing the world economy that is now in a complete mess on account of the strong influence of neoclassical economics.

As I have emphasized, the classical theory of value is not yet complete. A value theory within a country and an international value theory are provided. Rent theory (including the price theory of exhaustible resources) is being developed within the work of Cristian Bidard, Toichro Asada, and others. Still, there are at least two areas in which the classical value tradition has no satisfactory theory: (1) the labor market and (2) the financial economy.

The labor market problem lies in the question of how wages related to different kinds of work are determined. If the work force of a country is uniform, there will be no value problem. It is sufficient to assume that a nominal wage rate w is given. The nominal wage rate produces only a temporary effect on the real wage level. In fact, the real wage level is not determined by w; it is determined by the prices of products, which in turn are determined by the markup principle of firms. However, if there are variously qualified workers, it is necessary to derive a theory as to how the wages of different kinds of work forces are determined. Marx talked about a reduction of complex labor into multiples of simple labor; however, the process of that reduction is not sufficiently clear. One normally refers to the cost of reproduction of a specific kind of labor force; however, it is doubtful whether the cost of production theory of value applies to the labor market. Labor power is not reproduced in a capitalist production process. Rather, it is reproduced outside the capitalist mode of production. Value theory of labor forces must be constructed on the basis of this special feature.

Although the financial economy has an enormous impact on the course of the real economy, the classical tradition contains practically no theory at all. Stock prices may seem to be determined by a demand-and-supply mechanism, and in terms of price-setting procedures, this is correct. Every board of exchange has its own price-setting algorithm and matching methods to connect bids with offers. However, this is not yet a theory of prices, as we know very little about how bids and offers fluctuate as time passes. The neoclassical theory of value, which depends on utility, does not apply, either. Major parts of bids and offers are made for speculative purposes. The same observation can be applied to the foreign exchange market: prices in financial markets obey random walking rules, and yet they are markets where fundamentals can influence prices in the medium or long term (Economic Sciences Prize Committee 2013 gives an excellent account on the state of our knowledge today). Stochastic process theory must be used as an essential tool to analyze these complex movements, but we need to note that these processes are much more complicated than standard stationary processes where variations are independent of previous ones. Financial engineering may give us a first-step overview of what is happening in the financial markets, but this is only one of the starting points. A vast field that requires theory is waiting for us.

Notes

1 This chapter is based on my two recent books, Shiozawa (2014) and Shiozawa and Aruka (2014). Those who can read Japanese are asked to consult these books for the details of my contentions and the logical framework of my theories.

2 There are many other misformulations within the *General Theory*. I cite only one of the most conspicuous examples.

3 See for a more detailed argument Shiozawa and Aruka (2014), Chap.1 and 2.

4 See John Stuart Mill (1848) and Marx (1894, p.129). Note that the two concepts "center of gravity" and "center of gravitation" are sometimes confused. The internal logic of the gravitation thesis is competently examined by Dupertuis and Sinha (2009).

5 We do not enter into details of the characterization of R. If the input matrix is decomposable, we must differentiate basic and nonbasic products.

6 Inequality 5 holds in a wide case where there is fixed capital and a choice of techniques. See Shiozawa (1975).

7 For a short but rather critical review of the research, see Kahn (1952).

8 In reality, there are two ambiguities inherent in the concept of average unit cost. Some consider unit cost to include overhead costs, whereas others exclude the latter from the unit cost. If the unit cost includes overhead costs, the unit cost varies according to changes in sales volume. In such a case, the full cost may change in line with managers' sales expectations. In this chapter, I treat the unit cost as an entity that remains constant, irrespective of sales volume. Fujimoto (2012) proposes a *full and direct costing* (or *full variable costing*) concept in cost accounting. This concept keeps the full unit cost constant, irrespective of sales volume. Professor Fujimoto proposes this costing in view of building competitive capacity among firms and *genba* (or processing sites). Another ambiguity lies in the word "average": it may stand for "average" in terms of time, or "average" among the firms in an industry.

9 For these details, see Lee (1984), note 10 (p.1127).
10 Judging from the fact that neoclassical price theory remained intact, we should say the opposite.
11 For a compact history of the controversy, see Lee (1984).

References

Dupertuis, M-S and A. Sinha (2009) "A Sraffian Critique of the Classical Notion of Center of Gravitation", *Cambridge Journal of Economics*, **33**(6) pp. 1065–87.

Economic Sciences Prize Committee of the Royal Swedish Academy of Sciences (2013) "Scientific Background on the Sveriges Riksbank Prize in Economic Sciences in Memory of Alfred Nobel 2013," http://www.nobelprize.org/nobel_prizes/economic-sciences/laureates/2013/advanced-economicsciences2013.pdf

Fujimoto, T. (2012) "A Preliminary Note on Harmonizing Manufacturing (Monozukuri) Management and Cost Accounting," (in Japanese) Monozukuri Management Research Center (University of Tokyo) Discussion Paper Series No. 410.

Hall, R.L. and C.J. Hitch (1939) "Price Theory and Business Behavior", *Oxford Economic Papers* (old series), **2** pp. 12–45.

Hotelling, H. (1929) "Stability in Competition," *Economic Journal*, **39**(153) pp.41–57.

Jacobs, J. (1984) *Cities and the Wealth of Nations*, New York, NY: Random House.

Kahn, F.R. (1952) "Oxford Studies in the Price Mechanism", *Economic Journal* **62**(245) pp. 119–30.

Kaldor, N. (1972) "The Irrelevance of Equilibrium Economics", *Economic Journal* **82**(328) pp. 1237–55.

Keynes, J.M. (1936) *General Theory of Employment, Interest and Money*. Cambridge: Cambridge University Press for Royal Economic Society.

Koopmans, T.C. (Ed.) (1951) *Activity Analysis of Production and Allocation*, New York, NY: John Wiley and Sons.

Kurz, H.D. (2014) "David Ricardo: On the Art of Elucidating Economic Principles in the Face of a Labyrinth of Difficulties", Paper presented at the International Conference on New Thinking in Economic Theory and Policy, held at Meiji University, Tokyo on 13–15 September 2014.

Kurz, H.D. and N. Salavadori (1995) *Theory of Production, a Long Period Analysis*, Cambridge: Cambridge University Press.

Lee, F.S. (1984) "The Marginalist Controversy and the Demise of Full Cost Pricing", *Journal of Economic Issues* **18**(4) pp. 1107–32.

Lee, F.S. ([1998] 2006) *Post Keynesian Price Theory*, Cambridge: Cambridge University Press. Reissued in paperback in 2006.

Lester, R.A. (1946) "Shortcomings of Marginal Analysis for Wage-Employment Problems", *American Economic Review* **36**(1) pp. 63–82.

Machlup, F. (1946) "Marginal Analysis and Empirical Research", *American Economic Review* **36**(4) pp. 519–57.

Machlup, F. (1967) "Theories of the Firm: Marginalist, Behavioral, Managerial", *American Economic Review* **57**(1) pp. 1–33.

Marx, K. (1867) *Das Kapital* I. English translation 1887: *Capital / A Critique of Political Economy*. Volume I. Moscow ed. 2010: https://www.marxists.org/archive/marx/works/download/pdf/Capital-Volume-I.pdf

Marx, K. (1894) *Das Kapital* III. English translation 1909: *Capital / A Critique of Political Economy*. Volume 3. *The Process of Capitalist Production as a Whole*.

Library of Economics and Liberty: http://www.econlib.org/library/YPDBooks/Marx/mrxCpB.html

Mill, J.S. (1844) *Essays on Some Unsettled Questions of Political Economy*, Library of Economics and Liberty: http://www.econlib.org/library/Mill/mlUQP.html

Mill, J.S. (1848) *Principles of Political Economy*, Library of Economic and Liberty: http://www.econlib.org/library/Mill/mlPCover.html (7th ed., 1909, Longman, Green and Co.)

O'Brien, D.P. (2004) *The Classical Economists Revisited* (2nd Edition), Princeton University Press.

Ricardo, D. ([1821] 1951) *On the Principles of Political Economy and Taxation*, Ed. by P. Sraffa with the collaboration of M. Dobb, *Works and Correspondence of David Ricardo*, Volume 1, Cambridge: Cambridge University Press.

Robinson, A. (1939) "Review of Oxford Economic Papers", *Economic Journal*, 49(195) pp. 538–43.

Schumpeter, J.A. ([1954] 2006) *History of Economics Analysis*, First published by London: Allen & Unwin, 1954. E-books by Taylor and Francis, 2006.

Shiozawa, Y. (1975) "Durable Capital Gods and their Valuation", KIER Discussion Paper No.8, Institute of Economic Research, Kyoto University.

——— (1978) "A Theory of Depression and the Sraffa's Principle" (in Japanese), *Keizai Semina*, No. 287, pp. 48–57. Reprinted as Chapter 6 in Y. Shiozawa, *The Science of the Market Order* (in Japanese), Tokyo: Chikuma Shobo, 1990.

——— (1984) "Duopoly Competition which Implies Markup Pricing" (in Japanese), *Keizaigaku Zasshi* (Osaka City University) 84(6) pp. 12–24. Reproduced in Shiozawa (2014a) with a correction.

——— (1989) "The Primacy of Stationarity: A Case Against General Equilibrium Theory", *Osaka City University Economic Review* 24(1) pp. 85–110.

_____(2007) "A New Construction of Ricardian Trade Theory – A Many-country, Many-commodity Case with Intermediate Goods and Choice of Techniques," *Evolutionary and Institutional Economics Review*, 3(2), pp.141–187.

——— (2012) "Estimating Optimal Product Variety of Firms", *Evolutionary and Institutional Economics Review* 9(1) pp. 11–35.

——— (2014a) *A Final Solution of Ricardo Problem on International Values* (in Japanese, original title: Rikādo bōeki mondai no saishū kaiketsu), Tokyo: Iwanami Shoten.

——— (2014b) "The New International Value Theory and Its Applications", unpublished draft paper.

——— (2014c) "On Ricardo's Two Rectification Problems", a paper presented at the International Conference on Ricardo (organized by Ricardo Society) on 11 September at Waseda University. A revised version is to be published in Senga, Fujimoto, and Tabuchi (Eds.) Ricardo and International Trade Theory, by Routledge, as Chapter 10.

Shiozawa, Y. and Y. Aruka (2014) *Reconstructing Economics* (in Japanese, original title: Keizaigaku o saiken suru), Tokyo: Chuo University Press.

Smith, A. (1776) *An Inquiry into the Nature and Causes of the Wealth of Nations*, Survey is based on the *Library of Economics and Liberty* edition.

Sraffa, P. (1926) "The Laws of Returns under Competitive Conditions", *Economic Journal* 36(1444) pp. 535–50.

Sraffa, P. (1960) *Production of commodities by Means of Commodities*, Cambridge: Cambridge University Press.

Wilson, T. and P.W.S. Andrews (Eds.) (1951) *Oxford Studies in the Price Mechanism*, Oxford: Clarendon Press.

Part II

Cataclysm of global economy and future of capitalism

Political economy of
global interdependence

9 Dynamic comparative advantage and the new flying geese theory of capitalist development

Nobuharu Yokokawa

In this chapter I will examine the development of the capitalist world system after World War II, building a new framework of capitalist development.[1] The capitalist world system fell into a structural crisis in the 1970s. In the new capital accumulation regime the center of capital accumulation shifted to Asia. Asia's world share of the GDP including India was 60 percent in 1820. It fell to 15 percent in 1950 (Maddison 2007). It is now growing to 35 percent and may return to 60 percent by the latter half of this century at the expense of Europe and North America. In the first section I build a new flying geese theory incorporating dynamic comparative advantage theory and financial instability hypothesis with Akamatsu's flying geese theory within Kozo Uno's three-level analysis of the capitalist economy (Yokokawa 2001; 2012; 2013). Uno's three-level analysis is still a useful analytical framework. The first level comprises the basic principles. The next level develops a "stages theory of world capitalist development" which involved the concrete examination of the historical development of the leading industries, together with their main policies. At the third level of research, individual capitalist economies in their concrete historical situation are analyzed (Sekine 1975). In my framework, I call these three levels the basic theory, intermediate theory and historical analysis (Yokokawa 2001). I am especially interested in rebuilding intermediate theory which is a long-running institutionalist analysis. It can incorporate Marx's theory of forces of production (dynamic industries in this chapter) and relations of production (combinations of production and finance), theory of financial instability and theory of industrialization (flying geese theory). I argue that Akamatsu's flying geese theory is a proto-dynamic comparative advantage theory, and that Minsky's intermediate and open financial instability theory is indispensable to analyze capitalist development where finance plays crucial roles. In the second section, long waves and super long waves are examined using the new flying geese theory. In the third section, I follow the flying geese pattern of industrialization and re-emergence of Asia after World War II, and examine new dynamic industries comparing Japanese closed integral architecture and US open modular architecture. Then, in the fourth section, I answer the three questions: (1) why did a structural crisis occur in East Asia in the 1990s; (2) is an open modular architecture of global value chain (GVC) with core chipsets a new dynamic industry; and

(3) is the world financial crisis since 2007 a systemic crisis of the present capitalist world system?

A new flying geese theory

Theory of dynamic comparative advantage

Among theories of capitalist development, I am most interested in the works of the Other Canon. The Other Canon is critical of free trade and emphasizes the importance of dynamic industries and the role of government intervention for promoting industrialization. It is an older tradition than classical political economy and neo-classical economics. It started with mercantilists and Alexander Hamilton, and was developed by Karl Marx and Joseph Schumpeter. It has been rehabilitated by Ha-Joon Chang (2002), Carlota Perez (2003) and Erik Reinert (2007). I shall investigate Ricardo's comparative advantage theory, the most important theoretical foundation of free trade, and then build a dynamic theory of comparative advantage to support the argument of the Other Canon.

According to Ricardo's comparative advantage theory, specialization and international free trade are beneficial for two countries as long as there is a relative difference in the degree of productivity, even if one country's productivity is superior in all industries (Ricardo 1817). Ricardo's theory of comparative advantage was most useful for Britain in the mid-19th century. Exporting manufactured products and importing food and raw material allowed Britain to accumulate capital without demand and supply-side constraints, to prolong the period of extra profit, and then to enjoy the production of relative surplus value through both domestic productivity growth and better terms of international trade (Yokokawa 2013). It was not acceptable for catching-up countries which attempted to promote industries with high productivity growth potential and knew that their infant industries could not compete with British industries on a level playing field (Yokokawa 2013).

What is missing in Ricardo's theory is a concept of dynamic industries. In the history of capitalism, clusters of new technological innovations emerged several times. Following Reinert, I use the term "dynamic industries" to denote these revolutionary clusters of new technologies. Perez (2003) summarized evolution of dynamic industries as follows: (1) between the mid-18th and mid-19th centuries, mechanization of the cotton industry, wrought iron, the steam engine and railways; (2) between the 1860s and the 1910s, cheap steel, electrical machinery, the internal combustion engine, synthetic dyes and artificial fertilizers; (3) between the 1920s and the 1960s, mass-produced automobiles, cheap oil fuels, petrochemicals, air planes, electricity and home electrical appliances; (4) since the 1980s, information revolution, cheap microelectronics, computers, software, telecommunications, computer control instruments and new materials.

I built the theory of dynamic comparative advantage as a theoretical foundation of the Other Canon introducing the concept of value added per labour hour (VAL) (Yokokawa 2012; 2013). VAL is the amount of value added which is produced by one hour's labour. VAL is broken down to the number or volume of commodities and value added per unit of product.

VAL = the volume of product × value-added per product

In dynamic industries the volume of product increases with productivity growth. The value added per unit of product is large when a new product is exclusively supplied by a limited number of firms. When a new technology spreads, the price of a product becomes cheaper, and value added per product is reduced. As a result, dynamic industry's VAL increases with the increase in productivity and eventually decreases.

Dynamic comparative advantage depends on the difference between VAL and wages. Historically, real wages increased in proportion to average productivity growth. Then the dynamic comparative advantage of an industry does not last forever, because of the eventual decrease of VAL and increases in wages. If a country does not upgrade its industry when a dynamic comparative advantage is lost, its international status will be degraded.

It is difficult to obtain historical data of VAL of dynamic industries. Maddison's estimate of per capita real income is the best available data as an indicator of average VAL. Figure 9.1 shows that the center of dynamic industries shifted from The Netherlands (wool industry) to the UK (cotton industry), then to the USA (heavy and chemical industries, then mass-produced machinery), and

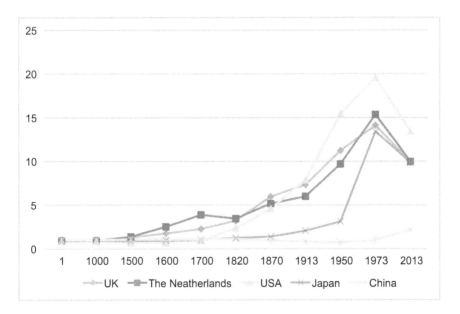

Figure 9.1 Per capita real income (India = 1)

Source: Maddison (2007) until 1998, then IMF *World Economic Outlook* (2014)

that industrialization increases diversion of VAL at first, and among advanced countries conversion of VAL is nearly completed.

In order to find the relation between per capita real income (y) and average VAL it is useful to break down growth of per capita income into three factors following Aoki (2011): (1) demographic factors such as increases of working-age population and labour participation rate; (2) structural change such as increasing employment in secondary and tertiary sectors reducing that in primary sector; and (3) increasing VAL in secondary and tertiary sectors.

$$y = \frac{\Upsilon}{N} = \left(\frac{E}{N}\right)\left[\left(\frac{E_A}{E}\right)\left(\frac{\Upsilon_A}{E_A}\right) + \left(\frac{E_I}{E}\right)\left(\frac{\Upsilon_I}{E_I}\right)\right] = \left(\frac{E}{N}\right)(1 - \alpha\beta)\left(\frac{\Upsilon_I}{E_I}\right)$$

where Υ = GDP, N = population, E = total employment, Υ_A = output in primary sector, Υ_I = output in secondary and tertiary sectors, E_A = employment in primary sector, E_I = employment in secondary and tertiary sectors; α is the employment share of the primary sector.

$$\alpha = \frac{E_A}{E}$$

β is the productivity differential between primary and other sectors.

$$\beta = 1 - \left(\frac{\Upsilon_A}{E_A}\right)\left(\frac{E_I}{\Upsilon_I}\right)$$

Let $(1 - \alpha\beta) = S$, which means impacts of structural effects. The rate of growth of GDP per capita is broken down as follows.

$$\Delta y = \Delta\left(\frac{E}{N}\right) + \Delta S + \Delta\left(\frac{\Upsilon_I}{E_I}\right)$$

Table 9.1 shows the following:

(1) Contributions by demographic factors $\left(\Delta\frac{E}{N}\right)$ such as increases of working-age population and labour participation rate are quite large in the beginning of industrialization. Once industrialization is completed this factor becomes smaller or even negative.

(2) Contribution by the structural change (ΔS) is quite large in the process of industrialization shifting employment from the primary sector to the more productive secondary and tertiary sectors. Once industrialization is completed it becomes minimal.

(3) The increase of VAL in the secondary and tertiary sectors $\left(\Delta\frac{\Upsilon_I}{E_I}\right)$ is the main source of growth once industrialization is completed. In the

Table 9.1 Contributions to per capita real income growth (percent)

	Japan			South Korea			China		
	$\left(\Delta\dfrac{E}{N}\right)$	ΔS	$\left(\Delta\dfrac{Y_I}{E_I}\right)$	$\left(\Delta\dfrac{E}{N}\right)$	ΔS	$\left(\Delta\dfrac{Y_I}{E_I}\right)$	$\left(\Delta\dfrac{E}{N}\right)$	ΔS	$\left(\Delta\dfrac{Y_I}{E_I}\right)$
1950s	1.43	2.34	2.54						
1960s	0.091	0.98	6.24				0.76	0.58	0.77
1970s	−0.41	0.62	3.59	2.22	2.29	3.29	0.28	1.65	0.28
1980s	0.23	0.40	3.18	1.60	2.27	4.74	1.44	3.47	3.21
1990s	0.10	0.28	0.53	0.51	0.11	4.86	0.03	1.07	8.39
2000s	−0.34	0.10	1.93	1.22	0.11	3.28	0.30	1.60	7.41

Source: derived from Aoki 2011; however, periodization is approximate.

catching-up period, it is exceptionally large because of the gains to be had from emulating the dynamic industries of the advanced countries. In more advanced countries, it depends on the creation of new dynamic industries and their development.

Financial instability

A new combination of production and finance is one of the most important prerequisites for the development of new dynamic industries. I will build an intermediate theory of financial instability in an open economy.

Minsky's financial instability hypothesis (i.e. the basic Minsky theory) explains monetary aspects of a cyclical crisis. Stable financial circumstances create conditions that produce instability (Minsky 1982). In prosperity, with an increase of profit flow, both borrowers' and lenders' expectations become progressively more optimistic. This unwittingly reduces the margin of safety (created by the cash inflow relative to the cash commitment). Financial arrangements change from hedge finance (revenues cover repayment of interest and loan principal), to speculative finance (revenues cover only interest), then to Ponzi finance (revenues are insufficient to cover interest). At the end of the boom, an external shock such as a tight monetary policy triggers a crisis.

In the financial instability theory it is important to distinguish saving from financing (Borio and Disyatat 2011). Saving is a national account concept which is defined as income not consumed. In a closed economy, saving is equal to investment by definition. Saving does not represent the availability of financing which is created by financial institutions by issuance of financial claims (for example credit or shares). Borio and Disyatat (2011) illustrate the differences between saving and financing in two ways. First, when income is all spent in consumption and saving and investment are zero (or in a simple social reproduction, in Marx's term), financing is positive (or simple social production may be realized by substantial borrowing and lending). Second, "the change in financial asset and liability in any given period bears no relationship to saving (and investment) in the national account sense . . . increase in assets and liability greatly exceed saving in any given period" (Borio and Disyatat 2011). In an open economy, the distinction between saving and financing is partly reflected in the concepts of net versus gross capital flows (Borio and Disyatat 2011). Net and gross capital flows are defined as follows:

> Net capital flows = Capital inflows by foreign agents – capital outflows by domestic agents
> Gross capital flows = Capital inflows by foreign agents + capital outflows by domestic agents

Current accounts show only net capital flows that arise from trade in real goods and services, and exclude changes in gross flows. An economy with a balanced current account can be engaged in large-scale foreign borrowing and lending (Borio and Disyatat 2011).

Little is known about Minsky's longer-term financial instability theory (i.e. the intermediate Minsky theory). Minsky argues that combinations of production and finance drive the evolution of the economy, and internal contradictions of these combinations make a previously robust financial system fragile and lead to eventual collapse. He distinguishes four stages of development of combinations of production and finance (Minsky 1992).

(1) "Commercial capitalism" in the British golden age in the 19th century is characterized as a "production-led economy". The role of a financial institution is limited to supplying transaction accounts and short-term credit (Minsky 1992, p. 108).
(2) "Finance capitalism" in the period of imperialism is characterized as a "finance-led economy". The financial system expanded to encompass longer-term capital credit, and investment bankers dominated financial markets. Bankers controlled industrial capital: "bankers were aware that cut-throat competition was hazardous to the health of their clients . . . They sought to protect the cash flows that the firm they financed generated by forming trusts, cartels and monopolies" (Minsky 1992, p. 109).
(3) "Managerial capitalism" in the golden age after World War II is characterized as a "production-led economy" (Minsky 1992, p. 110). Minsky gives three causes for the reestablishment of a production-led economy. First, government intervention in the market reduced the bankers' role (Minsky 1992, p. 110). Second, investment was mainly financed by an internal reserve (Minsky 1992, p.110). Third, management control was established which reduced the power of shareholders (Minsky 1992, p. 110).
(4) Money manager capitalism in the period of neoliberalism is characterized as a "finance-led economy". Minsky emphasized the parasitic character of the new finance-led economy: "unlike the earlier epoch of finance

capitalism, the emphasis was not upon the capitalist development of the economy but rather upon the quick turn of the speculator, upon trading profits" (Minsky 1992, p. 110).

Volatility of international capital flows

Historically net capital flows from surplus countries to deficit countries in the beginning of the robust international monetary system were eventually dwarfed by the increase of gross capital flows. Under the gold standard system, most international debts and credits were cancelled out in the bank clearing system in the City. The Bank of England was the de facto central bank of the capitalist world system. Volatility of international capital flows increased in the three stages. (1) In the latter half of the 19th century Britain had a large current account surplus and increased capital investment in such countries as the US and other British offshoots. (2) After World War I the US was the only structural surplus country and the continuation of international trade depended on the recycling of the US surplus. Britain, whose current account surplus decreased, attracted short-term capital by raising interest rates and invested it longer-term in British colonies. (3) In the latter half of the 1920s, gross capital flows involving current account deficit countries increased significantly so as to invest in the US stock market, the collapse of which became a cause of the great depression.

After World War II volatility of international capital flows increased in the three stages.

(1) After the experience of the Great Depression, the Bretton Woods system was designed to minimize the role of private financial institutions in the intermediation of international capital flows and exchange rates. In this system the global economy has anchors to prevent the overall expansion of gross capital flows from fuelling the unstable build-up of current account imbalances. Keynes proposed an International Clearing Union (ICU) as the international payment system (Keynes 1980). All international trade was to be carried out in bancor, which was supposed to have a given exchange rate with each national currency. Under this proposed system, exports add bancors to a country's account at the ICU, while imports subtract them. There is a built-in symmetric balance adjustment mechanism. If a nation exports more than it imports the ICU takes a percentage of that surplus and puts it into the ICU's reserve fund. If a nation imports more than its exports, the ICU members depreciate their currency against the bancor. However, the Bretton Woods system was realized following White's plan, where international currency was supplied by the key currency country and the adjustment mechanism of international imbalance was asymmetric. In this system trade and financial imbalance were tightly constrained within the limits given by existing reserves and potential IMF lending (Kregel 2004, p. 156). These factors eventually collapsed the Bretton Woods system. First, the long boom

of the 1950s and 1960s was much stronger in Japan and Europe than in the USA, which reduced US international competitiveness. In spite of the decline in its current account surplus, the USA did not decrease its capital exports and eventually undermined confidence in the US dollar (the Triffin dilemma). As a result, the US had to stop conversion in 1971. Second, deficit countries were required to restrain monetary and fiscal policies in order to reduce income and imports, while surplus countries were not required to increase their level of demand and imports. This asymmetry created diversion in productivity growth and inflation rates which undermined the fixed exchange rate system.

(2) The international monetary system that replaced the Bretton Wood system is characterized by large private capital flows. While increased private capital flows made larger imbalances possible, the global economy lost anchors to prevent excess capital flows. The traditional adjustment mechanism through exchange-rate adjustment stopped working. If deficit countries attempt to tighten monetary policy to reduce the level of activity, it may not be effective for the following reasons. First, their current account balance is mainly determined by the size of net borrowing and by interest rates, which are little affected by the level of income. Second, in a floating exchange rate system it may be met by flows of interest rate arbitrage funds, which increase capital inflows and cause the currency to appreciate even in the presence of deteriorating external balances. As a result, the only limit on external imbalance becomes the expectations of speculators. When deficit countries fail to ensure the lenders of their ability to borrow, international financial markets stop lending and capital reversal generates a financial crisis, which then imposes external adjustment (Kregel 2016).

Kregel (2004; 2016) applies Minsky's different types of repayment profiles to net capital flows. An economy with current account surplus is in a "hedge" finance position, a country with a current account deficit is in a "Ponzi" finance position, and a country with a more or less balanced position is in a speculative position. We distinguish four national economic growth strategies with capital flows.

(a) *Domestic demand-led hedge finance.* A surplus country may use domestic debt to finance domestic demand.

(b) *Export-led hedge finance.* A surplus country may use foreign lending to finance external demand.

(c) *Export-led speculative finance.* A deficit country may use foreign debt to build "real capital", which means using the foreign lending to invest in projects that ensure that the share of net exports in gross domestic product rises so that foreign exchange earnings eventually rise to the point at which they cover financing commitments created by the borrowing (Kregel 2004, p. 580).

(d) *International Ponzi finance.* As far as it can ensure the lenders of its ability to borrow, a deficit country may use foreign debt to finance domestic demand or to service foreign currency commitments.

In the longer run, deficit countries tended to fall into the international Ponzi position for the following reasons. First, in the case of sustained success in building up their real capital, both borrowers' and lenders' expectations become progressively more optimistic, which generates an international Ponzi position. Second, an international speculative finance country may not be able to build real capital to borrow in order to meet the rising current account deficits necessary. Third, external shocks may weaken the exchange rate and raise interest rate, which shifts the international speculative position to a Ponzi position. It was the international Ponzi finance that caused the Asian Crisis in 1997.

(3) After the Asian Crisis in 1997 net capital flows to the USA increased significantly. At the same time, gross capital flows increased far more than net capital flows. It was the volatility of gross capital flows that caused a boom and bust in the 2000s.

A new flying geese theory

Industrialization in East Asia has been studied in the framework of Akamatsu's flying geese theory (Akamatsu 1962), which is a proto-dynamic comparative advantage theory and the most original framework for the analysis of East Asian industrialization (Yokokawa 2013). Akamatsu's flying geese theory examines capitalist development from the point of view of developing countries. The first thesis of the flying geese theory starts from the second stage of Vernon's product cycle theory (Vernon 1966): (1) a new product is imported from advanced countries; (2) "previously imported goods" are domestically produced; (3) "the domestic industry develops into the export industry"; (4) with the increase in wages and falling prices of the product due to international competition, the dynamic comparative advantage is reduced, and production declines. The second thesis is "development from crude goods to elaborate goods" (Vernon 1966), i.e. the shift to more sophisticated products or industries when they lose existing dynamic comparative advantages. The third thesis is the "development of advanced and less-advanced countries in a wild-geese-flying pattern".

The theory of dynamic comparative advantage complements Akamatsu's flying geese theory, and creates a new flying geese theory.

First, it examines capitalist development from the point of view of the most advanced country, as in the case of Vernon's product cycle theory: (1) A dynamic industry is first developed in advanced countries. Demand for its products develops in advanced countries. (2) As the dynamic industry develops in advanced countries VAL increases. Production expands to achieve economies of scale, and exports begin. (3) With the further spread of production the VAL falls. Decreasing dynamic comparative advantage forces reductions in domestic production, and production moves to less-developed countries with lower wages. (4) Finally, the foreign-produced commodity is imported.

Second, the new theory enables one to analyze national economic growth strategies with capital flows. Advanced countries may use domestic demand–led hedge finance strategy in the first and second stages and export-led hedge finance strategy in the third stage, while catching-up countries may use export-led speculative finance strategy in the third and fourth stages.

Third, in its original form, the flying geese theory does not cover uneven development. According to Akamatsu, the flying geese pattern of development is on the one hand a catching-up process, where differences in productivity are reduced by conversion, and on the other hand a diversion process, where advanced countries try to improve productivity further by upgrading their dynamic industries. In the new flying geese theory, changes in the leaders of dynamic industries, such as the USA and Germany taking the lead from Britain at the end of the 19th century, are explained by the uneven development and the strategies adopted by the countries when they face structural crises in a capital accumulation regime (Yokokawa 2012).

Fourth, in its original form, the flying geese theory is mainly applied to industrialization in East Asia in the post–World War II period. Our theory is applicable to both linear (catching-up) and nonlinear (uneven) industrialization in any countries including advanced, catching-up and developing countries and in any capitalist world systems.

Stages of development in capitalist economy

Dynamic industries and long waves

Long waves (Perez 2003) may be better explained using the new flying geese theory as follows. Figure 9.2 shows that maturity of the old dynamic industry and the big-bang and bubble of the new dynamic industry overlap, and that the structural crisis of the old capital accumulation regime is creative destruction from the viewpoint of a new dynamic industry at the turning point.

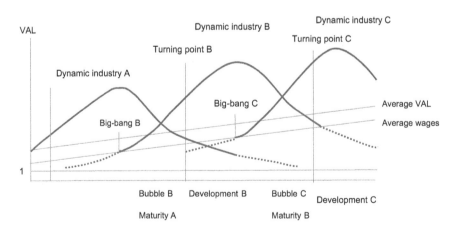

Figure 9.2 VAL of dynamic industries (Developing country's average VAL = 1)

(1) Big-bang: When a new dynamic industry B takes off (Big-bang B), as VAL grows faster than wages, its dynamic comparative advantage and profits increase. Then investment concentrates in this new industry, and often speculation causes bubble and bust (creative destruction B = structural crisis A).

(2) Turning point: In the structural depression (turning point B) new financial and other institutions are created to accommodate the new dynamic industries B.

(3) Development and Cyclical Crises: In a production-led economy, the new technology becomes an engine of economic growth and creates a new production-led capital accumulation regime. Production expands to achieve economies of scale, and exports begin.

When capital accumulation increases in the dynamic industry, capital accumulation in other sectors also increases. With the progress of prosperity, some types of labour in the dynamic industries become scarce, and wages rise. This reduces the rate of profits and eventually causes a cyclical crisis which spreads to other sectors. In dynamic industries, productivity continuously increases by means of a new method of production, which is introduced by replacing old fixed capital with new and more productive fixed capital in a depression. It increases VAL and the dynamic comparative advantage in the dynamic industry. Then the accumulation of capital recommences under sound conditions of exploitation, starting a new business cycle.

(4) Maturity: Through business cycles the expansion of dynamic industries at first increases their VAL, since the growth rate of productivity is larger than the decrease rate of the prices of their products. With diffusion of technology, competition between firms increases, and the reduction of the prices of their products eventually decrease their VAL. On the other hand, reduction of their prices revitalizes mature industries, either through lower input prices or through production of relative surplus value with cheaper wage goods. While VAL in the dynamic industries decreases, average VAL increases, and economic growth continues. When the available labour of the industrial reserve army is eventually absorbed with economic growth, wages in lagging sectors have to be increased in order to secure workers. A large increase in wages in the dynamic sectors spills over into the lagging sectors, and those higher wages are mostly passed on to consumers in the form of higher prices. Unlike wage increases in dynamic sectors, higher prices are not compensated for by productivity growth.

(5) Structural Crisis: When average wages eventually become higher than the average VAL, production in many industries cannot continue, which causes serious structural crises of the accumulation regime B.

(6) Turning point: If a new dynamic industry C has been created and new financial and other institutions are created to accommodate the new dynamic industry C in the following structural depression (turning point C), a new long wave starts.

Historically, finance-led economies were created after the structural crises of production-led economies, whereas dynamic industries did not develop fully due to a lack of effective demand. Under-consumption often became a cause of cyclical crises. In the longer run, financial deepening became an engine of profit growth and the structural crises took a form of a systemic crisis of the financial system.

Systemic crises of capitalist world systems and super long waves

The systemic crisis of a capitalist world system, such as the Great Depression in the 1930s, is the most serious crisis that abolishes not only the present capital accumulation regime but also the current capitalist world system. The first capitalist world system, market capitalism, was established when Britain created a production-led economy in the early 19th century, with cotton and railway industries as the dynamic industries. The dynamic comparative advantages of British cotton and railway industries were fully developed in this capital accumulation regime with foreign demand as the engine of demand growth. This created the first golden age of capitalism. After the structural crisis in the late 19th century, the locus of dynamism shifted to heavy and chemical industries, and the centers of economic growth shifted from the UK to the US and Germany (diversification). A new capital accumulation regime, imperialism, was created with two challengers and one old hegemon. It was a finance-led economy, and the structural crisis in the US took the form of a systemic crisis of finance. It developed into a systemic crisis of market capitalism in the 1930s.

The periods of diversification and systemic crisis of market capitalism overlapped with the formation period of a new capitalist world system. After World War II, bureaucratic capitalism was established when the US created a production-led economy with the mass production system of machinery industries as the dynamic industry. The dynamic comparative advantage of the mass production system was fully developed in this capital accumulation regime, with wages as the engine of demand growth. This created the second golden age of capitalism. After the structural crisis in the 1970s, a new finance-led accumulation regime,

Table 9.2 Capitalist world systems and super long waves

Capitalist World System (Hegemon)	Formation	Establishment (Golden age)	Diversification (Globalization)	Systemic Crisis
Market Capitalism (England)	Mercantilism (1750s–1810s)	Liberalism (1820s–1870s)	Imperialism (1870s–1910s,)	Interregnum (1920s–1940s)
Bureaucratic capitalism (the USA)	Imperialism to interregnum (1870s–1940s)	Welfare state (1950s–1970s)	Neoliberalism (1980s–)	

neoliberalism, was created, and the centers of economic growth shifted from the US and Europe to Asia (diversification). The question to be asked is whether the same process will be repeated and the world financial crisis since 2007 will develop into the systemic crisis of bureaucratic capitalism.

Dynamic industries and flying geese pattern of industrialization

Development and maturity of mass production system

After World War II bureaucratic capitalism successfully established the mutually reinforcing mechanism between productivity growth and domestic economic growth with strong support from the state and international institutions, resulting in the long-lasting high-rate capital accumulation of the 1950s–1960s (Yokokawa 2012). In the US, the locus of dynamism shifted from heavy and chemical industries to machine and electrical industries in the 1920s and 1930s. The US mass production system in machine and electrical industries known as "Fordism" was established in the early 1950s and introduced into Europe in the 1950s and 1960s. Japan shifted its dynamic industry from textile to heavy and chemical industries in the 1950s and the 1960s. The upgrading of Japanese industries left room for less-developed East Asian countries to industrialize in the flying geese pattern. Asian NIEs started industrialization with labour intensive industries.

The long-lasting high-rate capital accumulation itself made further accumulation difficult in the 1970s. It eventually reduced productivity growth in dynamic industries. First, Fordism reached the saturation stage in many advanced countries by the early 1970s. In Europe the scope for catching up with the US had declined. Second, part of the productivity slowdown stemmed from a slower output growth in industries characterized by economies of scale. Third, the relative backwardness of productivity growth in the service sector forced de-industrialization (Rowthorn and Wells 1987). Productivity growth in the service sector was difficult with the available technology. On the other hand, the diffusion of technology increased competition both domestically and internationally and reduced the price of products and value added. As a result, VAL was reduced. Long-lasting capital accumulation eventually exhausted the available industrial reserve army in advanced countries. With the over-accumulation of capital relative to available labour, labour unions became militant, and wage bargaining changed from Keynesian with sticky money wages to Marxist with sticky real wages. Large wage increases in the dynamic sectors spilled over into the lagging sectors and were mostly passed on to consumers in the form of higher prices, which further increased wages under Marxist wage bargaining with sticky real wages. Increases in wages under a declining VAL reduced the dynamic comparative advantage.

When demand for higher real wages surpassed limping VAL growth, wage pressure contributed to a squeeze on profitability. The USA and Europe suffered from a structural crisis of the mass production system. Japan lost dynamic comparative advantage in the heavy and chemical industries in the 1970s and shifted its dynamic industries successfully to mass production methods in machinery industries, such as automobiles and electrical machinery, from the mid-1970s onwards. The upgrading of Japanese industries left room for Asian NIEs to promote heavy and chemical industries and other more sophisticated industries with export-led international speculative finance strategy.

Industrialization of Asia under neoliberal accumulation regime

After the structural crisis of the 1970s the Anglo-American neoliberal accumulation regime reshaped the capitalist world system. In this finance-led economy, the US promoted globalization by increasing foreign direct investment through global value chain (GVC). The US monetary authority kept a strong dollar policy to encourage capital inflow as Britain did in the 1920s. Developing countries in East Asia happily accepted the US model of globalization with a strong dollar policy, since it allowed them to pursue export-led industrialization policies, and successfully built real capital. The center of economic growth shifted from the US and Europe to East Asia in the 1980s.

Japan and NIES's export-led growth strategies were hugely successful in the first half of the 1980s. The total current account surpluses of Japan, Korea and Taiwan were more than 50 percent of the world's combined surplus. After the Plaza Accord of 1985, these countries' currencies appreciated rapidly. A current account balance surplus reversal[2] triggered structural changes of their accumulation regimes. First, they increased foreign direct investment initially to ASEAN4 (i.e. Indonesia, Malaysia, Philippines and Thailand) and then to China to reallocate lower value-added open area. Second, they changed their export-led growth strategy to a domestic demand-led growth strategy. Korea and Taiwan established the link between wages and productivity growth to make wages the engine of demand growth, while Japan adopted neoliberal financial relaxation to increase domestic demand. Third, in this period, Japan built a Pacific Rim triangle trade regime, whereby Japan exported capital goods to the ASEAN and China, and the ASEAN and China exported completed products to the US.

New dynamic industries: standardization and platform business

When Japan shifted its dynamic industry to the automobile industry in the 1970s, the industry had already reached maturity in the USA and Europe. The Japanese car industry improved productivity by introducing the flexible production system. The system include institutionalized incentives to develop contextual skills; systems of centralized personnel administration; subcontracting systems through which diverse components are efficiently supplied (just-in-time system) and through which subcontractors work closely with prime contracting firms in product development. This method is now called closed integral architecture. Fujimoto (2014) defines it as follows. "Each component is functionally incomplete and interdependent with other components functionally and/or structurally. Designs of the components tend to be specific to each variation of the total system. For each product, components have to be optimized with the other component designs by mutual adjustment". This method was very effective, and quality and productivity in automobile and other electronic machinery industries improved significantly.

In the 1980s, facing declining international competitiveness, the US encouraged joint R and D based on consortia of firms to develop an industry-wide consensus standard (Tatsumoto, Ogawa and Shintaku 2010). In consensus standardization, multiple firms agreed on a set of industry-wide standards in a cooperative manner.[3] It changed the distribution of VAL. In the standardized open area, implicit knowledge and know-how were revealed and became explicit (Tatsumoto, Ogawa and Shintaku 2010). This enabled new companies to compete with existing companies under the same conditions in the standardized open area, where fierce price competition reduced VAL. By contrast, in the protected closed area that required high technology, existing companies could enjoy high VAL. This change in the distribution of VAL led to a drastic change in the division of international labour. Firms in emerging countries welcomed an open area with detailed standardization as a good opportunity for industrialization. Fujimoto (2014) defines their production architecture as open modular architecture: "*Open architecture* is a type of modular architecture, in which 'mix and match' of component designs is technically and commercially feasible not only within a firm but also across firms." Firms in advanced countries specialized in closed-area differentiating products by technological accumulation and implicit knowledge.

In the US, the platform business in the closed area has been most successful. The platform is composed of a core component and other peripheries with standardized interfaces. In the 1990s, US platform leaders successfully implemented their core technology into chipsets. For example, Intel integrated peripheral circuits on the CPU as a chipset to form a platform, and then supplied this platform to companies in the emerging world. It increased Intel's VAL and enabled assembly makers in developing countries to produce quality products easier and in a more competitive way. Design and production makers in advanced countries are losing competitiveness to the combination of platform leaders and assembly makers in developing countries. For example design and production makers in personal computer such as IBM, Compaq and Hewlett-Packard are losing competitiveness to the combination of Intel and assembly makers in developing countries (such as Quanta, Compal, Inventec and other Chinese makers); in LCD TV, Sharp, Panasonic and Sony are losing their competitiveness to the combinations of chipset makers (Genesis Microchip, Pixelworks and Philips) and assembly makers in Korea, Taiwan and China; and in mobile phones, Nokia is losing its competitiveness to the combinations of chipset makers (Texas Instruments, Infineon Technologies and MediaTek) and assembly makers in Korea, Taiwan and China (Suehiro 2014). It is the open modular architecture with core chipsets that has become a new dynamic industry.

Three questions

Belated structural crises in Asia in the 1990s

There are two reasons why a structural crisis occurred in Japan in the 1990s. First, Japanese closed integral architecture was a modification of mass production system and did not become the next dynamic industry, and eventually lost competitiveness to open modular architecture. Second, Japan was unsuccessful in switching from an export-led growth strategy to a domestic demand-led growth strategy. Japan adopted financial liberalization which was based on Ponzi finance, since demand growth is based on the expectation of asset price increase. Increasing income from capital gains and the availability of many kinds of loans increased consumption then investment. Minsky's financial instability process then started: increased profit flows made both borrowers' and lenders' expectations progressively more optimistic, and accelerated Ponzi finance. When the monetary authority tightened credit, the boom collapsed. Both investment and consumption had been heavily dependent on credit, which caused severe debt deflation.

In the 1990s, neoliberal world organizations forced Asian countries to follow free trade and capital liberalization policies, which became a cause of the Asian crisis. First, on the one hand, free trade made it difficult for newly developing ASEAN countries to use foreign debt to build real capital, since it does not allow domestic producers the time to upgrade industrial structures and improve productivity to compete with international producers (including China, which fully used the industrial, technological and trade policies), turning their international financial position to Ponzi finance. On the other hand, sustained expansions in more advanced Asian countries in the first half of the 1990s eroded safety cushions, turning their international financial position to Ponzi finance. Second, capital liberalisation had disabled the role of a central bank as the lender of last resort in the 1990s, when the amount of official foreign reserves was dwarfed by private gross capital flows. The historical process of financial crisis in Asia is summarized as follows. Gross capital flows increased significantly after the mid-1990s when the reversal of the trend appreciation of the Yen, along with historically low Japanese interest rates, created an incentive for substantial short-term flows from the Japanese financial market to Asia. International banks and other international investors could borrow short-term funds in Japan and lend them to Asian banks and firms for a substantial interest rate differential. Firms and banks in Asian countries took on huge levels of foreign debt. Under these circumstances hedge funds attacked the Thai baht. Failure of the Thai government to defend the baht against international speculators reversed capital flows and triggered a financial crisis in May 1997. A sharp rise in international interest rates accompanied by a sharp appreciation of the currency in which Asian countries borrowed abroad quickly converted international speculative positions into international Ponzi positions in many Asian Countries, and the crisis spread. It was IBM's conditionality to produce current account surpluses to meet the debt service that created conditions for full-scale debt deflation.

A new dynamic industry and China's compressed industrialization

Various pieces of evidence show that US productivity and VAL are recovering. First, US VAL increased significantly after the mid-1990s. Glyn (2006, p. 79) wrote: "Manufacturing industry in Europe and Japan . . . got within striking distance (80–90 per cent) of US productivity by the mid-1990s, then sank back to around 65–75 per cent of the US level". Second, the net earnings of US companies operating aboard increased. Kregel (2008, p. 177) wrote, "The Bureau of Economic Analysis provides a measure of the US trade account that takes the net earnings of US companies operating abroad into account. On this basis, the US deficit on goods and services for 2005 was $134.4 billion less than the $716.7 billion deficit recorded in the conventional international accounts framework." Third, "the income account has remained positive for the United States despite gross liability exceeding assets by approximately 34 percent in 2004" (Gourinchas and Rey 2007, p. 18). This evidence may be explained by the creation of new dynamic industries and new combinations of production and finance. First, in the 1990s, US platform leaders successfully implemented their core technology into chipsets. Second, the net earnings of US companies operating abroad may reflect the export of a new technology (Kregel 2008). Third, the United States created a new combination of production and finance. The US shifted its role from the "Banker of the World" to the "Venture Capitalist of the World", issuing short-term liabilities and investing in equity and direct investment abroad (Gourinchas and Rey 2007, p. 19). In this new combination of production and finance, the US international financial position is not a Ponzi position but a speculative position creating real capital by FDI and equity investment.

Chinese industrialization until the mid-1990s was based on cheap labour. Chinese wages were kept at 5 percent of US levels by a devaluation of the yuan until then (Yokokawa 2013). When its market exchange rate and real effective exchange rate were stabilized in the mid-1990s, Chinese quasi Lewis-type industrialization reached its limits (Yokokawa 2013). Its rapid wage rise was reflected in its dynamic comparative advantage in light industries such as textiles, toys and electrical appliances which peaked in the late 1990s. Then open modular architecture with core chipsets enabled China's compressed industrialization. Chinese dynamic comparative advantage in machinery such as electrical and general machinery increased rapidly from the mid-1990s onwards. In this new architecture, investment can help them catch up more quickly, and research and development may enable late-comers to leapfrog industry leaders. Japanese influence in Asia peaked in the mid-1990s, and the Japan-led Pacific Rim triangle trade regime in the 1990s has been replaced by a China-centric Asian production network in the 2000s (Yokokawa 2013). Now

China imports capital goods from Japan, Korea and Taiwan and food and raw material from less developed countries, and exports completed products to the EU, US, Asia and other areas. On the other hand, Chinese colonial-type trade and capital exports to less developed countries resulted in their premature de-industrialization (Rowthorn 2016).

In short, US productivity and VAL are recovering by the creation of new dynamic industries and new combinations of production and finance since the mid-1990s. US platform leaders successfully implemented their core technology into chipsets and created combinations of US platform leaders and assembly makers in developing countries with open modular architecture. The US financial role shifted from the "Banker of the World" to the "Venture Capitalist of the World". It made production of quality products easier, assembly makers in developing countries more competitive, and China's compressed industrialization possible.

The world financial crisis

There are two commonly accepted theories about the world financial crisis since 2008. I disagree with these theories.

First, at the international level theory of global imbalances argues that the Savings Glut in Asia caused the world financial crisis. There are three reasons to deny the global imbalance theory. (1) Gross capital flows were far more volatile than net capital flows. Gross capital flows increased significantly before the collapse of the IT bubble and the subprime loan bubble, and they were reduced significantly after both crises, while the changes in the net capital flows between Asia and the USA were modest (Borio and Disyatat 2011, p. 14). (2) Gross flows between the USA and Europe are four times bigger than that between the USA and East Asia.[4] European banks' branches and subsidiaries raise wholesale funding in the United States through money market funds. European banks then purchased private label mortgage-backed securities and structured products (Shin 2012). European banks earned fees by this intermediation while American banks shifted the financial risk to European banks. (3) Global imbalances increased Asian savings, rather than Asian savings creating global imbalances. Unusually low policy rates in advanced economies after the collapse of the IT bubble encouraged capital flows to developing Asian countries. Asian countries resisted unwanted upward pressure on their exchange rate by accumulating foreign exchange reserves (Borio and Disyatat 2011). In conclusion, it was the volatility of gross capital flows that caused the boom and bust in the 2000s.

Second, at the domestic level Paul McCulley (2009) and others characterized the world financial crisis as a "Minsky moment". I disagree with this characterization, since the subprime mortgages instruments were created from the beginning as fragile financial instruments based on a Ponzi scheme. Securitization shifted the robust structure of domestic finance into the Ponzi structure and became a cause of a systemic crisis of the finance system.

In the world financial crisis, not only the floating dollar standard system but also the Euro has shown their limits as international monetary systems. The Euro-Crisis may be analyzed by our framework as follows. There are two contradictions in the Euro. First, northern European countries have been successful in upgrading dynamic industries and took an export-led international hedge finance position, while southern European countries such as Greece have been unsuccessful in upgrading their dynamic industries. A currency union is an extreme case of free trade and capital market liberalization. It made it difficult for southern European countries to use foreign debt to build real capital, since it does not allow domestic producers the time to improve productivity to compete with northern Europeans. Second, there was no built-in symmetric adjustment mechanism for current account imbalance. Once crisis started, the asymmetrical adjustment process forced southern European countries to adopt an austerity policy to service debt, which deepened crisis into full-scale debt deflation.

The present world financial crisis has not developed into the systemic crisis of bureaucratic capitalism for two reasons. First, it was not the US but the EU that took an international Ponzi position. It was European financial institutions that mainly suffered from the US subprime loan crisis. Second, in the US, domestic financial fragility was damped by Big Government and a Big Bank, which prevented a systemic crisis of finance to develop into debt deflation. Third, current account surplus reversal, especially in China, was successful. China has changed policies from export-led international hedge finance to domestic demand-led international hedge finance.

In short the world financial crisis is a creative destruction of the neoliberal capital accumulation regime. The new platform business with core chipsets increased US profits. Gross capital flow increased investment in the US and caused the bubble and bust. If a new combination of production and finance that accommodate new dynamic industries is created, a new long wave may restart.

Conclusion: can we recreate a stable combination of production and finance?

In this chapter I examined the development of the capitalist world system after World War II, incorporating concepts of dynamic comparative advantage and financial instability hypothesis with Akamatsu's flying geese theory. Then I answered the three questions and concluded that if a new combination of production and finance that accommodate open modular architecture of the GVC with core chipsets is created, a new long wave may restart. It depends on the following conditions. At the international level, there are three requirements for the new international financial system. First, the exchange rate is a useful policy tool for less developed countries to upgrade their industrial structure, and to insulate domestic monetary conditions from those prevailing elsewhere. Second, a built-in symmetric adjustment mechanism is needed for stable economic growth. Third, export-led international speculative finance is a useful strategy for developing countries to create real capital. From the first and second points of view, Keynes's International Clearing Union (ICU) may be introduced as the international payment system. From the third point of view the ICU, which focuses only on trade balances, is not realistic. It is better for the ICU than the USA to play the role of the venture capitalist of the world, recirculating surplus countries' funds so as to allow deficit countries to build real capital. Then the ICU becomes the full-fledged world central bank. At the domestic level, securitization must be reformed from the point of view of the socialization of risk. A domestic policy framework should be expanded to control the build-up of financial fragility and to prevent speculative finance from developing into Ponzi finance.

Notes

1 I am grateful to Bob Rowthorn, Gary Dymski, Jayati Ghosh, Jan Kregel, Makoto Itoh, Yoshinori Shiozawa, Hiroyasu Uemura and members of JSPE for discussion and comments.
2 "A surplus reversal is a sustained and significant decline (2 percentage points of GDP or more) in the current account balance from a period of large and persistent surpluses" (IMF, WEO 2010, p.111).
3 Consensus standards are quite different from de facto standards. With de facto standards, a winner of a standard war takes significant profits and others face significant losses (Tatsumoto, Ogawa and Shintaku 2010).
4 Gross flows between the USA and Europe were $1960 billion and that between the USA and East Asia (China and Japan) were $461 billion before the crisis (BEA).

References

Akamatsu, K. (1962) "A Historical Pattern of Economic Growth in Developing Countries", *The Developing Economies*, Institute of Asian Economic Affairs, Preliminary Issue No.1, pp. 3–25.

Aoki, M. (2011) "The Five-Phases of Economic Development and Institutional Evolution in China and Japan", *ADBI Working Paper 340*, Tokyo: Asian Development Bank Institute. www.adbi.org/working-paper/2011/12/30/4836.five.phases.economic.dev.evolution.prc.japan/.

Borio, Claudio and Disyatat, Piti (2011) "Global Imbalances and the Financial Crisis: Link or no Link?", *BIS Working Papers, No 346*, Basel: Bank for International Settlements.

Chang, Ha-Joon (2002) *Kicking Away the Ladder – Development Strategy in Historical Perspective*, London: Anthem Press.

Glyn, Andrew (2006) *Capitalism Unleashed*, Oxford: Oxford University Press.

Gourinchas, Pierre-Olivier and Rey, Hélène (2007) "From World Banker to World Venture Capitalist: U.S. External Adjustment and the Exorbitant Privilege", National Bureau of Economic Research http://www.nber.org/chapters/c0121

Fujimoto, Takahiro (2014) "Architecture, Capability, and Competitiveness of Firms and Industries", National Bureau of Economic Research http://www.nber.org/chapters/c0121

IMF (2014) *World Economic Outlook* April 2014 http://www.imf.org/external/pubs/ft/weo/2014/01/weodata/download.aspx

Keynes, John Maynard (1980) *The Collected Writings of John Maynard Keynes, Activities 1940–44 Shaping the Post-war World the Clearing Union*, Vol. XXV, London: Macmillan for the Royal Economic Society.

Kregel, Jan A. (2004) "Can We Create a Stable International Financial Environment that Ensures Net Resource Transfers to Developing Countries?", *Journal of Post Keynesian Economics*, Vol. 26, No. 4, pp. 573–590.

Kregel, Jan A. (2008) "Using Minsky's Cushion of Safety to Analyze the Crisis in the U.S. Subprime Mortgage Market", in *International Journal of Political Economy*, Vol. 37. No. 1, pp. 3–23.

Kregel, Jan A. (2016) "Minsky's financial instability analysis: Financial Flows and International Imbalances" in this volume.

Maddison, Angus (2007) *The World Economy: A Millennial Perspective/ Historical Statistics*, Paris: OECD Publishing.

McCulley, Paul (2009) "The Shadow Banking System and Hyman Minsky's Economic Journey" http://www.cfapubs.org/doi/pdf/10.2470/rf.v2009.n5.15

Minsky, H. P. (1982) *Can It Happen Again?*, New York: M. E. Sharpe.

Minsky, H. P. (1992) "Chapter 7: Schumpeter and Finance," in Biasco, S., Roncaglia, A. and Salvati, M. (eds.), *Market and Institutions in Economic Development: Essays in Honor of Paulo Sylos Labini*, London, England, New York, NY: MacMillan, 1992, pp. 103–115.

Perez, Carlota (2003) *Technological Revolutions and Financial Capital: The Dynamics of Bubbles and Golden Ages,* Cheltenham: Edward Elgar.

Reinert, Erik (2007) *How Rich Countries Got Rich . . . and Why Poor Countries Stay Poor*, London: Constable.

Ricardo, David (1817) *Principles of Political Economy*, in *The Works and Correspondence* I. Cambridge: Cambridge University Press, 1951.

Rowthorn, Robert E. (2016) "The Emergence of China and India as Great Powers", in this volume.

Rowthorn, R. E. and Wells, J. R. (1987) *De-industrialization and Foreign Trade*, Cambridge: Cambridge University Press.

Sekine, Thomas T. (1975) "Uno-Riron: A Japanese Contribution to Marxian Political Economy", *Journal of Economic Literature*, Vol. 8, pp. 847–877.

Shin, Hyun Song (2012) "Global Banking Glut and Loan Risk Premium", *IMF Economic Review* Vol. 60, No. 2, pp. 155–192.

Suehiro, Akira (2014) *Shinko Ajia Keizairon* (in Japanese), Tokyo: Iwanami.

Tatsumoto, Hirofumi, Ogawa, Koichi, and Shintaku, Junjiro (2010) "Standardization, International Division of Labor and Platform Business", *Tokyo University MMRC DISCUSSION PAPER SERIES*.

Vernon, Raymond (1966) "International Investment and International Trade in the Product Cycle", *Quarterly Journal of Economics,* Vol. 80, May, pp. 190–207.

Yokokawa, Nobuharu (2001) "From Bureaucratic Capitalism to Transnational Capitalism: An Intermediate Theory", in Hodgson, G., Itoh, M. and Yokokawa, N. (eds.), *Capitalism in Evolution: Global Contentions-East and West*, Cheltenham: Edward Elgar.

Yokokawa, Nobuharu (2012) "Cyclical Crisis, Structural Crisis, Systemic Crisis, and Future of Capitalism" in Kiichiro Yagi, Nobuharu Yokokawa, Hagiwara Shinjiro, and Gary Dymski (eds.), *Crises of Global Economies and the Future of Capitalism: Reviving Marxian Crisis Theory*, London: Routledge.

Yokokawa, Nobuharu (2013) "The Renaissance of Asia and the Emerging World System" in Nobuharu Yokokawa, Jayati Ghosh, and Bob Rowthorn (eds.), *Industrialization of China and India: Their Impacts on the World Economy: Their Impacts on the World Economy*, London: Routledge.

10 The emergence of China and India as great powers

Robert Rowthorn

Introduction

The OECD projects that China will soon have the largest GDP in the world and that India will overtake the United States shortly after mid-century. On the assumption that these projections are accurate, this chapter explores their long-term implications for international trade and investment. The chapter goes on to consider the impact of China and India on the economies of sub-Saharan Africa. This is followed by a discussion of the changing balance of power in the world. This includes a discussion of the military balance. The chapter concludes with a brief summary.

Take-off

China's modern economic growth has been remarkable. Growth has been widely spread across the country and not merely concentrated on the coastal region where most export industries are located. As a recent World Bank report noted, if mainland China's 31 provinces were regarded as independent economies, they would be among the 32 fastest-growing economies in the world (World Bank 2013, p. 5). China has grown somewhat faster than South Korea and Taiwan at a similar stage of development, but its trajectory has been broadly similar with a lag of about 25–30 years. Indian economic growth was also impressive during the first decade of this century, although its performance has recently deteriorated and its per capita income is still well below that of China. The causes and exact timing of the Indian acceleration are disputed.[1]

Future growth

Forecasting economic growth is always hazardous. It was widely thought in the 1980s that Japan was poised to overtake the USA in terms of per capita income. This did not happen. On the contrary, Japanese growth faltered and the country entered a long period of near stagnation. The Soviet Union provides a more dramatic example. With its impressive postwar expansion and its achievements in areas such as space technology, the Soviet Union was regarded by many as a formidable rival to the West. Its implosion during the Gorbachev era and subsequent economic woes took most of the world by surprise. These examples are a warning against uncritical acceptance of current optimistic projections regarding economic growth in China and India.

The OECD has recently produced annual projections of GDP for China, India and certain other countries up to 2060 (OECD 2014). The Chinese annual growth rate is projected to decline from 9.3 per cent in 2011 to 1.5 per cent by 2060 (Figure 10.1). Following a recovery from its present difficulties, the Indian economy is also projected to experience falling growth rates, although the pace of decline is slower than for China. This is partly because India is currently poorer than China and has more scope for catching up. It is also because the working-age population of India is projected to grow whilst that of China is projected to fall. The UN projects that by 2060 India will have 50 per cent more people in the age group 20–69 than China (UN 2013).

The OECD projections assume that both China and India will be politically stable. They also assume that both countries will overcome their various macroeconomic and structural difficulties. This is by no means certain.

The projected growth rates have dramatic consequences. China soon overtakes the USA to become the largest economy in the world with a peak share equal to 25 per cent of world GDP in 2043 (Figure 10.2). India is initially well behind China and, despite its higher growth rate, fails to close the gap completely by the end of the projection period. Even so, in terms of total GDP it easily outstrips the Euro-area and just overtakes the USA by 2060. Assuming these projections are correct and can be extrapolated beyond 2060, they imply that around 2080, India, with its larger working-age population, will overtake China to become the biggest economy in the world.

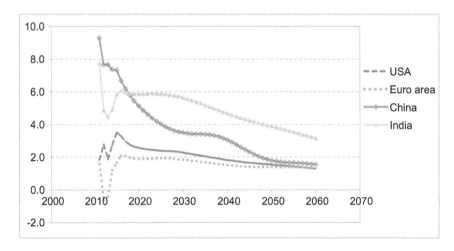

Figure 10.1 Projected growth rates of GDP per cent per annum

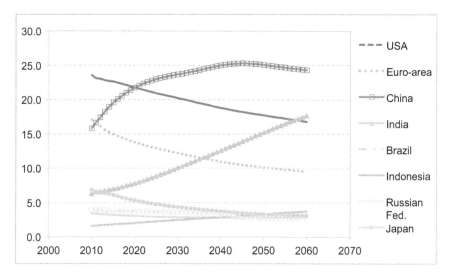

Figure 10.2 Shares of world GDP at 2005 PPP per cent

It is interesting how small the projected shares of Japan, Indonesia and the two BRIC countries, Brazil and Russia, are. By 2060, projected Indian GDP is considerably larger than the GDP of these four countries put together. Chinese GDP is even larger. For all the talk of Brazil and Indonesia as emerging giants, they will be relatively small on a world scale. The major players will be China, India, the USA and the Euro-area.

International trade

It is now a commonplace that as China develops it will move up the value-chain into more "knowledge-intensive" activities. Exports of labor-intensive goods such as clothing are still rising, and many of China's more sophisticated exports, such as consumer electronics, still have a significant local labor-intensive content. But wages are increasing rapidly and such labor-intensive activities will be phased out as China loses the ability to compete with cheaper foreign producers. South Korea and Taiwan reached this turning point in the late 1980s, and both of them eventually became net importers of clothing and the like. Given that China is following a similar trajectory to these countries with a lag of about 25–30 years, this would suggest that labor-intensive exports from China are approaching a peak. Their share of Chinese exports is already falling but it may not be long before they start to fall in absolute terms.

As China moves up the value-chain, this will create space for other countries to take over the abandoned activities. Some will be established exporters, such as Bangladesh, Indonesia or Viet Nam, whose exports of clothing, for example, have been rising strongly in recent years. India is also a contender. Despite recent growth, India's labor-intensive exports are still small in relation to the size of its economy, and there are huge reserves of underemployed labor that could be used to produce cheap labor-intensive manufactures. Africa is also a possibility. Wages are now comparatively low in some sub-Saharan countries, and if other conditions could be sorted out, these countries would be attractive locations for labor-intensive manufacturing. This issue is discussed below.

The growth of China, and also India, has created a hunger for commodities, especially oil and minerals. This is partly why most commodity prices are currently much higher in real terms than they were 25 years ago. It is difficult to know what will happen in the future. Commodity prices are notoriously hard to predict, since they depend on both supply and demand, and there are so many unknowns involved. For example, in its reference scenario, the American Energy Information Administration projects that world energy consumption will increase by 56 per cent between 2010 and 2040 (EIA 2013 slide 2). Half of the increase is attributable to China and India. This projection assumes that the real price of oil will rise by approximately 45 per cent over the period. The EIA also presents high and low oil price scenarios under which oil prices in 2040 differ by a factor of more than three.

World consumption of most commodities is likely to increase as population and per capita incomes rise. What happens to prices will depend on the evolution of supply. It is conceivable that developments, such as the use of substitutes, new sources of supply and methods of production, will make many commodities so plentiful that their real prices will fall on a permanent basis despite higher levels of output. A more plausible scenario is that real commodity prices will exhibit an upward trend, punctuated by large fluctuations.

Going global: will China (or India) buy the world?

The emergence of China as an economic giant, and a formidable manufacturing exporter with a voracious appetite for oil and minerals, has caused widespread unease and even fear in the rest of the world.

Fear of Chinese economic prowess is nothing new. Many years ago the still popular left-wing children's writer Jack London wrote a short story called "The Unparalleled Invasion" (London 1910). This story describes a fictional world in which the Chinese out-compete other nations through hard work and intelligence, and they threaten to dominate the world peacefully without the need for warfare. The story ends when the governments of other countries unite to exterminate the entire Chinese population by infecting them with the plague and other deadly viruses. Such fears have surfaced once again, although in less extreme form. A few years ago, it was the fear that low-wage imports from China would wipe out manufacturing industry in rich countries. Now it is the fear that the Chinese are using their supposedly vast financial wealth to buy up swathes of foreign business, and to monopolise natural resources in Africa, Latin America and elsewhere.

The above fears have been challenged in a well-documented book by Peter Nolan (Nolan 2012). He argues that the scale of overseas investment by Chinese firms is grossly exaggerated, and that while some of these firms may have large operations at home, they are relatively small players on the world stage. This is true even in the case of natural resources, where Chinese overseas investment in oil and mineral extraction has given rise to claims of a new imperialism. Nolan's central theme is that China is vulnerable. It is highly dependent on imported commodities, and many of its overseas investments in natural resources are defensive in character and designed to ensure security of supply. Nolan points out that foreign multinationals have invested far more in China than Chinese firms have invested overseas. He also defends the role of the Chinese government in encouraging and supporting the outward thrust of state-owned firms because it is the only way for China to break into global markets, which in many industries are currently dominated by a handful of established giants from the advanced economies.

The evidence mostly supports Nolan's argument. Despite recent developments, Chinese firms are still, for the most part, minor players on the world stage, although the situation may change if China continues on its planned trajectory. Let us review some of this evidence. The following remarks mostly concern China, but there is also some reference to India.

In 2000, the Chinese government announced its "go global" policy. One objective was to improve the operations of China's large state-owned enterprises (SOEs) by exposing them to the challenge of global markets. Another was to secure future supplies of energy and raw materials (Davies 2010). Since then, foreign direct investment (FDI) by firms from mainland China has mushroomed. It is this development above all that has fed concerns about Chinese expansion.[2] However, official statistics exaggerate the scale of Chinese expansion, since they include investment in Hong Kong, which is part of China. More than half of the outward FDI stock of mainland China is located in Hong Kong and about 40 per cent of the Hong Kong outward FDI stock is located in mainland China (Table 10.1). When cross-holdings are eliminated, the total FDI stock held by China (including Hong Kong) in the rest of the world in 2010 was equal to US$701 billion. In the same year, the American direct investment abroad was valued at $4,767 billon which is almost 7 times the Chinese total and 49 times the Indian total.

There has been extensive, mostly negative publicity in the Western media about Chinese investment in Africa. Yet despite its recent growth, China's stake in Africa is still small compared to that of Western countries. The same is true for India. In 2011, the stocks of Chinese and Indian direct investment in Africa were US$16 billion and US$14 billion, respectively (UNCTAD 2013, pp. 7–8). In the same year, the combined total for France, the USA and the UK exceeded US$150 billion. The Heritage China Global Investment Tracker records Chinese investment projects abroad worth at least US$100 million each (Heritage Foundation 2013).

Because of their large size these projects are disproportionately concentrated in energy and mining. Of the 405 projects recorded over the period 2005–2012 a total of 45 were located in Africa, and the rest were scattered throughout the globe, including many in developed economies.

Table 10.1 Outward FDI stocks of mainland China, Hong Kong and India

US$ billions			
	2003	*2010*	*Growth rate (% p.a.)*
Mainland China	33.2	317.2	38.0
of which to			
Hong Kong	24.6	199.1	34.8
Rest of world	8.6	118.1	45.4
Hong Kong	414.6	1,039.0	14.0
of which to			
Mainland China	146.4	426.8	16.5
Rest of world	268.1	582.7	11.7
China (incl. HK) to			
Rest of world	**276.7**	**700.8**	**14.2**
India	**6.1**	**96.9**	**48.5**
For comparison:			
USA	2,729.1	4,766.7	8.3

Source: China: Davies (2012), Hong Kong Government (2006, 2012): India, USA: UNCTAD database. The estimates for Hong Kong FDI are derived by converting the original figures from Hong Kong dollars into US dollars.

Chinese and Indian direct investments abroad are still relatively small, but they are growing rapidly. Between 2003 and 2010, the combined direct investments of mainland China and Hong Kong in the outside world grew at 14.2 per cent p.a. (Table 10.1). For India and the USA, the growth rates were 48.5 per cent and 8.3 per cent, respectively. If such growth rates were to continue unchanged into the future, India would overtake the USA in 2023, and for China (including Hong Kong) this would occur in 2047. The Indian projection is beyond the bounds of possibility, but it is conceivable that China may begin to rival the USA as an overseas investor by mid-century.

A new imperialism in the making?

Book titles like *When China Rules the World* by Martin Jacques imply that we are witnessing a new imperialism in the making (Jacques 2012).

The term "imperialism" has many different meanings. In the *Dictionary of Human Geography*, it is defined as "an unequal human and territorial relationship, usually in the form of an empire, based on ideas of superiority and practices of dominance, and involving the extension of authority and control of one state or people over another".[3]

Rivalry

In his classic work *Imperialism, the Highest Stage of Capitalism*, Lenin identified imperialism as a special stage of capitalism

> with the following five basic features: (1) the concentration of production and capital has developed to such a high stage that it has created monopolies which play a decisive role in economic life; (2) the merging of bank capital with industrial capital, and the creation, on the basis of this "finance capital", of a financial oligarchy; (3) the export of capital as distinguished from the export of commodities acquires exceptional importance; (4) the formation of international monopolist capitalist associations which share the world among themselves, and (5) the territorial division of the whole world among the biggest capitalist powers is completed. Imperialism is capitalism at that stage of development at which the dominance of monopolies and finance capital is established.
>
> (Lenin (1917)

The world has not evolved as Lenin expected. The old empires have collapsed and the whole world is not divided amongst the biggest capitalist powers. However, some of his predictions have come true. Large swathes of the world economy are now dominated by giant global firms ("monopolies" in Lenin's terminology) that compete fiercely with each other. And as he predicted, the export of capital as distinguished from the export of commodities has acquired exceptional importance.

Implicit in Lenin's thinking was the idea that individual states in the leading capitalist economies would support "their" firms in the global struggle. It has been argued that, with the growing internationalisation of their activities, today's giant firms are losing their national identity. No matter where their headquarters are located, no matter what national label they bear they are all becoming similar in terms of global spread and objectives (Nolan 2012; Reich 1991; 2013; Rowthorn 1971). There may something in this view. As the operations of large firms become more international, their interests are becoming more global in nature and less closely tied to the fate of their home economies. However, one should not exaggerate this tendency. Despite decades of globalisation, a substantial fraction, often a majority, of the operations and sales of large American firms are still located in their home country. The same is true for Japanese firms. The picture is more complex in the case of European firms, because their operations may be dispersed across several countries of the European Union. However, the EU as a whole still accounts for a substantial proportion of their operations and sales, and the fate of these firms depends to a significant extent on what happens to the European economy.

Geoffrey Jones has challenged the notion that large multinational firms are becoming stateless global webs and that corporate nationality is increasingly irrelevant. Writing in the *Harvard Business Review*, he says: "Today, technological advances may permit different parts of the value chain to operate in different places, companies may hold portfolios of brands with different national heritages, and leaders, shareholders, and customers may be dispersed. Still, the nationality of a firm is rarely ambiguous. It usually has a major influence on corporate strategy, and it seems to be growing in political importance" (Jones 2006).

National governments and the EU Commission support "their" firms in various ways. They lobby to gain better conditions for these firms in foreign markets, sometimes under the slogan of a "level playing field". For example, the USA and the EU have been pressing for the reduction of inward investment restrictions in China and India so that their firms can penetrate local markets more effectively. In the case of China, they seek to protect the intellectual property rights of American and European firms.

How do China and India fit into all this? Large firms from both countries are starting to push outward and extend their external operations. Outward investors from India are mostly private firms and, as such, pose no particular conceptual problem. They are driven primarily by the profit motive and are therefore similar in motivation to most existing multinationals. In the case of China, most outward FDI is undertaken by large state-owned enterprises (SOEs). The primary objectives of these enterprises are laid down by the government, and the profit motive plays a smaller role in their decision-making than in the classic capitalist enterprise.

The close relationship between the large SOEs and the government has sometimes inhibited Chinese expansion abroad. A country may be reluctant to allow large parts of its economy to fall under the control of firms whose actions may be guided by the political imperatives of a foreign government (Drysdale and Findlay 2009). There have been some high profile refusals. For example, in 2007 the Chinese company Huawei was prevented from taking over 3Com in collaboration with Bain capital, because of Huawei's alleged links with the People's Liberation Army.[4] One way to allay such fears is to reduce political control over the large SOEs and put their operations on a more transparent commercial basis, whilst retaining formal state ownership, perhaps with a minority private shareholding. This has been the practice so far. Full privatisation is a potential alternative. Many of the small and medium sized SOEs have been privatised, but so far the large firms which dominate the "commanding heights" of the economy remain in public hands.

The rise of China and India will not alter fundamentally the nature of global rivalry between the large firms, although the fact that many of the large Chinese players are state-owned may alter the rules of the game somewhat. Moreover, as the external activities of the large Chinese SOEs increase in importance, there will be increasing pressure to relax government control of their activities or even to privatise them. This is already happening to some degree anyway, but the going global policy may accelerate the move towards commercialisation and, ultimately, privatisation of these firms. The "commanding heights" of the Chinese economy are at present still controlled by the government. It is an open question how far this will be compatible with continued global expansion of the large Chinese firms.

The scramble for resources

China's industrialisation has created a hunger for imported commodities, especially oil, from developing countries in Africa, Latin America and elsewhere. Developing countries are also valuable markets for Chinese exports. Many of these countries have welcomed their growing engagement with China, if only as a counterweight to the western powers. However, this engagement has its downside and some of the expected benefits have not materialised. In what follows, we shall focus mainly on China's relations with Africa, although there will be some mention of its relations with Latin America, and of India's role.

Until recently, Africa's political élites have been enamoured with China. In return for access to the continent's natural resources, China has offered generous aid, cheap credit and expertise for infrastructural and other projects. Such deals have come with few political strings attached, and are especially attractive to countries with poor records in terms of corruption or human rights. These generous and unconditional terms have allowed China to break into what was previously almost a European and American monopoly in Africa. However, there are signs of African discontent with the arrangement.

The governor of Nigeria's central bank, Lamido Sanusi, has warned that China is a "competitor as much as a partner . . . capable of the same exploitative practices as the old colonial powers . . ." (Wallace 2013). Africa is "opening itself up to a new form of imperialism. China takes from us primary goods and sells us manufactured ones. This was also the essence of colonialism. . . . China is a major contributor to the de-industrialisation of Africa and thus African underdevelopment."

Is Sanusi's picture of China's economic relations with Africa accurate? The answer is yes up to a point. A number of African countries now depend heavily on their exports of commodities, mainly oil and minerals, to China. Moreover, African producers of labor-intensive manufactures have been damaged by competition from Chinese exports. However, China is by no means the dominant player in Africa. As mentioned above, China's direct investments in Africa have grown rapidly but they are still modest in comparison to those of Europe and America. Trade between Africa and China has also grown rapidly but most of Africa's exports still go to non-Chinese destinations, such as Europe and the USA, and most of its imports come from these areas. Similar observations apply to Africa's links with India. Despite rapid growth, the combined share of China and India in Africa's exports of agricultural products in 2012 was still only

Table 10.2 Exports of selected products from Africa and Latin America, 2000 and 2012, US$ billions

	2000	2012	2000	2012	2000	2012
	Agricultural Products		Fuels & Mining Products		Manufactures	
Africa to:						
Africa	3.3	13.5	4.2	27.4	5.9	29.7
Latin America	0.2	1.5	3.3	25.8	0.5	2.9
China	0.4	3.1	3.4	61.7	0.2	2.1
India	0.5	1.5	1.0	29.8	0.8	2.6
Rest of world	13.9	37.7	74.9	293.1	28.5	66.2
World	18.3	57.4	86.8	437.7	35.8	103.4
Latin America to:						
Africa	1.6	14.8	0.3	1.9	0.8	4.1
Latin America	9.8	35.5	15.9	71.3	24.7	94.5
China	2.0	26.0	1.2	53.9	0.4	5.5
India	0.5	2.2	0.4	8.2	0.1	0.9
Rest of world	38.9	126.7	52.3	184.3	46.8	94.5
World	52.8	205.2	70.0	319.6	73.0	199.5

Source: WTO data base

10.5 per cent, excluding intra-African trade (Table 10.2). For fuels and minerals their combined share was 22.3 per cent. The same patterns are visible in Latin America, although on a smaller scale.

The impact of China on African manufacturing

Manufacturing in Sub-Saharan Africa and elsewhere has been damaged by competition from China.[5] The Chinese combination of superior organisation and low wages has proved unstoppable.

The situation is worst in countries which rely heavily on the export of commodities such as oil or food. If a country starts to export commodities on a large scale, this will drive up the real exchange rate, making locally-produced manufactured goods more expensive in comparison to foreign goods. Exports of such items will fall, imports will rise and the domestic manufacturing sector will shrink or fail to expand. This effect, which is known as the "Dutch disease", has been observed in a number of countries in Africa.[6] However, China is not the main culprit. Most of the increase in commodity exports from Africa did not go to China, but to other countries.

The impact of revenue from commodity exports depends on how it is used. If the revenue is invested wisely in areas such as health, education and infrastructure it will generate employment and provide the foundation for sustainable growth. However, all too often, especially in the case of oil and minerals, the export sector is an enclave which has few links to the rest of the economy and much of the revenue is siphoned off by a corrupt elite (Carmody 2011). The danger is summarised in the following quotation from the African Development Bank (UNCTAD 2013):

> The discovery of oil and minerals in a growing number of African countries is of enormous significance for Africa's development. However, it may also have the effect of sharply increasing the level of corruption and the risk of conflict. In addition, natural resource booms can suppress growth in other parts of the economy – a phenomenon that is often referred to as "Dutch disease".

In its pursuit of oil and minerals, China and India have been willing to tolerate a high level of corruption in the countries they deal with. However, China and India are not the only culprits. Despite some improvements in recent years, corruption is still rife in Africa, including countries where western firms have a dominant presence.[7]

Fuelled by income from natural resources, GDP in a number of African countries has grown rapidly but unemployment is rife and there has been little trickle down of income to the mass of the population. It is this experience that informs Lamido Sanusi's warning. However, the culprit is not simply China as he implies. Whilst China has supplied many of the cheap labor-intensive manufactures that have damaged African producers, the revenue which has been used to purchase these imports has come partly from commodity exports to non–Chinese destinations.

The future of African manufacturing

China's industrialisation has damaged African manufacturing in the past, but the situation may be about to change. Wages in many African countries are now lower than in China, and Chinese firms are starting to invest in labor-intensive manufacturing in Africa. However, this process is in its infancy and labor-intensive manufacturing, indeed manufacturing of any kind, is still virtually absent in many African countries. The whole of Africa currently produces 1.5 per cent of world manufacturing output (value-added). According to a recent World Bank report, employment in the apparel sector was 4,587,000 in China and 1,194,310 in Vietnam; the corresponding figures for African countries were: Ethiopia 9,746, Tanzania 2,000 and Zambia 1,500 (World Bank 2011, p 77). There are still many obstacles to overcome before manufacturing takes off in Africa. There is a scarcity of well-serviced land with suitable transport links and utilities, local workers often lack the required skills, and suitable inputs may be hard to obtain or expensive. When these factors are taken into account, despite lower wages, costs of production are often higher in Africa than China (Dinh, Palmade, Chandra and Cossar 2012). If such difficulties can be overcome, Africa may attract much of the labor-intensive manufacturing that will migrate from China to other countries.

When Africa eventually stops importing cheap labor-intensive manufactures from China, this does not mean that it will stop importing Chinese manufactured goods altogether. It may simply be that manufactured imports from China will become more sophisticated. For the foreseeable future, Africa will continue to export oil and minerals and it may use the revenue to import manufactures of some kind from China. This is not an intrinsically exploitative relationship. Provided African economies can utilise their revenue from oil and mineral exports to develop other sectors of their economy, including domestic manufacturing, the exchange with China will be of mutual benefit. So far this revenue has often been misused, but this is not inevitable. There are several examples, such as Canada, that export natural resources in return for manufactured imports, but also maintain a vibrant domestic manufacturing sector.

The shifting balance of power

The emergence of China and eventually India as economic giants has many implications for the global and regional balance of power.

In monetary sphere, the Chinese renminbi may eventually replace the US dollar as the world's leading reserve currency. This is not inevitable and is not an immediate prospect, but China is liberalising its capital account and is already eroding the lead of both the dollar and the euro (Prasad and Lei 2012). At the very least, the renminbi will become a major reserve currency alongside the dollar. The rupee should also become a major reserve currency one day.

Both China and India will expect greater representation in international institutions. Failing this, they may set up their own rival institutions. An example is the new BRICS bank. On the 70th anniversary of the Bretton Woods conference, which established the IMF and the World Bank, the formation of a new development bank was announced by the BRICS countries: Brazil, Russia, India, China and South Africa. The new bank will focus mainly on infrastructure projects and will have initial capital of $50 billion building up to $100 billion. Its headquarters will be in Shanghai. This move was partly motivated by dissatisfaction with the present voting arrangements and with the cosy arrangement whereby the head of the IMF is European and the head of the World Bank is American. The BRICS countries already account for almost 34 per cent of global output at purchasing power parity, but their voting power in the IMF is less than 12 per cent. It was agreed to reduce this distortion at the 2010 G20 summit, but this proposal has yet to be implemented.

The aid to be channelled through the BRICS bank is only a small fraction of the Chinese total aid. The amount of Chinese foreign aid newly pledged in

2011 was an estimated $189 billion including government sponsored investment (Wolf, Wang and Warner 2011).

The cumulative total of pledged aid over the period 2001–2011 was $671 billion, of which 42 per cent was in natural resource projects and 40 per cent in infrastructure. In contrast, US official economic assistance to developing countries in 2011 was $33 billion (new commitments).[8] The scale of Chinese aid will presumably continue to increase as the country becomes richer and seeks to promote its diplomatic and economic interests through grants and loans. The Indian foreign aid budget is still very small at $1.3 billion in 2013–14, but is growing fast, having trebled in the past four years.[9]

The above developments will reduce the ability of western countries to set the international economic agenda and to shape global trade and investment rules. The result may be greater policy freedom for developing countries. For example, there may be some relaxation of the WTO rules that currently outlaw many types of useful government trade-related intervention, such as domestic content conditions on inward FDI. Moreover, given the professed support of its members for the principle of non-interference in the domestic affairs of other countries, the BRICS bank is likely to attach fewer strings to its loans than western countries or the IMF and World Bank. Non-interference is already a feature of China's existing development assistance.

The military balance

In addition to its economic implications, the rise of China and India will affect the military balance in Asia and beyond.

The United States is still the strongest military power in the world by far. However, the balance is shifting. The International Institute of Strategic Studies projects that in terms of military expenditure China will overtake the United States at some time between 2025 and 2050 (IISS 2013, p. 256). Uncertainty about the timing of this event derives from uncertainty about future economic growth rates and about the shares of GDP that the two countries will in future commit to military expenditure. India is a long way behind but it is also upgrading its armed forces. Over the decade, 2002–2012, annual military expenditure by China increased by almost 200 per cent. For India the figure was 68 per cent.[10]

Concern about China's increasing military strength and assertiveness is leading many countries in the region to upgrade their own military capabilities and to forge new alliances or strengthen old ones. China's military strategy was outlined as follows by President Hu Jintao's in his report at 18th Party Congress:[11]

> China pursues a national defence policy that is defensive in nature. Our endeavours to strengthen national defence aim to safeguard China's sovereignty, security and territorial integrity and ensure its peaceful development.

This statement ignores the fact there is no universal agreement about what constitutes Chinese territory or, ultimately, China's maritime rights. China has settled its former border disputes with Pakistan and Russia, but points of conflict with other countries remain. There are unresolved territorial disputes with India, which have already given rise to one major war between the two countries and are still the cause of frequent skirmishes between their armed forces. There are also on-going disputes with most of China's coastal neighbours. What China regards as legitimate defence of its territorial integrity is seen by many of its neighbours as territorial aggrandisement.

In response to China's growing military prowess the United States has announced a rebalancing of its strategic priorities with greater emphasis on the Asia-Pacific region. China has one great advantage in this context. The United States still sees itself as a global power which, despite its new priorities, cannot afford to divert too many of its military resources to the Asia-Pacific region. In contrast, China's military objectives, for the time being at least, are mainly confined to its geographical periphery where it can concentrate its armed forces[12] Faced with this reality, the United States is hoping to share the military burden with China's regional neighbours. Indeed, this is already happening. In 2012, the combined military expenditures of the ASEAN countries plus Japan, South Korea and Taiwan amounted to $135 billion which is not far short of China's military expenditure of $166 billion.[13] The United States could in theory forge a formal alliance with China's Asia-Pacific neighbours similar to NATO in Europe. However, quite apart from the fact that many countries would refuse to join such an alliance, it is likely that such a policy would be seen by China as a threat to its security and would stoke up tension in the region.

The strategic dilemmas facing the United States in its future relations with China have been recently analysed by James Dobbins, formerly American ambassador to the European Community and Assistant Secretary of State (Dobbins 2012). He identifies the causes most likely to occasion a China–US military clash over the next 30 years as follows: "changes in the status of North Korea and Taiwan, Sino-American confrontation in cyberspace, disputes arising from China's uneasy relationships with Japan and India" (Dobbins 2012, pp. 7–8).

He goes on to argue that, although the United States still has the capacity to offer direct defence to China's neighbours in the event of a conflict, this capacity will decline as China grows stronger. The United States will eventually be forced to rely on some alternative to direct defence. The aim would be to deter China by threatening some form of escalation, such as a first-strike nuclear attack or a comprehensive economic boycott. The analogy here is with the containment of the Soviet Union in Europe after World War Two. However, there is a problem with such threats. A nuclear first-strike on China would be suicidal for the United States since China could retaliate by using the second-strike force of land and submarine launched missiles that it is now developing. It is hard to believe that the United States would launch a nuclear strike in defence of Taiwan or the Philippines. A comprehensive trade war with China could also be damaging to the United States, although it might develop out of a tit for tat escalation.

On a more positive note, Dobbins argues that China is seeking neither territorial aggrandisement nor ideological sway over its neighbours, although he warns that:

> A climate of mutual distrust and suspicion clouds the US–China relationship, producing a potent security dilemma. If ignored, this dynamic could spiral out of control. Altering it will require both the United States and China to fundamentally rethink their national security goals and strategic assumptions in Asia and beyond. . . . As China becomes a true peer competitor, it will also potentially become a stronger partner. . . . Even as the United States seeks over the next several decades to sustain its defence commitments and advance its interests in East Asia, it will also have an interest in encouraging the world's other emerging superpower to assume greater responsibility for international peace and security. China's efforts to combat piracy in the Indian Ocean, and its growing interest in United Nations peacekeeping, should become the basis for enhanced US–Chinese cooperation. In the long term, the United States will want to look for other ways to leverage Chinese power as well as restrain it
>
> (Dobbins 2012, p. 22)

The theme of power-sharing is explored in depth by the Australian military analyst, Hugh White (White 2013). He proposes a new political settlement in which leadership in Asia would be shared between four great powers: China, India, the USA and Japan. These countries would negotiate agreed ground rules to regulate competition and cooperation between them. They would also establish a framework for the regulation of interstate relations involving other Asian countries. Japan appears as an independent power in this list because, in White's view, a rising China will become increasingly hostile to the present status of Japan as an American strategic client. Conversely, the USA would not tolerate the absorption of Japan into China's sphere of influence. White's vision involves the full-scale re-armament of Japan, including the proposal that Japan should acquire sufficient nuclear weapons to act as a minimal deterrent against a Chinese nuclear attack (White 2013, pp. 84–5)

Such a proposal would have few supporters in present-day Japan, but who knows what could happen in the future.

It is conceivable that the USA will gradually scale back its military engagement in the Asia Pacific region, because it is too expensive to compete with China and the region is no longer seen as of vital interest to America. A precedent for this would be the withdrawal of most British armed forces from "East of Suez" from the 1970s onwards, partly on grounds of expense and partly because British interests in Asia were no longer deemed sufficient to justify a large military presence there. The gap left by the departure of the USA might open the way for China to become a hegemon in the Asia-Pacific region to which other countries in the region must defer. Even if the USA remains a major military power in the Asia-Pacific region, China will have a growing influence over its neighbours, if only because of the enormous size of its future economy and its ability to confer economic costs and benefits on these neighbours.

Concluding remarks

Despite its large GDP and its newly acquired status as the world's leading exporter of goods and services, China is still what David Shambaugh calls a "partial power" (Shambaugh 2013). It has few truly global companies and the overseas operations of Chinese firms are still small in comparison with those from the advanced economies. In military terms it is no match for the United States at a global level, although it now has sufficient military capacity to challenge America's previous dominance of Chinese coastal waters. China is also using its economic muscle to win diplomatic influence and to challenge the western dominance of international economic and financial institutions. If China continues to grow at the rate projected by the OECD, it will become a truly global power by mid-century. Its overseas investments will begin to rival those of the United States and it will be easily the world's largest trading nation. It will have enormous economic clout which it can use to buy friends abroad or neutralise potential opponents. China may also become a global military power, with the ability to project force anywhere in the world. Similar observations apply to India, although it will be a long time before India rivals China as a great power.

The United States has a number of choices. (1) It can accept the rise of China and eventually India as great powers and seek to establish a modus vivendi in which leadership is shared between these countries, perhaps with the participation of a few select partners on a regional basis, such as Japan in Asia or Brazil in Latin America. This might involve a division of the world into spheres of influence of a traditional imperialist character. Alternatively, their shared leadership could be exerted within the framework of cooperative institutions such as the UN or APEC (Asia Pacific Economic Cooperation). (2) The United States can refuse to accept China or India as equals and seek to restore or preserve its position as undisputed global leader. This is a losing game which is fraught with danger. (3) The United States can simply throw in the towel and retreat into isolation, leaving the rest of the world outside of North America for other countries to squabble over. This might be a feasible option from an economic or military point of view, but there is always the danger that events in the outside world might eventually force the United States to play a more active role.

The economic impact of China on other developing countries has so far been mixed. China has made infrastructural investments in these countries and has provided a valuable market for their commodity exports, but competition from Chinese exports has damaged their manufacturing industry. However, rising wage costs are making Chinese labor-intensive goods uncompetitive and the production of such items this is moving to other countries. This will provide new opportunities for the producers of labor-intensive manufacturing in Africa, although there is always the danger of future competition from India if it emerges as a great exporter of labor-intensive goods.

Notes

1 For a good discussion of this issue see chapter 3 of Corbridge, Harriss and Craig (2013)
2 Foreign direct investment (FDI) refers to an external investment whereby an investor who is a resident (individual or organisation) in one economy acquires a lasting interest and a significant degree of influence or an effective voice in the management of an enterprise located in another economy.
3 Gregory, Johnston, Pratt, Watts and Whatmore (2009) p. 373. The quotation in the text is taken from the Wikipedia entry on imperialism.
4 See Davies (2013).
5 See Hardy (2013) on Latin America, and Geda and Meske (2007), Kaplinsky, McCormick and Morris (2007), and Morrissey and Zgovu (2011) on Africa.
6 See Van der Ploeg and Venables (2013) for a general discussion of the Dutch disease.
7 Of the bottom 38 countries Transparency International's 2012 Corruption Perceptions Index 16 are in sub-Saharan Africa (Transparency International 2012).
8 OECD database. http://stats.oecd.org/Index.aspx?datasetcode=TABLE1
9 http://www.respondanet.com/Asia/indias-foreign-aid-program-catches-up-with-its-global-ambitions.html
10 The figures for China and India are from the SIPRI (Stockholm International Peace Research Institute) database. http://www.sipri.org/research/armaments/milex/milex_database
 Expenditure is measured at constant (2011) US dollars.
11 http://news.xinhuanet.com/english/special/18cpcnc/2012–11/17/c_1319 81259_11.htm
12 See Shambaugh (2013) chapter 7.
13 Data from the SIPRI database.

References

African Development Bank (2013) *African Development Effectiveness Review 2013* http://www.afdb.org/fileadmin/uploads/afdb/Documents/Project-and-Operations/ADER-%20Annual%20Development%20Effectiveness%20Review%202013.pdf

Carmody, P. (2011) *The New Scramble for Africa* (Cambridge: Polity).

Corbridge, S., J. Harriss and J. Craig (2013) *India Today* (Cambridge: Polity).

Davies, K. (2010) *Outward FDI from China and Its Policy Context* Vale Columbia Center (New York: Columbia University). http://www.vcc.columbia.edu/files/vale/documents/China_OFDI_final_Oct_18.pdf

Davies, K. (2012), Outward FDI from China and its policy context, 2012, Columbia University Academic Commons, http://hdl.handle.net/10022/AC:P:13645

Davies K. (2013), "China Investment Policy: An Update", OECD Working Papers on International Investment, 2013/01, OECD Publishing.http://dx.doi.org/10.1787/5k469ll1hmvbt-en

Dinh, H. T., V. Palmade, V. Chandra and F. Cossar (2012) *Light Manufacturing in Africa* Vol. 1, Africa Development Forum, World Bank. http://siteresources. worldbank.org/DEC/Resources/LightManufacturingInAfrica-FullReport.pdf

Dobbins, J. (2012) "War with China", *Survival*, Vol. 54, No. 4, August–September, pp. 7–24. International Institute of Strategic Studies. http://www.ingentaconnect. com/content/routledg/surviv/2012/00000054/00000004/art00001

Drysdale, P. and C. Findlay (2009) "Chinese foreign direct investment in the Australian resource sector" in R. Garnaut, L. Song and W.T. Woo eds. *China's new place in a world in crisis* (Canberra: ANU E Press) pp. 349–38 http://epress. anu.edu.au/wp-content/uploads/2011/06/ch162.pdf

EIA (2013) *International Energy Outlook 2013*, 25 July 2013, US Energy Information Administration http://www.eia.gov/pressroom/presentations/sieminski_ 07252013.pdf

Ernst and Young (2012) *Indian Infrastructure Summit 2012: Accelerating Implementation of Infrastructure Projects* (London: Ernst & Young). http://www. ey.com/Publication/vwLUAssets/FICCI_Infra_report_final/$FILE/FICCI_ Infra_report_final.pdf

Geda, A. and A. G. Meskel (2007) *China and India Growth Surge: Is It a Curse or Blessing for Africa? The Case of Manufactured Exports*,

African Development Review, vol.20, issue 2, pp. 247–272 (Hoboken: Wiley-Blackwell Publishing).

Gregory, D., R. Johnston, G. Prattt, M. J. Watts and S. Whatmore (2009) *The Dictionary of Human Geography* 5th edition (Chichester: Wiley-Blackwell).

Hardy, A. T. (2013) *The World Turned Upside Down: The Complex Partnership between China and Latin America* (New Jersey: World Scientific).

Heritage Foundation (2013) *China Global Investment Tracker Interactive Map* http:// www.heritage.org/research/projects/china-global-investment-tracker-interactive-map

Hong Kong Government (2006) *External Direct Investment Statistics Hong Kong 2005* http://www.statistics.gov.hk/pub/B10400032004AN04B0300.pdf

Hong Kong Government (2012) *External Direct Investment Statistics Hong Kong 2011* http://www.statistics.gov.hk/pub/B10400032011AN11B0100.pdf

IISS (2013) *The Military Balance 2013*, International Institute for Strategic Studies, http://www.iiss.org/en/publications/military%20balance/issues/the-military-balance-2013–2003

Jacques, M. (2012) *When China Rules the World: The End of the Western World and the Birth of a New Global Order* 2nd edition (London: Penguin Books).

Jones, G. (2006) "The rise of Corporate Nationality", *Harvard Business Review*, Vol. 84, No. 10, October, pp. 20–22.

Kaplinsky, R., D. McCormick and M. Morris (2007) "The Impact of china on Sub-Saharan Africa" February http://asiandrivers.open.ac.uk/documents/china_and_ ssa_dfid_agenda_paper_v3_%20feb_%2007.pdf

Lenin, V. I. (1917) *Imperialism the Highest Stage of Capitalism* reproduced from V. I. Lenin *Selected Works* (Moscow: Progress Publishers, 1963) Volume 1 pp. 667–766 http://www.marxists.org/archive/lenin/works/1916/imp-hsc/

London, J. (1910) *The Unparalleled Invasion* http://www.jacklondons.net/writings/ StrengthStrong/invasion.html

Morrissey, O. and E. Zgovu (2011) *The Impact of China and India on Sub-Saharan Africa: Opportunities, Challenges and Policies* (London: The Commonwealth Secretariat).

Nolan, P. (2012) *Is China Buying the World?* (Cambridge: Polity).

OECD (2014) "Long-term baseline projections", *Economic Outlook,* No. 95, May, http://stats.oecd.org/index.aspx?queryid=51396

Prasad, E and Lei, Y (2012) "Will the Renminbi Rule", *Finance & Development,* March 2012, Vol. 49, No. 1. (Washington, International Monetary Fund) http://www.imf.org/external/pubs/ft/fandd/2012/03/prasad.htm

Reich, R. (1991) *The Work of Nations: Preparing Ourselves for 21 Century Capitalism* (New York: Vintage Press).

Reich, R. (2013) "Global Capital and the Nation State (2013)" http://robertreich.org/post/50890974932

Rowthorn, B. (1971) "Imperialism in the Seventies", *New Left Review,* September–October.

Shambaugh, D. (2013) *China Goes Global: The Partial Power* (Oxford: Oxford University Press).

Transparency International (2012) *Corruption Perceptions Index* http://cpi.transparency.org/cpi2012/results/

UN (2013) *World Population Prospects: The 2012 Revision* United Nations Population Division (New York: United Nations).

UNCTAD (2013) "The Rise of BRICS FDI and Africa", *Global Investment Trends Monitor,* No. 25, March, http://unctad.org/en/PublicationsLibrary/webdiaeia2013d6_en.pdf

Van der Ploeg, F. and A. J. Venables (2013) *Absorbing a Windfall of Foreign Exchange: Dutch disease dynamics* Oxcarre Research Paper 52, 14th February, Department of Economics, (Oxford: Oxford University) http://www.oxcarre.ox.ac.uk/files/OxCarreRP201052.pdf

Wallace, W. (2013) "Africa told to view China as a competitor", *Financial Times,* March 11. http://www.ft.com/cms/s/0/58b08eb0–8a6c-11e2–9da4–00144feabdc0.html#axzz2HEYdJE3P

White, H. (2012) *The China Choice* (Oxford, Oxford University Press).

Wolf, C. Jr., X. Wang and E. Warner (2011) *China's Foreign Aid and Government-Sponsored Investment Activities* National Defense Research Institute (Santa Monica: Rand Corporation) http://www.rand.org/content/dam/rand/pubs/research_reports/RR100/RR118/RAND_RR118.pdf

World Bank (2011) *Light Manufacturing in Africa,* Vol. II, (Washington, D.C.: World Bank) http://siteresources.worldbank.org/DEC/Resources/FinalVolumeII.pdf

World Bank (2013) *China 2030: Building a Modern, Harmonious and Creative Society* The World Bank and the Development Research Center of the State Council, the People's Republic of China. http://www.worldbank.org/content/dam/Worldbank/document/China-2030-complete.pdf

11 Asia

Renewal of the diversity of capitalisms, tipping in international relations

Robert Boyer (translated by Heger Attaya)

Introduction

For economists, the industrial countries had become a closed club excluding other countries after World War II, mainly because of their advanced innovations, capabilities to create increasing returns to scale and even to control the rules of the international system. This assumption was emphasized by the recurring difficulties and the inability of Latin American countries to develop a strong industrial base and to promote a steady growth. Consequently, the trade among countries had evolved according to a dual scheme establishing complementarity and confrontation between the center and the periphery: developed countries exchanged industrial goods with the others in return for their supply of natural resources.

Since the 1960s, the specific case of Japan has received much attention. Although Japan was industrialized for a long time, it was surprising to observe how rapidly Japanese companies were able to overcome their technological backwardness and how the economy reached a high growth rate. Similarly, China has followed the same path since the 1990s. These two cases are not an exception. Indeed, some other Asian countries also conducted with success their industrialization strategies. To explain why, a vast literature has been written about the emergence of Asian dragons even before they appeared as emergent countries in the 2000s.

In this context, Asia represents a remarkable challenge both for growth theories that are applied for developed countries and for underdevelopment theories that emerged to show the specificities of developing economies compared to the old industrial ones. Therefore, it is essential to understand the circumstances and processes that have allowed Japan, then Asian dragons, and finally China, to build their original forms of capitalism. The *régulation* theory will be a guideline for this analysis, as it is precisely a research strategy that identifies the factors shaping the transformation of each capitalism and the renewal of their diversity.

Such success of Asian countries is dependent on the gradual opening of the old industrialized economies as well as the internationalization of production chains, but in return, this shift in economic dynamism affects the organization of international relations which become less and less dominated by the absolute supremacy of the US. Is there any regionalization trend of the division of labor in Asia? Does the concentration of both manufacturing production capacity and reserve currency in Asia give a new configuration for the international system? Is China the future hegemonic power or the current multipolar world already anticipating the international system of the 21st century? The extension of the analytical framework of the *régulation* theory to the geopolitical analysis emphasizes complementary relations in the economic sphere and, simultaneously, rivalry in the political sphere that lead to a largely original configuration of international relations.

History and theory of capitalism revised by the dynamism of Asia

A historical perspective must examine both the miracle of Japan after World War II and the surprising growth of China since 1978: should we not review the idea of capitalism built from the experience of Europe and then the US?

"Japan as number one", a challenge for American capitalism and the theorists

In an American conception, the firm is considered an entity dedicated to maximize profits for its shareholders. The Japanese firms during the 1970s appeared as an anomaly, a kind of irrationality: job stability for the polyvalent employees contributing to a firm's performance, no power for shareholders paid with a flat rate, and bank financing preference instead of the financial market, all are features that should have hypothecated the success for major Japanese companies. Based on this observation, Masahiko Aoki, Japanese researcher and professor at a prestigious American university, showed that both the American "A" firm and the Japanese "J" firm are viable forms of capitalist enterprise, but that they are based on two different compromises between shareholders, managers and employees along with different information flow and decision-making hierarchy (Aoki 1988; 2001). Other Japanese researchers have also emphasized how this originality explains that firms are more interested in growth and market share than in just making a profit. This feature was not without consequence on the growth regime in Japan.

Similarly, Japanese researchers utilized the research developed in the *régulation* theory which was applied initially to the US and France to shed light on the specificities of these countries. They pointed out a strong contrast between the wage–labor nexus in the classic American Fordism and a wage–labor nexus existing in large Japanese firms. In the first case, wage growth is codified and institutionalized as a counterpart of more flexible employment, for instance via layoffs. In the second case, it is the permanence of the "companyist" relation that makes all the other components of the labor contract adjustment variables (Boyer and Yamada 2000). Basically, the organization of the labor process is different in both cases, as evidenced, for instance, by a comparative study between the organization of automobile production in Japan and the US. Hence, the name of Toyotist wage–labor nexus is given to this original configuration, and extended to the corresponding growth regime.

Both cases led to the interesting concept of "hybridization" (Freyssenet 2001). Indeed, after World War II, the attempt to import American mass production methods into Japan was faced with some obstacles which were related mainly to the nature of business relationships, the degree of industrial concentration, the small size of the market and the consequences of the destruction caused by the war (Freyssenet and Boyer 2000), as well as the social values and culture which prevailed at that time. Is it not remarkable that a Japanese mathematical economist, Michio Morishima, has presented the assumption that Confucianism is the equivalent of Protestantism as the key explanatory variable in the development of Asian capitalism? Therefore, what literature continuously called Americanization was, in fact, a slow and groping adaptation process rather than an imitation, which finally led to a hybridization and innovation process creating an original form of capitalism. *Mutatis mutandis* such process will be repeated in most other East Asian countries, providing many new socioeconomic paths in all of South Korea, Taiwan, Hong Kong and Singapore.

The boom, the crisis, the stagnation: it was necessary to re-evaluate the "Japanese model"

The diffusion of production methods and organizational forms towards new territories becomes a factor of socioeconomic transformation. However, this hybridization process is not the only mechanism in action. Indeed, the studies in the *régulation* theory illustrated that the slow transformation of technical systems, organizations and institutions can lead to a sudden tipping point in an economic conjuncture. The notion of *endometabolism* developed for this purpose (Lordon 1996) to describe why the Japanese economy, which had become in the 1980s a reference for economists, first experiences a speculative boom raising great optimism for the future, but then is beset by a sudden reversal causing a long process of declining real estate prices and stock market valuation, so dramatic that the growth rate never again reaches the previous levels.

Indeed, Japan was recognized as a model to imitate, but it entered a crisis because of the same factors that led to its emergence and success: the intensification of work typical of the Toyotist wage–labor nexus encountered both social and economic limits (Freyssenet 2001); the remarkable productive efficiency generated a surplus in the trade balance which brought North American liberalization pressures on the Japanese economy and its openness to the international financial flows. The Bank of Japan and the Ministry of Finance both lost control of the conjuncture, and the Japanese economy showed a speculative boom which was suddenly inverted, announcing the beginning of a new phase: the companyist mode prevented a cumulative depression but did not allow a return to the trends of the 1970s and 1980s, and the absence of clear strategy of the government and the administration did not allow the emergence of a new growth regime (Boyer and Yamada 2000). This is a great crisis, or a structural crisis according to *régulation* theory. In this regard, Japan is a developed country that has anticipated the successive crises which have, as a common origin, the explicit conflict between commercial and financial globalization and the persistence of long, historical domestic institutionalized compromises. In 1997 many other Asian countries experienced similar crises, even if these did not have the same consequences.

This turning point suggests three lessons. First, it challenges the naive admiration of models that are supposed to ensure the success and unlimited growth of capitalism. Second, one should admit that a big crisis can occur even with the existence of sophisticated monetary and fiscal tools, especially if the illusion of an unfailing economic model is maintained for a long time. Unfortunately, these lessons from Asian history were not taken seriously, neither by the European Union (for the German model is still a pattern to follow) nor by the North American authorities. Finally, one should beware of the naive assumption that any new emerging industrial power is intended to replace the hegemon since it ensures economic performance and may stabilize the international economy. Many analysts had concluded that Japan would become No. 1, substituting the US as a center to launch a new configuration of international relations. History has denied this prediction. It is useful to remember this today when we consider the expectations raised by China.

The great transformation of China: the domestic and the global

After the dissolution of the Soviet Union, the dominant vision of economists stressed the convergence to a canonical model which was marked by the primacy of the market, privatization, internationalization, trust in finance to anticipate and prepare the future, the limited role of public intervention, and a full initiative left to companies. The US is the most illustrative of this new configuration of contemporary economies. The rapid and resilient growth of China after 1968 disturbs this consensus. Indeed, all the principles of Washington Consensus are violated by the uncertainty about property rights, the absence of a constitutional state, strong political interventions in the economy, and administrative control of credit and the exchange rate. Mainstream economics as taught across Western universities is unable to explain the success of this original configuration.

This lasting divergence has already generated the renewal of research in most social sciences. First, in the *economic history*: how should we explain the stopping of the Chinese economy dynamism in 1820, which extended until the first half of the 20th century, as revealed by the long-period analysis (Maddison 2007)? Compared with Europe and the US, should we attribute this stoppage to political factors or to the unequal natural resource endowments (Pomeranz 2001)? Should we return to the analysis of Fernand Braudel to highlight the similarities and differences with the constitution of Europe (Gipouloux 2009) and much more to highlight the long-term continuities that mark the successive socioeconomic regimes in China (Aglietta and Bai 2012)? Is there any common *cultural model* explaining the development of the East Asian countries, whereby China would follow the experience of both Japan and Korea (Aoki 2011)? It is in this context that analysts refer to Confucianism, not only for Japan but also for China.

Here, the question naturally arises: what is that capitalism? In this regard, the creativity of China analysts is unlimited since there are as many definitions as authors: authoritarian capitalism, market Leninism, state capitalism, bureaucratic capitalism, market socialism, etc. Would the actual Chinese economy be illustrative of Adam Smith's ideas, a market economy rather than capitalist economy (Arrighi 2007)? So far, it is the crucial question addressed by *régulation* theory about distinguishing between the market economy and capitalism and the reasons for the multiplicity of paths explored by various nation states: a variety of capitalist forms coexists, largely complementary, since they result from a great variety of sociopolitical compromises in the wage–labor nexus, competition regime or the State/Economy relationship (Boyer and Saillard 1995). Recent collaborative research made by Asian and European researchers proposes a characterization of different Asian capitalisms; China has a special place in this overview (Boyer, Uemura and Isogai 2012). This is the point on which this chapter is based.

Finally, given the size and dynamism of the Chinese economy, its growth raises the question of the transformation of an *international system* as a result of contrasting *geopolitical strategies* confrontation. Is it the same handover which occurred between Britain and the US in the interwar period that is setting up China as a successor to the US as a hegemonic stabilizer of international order (Kindleberger 1995)? Furthermore, should we reintroduce the concept of *world economy*, in which the global stability does not necessarily require the presence of a hegemonic power, in order that a multipolar world would be conceivable for the 21st century (Wallerstein 1979)? This article explores this second point based on a central assumption: the domestic growth pattern shapes largely the strategies of nation states in geopolitical terms.

A capitalism based on a competition among a series of local corporatism

China seems to have succeeded in aligning, at least partially, the interests of the political class with those of the local and national entrepreneurs. The starting point is a *tax reform* providing greater responsibilities for the local public entities. The public sector is maintained, but local authorities are strongly encouraged to facilitate the emergence of entrepreneurs, sources of greater wealth and larger taxes, which finally increase the resources for public spending. The *local corporatism assumption* provides a perfect definition of this hybridization (Oi 1992; Peng 2001). This cooperation between politicians and entrepreneurs is a logical consequence of the partial conciliation of their respective objectives: on one hand, gathering much tax, on the other hand, improving the

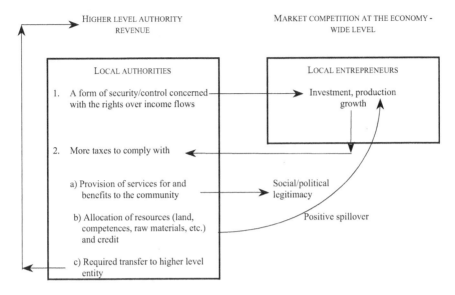

Figure 11.1 The local corporatism and basic institutions of the Chinese economy

competitive advantage of each locality by stimulating investment, production and employment (Krug and Hendrischke 2007). However, the competition among local communities is neither totally chaotic nor highly conflictive due to the contribution of an important network between companies and the government, as well as between the micro and macro levels, maybe as a result of the Communist Party or of the networks of Guanxi (Xin and Pearce 1996).

At the national level, the extended activities and the multiple junctions of the single-party political state allow continuous sharing between the economic and the political spheres (Bergère 2007). It is visible at all levels of Chinese society in which the political elite class is switching to the economic sphere, and vice versa. How can such a complex architecture remain consistent? Many political analysts suggest that the Chinese growth pattern is based on an *implicit compromise*: "a higher standard of living for the population against the political monopoly of the Communist Party." This compromise concerns all the dynamic groups of the society, from the intellectuals to the most brilliant entrepreneurs (Domenach 2008).

Based on this assumption, the Chinese economy is not a typical capitalism based upon profit seeking by private firms. The Chinese elites hold both the political power and the ability to distribute economic resources in order to get implicit social support. Consequently, the first criterion for Chinese capitalism is neither the welfare of consumers nor the increase in shareholder value; but it is *a combination of political and economic targets*, finally pursuing the maximization of growth (Zou 1991). Under the name of "mixed economy capitalism" (Shonfield 1967), the same combination of political and economic factors was observed in Europe after World War II, and it has proved to be completely favorable to long-term growth and the legitimization of an original socioeconomic regime.

An increased openness to the world economy for stimulating growth and modernization

In fact, the integration of China into the international economy is a consequence of the architecture of national institutional form. However, Chinese leaders are not completely free to conduct a foreign policy autonomously. They have to face the dynamism of the accumulation regime driven by an intense competition that creates a tendency to overinvestment. The arising overcapacity cannot be reduced only by the dynamism of household consumption, because of the wage–labor nexus which is dependent, segmented, serialized and, for many workers, competitive. Indeed, the low bargaining power of the working class is associated with a nearly continuous decline in the wage share in national incomes. This factor can help to stabilize the decline of the average rate of profit, but it does not reduce the gap between productive capacity and domestic demand.

Additionally, the difficulty for private firms to access credit induces an investment financed only by past profits (Riedel and Jin 2007); whereas a quite modest social welfare system (unemployment compensation, health care and housing) promotes a high household savings, in order to manage the families' and individual's risk. The increasing trend of the trade surplus for more than ten years in China is due to the unbalanced national accumulation regime. In other words, contemporary China is an illustrative type of the hierarchical domination of the competition on a national and global scale (Figure 11.2).

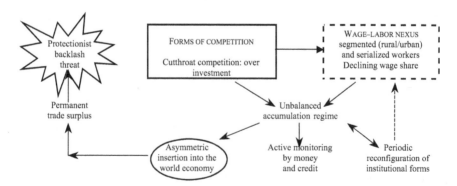

Figure 11.2 Competition and overinvestment promote the international opening of China

A spectacular adjustment of an empire-economy

In this regard, it is paradoxical that such a large country is one of the leading exporters in the world, while generally speaking, the economic openness is inversely proportional to the size of its domestic market. The explanation of this paradox points to a productive dualism in the Chinese economy: in fact the majority of exports come from the multinationals established in China that import, for their activities, a large proportion of components, machine tools and patents. In parallel, Chinese companies used to be focused on the domestic market and export only less technologically advanced products and this drawback is progressively overcome by the emergence of chinese multinationals in some high tech sectors. In this context, the Chinese growth regime is essentially driven by the dynamics of investment, supported by exports. Therefore, the Chinese regime is not a typical regime driven by insertion into the international economy (export-led).

Since 1978, and especially during the 1990s, the performance of the Chinese economy can be explained by the combination of three main factors.

- First, the switching of rural laborers to the most attractive urban industries: the productivity differentials had an impact on the growth rate, which maintained the level of 10 percent for more than two decades. However, it should be stressed that this is also the reason for the rise in social inequality, since the gap between the incomes of rural and urban has continued to increase until now.
- Second, as the industrialization process in China has occurred quite late, the Chinese companies got the most modern machines which are at the technological frontier: these investments are essential for Chinese competitiveness and are imported from everywhere in the world. On the contrary, European countries and even the United States have not enjoyed such an advantage because of their modest productive investment rates. Consequently, in China the economies of scale are similar to the ones that made Fordism successful, with the difference that they concern the international market as well as the domestic market. As the coordination of workers' demands between companies and regions is hard, the *régulation* mode is based on wage competition: knowing that the rural labor offer is important, the real wage has increased less than the productivity for most of the period. The consequence is a high competitive pressure on almost all other national production systems.
- Finally, the investment rate on productive capital and on infrastructure has reached more than the half of the GDP in the 2010s, after the economic plan launched in response to the crisis of 2008–2009. Thus, the renewal of the capital in China is two to three times faster than in old industrial countries like the United States or even most European countries.

This technological catching-up is the main goal of the economic policy, as it is the condition allowing the implicit compromise of the Chinese society to be realized: "A promise of a continuous life standards improvement under the condition of acceptance of the complete and exclusive power by the communist party". The two main tools of the economic policy are the control of the allocation of credit by sectors, companies and regions, and the control of the exchange rate in order to balance the trend in income distribution which is in favor mainly of profits and investments. Thereby, China has succeeded in confronting the subprime crisis, even if a deceleration has been obvious since 2012.

Multiple structural imbalances accumulated

These successes do not hide the imbalance of such a growth regime. One might even ask how this regime has so far avoided its stock market crashes turning into a major crisis. The sources of weakness are diverse (Table 11.1):

- Doubtlessly the most important factor is the *permanent over-accumulation* due to the overproduction and the inefficient allocation of credit attributed to companies unable to repay given the intense competition. As long as the growth is strong, the resulting profits allow compensation for the previous losses. However, such mechanism will be no more relevant when the Chinese economy is in deceleration. Actually, the Chinese government tried to avoid such a situation in 2009–2010 and even in 2012 by applying intense infrastructure plans. But in 2016, the deceleration of growth is clear after the bursting of a real estate bubble and the reversal of stock market speculation.
- The *inequality between urban and rural individuals* represents a real threat for the acceptance of the Chinese regime. Indeed, rural laborers who work in some urban sectors, such as industries or construction, do not have the same social advantage as the urban laborers (health, education, accommodation and pension). In parallel, the rural population suffers from much abuse: expropriation of their land without a just compensation as well as abuses by local political authorities (delay on wages payment, no recourse against manifest abuses, corruptions, and so on). This explains the frequency and extent of social protests that are tens of thousands each year, showing the limits of the acceptance of the Communist Party monopoly, beyond even the modest attempts of democratization at the local level.
- The success in *reducing poverty* cannot conceal the *explosion of inequalities*, particularly spectacular in the light of the relative homogeneity of the living conditions after the post-1949 collectivist regime. In fact, the inequality of income is obvious, as well as the access to public services such as health, education and retirement; all these accommodations have been compromised by the massive privatization. During the first decade of the 2000s, public authorities have become aware of this situation, but for now, the social polarization tendency has not been halted by the launch of a collective social security system, which is still minimalist.

Table 11.1 The blocking factors of China: the economy

Areas	Nature of the tensions	Policies	Their effectiveness
1. Growth Regime	• Imbalance of growth driven by investment/ exports • Over-accumulation strengthened after 2008	• Minimum wage increase • Constitution of a minimum and limited social security system (health, retirement, unemployment, etc.)	• Limited by the competitive struggle between regions • Modesty of these transfers facing imbalances in salary/profit and consumption/ investment
2. Integration into the world economy	• Friction with the United States (exchange rate, intellectual property)	• Prudent revaluation of the real exchange rate	• By gradual adjustment of production to domestic demand
3. Financial system	• Promotes over-accumulation for some companies, but penalizes others • Poor quality loans, bad debts recurrence • Few investments for investors	• Attempt to control the credit allocation by the central government • Responsiveness thanks to the abundance of reserves • Prudent but multifaceted reforms	• Annoyed by the relative autonomy of local authorities • Risk of negative impact on growth • Risk of a future loss of control after the completion of these reforms
4. Real estate sector	• Major needs but trends to overcapacity with respect to purchasing power	• Use the control of the credit allocation	• Intrinsic delay of public intervention in response to speculation
5. Innovation system	• Tension on intellectual property rights • A duality in multinational/ national companies	• Strong and continuous growth of expenditures for research and development Quest for an endogenous and indigenous innovation	• Large volume of funding but quality problems of the research • Catch-up time longer than expected, open conflict with foreign capital

- The *environmental problems* are particularly severe in large metropolises. The rapid growth of traffic and the non-enforcement of environmental rules for many industries have strongly affected the quality of the air; the massive use of coal and the increasing appropriation of natural resources by China involve a high environmental impact, in addition to the problems related to the food quality, water and the deterioration of agricultural lands. In fact, the continuation of current trends is hardly sustainable. The Chinese government has recognized clearly the seriousness of these imbalances, but the importance given to growth is contradictory, at least in the short–medium term, with the environment preservation (Table 11.2).

Table 11.2 The blocking factors of China: the social and the environmental

Areas	Nature of the tensions	Policies	Their effectiveness
1. Social	• Opposition between rural and urban Hukou • Urbanization and change of social relations • Inequality of social protection • Less poverty but inequality explosion	• Mitigation of their differences • Rehabilitation of Confucianism as a possible ideological link • Movement towards homogenization, more redistribution through the state • Action on minimum wage	• Partial, conditioned by the continued growth • Risk of anomia • Negative impact of corruption • Major obstacle: the diversity of local situations
2. Environment	• Reduction of agricultural land • Pollution (air, water) • Food poisoning • Climate Change	• Better defense of individual rights • Administrative restrictions (plant closures, traffic bans) • Exemplary sanctions • Accelerated development of green technologies	• To be confirmed over time • Conflict with domestic market growth (automotive) • A long transition accelerated by the intensity of productive investment and technological modernity • China, leader in many of these sectors (solar panels, etc.)

- The nature of Chinese growth itself led to an increase in the *trade frictions* with the United States and Europe. On one hand, the US government has developed the habit of attributing Chinese trade surpluses to a manipulation of the yuan, even though the real exchange has finally appreciated until 2014. On the other hand, the competition for *access to raw materials*, especially in Africa and Latin America, creates multiple sources of conflict with national governments, knowing that the paucity of natural resources in China makes these procurements absolutely necessary. In addition, the formal or smuggled import of Chinese manufactured goods weakens the industrial producers in those countries, to the point that China can be accused of contributing to their *deindustrialization*.

The long-term emergence of another mode of Chinese development

As of the mid-2010s, leaders have sought to correct the obvious imbalance of the Chinese development mode. First, they have encouraged technological improvement by reforming the research organizations and by encouraging R & D expenditures that have reached a high level compared with other countries with similar income per capita. The purpose was to guarantee the independence of the social innovation system and to get a better response to the specific needs of the country. Second, they have fixed a central objective that makes rebalance between investment, exports and consumption. In the 2010s, the relative depletion of skilled labor reserves have favored the effectiveness of Beijing's encouragement to increase wages, evaluated according to the local corporatism initiative.

In addition, the explosion of economic inequality and the poor access to health and education services that became private have compelled a social security program. This program, initially modest, is essentially to reduce the insecurity caused by the rapid modernization which surpasses numbers of previous solidarities. Finally, the concern with preserving the domestic environment but not with preventing global warming is no longer a second goal, but a priority that must shape the methods of production, urbanization and lifestyle.

In 2015, the results failed to live up to the Chinese government's expectations (Table 11.1). The multinational companies which are controlling the most advanced components and machines continue to supply the majority of high technology exports in China. The uncertainty about the success of the new government strategy weighs on the consumption growth which remains compromised by the volatility of the credit policy since September 2008. Actually, the transfers through the state budget, taxation, new health coverage, unemployment and pensions have not sufficient weight to pilot the transition to a growth driven by consumption.

However, in the longer term this should not be interpreted as evidence of sustainability by the previous regime drawn by an exacerbated domestic competition. First, the growth will not regain its previous pace as China follows a path already explored partly by Japan and Korea (Reidel and Jin 2007), knowing that the assumption of steady and unlimited growth should be abandoned at least because of the changing productive paradigms and the increase of ecological limits occurring in many areas. Second, the historical research (Boyer and Saillard 1995) has shown repeatedly that the change in institutional forms does not result initially in the emergence of a new mode of development, since this requires a groping process that extends several decades. Then, the hope of a return to a previous socioeconomic system after a structural crisis was always disappointed. The history of capitalism is not a repetition, but a spiral progression. Finally, the statements of the government which arrived in power in 2013 have introduced the new idea of a Chinese dream, meaning a long-term reorientation to satisfy Chinese demands and expectations with higher incomes and better quality of life for the largest part of the population.

South Korea, Hong Kong, Singapore and Taiwan: some other forms of capitalism

The economic literature often introduces the categorization of capitalism based on their geographical origin, in which Asia is frequently opposed to Latin America. Some other research about the categorization of capitalism tends also to present all European countries as belonging to the same model based on the coordination by institutions, by opposition to the Anglo-Saxon capitalism in which the market is assumed to be the essential, and sometimes exclusive, factor of coordination.

In parallel, the *régulation* theory emphasizes the dependence of the forms of capitalism based on certain core founding compromises which are updated and revised continuously, but which retain the same style for the *régulation* mode and growth regime. Therefore, the industrialization of South Korea is realized later than Japan. The *chaebol* are not exactly similar to the *keiretsu*. With regard to the wage–labor nexus, for instance, the labor movement of 1985 had an essential role in shaping an original form of capitalism. Similarly, the success of Taiwan is due partly to the institutions it inherited from the Japanese colonization. But the importance of small- and medium-sized enterprises and their link with China provide Taiwan with another form of capitalism with some specific features.

Consequently, it would be improper to speak about an Asian model of capitalism, as well as to propose the assumption of a European capitalism, invalidated by the euro crisis that shows the opposition between the northern and the southern European growth regimes. Nevertheless, the sociopolitical history is not only specific to each national entity. A cross-sectional international study of contemporary capitalism and their institutional, organizational and technical characteristics shows that the rise of Asia increases the diversity of capitalism, as Asian countries depend on diverse schemes that may present contrasting – or extreme – configurations. A first group, mainly Hong Kong and Singapore, is constituted by city capitalism while the second group, such as Indonesia and

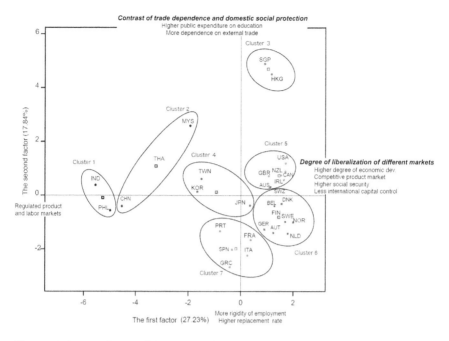

Figure 11.3 Four forms of Asian capitalism and their position within the ensemble of capitalisms

the Philippines, consists of semi-agrarian capitalism. The similitude of Malaysia, Thailand and, to a certain extent, China is that their industrialization is piloted by the development of international trade, whereas the capitalism in South Korea, Taiwan and Japan is driven by innovation and export, similar to the others in terms of industrialized capitalism; however, these three countries are different (Figure 11.3).

This diversity of Asian capitalisms plays a decisive role in the intensification of the division of labor in this area. The analysis of both international and interindustry trade shows the increasing intensity of the upstream and downstream linkages among sectors and countries (Wang, Shrestha and Uemura 2012). Japan, a good illustration of a capitalism driven by innovation, supplies China with sophisticated intermediate goods and machines, whereas the other Asian countries, less developed, benefit from the relocation of Chinese industries that are intensive in low skilled labor. This dynamism of the regional demand also stimulates the economies that are still dominated by agriculture. Therefore, a regionalization process is initiated by private actors among which the multinationals are on the first line. Contrary to what is observed in the European Union, the political authorities play a secondary role in this original form of regionalization.

Tipping in international relations challenges the theory

The transformations discussed previously do not affect only the mode of the development of the Asian countries because they imply also major changes for the relations that Asian countries have both with each other and with the rest of the world, especially with the United States.

A look back at the history

How do North America, China and Japan, interact? The answer to this question is crucial if one wants to understand the trajectory adopted by each of these countries. In a way, the current configuration is new, but one can learn some valuable lessons or intuitions from the history of the world economic development. Indeed, we owe to Fernand Braudel and Immanuel Wallerstein credit for having helped to place the contemporary world economy in the long-term perspective of the emergence of capitalism.

- A first lesson relates to the *periodic reconfiguration* of relations between the various local entities, which have evolved from the city-state during the rise of commercial capitalism (Antwerp and Genoa in the 16th century and Amsterdam in the 17th and early 18th centuries) to the nation-state after the industrial revolution, without forgetting the empire form inspired by the Byzantine Empire model. In view of the previous considerations, we are probably experiencing a switch towards a *new international system*.
- We owe to Immanuel Wallerstein the explanation of the opposition between two world systems, one under a form of *empire* when the unity derives from politics, the other under a form of *world-economy* when it is the economic relations which guaranteed the consistency of the system (Wallerstein 1980; 1984). We can therefore consider that after the Second World War, the United States was the organizer of a *world-economy* that is the result of the emergence of mass production and consumption, in additional to their geopolitical domination accompanying this economic hegemony to the point that some political scientists argue for a possible "American empire". As this configuration creates the emulation and competition, the accumulation process is extended to other nation-states: Germany, Japan, etc. In a sense, the erosion of American dominance is endogenous. By contrast, traditionally, China was an empire, since it was perceived during centuries as a self-referential entity, built on a cultural identity and strong political control. The novelty of the past three decades is due to extraversion of this imperial conception in favor of a participation in the world-economy, since the internal dynamics of the division of labor has far-reaching effects, well beyond the borders of China.
- According to Charles Kindleberger, the stability of the international regime is due to the existence of a hegemon that, by defending its national interests, ensures the viability of the whole system. He analyzed the crisis of

international relations in the interwar period: the British Empire wanted to retain its status, but it no longer had the economic means to keep this role, while that the United States was the rising economic power without any intention to play the stabilization role of hegemon (Kindleberger 1986). The contradiction was resolved after the Second World War, since the system of Breton Woods is an expression of the American plan to reconstruct the international order based on the central role of the dollar. This framework of analysis provides one of the interpretations of the current period: the United States, whose economic power is decreasing but whose financial role is still determinant, has the intention to maintain its superpower status, while the Chinese leaders who are very concerned about their internal economic and social stability do not intend to sacrifice this purpose for the reduction of the imbalances of the global economy, for instance, by renouncing their exchange rate policy as a support to competitiveness and domestic growth.

- The research of Angus Maddison about the long-term national accounting provides another interpretation (Maddison 2001). In fact, in 1820 the standard of living was relatively similar in Europe and in Asia as well as in the main regions of the world. As the industrial revolution took its rise in Europe, the main countries on this continent organized the division of labor for their benefit, creating consequently a division between *the center and the periphery*. Africa, Latin America and Asia fell into the second category, and they experienced what one has called dependent underdevelopment. The originality of the last half-century is due to the re-emergence of Asia as a field for the rise of original forms of capitalism: Japan, South Korea, Taiwan, China and Vietnam. As the distribution of the population evolves in favor of Asia – in India as well as in China – this means a shift in *the most dynamic accumulation pattern*, to the detriment of North America and especially of Europe. As Gérard Chaliand and Jean-Pierre Rageau (2012) concluded in their book, "No doubt that we are witnessing the dwindling of the supremacy of the United States on the world economy but through that one can observe, beyond the opacity of the crisis, this signals the end of the absolute hegemony of the West that has been exercised since some centuries" (p.244).

A repetition of the past, or a renewal in international relations?

The major conceptions of history are divided into two categories. On one hand, time is cyclic insofar as the sequences of the same type tend to be repeated, especially at the world economy level. For instance, the decline of the British Empire is followed by the rise of the power of the American model. According to this line of analysis, China is expected to replace the hegemonic power of the United States. On the other hand, historical time tends to the formation of a global economy in the long run, according to a progression through various configurations that are mainly attached to innovations. If we adopt this point of view, the high degree of interdependence between the various zones of the contemporary world economy requires the construction of an international multipolar system, without the emergence of any hegemonic power appearing.

The first conception is the result of important historians such as Fernand Braudel (1985) or also of Chinese thinking, while the second conception is the consequence both German and European philosophy in the wake of Hegel and Marx. These two points of view are of great interest and are used in this present chapter, but they are not the only theoretical inspirations. Indeed, this chapter utilizes one of the major teachings of the *régulation* theory, which are essentially meant to set in history the categories of contemporary social sciences (Boyer 2004). Based on the previous works about the long-term transformations of American, French and Japanese capitalisms, it becomes crucial to distinguish two different periods.

- Sometimes, the relative and transitory coherence of an institutional configuration sustains an economic regime whose evolutions reinforce the daily anticipations of different economic actors. Here, the complementarity between the accumulation regime and the *régulation* mode is so important that a mainly economic determinism shapes the overall evolution.
- Sometimes, this institutional edifice is in crisis, in the sense that the rules and the previous institutions no longer allow coherence of individuals and collective strategies, which become contradictory. Faced with this failure of the previous determinisms, the different collective actors search for new political and social strategies that aim to reconfigure the socioeconomic regime. It is then time for the politics to intervene, but it takes longer to construct new institutional forms than to realize a succession of political coalitions. Here, one can understand why the great crises are long lasting, such as the crisis of the 1930s.

Based on what was developed above, Asian regions, as well as the global economy, are in a reconfiguration phase, and they are not following the past path trajectory.

The United States: the disadvantage of being a superpower

One major obstacle stands opposite to the project of the US to remain the superpower of the 21st century. Certainly, the US remains the only superpower in terms of geopolitics and conception of modernity. The consequence is a real underestimation of the challenges addressed to the US (Table 11.3). However, the American financial balance is dependent on some Chinese leaders who still accept buying American treasury bonds. Their long-run project is to become less dependent on the dollar as a reserve currency and thus to support moderately the implementation of the euro. It is no surprise that the best experts of the international economy consider highly probable a reconsideration of the dollar's future as a unique reserve currency, and it is not sure that the politicians and the American opinion are completely aware of it.

Table 11.3 Strength and weakness of the United States in 2014

	Strengths	*Weaknesses*
Economy	• Innovation System • Control of high-tech sectors • Size of the domestic market • Networks of strong multinationals • Towards energy independence (shale gas)	• Obsolescence of public infrastructure (transport, public education) • Long-term deindustrialization • High and long-lasting external deficit • Explosion of the public debt and dependence on world savings • Strong ecological imprint
Society	• Business dynamism • Geographic internal mobility • Growing and young population	• Explosion of inequality of income and wealth • Low social mobility • Rise of minorities and erosion of the middle class
Political	• Stability of the constitutional and legal order • Strength of American democracy as a reference • Political alternation of Democrats and Republicans	• Deadlock by "checks and balances" of needed reforms • Control by interest groups (Wall Street, oil and military industrial complex) • New compromise unattainable by ideological polarization
Geopolitics	• Still the only military superpower • The dollar, the de facto reserve currency • Military superpower through technological advances • The soft power of universities, research centers, cultural institutions (theater)	• Dependence on China (value chains, buying Treasury bonds) • Emerging countries might challenge the dollar as key currency (Brazil) • Loss of influence in the Middle East, difficulties in Asia by inadequacy of diplomacy, military means and economic interests • Penalized by a clumsy use of hard power (military intervention) and innovation is reduced by the restriction on guest researchers

Similarly, under both Bush presidents, the US had privileged hard power, which- means the use of military power during the wars in Iraq and Afghanistan – at the expense of the soft power associated with American research centers, universities and culture, and above all, the cinema. The decision to make it more difficult for guest researchers to obtain visas in the United States seems to have eroded the dynamism of the innovations, especially if we observe actual scientific production and patents activity. Both presidencies of Obama have rectified or will partially rectify this situation, but the incapacity to find a solution to the Israeli–Palestinian conflict has emphasized the decline of the American superpower.

Finally, the provincialism of many American politicians leads them to believe that their country is the most advanced in every domain. By contrast, Asia and Europe are often considered unable to be at the technological frontier or to define another form of modernity. Is it not strange that after having caused a global crisis because of their reckless financial deregulation, Americans permanently give lessons to the Chinese and Europeans regarding good economic management? Such arrogance is far from favorable to the self-consciousness that it is essential to have. However, an increasing fraction of experts in geopolitics predict nowadays the start of the decline of American power, although the United States will remain, for a while, the possessor of a power related to their dynamism in terms of technologies and of their domination in military technologies and spending. Unfortunately, this military dominance, actually undeniable, is far from being a solution for the crisis in American hegemony.

Europe in crisis and without any geopolitical strategy

In terms of GDP, the European Union is in line with the North American continent: it remains the largest regional market and the continent where the advances in terms of social welfare are among the most remarkable. In addition, the Europeans defend a negotiated and multilateral approach to the major contemporary issues such as poverty, epidemics, global warming and development aid. But the paradox is that the severity and the duration of the Euro Crisis have weakened the European governments that are unable to show how their models of mixed economy, of the social market economy or social democracy, could help to resolve the imbalances of the global economy.

Thus, given these weaknesses, they contribute less to the redefinition of the international institutions which are expected to replace the ones inherited after World War II. Obviously in the early 2010s, China, Brazil and other emerging countries have been pushing for reforms because these countries are strong by their economic dynamism and by their claim for a power rebalancing within these international institutions.

Therefore, the European Union, despite its vocation to promote welfare capitalism and a multilateral approach to international relations, is relatively powerless to negotiate the rules of the global economy. At the macroeconomic level, the European Union is passively adjusting to the strategies deployed by the US and China, as evidenced, for instance, by the evolution in the exchange rate of the euro, which is more often imposed than chosen to enhance a return to economic growth.

China becomes the impulsion center of Asia and transforms the global economy

Although it is exaggerating, one might think that the G20 and G8 hide in reality a G2, that is a confrontation between two strategic actors: China and the United States, which determine the constraints and the opportunities for the rest of the countries of Asia, Europe, Latin America and Africa.

- On one hand, Chinese dynamics have an attraction effect on the majority of the countries in its neighborhood, as illustrated, for instance, by the progressive synchronization of the economic activity of South Korea, Taiwan, Vietnam and Thailand with the Chinese (Missions économiques 2006). The division of labor is occurring more and more inside Asia, and the impulsion center is in China, given the accumulation dynamism and the size of the economy.

As a result, the international trade frictions with the US have moved from Japan (Figure 11.4) to China (Figure 11.5), as it is China that starts the export of consumption goods. This gives the Chinese leaders a decisive role

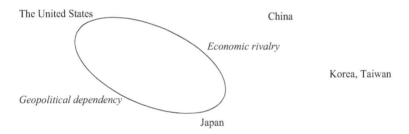

Figure 11.4 The 1980s: Japan focuses on the relations of the United States with Southeast Asia

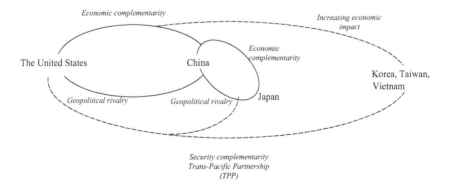

Figure 11.5 The 2010s: A complex and contradictory configuration

in the evolution of international relations, and, especially, the importance of the reserves accumulated in American Treasury bonds seems to stabilize the dollar parity.

- Natural resources producers such as Latin American and African countries are reorienting their export to China. For an illustration, the Brazilian macroeconomic evolution today is dependent on the Chinese one through the volume and the prices of the export of primary goods. Consequently, the Latin American countries that were traditionally under the influence of the United States start to be closer and closer to China. Mutatis mutandis, Africa is starting to be less dependent on Europe and closer to China.
- Finally, Chinese leaders would like to use their reserves to acquire companies all over the world and in all fields that have high scientific and technological potentials (biotechnology, airspace, transports, green techniques, etc.). One can easily imagine the extent of the future conflicts about the free access to these technologies.

Thus, the assertion of China is in a way a contribution to the stability of the world economy, as it is also one of the sources of potentially dangerous conflicts both economic and territorial.

The Chinese reference and the rise in the South/South relations

Beyond the uncertainties about the exact features of the future development mode as well as the pace of growth, the weight of China's production and market has provided to that country a key role, which may accentuate the divergent path between the old industrialized countries and the others, called for convenience the emerging countries.

Indeed, the increasing returns to scale due to the globalization of the markets is the result of an unprecedented deepening of the division of labor that gives China a competitive advantage: its industrialization is launched when value chains become international due to globalization, the low transport costs and the contribution of information and communication techniques. The consequence is the diverging paths of the mature economies. If they continue their specialization in low-quality products, they register an acceleration of their deindustrialization (Southern Europe). If they are at the forefront of innovation and adapt to the new demands of a globalized economy, they prosper and the deindustrialization will be limited (Japan, South Korea, Germany and Nordic countries).

The dynamism of the Chinese industry, even slower, could be confronted with the limits of the environment: reduction of the agricultural lands as a result of the construction of factories, housing and urbanization, the depletion of domestic natural resources, so there is a need to import raw materials from all over the world, including Latin America and Africa. However, these sectors are characterized by decreasing returns, since new investments require time to find and exploit new deposits, particularly in the energy field. Thus, it also explains the surge in natural resources prices from 2013 to 2014. On one hand, the nations which thrive thanks to these rents see their growth to take off, which motivates a diagnostic about a future way out of underdevelopment, for example in Africa, hit in the past by crises, wars and stagnation. On the other hand, the nations which try to convert their agricultural rents in an industrialization process are obtaining high revenue growth but often at the cost of a slow and barely reversible loss of industrial substance (Brazil, Argentina).

There are other consequences more favorable to the economies of the South. First, the shift of the world economy towards Asia leads China to be the economic reference for many governments, thus suggesting that the consensus of Beijing is replacing the one of Washington in terms of development strategy. Then, the erosion of the American superpower and the uncertainty of its new growth regime leave open the possibility of a reorientation of international trade flows in favor of China, which becomes the first partner for a growing number of countries (for instance, Brazil). One can imagine in the long run that the South/South relations are substituting the previous North/South or Center/Periphery opposition. Finally, this divergence of interest is susceptible to influence in a determinant way the reconfiguration of an international system characterized by a possible abandonment of the dollar as a pivot of international and financial relations. Compared with India, China is at the origins of most of these changes.

The geopolitics from Beijing: an illuminating thought experience

According to the maps established in the US and Europe, China is more distant than India, marginalized by one century of troubles and nondevelopment. Based on the previous analyses, a different representation emerges. In fact, contemporary China is full of contradictions: between complementarities of economic specialization and geopolitical rivalry in Asia, especially with Japan; between cooperation constrained and open conflict with the United States; between alliance for reforming the international institutions and asymmetrical economic integration with Latin America and Africa; between the need to maintain the euro as a currency susceptible to compete with the dollar and the pressure to make the yuan an international currency while the autonomy of the monetary policy and the exchange policy constitute essential tools of the Chinese macroeconomic management. In this planetary game, the European Union occupies a less enviable position than Japan: it is dominated by American finance, open to intense Asian competition, and consists of old nation-states that have decided to abandon to the joint exercise of any kind of geopolitical power in the reorganization of the new world (Figure 11.6).

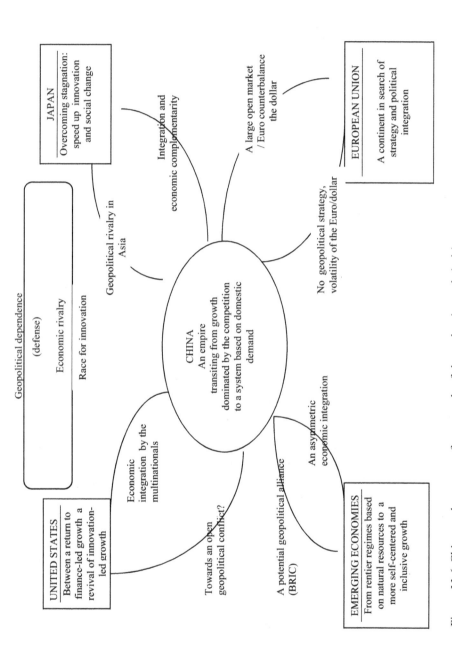

Geopolitical dependence

(defense)

Economic rivalry

Race for innovation

UNITED STATES

Between a return to finance-led growth a revival of innovation-led growth

JAPAN

Overcoming stagnation: speed up innovation and social change

Geopolitical rivalry in Asia

Integration and economic complementarity

A large open market / Euro counterbalance the dollar

EUROPEAN UNION

A continent in search of strategy and political integration

No geopolitical strategy, volatility of the Euro/dollar

CHINA

An empire transiting from growth dominated by the competition to a system based on domestic demand

Economic integration by the multinationals

Towards an open geopolitical conflict?

A potential geopolitical alliance (BRIC)

An asymmetric economic integration

EMERGING ECONOMIES

From rentier regimes based on natural resources to a more self-centered and inclusive growth

Figure 11.6 China at the center of a network of dependencies and rivalries

Conclusion

The fall of the Berlin wall had been interpreted as announcing the coming *convergence of socioeconomic regimes* to a single canonical form that combines democratic principles and the market economy. Nothing like this has been observed over the past two decades: it is obvious that the competition has become intense both in the domestic markets and, as a consequence of liberalization, at the international level, but it leads to a *deepening of the diversity of capitalism forms*. This is the case for the Central and Eastern European countries and more particularly of the Asian countries.

This chapter has aimed to show how the observations of the rise of Japan as an industrial power and then the dysfunction of its original development pattern have allowed the *renewal of the analysis and the theory of capitalism*, by showing how a hybridization process between imported productive modernity and resilience of domestic social relations has allowed the emergence of an original configuration. The growth of the Chinese economy since 1978 defines a new form of capitalism that is different, since it is built on the dynamism of a myriad of local corporatism whose compatibility is ensured by the capability of Beijing to fully utilize the key instruments of economic policy.

While the crisis in the euro zone has showed the heterogeneity of the socio-economic regimes of the member states, the Asian countries also confirm that a geographical or cultural proximity is far from including an identity of development mode: South Korean capitalism is not a replica of the Japanese model, nor of the Taiwanese economy. On the contrary, it appears instead that the deepening of the division of labor in Asia is consolidating *the complementarity of the capitalism forms* that involves institutionally constructed advantages, largely different from one country to another.

In this process, *China has a determinant influence*, since not all the national economies have the same capacity and the degree of freedom to be inserted into international trade, the capital flows and the definition of the rules. Thus, China has the capability to defer, on its neighbors and more generally on the rest of the world, one part of its imbalances that affects its domestic development pattern; attributes that it is still sharing with the American economy for which the dollar is still a pivot for the international financial system. This is not the case of second-level countries that need instead to adjust the level of their activities, their institutions and their economic politics to the impulsions and constraints of the global economy.

Under such conditions, one can analyze international relations as a result of the *interaction* between dynamics bringing the *complementarity* of the division of labor and specialization in the economic field and *geopolitical rivalries*. Therefore, the 1980s was analyzed in terms of acute competition between the United States and Japan, while the present decade shows the contradictory character of the interdependence that connect the US with China: on one hand, certain complementarities in the organization of the value chains and the adjustment of investment and saving at the international level, on the other hand, a political rivalry to reorganize international relations. However, one must also introduce the increasing role of countries that produce natural resources. Furthermore, we should not forget that the European Union is still representing the largest continental market, although the economic crisis has reduced its ability to diffuse a multilateral and negotiated approach of the major imbalances that affect the global economy.

These developments lead to putting into perspective the concept of globalization. Indeed, consequently to the long phase of openness to international trade, to productive investment and to financial capital, an interdependence of an unprecedented intensity between these various forms of capitalism has been organized. *China's externalization of the internal imbalances* of its accumulation regime leads to renewed analysis of the global economy, without China's acquisition of the hegemonic form that the US had after World War II, because no longer does any country have all the attributes of power enabling it to unilaterally decide its future. A *multipolar world* exists because of the catching up of Asia, the eroding of the US economic domination, the new status of both Latin America and Africa, which face the opportunity and limits associated to the supply of raw materials, as well as the inertia of the European Union.

This work is a first step towards a geopolitical approach that focuses on the *compatibility, the complementarit /or conflict* between contrasted accumulation regimes and simultaneously their *rivalry* in defining new rules of the game.

References

Aglietta, M. and G. Bai (2012) *La voie Chinoise. Capitalisme et empire*, Paris: Odile Jacob.

Aoki, M. (1988) *Information, Incentives, and Bargaining in the Japanese Economy*, Cambridge: Cambridge University Press.

Aoki, M. (2001) *Toward a Comparative Institutional Analysis*, Cambridge, MA: MIT Press.

Aoki, M. (2011) "The Five-Phases of Economic Development and Institutional Evolution in China and Japan", *Working Paper*, Stanford University, July.

Arrighi, G. (2007) *Adam Smith in Beijing: Lineages of the Twenty-First Century*, Verso.

Bergère, M. C. (2007) *Capitalismes et capitalistes en chine: XIXe-XXe siècle*, Perrin Asie.

Boyer, R. (2004) *La théorie de la régulation: les fondamentaux*, Repères, Paris: La Découverte.

Boyer, R. and Y. Saillard (eds.) (1995) *Théorie de la régulation. L'état des savoirs*, Paris: La Découverte.

Boyer, R., H. Uemura and A. Isogai (eds.) (2012) *Diversity and Transformations of Asian Capitalisms*, Oxon: Routledge.

Boyer, R. and T. Yamada (eds.) (2000) *Japanese Capitalism in Crisis: A Regulationist Interpretation*, London: Routledge.

Braudel, F. (1985) *La dynamique du capitalisme*, Paris: Éditions Flammarion.

Chaliand, G. and J.-P. Rageau (2012) *Géopolitique des empires. Des Pharaons à l'Imperium Americain*, Champs, Essais.

Diplomatie (2012a) 'Chine: l'inévitable décrochage économique,' pp. 69–76.

Diplomatie (2012b) 'Quel bilan de la politique étrangère américaine,' pp. 44–68.

Domenach, J.-L. (2008) *La Chine m'inquiète*, Perrin.

Freyssenet, M. (2001) "Le modèle productif japonais n'a jamais existé" in R. Boyer and P.-F. Souyri (eds.) *Mondialisation et régulations. Europe et Japon face à la singularité américaine*, Paris: La Découverte.

Freyssenet, M. and R. Boyer (2000) *Les modèles productifs*, Collection Repères, Paris: La Découverte.

Gipouloux, F. (2009) *La Méditerranée asiatique: Villes portuaires et réseaux marchands en Chine, au Japon et en Asie du Sud-Est, XVIe-XXIe siècle*, CNRS éd. Paris.

Golub, P. (2010) *Power, Profit, Prestige. A History of American Imperial Expansion*, Pluto Press.

Harada, Y. and H. Tohyama (2012) "Asian Capitalisms: Institutional Configurations and Firm Heterogeneity", in R. Boyer, H. Uemura and A. Isogai (eds.) (2012), pp. 243–263.

Kindleberger, C. (1986) *La grande crise mondiale*, Economica, Paris. *Le monde en dépression: 1929–1939*, The first American Edition (1973).

Kindleberger, C. (1995) *World Economic Primacy*: 1500-1990, Oxford: Oxford University Press.

Krug, B. and Hendrischke, H. (2007) "Framing China: Transformation and Institutional Change through Co-evolution", *Management and Organization Review*, Vol. 4, No.1 pp. 81–108.

Lordon, F. (1996) "Formaliser la dynamique historique", *Economie Appliquée*, Tom XLIX, No. 1.

Maddison, A. (2001) *Une perspective millénaire*, Centre de Développement de l'OCDE, Paris.

Mission Economique (2006) " L'impact de la croissance chinoise sur l'économie japonaise", Fiche de synthèse, 23 juin 2006, p. 1 and 2. Tokyo: Ambassade de France.

New York Times (2012) "A Troubling Trend in Life Expectancy", September 20.

Oi, J. C. (1992) "Fiscal Reform and the Economic Foundation of Local State Corporatism in China", *World Politics*, Vol. 45, No.1.

Peng, Y. (2001) "Chinese Villages and Township as Industrial Corporations: Ownership, Governance and Market Discipline", *The American Journal of Sociology*, Vol. 106, No. 3.

Pomeranz, K. (2001) *The Great Divergence: China, Europe, and the Making of the Modern World Economy*, Princeton: Princeton University Press.

Riedel, J., J. Jin and J. Gao (2007) *How China Grows: Investment, Finance and Reform*, Princeton: Princeton University Press.

Shonfield, A. (1967) *Le capitalisme d'aujourd'hui: L'etat et l'entreprise*, Paris: Gallimard.

Védrine, H. (2012) *Dans la mêlée mondiale*, Paris: Fayard.

Wallerstein, I. (1979) *The Capitalist world economy*, Maison des sciences de l'Homme Paris. Cambridge: Cambridge University Press.

Wallerstein, I. ([1980] 1984) *Le système-monde du 15ᵉ siècle à nos jours*, Vol. 1 and Vol. 2, Paris: Flammarion.

Wang, J., N. Shrestha and H. Uemura (2012) "Chinese International Production Linkages and Japanese Multinationals: Evolving Industrial Interdependence and Coordination", in R. Boyer, H. Uemura and A. Isoigai (eds.) (2012), pp. 141–164.

Xin, K. R. and Pearce, J. L. (1996) 'Guanxi: Connections as Substitutes for Formal Institutional Support,' *The Academy of Management Journal*, Vol. 39, No.6, pp. 1641–1658.

Zou, H.-F. (1991) "Socialist Economic Growth and Political Investment Cycles", *Working Paper* WPS 615, World Bank.

12 Minsky's financial instability analysis

Financial flows and international imbalances

Jan Kregel

Introduction: Minsky on financial fragility

Minsky's explanation of the endogenous crisis dynamic of capitalist economies was not limited to closed economies (Minsky 1986). Although he was
most concerned with the dynamic of American capitalism, he did analyze
the financial stability of the global economy and it is quite easy to extend
his analysis to international economic instability on the basis of his suggestions (Kregel 1998a; 1998b; 1999). This has been particularly useful in the
analysis of financial crises that have become endemic in developing economies, since they have adopted policies to open their economies to direct
investment by international corporations and their financial markets to
international money managers.

But there is a substantial difference between Minsky's analysis of a closed,
national economy and an economy open to international trade and capital flows.
While it is possible to formulate the conditions of hedge finance for a national
economy operating in a globalized international system, what has been less
evident is that these flows cannot produce global stability.

Minsky's analysis of the financial instability of an economic unit operating in
a national economy is based on a debt repayment profile given the balance sheet
position of a private firm with income-generating capital investments on the asset
side, financed by liabilities carrying cash payment commitments on the liability
side. The repayment profiles classify the relation between the future debt service
flows generated by the liabilities and the expected future income flows from
operating the capital assets. The most conservative financing profile, which
Minsky called "hedge" finance, is one in which in every future period the firm
has a large cushion of expected cash flow receipts over debt service. Even in the
case of a chance rise in interest costs or a decline in sales or prices or increases
in wage or other production costs, the cash cushion is always sufficient to meet
the servicing of the debt. The firm with a "hedge" financing profile is thus virtually a risk-free borrower.

But a capitalist system is one in which firms borrow to take risks and finance
investment. A period of successful investments in which expectations are generally satisfied will lead to a shift in financing profiles of the majority of firms as

cash cushions become smaller relative to the likely volatility in cash inflows leading to what Minsky calls a "speculative" profile. Here cash flows in some periods may not be sufficient to meet payment commitments, but over the life of the investment project the firm will have earnings excesses that enable it to make good on any periodic shortfall. Note that a speculative profile requires an accommodating financial system in which the banks are willing to fund any periodic shortfall in debt service. In the language of managerial finance, the net present value of the investment is positive.

The third profile arises when some unexpected and unforeseen event occurs to a firm with a speculative financing profile that makes it impossible to meet current and future cash commitments. To stay current in its commitments and remain operational, the firm has to contract new lending to pay what it owes in debt service each period. It thus has to convince the original lender to increase the size of the existing loan, or get new loans from other lenders, even though it has little prospect of being able to service its existing loans – unless it is successful in getting additional funding in the future. In reference to a pyramid scheme, Minsky calls this a "Ponzi" scheme, although it does not arise from intentionally illegal or fraudulent behavior.

Since in such conditions liabilities cannot be met by liquidating its assets at their current fair market value, the firm is insolvent. While lenders may be willing to provide financing to such a firm for some time, eventually they will withdraw support, and then activities will cease and the de facto insolvency becomes de jure bankruptcy.

The proportion of firms with particular financing profiles then indicates the potential for a financial crisis. An economy with the majority of firms showing hedge profiles requires the largest changes in receipts or commitments to transform the economy into speculative profiles; but once speculative profiles become dominant, Ponzi financing profiles may start to spread into the system with a much smaller variation in internal or external conditions, since its margin of safety represented by the excess of expected receipts over certain commitments is lower.[1]

Minsky argues that capitalist economies will evolve from "hedge" to "speculative" to "Ponzi" finance as a result of an endogenous process in which investors and lenders both underestimate the size of the cushion of safety to meet possible shortfalls in cash inflows. Thus a run of good results in which realizations exceed expectations may produce a historical distribution of results in which the size of the standard deviation around the mean expected performance declines in absolute magnitude. Thus, even though the lender and investor maintain a risk cushion of, say, two standard deviations, the size of the cushion will be smaller and thus less able to cover an unexpected shortfall in cash inflows. Note that this type of behavior is not irrational, nor does it require fat tails on the distribution, representing black swans or 100-year floods. It is the natural result of a run of sustained growth in what Joan Robinson (1956) called "tranquil" conditions.

Financial fragility on the global level

We can transfer this framework to the international context by noting that countries have cash inflows generated by export sales, factor earnings from abroad, emigrant remittances and capital inflows, while cash commitments are generated by imports, noncapital factor foreign services, foreign lending and debt servicing created by foreign borrowing to fund development strategies. Thus, a hedge profile for a country would be one in which it has a sufficiently large surplus of goods and services and other noncapital factor service earnings that it will always have available to meet its debt service commitments. This definition fits a country with a large "negative" net transfer of resources.

The cost of holding the foreign financial assets, which is the counterpart of the current account surplus, represents the cushion of safety in Minsky's terms. If the return on those assets is lower than the return on domestic assets used to sterilize the impact on domestic monetary conditions or to stabilize the exchange rate, this "negative net carry" will represent the cost of the hedge against a shortfall in export earnings, causing a failure to meet external payments or a withdrawal of foreign assets. It may be viewed in term of Keynes's "liquidity preference" and the costs of the hedge representing the liquidity premium on holding foreign money assets.

A speculative position for a country could then be defined as one in which there was an occasional deficit on external accounts which had to be funded by additional borrowing, since the cushion of safety was by definition not sufficient to meet any possible shortfall in debt service capacity.

Hedge and speculative profiles under Bretton Woods system

The Bretton Woods system may be interpreted as the imposition of speculative financing profiles on countries. By definition it would not be a "hedge" system, since that would require all countries to hold current account surpluses, which would be impossible.

Under Bretton Woods the reserve of foreign currencies represented the cushion of safety for a country to meet any shortfall in debt service from a decline in external earnings. When it was not sufficient, the International Monetary Fund (IMF) would be available to provide bridge financing until the country was able to return to current account surplus. The costs of the foreign exchange reserves in the form of negative net carry was thus augmented by the costs of IMF conditionality in the form of the declines in output and employment that were imposed on the country in order to return it to a hedge financing position, which allowed it to repay the short-term financing from the IMF. Thus, in addition to imposing financial stability on countries in the form of speculative financing profiles, it also had the global benefit of keeping exchange rates broadly stable, since no country could run an external imbalance that was larger than its cushion of safety in the form of foreign exchange reserves and its ability to use its gold tranche and program lending from the IMF.

Bretton Woods and developing countries

While this framework for international financial stability made a great deal of sense for developed countries, it worked against the interests of developing countries and was in sharp contradiction with the then prevailing economic development strategies. Since developed countries usually have a similar pattern of production and composition of trade, most trade involves goods within the same industry (e.g. import and export of automobiles), stable exchange rates thus insure that real productivity gains determine international competitiveness. It provided a defense against the "beggar thy neighbor" policies that prevailed after the Great Depression.

Developing countries, which depend on trade in natural resources, will seek to use these resources to finance the development of a more balanced production structure, by building up manufacturing exports. Here exchange rates may be crucial in promoting exports from a nascent industrial sector, and it may be important to have undervalued exchange rates overall, or at least for their manufactures. Here dual exchange rates may be more important than exchange rate stability.

At the same time, developing countries with natural resource dependence are encouraged to borrow from developed countries (indeed this has been the official policy of multilateral agencies and the United Nations since the Second World War) in order to finance their development. But external borrowing means a current account deficit, and under Bretton Woods the size of this deficit was limited; indeed, if a country grew too fast without a concomitant expansion in export earnings, it would soon meet what came to be baptized the "balance of payments constraint" and the necessity to appeal to the IMF to support exchange rate stability via a loan and conditionality that produced domestic recession which reversed the growth process. The best possible result would be a "stop-go" performance with the "go" period's growth exceeding the recessions of the "stops". But for many countries the opposite was the case, and the result was that the financial stability imposed by the IMF system of speculative financing leading to mediocre development results.

Post–Bretton Woods: from speculation to Ponzi

All of this changed radically in the 1970s as the crisis in the Middle East and the rise in energy prices led to large imbalances between petroleum producing countries and developed countries. The result for developing countries was two-fold. First, the collapse of the Bretton Woods system meant the elimination of exchange rate stability as the basis for international financial stability. Second, the decision to recycle the large petrodollar surplus gave a sharp boost to private international capital flows, and developing countries no longer faced an external constraint nor IMF conditionality if they could attract sufficient funding from private sector investors. The increased availability of private financing made it possible for countries to undergo external disequilibrium for more extended periods without recourse to the IMF or to the policy conditions attached to official lending. But it also meant that the sustained imbalances created increasing stocks of external indebtedness dominated in foreign currencies.

From Minsky's point of view these changes simply made it possible for developing countries to engage in Ponzi financing schemes such as had not been previously available from official lenders. The Latin American economies in the 1980s can be represented by a Ponzi financing scheme. They did not have a sufficiently large cushion of negative net transfers and thus had to purchase insurance in the form of an IMF "seal of approval" to convince lenders to continue to lend to them even though there was little real evidence of any ability to repay debt. And the result was as Minsky predicted: financial instability in the form of the 1980s Latin American debt crisis.

The changed role of the IMF under Ponzi finance: the "seal of approval"

The response of official financial institutions to the 1980s debt crisis brought about an important change in the impact of their support to developing countries for adjustment to external imbalances. Without the commitment to fixed exchange rates, the need for IMF bridge lending and the associated conditionality disappeared. In theory, under flexible exchange rates, central banks no longer needed to hold exchange reserves, since adjustment to external imbalances would take place through the impact of appropriate market adjustment of exchange rates producing changes in the relative prices of tradeable and nontradeable goods.

But, in the aftermath of a crisis caused by the withdrawal of private funding, developing countries again looked to the IMF to provide short-term adjustment lending. In this, the Fund found a new role, now as guarantor for the policies to be applied by developing countries to ensure private lenders of their creditworthiness.

However, the objective of policy to generate the foreign exchange earnings necessary to meet outstanding commitments remained the same, except that in the new circumstances, it was necessary to convince creditors to participate in debt restructuring programs and to continue to lend to distressed borrowers. The introduction of tight fiscal and monetary policy that had been used to reduce absorption was now viewed as the appropriate policy to convince foreign lenders to continue to provide the capital inflows that would allow the borrower to repay the Fund and other official lenders and to provide sufficient additional inflows to allow existing creditors to exit if they so desired. Thus, even though the Fund's resources were insufficient to meet the borrower's full financing needs, the existence of a Fund lending program was considered to provide the guarantee of recovery that would convince private lenders to restructure existing debt and for new lenders to commit fresh funds to insolvent countries. In the words of the IMF's Deputy Director, "the 'seal of approval' provided by IMF lending also reassures investors and donors that a country's economic policies are on the right track, and helps to generate additional financing from these sources. This means, of course, that the Fund has to be careful to maintain its credibility: if we lose that credibility, by lending in support of inadequate policies, such cata-lytic, complementary support would not be forthcoming" (Carstens 2004).

This view echoes that of the IMF's own Independent Evaluation Office: "creditors . . . tended to link increasing parts of their financing flows to the existence of an IMF lending arrangement acting as a 'seal of approval' on recipi-ent country policies" (IMF Independent Evaluation Office 2002).

Rather than providing bridging finance, under its new mandate the Fund was providing an implicit guarantee – through the conditionality on its lending programs and their surveillance – to external creditors concerning the probability of repayment. It was this new role in providing a "seal of approval" that created an implicit moral hazard that was reinforced by the various IMF rescue packages provided to countries experiencing financial crises after the Mexican declaration of default in 1982.

IMF support for Ponzi finance profiles on the global level

But there was an additional dimension to this new approach; to the extent that a Fund lending program succeeded in convincing the private sector to continue to lend, it implied that the debt would not be reduced; it would only be refi-nanced by allowing new lenders to bail out old lenders.[2] For this to be the case it also implied that the borrowing countries' domestic policies would be more or less permanently governed by IMF surveillance and conditionality, creating the need for a much more prolonged commitment of IMF funds.[3] From being a temporary lender of bridging funds in support of a short-term adjustment program, the IMF became the permanent supplier of "seal of approval" condi-tional loans that ensured the viability of long-term debt rollover and debt service. This in effect meant virtually permanent restrictive fiscal policies and tight monetary policies to ensure external borrowing to finance debt service.

The result has been a wide divergence between the financial performance of indebted developing countries and their real performance in terms of real per capital income growth and employment. Under the initial IMF mandate, growth rates and inflation rates tended to be higher than under the new mandate. However, under the new mandate, while most countries have been able to reduce extremely high inflation rates and to create primary fiscal surpluses and external surpluses to allow them to regain access to private international capital markets, these conditions have been associated with low domestic demand growth, high real interest rates and appreciation of real exchange rates that have produced disappointing real growth performance.

The IMF, development strategy and negative net resource transfers

The IMF's new mandate covered most of the 1980s' experience of Latin Ameri-can countries recovering from the 1982 debt crisis under IMF adjustment programs. Net transfers of resources from developing to developed countries again turned negative after the Asian financial crisis of 1997 and have remained so through the recent developed country financial crisis of 2007–2008. This pattern of financial flows reflects the cost of the IMF "seal of approval" in the form of policies to restrict demand that produce a surplus on trade in goods and services that is not sufficient to cover the negative net capital factor services balance due to the servicing of the existing debt stock. As a result, countries continue to depend on new external private capital inflows to remain current with their external payments commitments. And, to maintain the Fund "seal of approval" to ensure these flows, it requires continued policies of monetary restraint, high real interest rates and primary fiscal surpluses that make return to rapid domestic growth difficult.

Negative net resource transfers are usually considered to have a negative impact on domestic growth; because they represent the export of real goods and services, they reduce the resources available for domestic consumption and investment, lowering real per capita incomes. However, it is important to distinguish between the impact of the negative transfers and the policies that cause them. It might be more correct to note that policies that reduce domestic demand will in general have a negative impact on domestic growth and employment.

At the same time, this means that the transfer of real resources abroad may be part of a rational development plan if they are the result of policies to support domestic income growth and increased domestic savings. In such conditions it is possible to maximize domestic per capita incomes by investing resources abroad if the returns are higher than from using them at home. The possible benefits to growth from negative net resource flows arise from the fact that they create claims on foreigners that can be used to acquire foreign assets that will produce additional foreign claims.

Alternatively, the foreign claims can be used to extinguish foreign liabilities, which reduce debt service. Both reduce the size of negative net resource flows. The importance of domestic policy and the use of net resource outflows may be seen in the behavior of Asian economies in the aftermath of the 1997 financial crisis, compared to the experience in Latin America after the 1982 debt crisis in that region. Many crisis-stricken economies in the Asian region have used negative net resource transfers, averaging well over $100 billion per year for the region as a whole since the crisis, to reduce their private sector liabilities to foreigners, and have started to use their negative net resource flows to make foreign investments. In Latin America, on the other hand, the increase in claims on foreigners during the 1980s was used primarily to cover debt service and to repay arrears. In Asia the rise in net exports has allowed repayment of IMF loans and the possibility of using expansionary domestic policies so that economic growth and domestic savings rates have increased, while in Latin America the net outward transfer of resources has been the result of continued compression of domestic expenditure and continued implementation of IMF conditionality of domestic policy that prompted the lost decade of declining per capita incomes and falling savings rates.

This comparison between the behaviors of Asia and Latin America suggests that the former's policy provides the potential for higher growth. However, this conclusion must be approached with caution. In particular this is because rather than being invested in productive activities abroad, the counterpart to strengthened commercial account positions and rising net private capital flows in the Asian region was an accumulation of international foreign exchange reserves on the order of $364 billion in 2003.

The accumulation of reserves has been mainly in low-risk and comparatively low-yield government securities of developed countries, primarily the United States (US). Not only do these purchases reflect the net transfer of resources from developing to developed countries, but they are also a major component of the financing of the increasingly large external account imbalances of the US. But more importantly, just as the holding of any liquid asset has a cost, these reserve holdings represent an investment which has a negative return. This is the result of the attempt by central banks to maintain control over domestic monetary conditions by sterilizing the financial inflows that are the counterpart of the real resource transfers. It is often thought that sterilization is an optional decision, but it is not. In the absence of sterilization the net foreign earnings of domestic residents will be converted into domestic bank reserves, which will either provide the basis for additional lending by the banking system or, since they represent a net increase in supply of bank reserves to the banking system as a whole, will drive the rate on interbank lending to zero. Thus, if the central bank wishes to retain control over its domestic monetary aggregates or its policy interest rate, sterilization is required. Since sterilization requires issuing a domestic claim in exchange for the foreign claim, and since the domestic claim will in virtually all cases carry an interest rate higher than the rate paid on short-term investments in the US dollar or the euro, this represents an investment with negative carry – the rate of interest paid to fund the foreign reserve position is greater than the rate of interest earned on the position. This translates into lower central bank earnings and a higher fiscal deficit, since such earnings are usually transferred to the Treasury. Reserves thus not only represent a negative transfer of resources, but they also have a negative impact on growth if the government is pursuing a fixed fiscal target, since fiscal expenditures will have to be cut to offset the decline in central bank earnings' contribution to fiscal resources.

However, it is clear that for many developing countries the costs of holding large international reserve balances are more than offset by the benefits they perceive from being able to use them to smooth sharp reversals in private capital flows and to provide a guarantee of solvency. These liquidity balances may thus be seen as the alternative to the IMF "seal of approval" in an active Fund borrowing arrangement and conditionalities on domestic policy. Clearly, when comparing the growth performance of the Asian economies that emerged as rapidly as possible from Fund programs with the performance of Latin American economies which have been subject to IMF "seal of approval" programs virtually continuously since the 1982 debt crisis, the relative cost is much lower.

The paradox of national stability and global instability

As a result of the reduced costs that appear to attach to the strategy of being a "hedge" country, most developing countries are now trying to emulate this strategy in order to increase financial stability. However, in an interdependent international trade and financial system it is not clear that this is a viable policy for all developing countries and whether it has a positive impact on global stability.

The first question can be answered by reference to historical precedent. In the immediate postwar period, the US had a large external trade surplus, and some economists suggested that it could be permanent, creating a situation of dollar scarcity. Others argued that it could provide the basis for generating the demand necessary to keep the US from returning to the Depression of the 1930s. As noted above, the trade balance is roughly the counterpart of what we have been calling the net transfer of resources and is balanced by the capital account plus the capital services account. Maintaining a constant trade surplus (or a constant trade surplus as a share of national income) requires an equivalent capital outflow (or share of income), given exchange rates. However, the increasing foreign lending that is required generates a return flow of debt service payments that produce a surplus on the capital factor services balance. In the absence of any change in the absolute amount of capital outflows the trade surplus thus has to fall to accommodate the increased factor services balance without exchange rate adjustment.

It also provides to conservatives a more acceptable alternative policy for full employment than the Keynesian proposals for deficit financing.

One possible solution would be for foreign lending to rise each year by an amount sufficient to cover the increasing debt service payments. Now, instead of the trade balance and the positive impact on demand, disappearing capital outflows would have to increase without limit. Evsey Domar (1950) provided an answer to whether this process could be sustained: as long as capital outflows increase at a rate equal to the rate of interest received in debt service from the rest of the world on the outstanding loans, the rising inflows on factor service accounts are just offset by the rising capital outflows, and there is no net impact on the trade balance and thus on demand. On the other hand, if interest rates are higher than the rate of increase in foreign lending, the policy becomes self-defeating and the trade balance eventually becomes negative to offset the rising net capital service inflows. Eventually, the continually rising factor service flows would turn the trade balance negative, and the negative net resources flows turn positive.

Thus, the sustainability of the hedge profile is similar to the problem analyzed by Domar – it can only work if the rate of interest on foreign assets is equal to or below the rate of increase of the negative net transfers. As long as the foreign assets acquired are highly liquid with low interest rates, it is more likely that the policy can be maintained.

However, with respect to the second question about the stability of the financial system, it is interesting to note that the Domar conditions for a sustained long-term development strategy based on external financing – on sustained positive net resource transfers – are the precise equivalent of the conditions required for a successful Ponzi financing scheme. As long as the rate of increase in inflows from new investors in a pyramid or Ponzi scheme is equal to or greater than the rate of interest paid to existing investors in the scheme, there is no difficulty in maintaining the payments promised to prior investors in the scheme. However, no such scheme in history has ever been successful – they are bound to fail eventually by the increasing size of the net debt stock of the operator of the scheme. On the other hand, if the rate of interest on foreign lending is greater than the rate of increase of foreign lending, then the system is absolutely unstable and cannot be sustained on even a short-term basis.

In the present case, it is the US that is the counterpart of the Asian developing countries accumulating dollar claims, so it is the US that is operating the Ponzi scheme. Any move to increase interest rates on US dollar claims thus increases the fragility of the scheme because it means that the US has to increase the rate of increase of its foreign borrowing and by implication the rate of increase in its trade deficit. On the other hand, any action to bring about a rapid reversal of the US deficit or a contraction in US growth would quickly counter Domar's stability conditions and make the system locally unstable, negating the hedge protection of developing countries with large negative net resource transfers invested in dollar claims.

Thus, while the hedge country strategy may provide liquidity protection for a single country, as Keynes (1946) warned, there is no such thing as liquidity for the system as a whole, and there is no such thing as a perfect hedge in an interdependent international trading and financial system: "It is obvious that no country can go on forever covering by new lending a chronic surplus on current account without eventually forcing a default from the other parties." The provision of global liquidity requires a global institution based on symmetrical adjustment through automatic provision of liquidity such as that proposed in Keynes Clearing Union (see Kregel 2014).

Notes

1 Minsky (e.g. 1990) formulated these profiles as part of his financial instability hypothesis based on the idea that financial crises are endogenous events inevitably generated by periods of financial stability.
2 For example in the solution to the Latin American crisis provided by the Brady Bonds, bank loans were repaid by selling bonded debt to institutional investors.
3 Indeed, the Report on Prolonged Use of IMF resources (op. cit.) notes that the increased commitment period for IMF funding programs was in part due to a shift, from its traditional balance of lending to developed country borrowers, to lending to developing country borrowers.

References

Carstens, A (2004) "Remarks of the Deputy Managing Director, International Monetary Fund", at the WCC-World Bank-IMF High-Level Encounter, Geneva, October 22, 2004 (http://www.imf.org/external/np/speeches/2004/102204a. htm).

Domar, E (1950) "The Effect of Foreign Investments on the Balance of Payments" *American Economic Review*, Vol. 40, (December), pp. 805–26.

IMF, Independent Evaluation Office (2002) *Evaluation of Prolonged Use of IMF Resources* (Washington, DC: International Monetary Fund).

Keynes, J M (1946) "The Balance of Payments of the United States" *The Economic Journal*, Vol. 56, No. 222 (June), pp. 172–87.

Kregel, J A (1998a) "Derivatives and Global Capital Flows: Applications to Asia" *Cambridge Journal of Economics*, Vol. 22, No. 6 (November), pp. 677–692.

—— (1998b) "East Asia Is Not Mexico: The Difference Between Balance of Payments Crises and Debt Deflations", in Jomo, K.S. ed., *Tigers in Trouble: Financial Governance, Liberalisation and Crises in East Asia* (London: Zed Press) 44–62.

—— (1999) "Alternatives to the Brazilian Crisis", *Brazilian Journal of Political Economy*, Vol. 19, No. 3 (75) (julho-setembro), 1999, pp. 23–38.

—— (2014) "The Chimera of Export Led Growth and External Debt Reduction After the Financial Crisis", *Keynes's Relevance to Today's World* (Tokyo: Sakuhinsha).

Minsky, H (1986) "Global Consequences of Financial Deregulation", *The Marcus Wallenberg Papers on International Finance*. Vol. 2, No. 1.

—— (1990) *Stabilizing and Unstable Economy*, Twentieth Century Fund Reports (New Haven: Yale University Press).

Robinson, J. (1956) *The Accumulation of Capital* (London: Macmillan).

13 Malfunction of capital accumulation regime in present-day Japan

Kenichi Haga

Introduction

Trends in Japan's recent capital accumulation regime can be classified into three phases: the bubble period (1986–91), the first half of the bubble bust period (1991–97), and the latter half of the bubble bust period, i.e. the malfunctioning period (1998 until now). With a focus on the last period, this chapter analyzes the mechanisms of the malfunctioning of Japan's capital accumulation regime since the watershed year of 1998, and gives perspectives for countermeasures.

This chapter begins by outlining its analytical framework. It then analyzes the current status of Japan's capital accumulation regime. In doing so, it first goes through economic indicators of malfunction; second, it investigates the financial crisis as a plausible suspect with regard to the malfunction since 1998, and confirms that the financial crisis as such is not the principle offender; third, it explains Japanese corporations' peculiar price-setting strategies; fourth, it points out that corporations' facile strategy of wage reduction to secure profits was facilitated by the old and new institutional peculiarities of the employment regime; fifth, it demonstrates that corporations' low-wage strategy stagnated the demand regime, and that the abnormality of the distribution regime caused by corporations' low-wage strategy endorsed deflation through firms' costs; and sixth, the stagnant demand regime caused abnormalities in the investment regime. The chapter goes on to discuss perspectives for overcoming the problem, together with their feasibilities. It concludes with a brief summary.

Analytical framework

As main factors constituting the methodological framework for analyzing the capital accumulation regime, the following four points should be mentioned. The first is the corporations' (as well as financial institutions') micro-level strategic behavior (or nano-level strategic behavior, which takes "species differences" into account). In accordance with their demand predictions, corporations invest, produce goods and services, and set prices to supply the market. The market is the stage on which to judge whether or not produced goods will be sold at the set prices. Money can purchase goods, but goods cannot purchase money. Equally important is the strategic behavior of organizations called corporations.

The market will not tell corporations the best strategy to adopt. Corporations, through addressing the market and production uncertainties, accumulate learning and nurture "organizational capabilities" within their organization.[1] If they fail, they are forced to exit. It is not only the "invisible hand" of the market, but also the "visible hand" of corporations, i.e. their planned and discretionary behaviors, that creates the dynamics of the accumulation regime.

The second factor is the socio-institutional framework that facilitates or limits corporations' strategies. If social institutions can successfully coordinate interfirm competition and conflicts between capital and labor, business confidence will be enhanced and corporations' innovative investment strategies will be facilitated. I will elaborate on this point while discussing employment strategy in the context of social institutions.

The third factor is the macroeconomic dynamism that is realized through corporate behaviors. The goods and services produced are sold. The values-added are distributed between wages and profits. Wages are expended on consumer goods, and profits are expended on capital and producer goods. The virtuous "circular relation" (Steindle 1983, p. 99) among the production regime, the distribution regime, and the expenditure (i.e. demand) regime helps the macro-economy to operate normally, and hence secures legitimacy of the social system. Moreover, if the increment of the value-added is properly distributed to wages with the result of increased household consumption, corporations expand fixed capital investment which will increase employment and realize expanded reproduction.

On the contrary, if accumulation stagnates and unemployment increases – as the SSA (social structure of accumulation) theory emphasizes – the legitimacy of the social structure will be shaken and there will be a rise in social conflicts, which will lead to efforts to find a new structure. This is the fourth point, the transformation theory of the "capital accumulation regime".

What these four points constitute is the framework generally called "capital accumulation regime". Rather than elaborating the methodology as such, I will demonstrate it more concretely while applying it in this chapter's analysis.

Malfunction of the accumulation regime: its mechanism

Indicators of malfunction

As macro-indicators show the current malfunction of the accumulation regime, let us check the declining nominal GDP in absolute terms since 1998, continuing deflation, and the persistently high unemployment rate.

The long-term trend of nominal GDP shows that it steadily increased since 1955, which was the first year of rapid economic growth (Figure 13.1). This trend continued after the 1970s, despite the drastic changes in the international environment that occurred approximately every five years, such as the two oil shocks, the switch to the floating exchange system, etc. The bursting of the economic bubble in 1991 brought about a downward kink in the trend, but in absolute terms, nominal GDP kept increasing. However, after reaching its

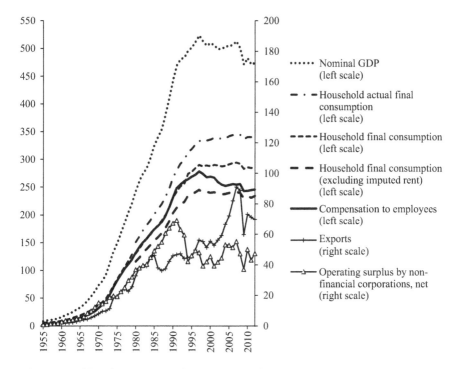

Figure 13.1 Trends in GDP and other GDP-related indicators in trillion yen

Source: ESRI (d) 1999, 2010 and 2013.

Note: There are statistical breaks in 1980 and 1994.

peak at 523 trillion yen in 1997, it declined steadily to 499 trillion yen in 2003. Thereafter, thanks to the increase in exports, it gradually recovered to the level of 513 trillion yen in 2007. However, following the bankruptcy of Lehman Brothers in 2008, it tumbled to 471 trillion yen in 2009. During the 12-year period from 1997 to 2009, it never returned to its peak. Rather, it declined by 52 trillion yen in absolute terms, or 10 percent less than the peak.

As can be seen in Figure 13.2, GDP deflator has been showing negative signs since the mid-1990s. Deflation, defined as the steady decrease in overall prices, is an abnormal phenomenon prominent only in Japan among developed countries. Further, unemployment (rate) has rapidly increased from 2.3 million persons (3.4 percent) in 1997 to 3.59 million (5.4 percent) in 2002, and remained high at 2.85 million (4.3 percent) in 2012.

Breakout of financial crisis and the malfunction mechanism

Why, then, is Japan's capital accumulation regime malfunctioning, and why has it never been able to escape this autonomously? If the turning point is 1998,

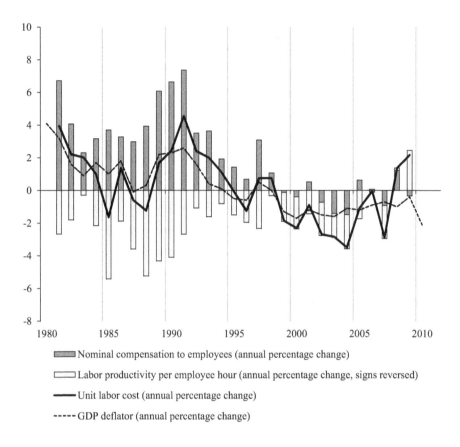

Nominal compensation to employees (annual percentage change)

Labor productivity per employee hour (annual percentage change, signs reversed)

——Unit labor cost (annual percentage change)

-----GDP deflator (annual percentage change)

Unit labor cost (OLS 1980–2009)
ULC = -.052379 +.005849*(PGDP)
        (-1.45)   (15.60)
R^2 = 0.8932 Standard Error = 0.011 Durbin-Watson Ratio = 0.364

ULC : Unit labor cost, PGDP : GDP deflator

Figure 13.2 Trends in unit labor costs percent

the suspect that immediately comes to mind is the financial crisis, which broke out in November 1997 and spread across the region thereafter.

Japanese financial institutions have been busy dealing with bad loans. These bad loans reflect those related to real estate (especially on commercial lands) during the bubble economy, as well as those added in line with the depression after the bubble burst. At first, the Ministry of Finance (MOF) dealt with those financial institutions on the verge of bankruptcy through "discretionary policies (merger of de facto bankrupt banks with healthy banks, establishment of new banks, etc.)" to contain a sudden and widespread financial crisis. When such polices reached their limits, the "Three Financial Laws" of 1996 were passed, enabling the government to provide credit unions (and housing-loan corporations) with financial assistance, including those to cover costs that exceeded the payoff cost while using tax money. The then cabinet led by Ryutaro Hashimoto misunderstood this as the completion of the financial management system. Combined with the recovery in fixed capital investment in the real economy since 1996, they switched their policy goal from financial management to the so-called six major reforms. One of these was fiscal structure reform, which increased the public burden by as much as 9 trillion yen for FY1997 (starting in April 1997), and the economy experienced a downturn from its peak in May of that year. And then, in November of the same year, triggered by the failure of the medium-sized securities house, Sanyo Securities, the interbank market was paralyzed and the crisis extended to major banks as well. However, it is difficult to think that the deterioration of the real economy caused by the government's "mismanagement of the economy" in April 1997 directly triggered the financial crisis in November. Rather than being based on the real economy, the financial crisis was presumably based on an enormous amount of bad debts and happened to emerge in November. Instability in the financial system continued until May 2005, when the government declared the financial normalization of major banks.

The number of failed financial institutions was 28 (7 of which were banks) during the period from 1991 to 1997. However, this number increased to 153 (13 banks) during the period from 1998 to 2005, and 181 during the two periods combined (*Deposit Insurance Corporation of Japan* [hereinafter DICJ] 2007, pp. 406–407). Further, according to "the write-off of bad debt (loans)" recorded in *Annual Report of National Accounts of 2013* (Economic and Social Research Institute, Cabinet Office, hereinafter ESRI 2013), the accumulated loss during the period from 1991 to 2005 was 113.8 trillion yen in "private financial institutions" and 1.8 trillion yen in "public financial institutions", totaling 115.6 trillion yen (the figure for "all banks" was approximately 96 trillion yen until March 2005). Such was the degree of financial asset value that has been destroyed and disappeared. Further, injection of public money through DICJ (for the full protection of deposits, capital injection, etc.) amounted to 47 trillion yen (out of which 10 trillion was ultimately borne by taxpayers). If other measures such as special credit guarantees to small- and medium-sized companies were included, the total cost of government intervention would amount to 88 trillion yen (Cabinet Office 2009, p. 189).

To deal with financial liberalization without a national strategy (government failure), banks had as early as around 1980 formulated an aggressive loan strategy – a strategy to overcome the margin squeeze due to interest-rate liberalization through expanding types of operations (bank management failure). This strategy was implemented against the backdrop of BOJ's ultra-low interest rate policy (BOJ's failure), and supported the land-price bubble from the financial aspect. When land prices started to decline in 1991, land-related loans became non-performing. Through amortizing large amounts of bad debt, financial institutions mutilated their equity capital, and some were forced into bankruptcy. What prevented the spread of systemic risk stands in direct opposition to the recently predominant economic thought of neoliberalism – bailout measures for financial institutions by the large government and by the large central bank, as well as the injection of public funds totaling 88 trillion yen and the burden on the public.

The financial crises, channeled through banks' reluctance to extend loans undoubtedly had negative effects on business activities. The total amount of outstanding loans by domestic banks declined from 493 trillion yen as of the year-end of 1997 to 404 trillion yen as of the year-end of 2004, a reduction of almost 90 trillion yen. As of the year-end of 2013, this amount only recovered to 449 trillion yen. In 1998, private banks' reluctance to extend loans, particularly to small- and medium-size firms, was severe, but the government's special credit guarantee and government financial institutions filled the gap. Further, without regard to firm size, the situation where net cash flow exceeds fixed capital investment has been continuing since the mid-1990s in manufacturing industries, and since around 2000 in nonmanufacturing industries. Thus it is difficult to think that financial aspects are constraining corporate behaviors (The Director General for Economic and Fiscal Management, Cabinet Office 2014, p. 130). Rather, the prime cause for the malfunction should be looked for in the real economic aspect of the capital accumulation regime. Moreover, the stagnant fixed capital investment in real economy is causing weak growth in outstanding bank loans in the financial regime, as well as "de-financialization" in the accumulation regime.

The price-setting strategy of corporations

The financial crisis merely triggered the malfunction of the capital accumulation regime. The capital accumulation regime started malfunctioning through its inherent mechanism. During the financial panic that started in 1998, the business confidence of corporations was shaken, and they pulled back investments. Households expected downsizing and wage cuts, and they restrained consumption. In the midst of rapidly contracting aggregate demand, corporations accelerated destructive price-cutting competition.

Japanese corporations' price-setting strategy is peculiar compared to US and European corporations. Recently, central banks in developing countries conducted a survey on price-setting behavior in various countries. As for corporations in the Euro area in 2003–04, the survey reported that the average "markup (on costs)" accounted for 54 percent (including 40 percent in France and 73 percent in Germany), "competitors' price" accounted for 27 percent (38 percent, and 17 percent), and others accounted for 19 percent (Fabiani et al. [eds.] 2007, p. 39). The Bank of Japan also conducted a survey during the period of April–May 2000 on the price-setting behavior of Japanese corporations listed in the First Section of the Tokyo Stock Exchange, and found that the top preference for both manufacturing and nonmanufacturing corporations was "price is set at the upper limit permitted by the market" ("weak relationship with costs, . . . and strong relationship with supply-demand conditions in the market"). Placing importance on "market share" rather than mark-up, which has hitherto been pointed out to be most peculiar among Japanese companies, was the second-biggest concern in manufacturing and the third-biggest in nonmanufacturing. "Direct cost plus fixed mark-up" was third in manufacturing and fourth in nonmanufacturing (Bank of Japan Research and Statistics Department 2000, pp. 8–9). While Fabiani et al. characterize this as "a particular form of markup pricing" (Fabiani et al. [eds.] 2007, p. 190), it tends to deal with the decline in demand through adjusting prices rather than adjusting production quantities, and hence it is a peculiar form of price-setting.[2]

On the other hand, the same BOJ survey demonstrates, "in comparison with 1996–97", "corporate management strategy" has changed from "focusing on market share" to "focusing on the rate of return". The reason for this is that it is "difficult to expect growth in the product market, compared with the past", according to "about 80 per cent of manufacturing and non-manufacturing companies" that responded (Bank of Japan Research and Statistics Department 2000, pp. 5–6). Presumably, corporations finally accepted the fact that low growth is firmly in place and changed their strategy. To cope with the new situation, more than 90 percent of companies indicated "productivity increase and reduction in costs" as possible means. Moreover, 54 percent of manufacturing companies indicated that they would adopt "product differentiation" measures and "not rely on price-cutting as before." However, these are only their hopes. In reality, to cope with fierce competition, corporations relying on price-cutting amounted to 62 percent in manufacturing and 64 percent in nonmanufacturing (Bank of Japan Research and Statistics Department 2000). Such a price-setting strategy implies the following: if one corporation adjusts its assumption for the "upper-limit price level" downwards in response to a sudden decline in demand, its rivals will follow suit, and price-cutting competition will start.

Corporate employment strategies and social institutions of the employment regime

Due to their traditional price-setting method, Japanese corporations' price-cutting strategy has been causing destructive price-cutting competition in the industry sector. Against this background, the measure taken by corporations to realize the management strategy of "putting weight on rate-of-return" was not the innovative strategy of productivity increase and product differentiation, but the most facile strategy of wage reduction. This causal relationship from price to wage is important. According to *FY 2002 Annual Survey of Corporate Behavior* by ESRI, 75.5 percent of corporations answered that "the decline in sales price is advancing more than the cost-cuts, putting pressure on profit margin" (ESRI (a) 2003). Thus, the authors of the survey summarized that "deflation is regarded as an external harsh pressure to bring prices down beyond reductions in costs", and therefore "prices affect wages in deflation, not the other way around".

Table 13.1 Number of employees by employment type, millions of persons

Year	1985	1991	1997	2012
Number of employees excluding executives	39.99	45.36(+5.37)	49.63(+4.27)	51.54(+1.91)
Of which: regular employees	33.43	36.39(+2.96)	3,812 (+1.73)	33.40(–4.72)
Non-regular employees	6.55	8.97(+2.42)	11.52(+2.55)	18.13(+6.61)

Source: Statistics Bureau, MIC (2013)

As can be seen in Figure 13.1, "nominal compensation to employees", a macro aggregate representing "wages and salaries" plus "employers' social contributions", reached its peak at 278 trillion yen in 1997, thereafter declining to 243 trillion yen in 2009. Wages and salaries declined from 240 trillion yen to 206 trillion yen in the same period. Since 1991, these two indicators kinked downwards, reflecting the first and the second downsizing by corporations. Even though the rate of growth declined, absolute value did not decline until 1998.

The decrease in employee compensation was due, aside from unemployment caused by bankruptcy, to corporate employment strategies of (1) reducing new employment, (2) holding down the age-wage profile for regular workers (those employed without term) and relying on long working hours, and (3) increasing the share of low-wage non-regular workers (those employed with term), which allow corporations to save "employers' social contributions" and to conduct employment adjustments easily. The third point was particularly important. As Table 13.1 shows, the total number of employees excluding executives increased by 4.27 million during the six-year period from 1991 to 1997, and the number of regular workers also increased by 1.73 million during the same period. However, during the 15 years from 1997 to 2012, not only did the total number of employees increase by only 1.91 million, but the number of regular employees also decreased by 4.72 million, and the number of non-regular employees increased by 6.61 million. Even though the share of non-regular employees has gradually been increasing, from 16.4 percent in 1985 to 23.2 percent in 1997, its increase since then has been accelerated, reaching 35.2 percent in 2012. According to the *Basic Survey of Wage Structure for 2012: National: Summary of Report* conducted by the Ministry of Health, Labour and Welfare (hereinafter MHLW), if we take the average wages of all male and female regular workers as 100, those of non-regular workers were only 62 (MHLW (a) 2012). Moreover, even when non-regular workers reach a higher age range, wage increases are rare. As discussed later, this implies exclusion from the education and training system of corporations.

Why, then, were corporations "successful" in curbing wages for regular employees and in increasing the share of non-regular employees? The answer can be found in socio-institutional characteristics of the employment regime, which encouraged corporations to choose the low-wage employment strategy. First, concerning regular employees, labor unions have been allowing voluntary retirement when corporations have been in deficit for two consecutive years (Koike 2005, pp. 143–144), and labor costs have been flexibly adjusted through cutting overtime payments, bonuses, etc. In addition, since the outbreak of oil crises, the management side has been pressing labor unions to choose "employment or wages". Against this backdrop, labor unions have been prioritizing employment security while accepting wage restraint. Thus, the employment regime for regular employees has long been "flexible (unstable)".

Moreover, as can be seen from the fact that non-regular employees accounted for 17 percent of the total in1985, the Japanese employment regime has been characterized by a "dual structure" or segmented labor market. Even during the period of rapid economic growth, corporations made most use of the temporary employees and day laborers; and during the post–oil crises period, the number of short-term workers, particularly that of part-timers, had been increasing. The already existing employment forms for non-regular workers were utilized as part of a low-wage strategy since 1998.

Further, the number of dispatched workers – a new employment form of non-regular workers – has been increasing. Enacted in 1986, the Worker Dispatching Law started with 16 occupations on the positive list. In December 1996, the number of listed occupations was increased to 26, and in December 1999, the scope of occupations was liberalized in principle, with the exception of some occupations. In March 2004, the ban on dispatching workers for those manufacturing occupations was lifted. The original aim of legally limiting occupations for non-regular workers was to prevent corporations from substituting non-regular workers (who should inherently be employed as regular workers) for regular workers. However, substitution has advanced without regard to the original aim of the law. Since 1999, growth in the number of part-time workers leveled off at around 10–11 million plus persons, whereas that of dispatched workers rapidly increased from 0.33 million persons in 2000 to 1.4 million in 2003, thereafter declining sharply at 0.9 million in 2012 due to the recession, indicating that this form of employment was utilized as a control valve (Statistics Bureau, MIC, various years).

Why in recent years has the age-wage profile for regular employees been maintained somewhat, even though it has been decreasing year by year, and why are wages for non-regular employees as little as 60 per cent of those of regular employees? Generally speaking, money wage is determined through institutional factors (the ratio of organized labor, the ways in which collective bargaining is carried out, etc.) and market factors (primarily unemployment rate). During the period of rapid economic growth, the "*shunto* (spring offensive) method (started in 1955)" was the most important of the former factors. It is a negotiation model where a series of collective bargaining sessions are concentrated in the spring to determine money wage raises for regular workers (especially males). During *shunto*, the leading corporation within a pattern-setting industry determines its wage raise rate through collective bargaining, followed by other corporations within the same industry. The negotiated raise has also functioned as the benchmark for negotiations in other industries and spread among unorganized workers, as well as the "going rate." If corporations within the same industry raised wages by the same rate, a particular corporation would not have a competitive disadvantage. This was important not only for the management side, but also for enterprise-based unions. *Shunto* was a good method to avoid the situation termed "co-ordination failure (between corporations and labor unions, as well as among themselves)" under the game theory (see Figure 1.9 and its explanations in Bowles (2012), pp. 27–32). Since the rate of increase of money wage was parallel with that of productivity, the management side was able to assure profits. Further, wage raises smoothly increased final consumption by households, which activated capital accumulation and decreased the unemployment rate. A lower unemployment rate made market factors favorable in wage negotiations and contributed to the strengthening of labor unions' bargaining power. Note, however, that even though *shunto* was a rational method, it was developed only as a "practice" and was not fully institutionalized. In addition, it was a method that was strongly affected by market factors.

This method of determining and disseminating money wage was the pivot of the income distribution regime during the high growth period. In neoclassical economics, the real wage of any worker is essentially determined by marginal productivity of his/her labor (which is not measurable), and therefore functional income distribution of the value added into wages and profits does not pose a problem. On the other hand, in Marxian economics, the money wage is defined by the value of labor power, and hence income distribution is out of the question. In reality, the labor–capital negotiation model has been implementing functional income distribution of the value-added and its increment.

As previously stated both labor and capital have been making this method of determining money wages into a mere formality since the oil crises. However, the age-wage profile for regular employees has been maintained, although it has been pressed downwards. The reason why the wages of regular workers are not reduced as much as those of non-regular workers is that management is concerned about hurting employee "morale" (Bewley 1999, pp. 47–52). Workers are not "commodities", nor those providing "supplementary assistance" to an "automatic system of machinery" (Marx 1976). Even though basically relying on workers' perception of "the threat of job loss", management has to obtain their spontaneous "consent" to extract maximum labor efforts from workers (Burawoy 1979 and 2012). The condition for obtaining such consent is to allow the workers to feel that the management is treating them with fairness. One such fair treatment is to set a money wage that is in line with the "criterion of employment" assumed by regular workers. Wages that differ greatly from the criterion will harm the feeling of fairness and the workers' consent, deteriorate morale and eventually bring about a decline in productivity that will exceed the degree of wage savings. Herein lay the reason why management considered, as a primary measure to reduce labor costs, increasing the share of non-regular employees. On the other hand, wages of non-regular workers are determined in line with the "criterion of employment" of housewives hoping to get supplementary household income, and students who are satisfied with supplementary income to cover their living expenses. However, labor supply structure has greatly changed. Young people who unfortunately graduated during the employment ice age formed a huge pool of unwilling non-regular workers.

Abnormality of the distribution regime and the demand regime

The old and new social institutions of the employment regime have made management choose the lowest wage strategy possible and transformed the distribution regime. Let us see how the transformation of the distribution regime caused the capital accumulation regime to malfunction from the viewpoint of the demand (expenditure) regime as well as the cost aspect of the production regime.

Under the capital accumulation regime, in addition to addressing workers' morale, money wage has two additional functions. Namely, wages are costs for corporations in the microeconomic sense, but they are also a source of household income in the macroeconomic sense. I will discuss the cost aspect in the next subsection. In this section I will focus on the relationship between wages and household consumption.

As a result of the low-wage strategy, "wages and salaries", a category under nominal employee compensation, have declined with slight fluctuations by as much as 34 trillion yen from 1997 to 2009. And this abnormality in the distribution regime caused the demand regime to hover around through declining household consumption. Stagnant GDE growth offered a perfect macroeconomic opportunity for corporations to deploy price-cutting competition. At first, it was the outbreak and the continuation of financial crises since 1997 that caused the contraction of household consumption. After that, external shocks continued to occur, including the bankruptcy of Lehman Brothers, natural disasters (the Great East Japan earthquake and tsunami) and a man-made disaster (Fukushima nuclear accident). The effects of these events on consumption were not temporary, and through the decline of "wages and salaries" in absolute terms, stagnant consumption was built into the mechanism of malfunction. This is a typical "fallacy of composition", where corporations' low-wage strategy in the micro aspect reduces consumption in the macro aspect.

However, as can be seen from Figure 13.1, unlike "wages and salaries", "final household consumption" shows little change since 1997. According to ESRI's *Annual Report on National Accounts of 2013*, it decreased from 1997 at 290 trillion yen to 2009 at 283 trillion, indicating a fairly small decline of 7 trillion yen (ESRI 2013). One of the reasons for such a trend in household consumption was the decline in the household saving rate. According to the above report, the household saving rate increased from 10.3 percent in 1997 to 11.4 percent in 1998, but thereafter it declined to 2.2 percent in 2009. A more important factor was the increase in the "social benefits other than social transfers in kind, receivable", which increased steadily from 59 trillion yen in 1997 to 78 trillion yen in 2009. Further, the "actual final consumption" by the household (the sum of "final consumption expenditure" by the household and social transfers in kind from the government to the household, such as education and medical services) slightly increased from 334 trillion yen in 1997 to 336 trillion in 2009. In 2009, "actual consumption expenditures" by the household accounted for as much as 70 percent of GDP. Thus, the welfare state system was working as a built-in-stabilizer, checking the spiral reduction of total demand, and preventing the capital accumulation regime from falling into a "great depression".

Figure 13.1 also shows that exports increased from 2001 at 53 trillion yen to 2007 at 91 trillion yen, and this increase contributed to the raising of the level of the capital accumulation regime. However, the increase in exports was due to the speculative housing boom in the US, and was an externally generated phenomenon. Following the bankruptcy of Lehman Brothers, exports tumbled to 59 trillion yen in 2009.

Abnormality of the distribution regime and the production regime

Abnormality of the distribution regime adversely affected the production regime. This subsection focuses on two points. One is that the low-wage strategy prompted deflation from the production cost aspect. The other is that the abnormality of the distribution regime caused the investment regime (a part of the production regime) to malfunction by stagnating the demand regime.

First, the low-wage strategy endorsed deflation from micro aspects. Corporations set prices by using a "peculiar" mark-up method on the unit cost of a product. When we look at the national economy as a whole, intermediate goods (excluding imported goods) will be cancelled out and nominal GDP can be divided into wages and profits (including consumption of fixed capital). The labor share (in GDP) can be written as follows:

$$\pi = WL/PY = W/P\lambda$$

where π is the labor share, W is nominal compensation to employees (per unit labor hour), L is the number of employees multiplied by annual working hours per person, Y is real GDP, P is GDP deflator, and λ is Y/L, i.e. the productivity per unit labor hour. In the above expression, $WL/Y = W/\lambda$ denotes unit labor cost (ULC).

If we express the above equation in terms of growth rates, we obtain:

$$\hat{\pi} = \hat{W} - \hat{\lambda} - \hat{P} = \widehat{ULC} - \hat{P}$$

For example, if W increases by 5 percent, and if we assume the growth rate of λ is 3 percent, then the management will offset the 3 percent through productivity increase, and transfer the unabsorbed 2 percent on the price to maintain the capital share. This represents moderate inflation.

Then, what about current deflation? Figure 13.2 breaks down ULC trends into nominal compensation to employees per hour and labor productivity. Since the mid-1990s, annual growth rates of both compensation to employees and ULC have been negative, and the GDP deflator is indicating a significant correlation with respect to ULC. Needless to say, correlation is not a causal relationship. As has been stated, the direction of causal relationship was that the prices have been reduced in the first place, and then wages have been cut down. Under normal circumstances, the cutting down of money wages lagged behind the reduction in prices. However, this time, the former paralleled the latter due to the increasing share of non-regular workers. During the period from 1998 to 2007, annual average rates of change for nominal compensation to employees and labor productivity were -0.31 percent and +1.47 percent, respectively, and that for ULC was -1.78 percent. Continuation of deflation is prompted by cost aspects of the production regime.[3] Thus the labor share (in national income) declined from 73.0 percent in 1997 to 67.1 percent in 2007. On the other hand, as shown in Figure 13.1, "operating surplus by non-financial corporations, net" declined from 48 trillion yen in 1997 to 39 trillion yen in 2001. Thereafter, it managed to exceed the level of 7 years ago in 2004. However, after the Lehman Brothers bankruptcy, it tumbled to 37 trillion yen in 2009. Even when capital share increases, it is natural for "operating surplus by non-financial corporations, net" to decline if the economic pie becomes smaller (ESRI (d) 2013). (Incidentally, its most recent peak was in the last year of the bubble economy in 1991 at 69 trillion yen, according to ESRI [d] [2010]. Through its low-wage strategy, the capital is not only putting pressure on workers' daily lives, but also reducing their essential profit, which is akin to putting a noose around their necks.Figure 13.2 Trends in unit labor costs percent

In addition, the abnormality of the distribution regime was channeled through the demand regime and caused the investment regime to malfunction. From the viewpoint of flow, fixed capital investment was stagnant. Growth in corporations' fixed capital stock is also deteriorating against the backdrop of accelerated disposal. According to Figure 13.3, during the period of the bubble economy in the latter half of the 1980s, the boom was not a superficial one where only asset prices rose sharply, but was deep-rooted in the real economy where almost all industries increased their fixed capital investment (the reason for the fixed capital stock increment in 1984 exceeding new investments was the privatization of Japan National Railways, the Nippon Telegraph and Telephone Public Corporation, etc., which added their fixed capital assets to the private sector). Since the start of the 1990s, not only have new investments declined, but growth in fixed capital stock has also deteriorated, because corporations have recognized that lower growth is rooted in and has accelerated the disposal of existing plants and equipment. During the six-year period of the investment boom in fixed capital (1986–91), capital stock increased by 259 trillion yen. During the six-year pre-bust period (1991–97) as well, it increased by 199 trillion yen. However, during the 12-year period from 1997 to 2009, it grew by only 235 trillion yen. In addition, not all of the fixed capital investment was for the strengthening of production capacity. According to the Development Bank of Japan's *Survey on Planned Capital Spending*, among the motives for investment by all industries

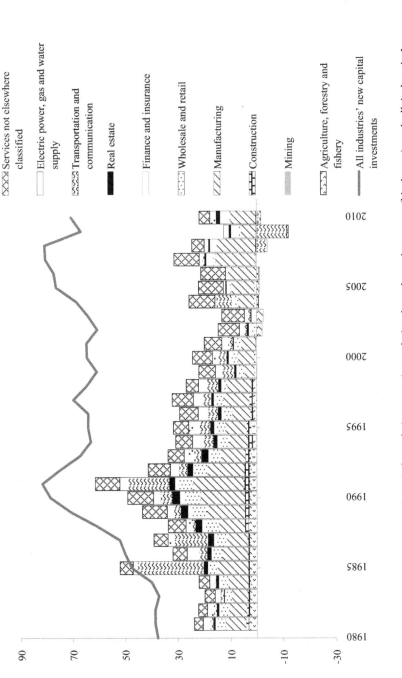

Figure 13.3 Private enterprises' capital stock increase (cumulative bar chart, by type of industry) and all industries' new capital investment (line graph)

Source: ESRI (e)

Note: Data are on "value-put-in-place" basis.

(actual record) in the peak year of 2007, "expansion of capabilities" accounted for 49 percent, and "maintenance and repair" for 21.5 percent, whereas in 2013 their shares respectively declined to 42 percent and 19.4 percent. It should also be noted that investments in "maintenance and repair", "new products" and "labor saving" totaled more than investments in "expansion of capabilities" in 2013.

ESRI frequently surveys "determining factors for plant and equipment investments" (multiple answers allowed). According to their *FY2000 Annual Survey of Corporate Behavior* (ESRI 2001), 77.1 percent and 60.7 percent of corporations respectively answered "domestic and overseas demand trends" and "level of earnings" as motives for "capacity expansion investments". Only 21.8 percent of corporations gave "other companies' movement" as a motive. The share of those that answered "interest rate" was only 8 percent (results are essentially the same in other survey years). Since fixed capital investment requires a long amortization period, they are implemented only after corporations are convinced of the increase in medium-term demand. If corporations adopted the mark-up method – regardless of the thin margin it may be – "level of earnings" would be in line with "demand trends".[4] The assumed "demand trends" are indicated in the "economic growth rate forecasts (all industries basis)" in the survey. According to *FY 2013 Annual Survey of Corporate Behavior*, "forecasts for real economic growth rate for the next three years" peaked at 3.8 percent in fiscal year (FY) 1989, and thereafter it continued declining to 0.6 percent in FY 2001. It recovered to 2.1 percent in FY 2006, but it declined again. The decline in actual growth rate has been leading to the lowering of forecasts for future years, thereby restraining fixed capital investment. New fixed capital investment embodies technical innovation. Their sluggishness will increase the average vintage of fixed capital (hereafter vintage)and have harmful effects on labor productivity increases (for information about the relationship between the vintage and the increase in capital coefficient, see Director General for Economic and Fiscal Management, Cabinet Office 2013, pp. 127–129). The organizational capability of corporations is deteriorating through the fixed capital aspect.

Abnormalities in the distribution regime are reducing household consumption and causing the demand regime to malfunction, leading to the lowering of forecasts for GDP growth rates, and thereby causing deterioration in the investment regime. The demand for labor is the derived demand of the increase in capital stock and its rate of operation. Unless demand, particularly domestic demand, recovers and increases fixed capital investment, unemployment cannot be reduced.

Measures to overcome the malfunction

Restoring the distribution regime and labor law policies

The key to circular relations – among the production, distribution and expenditure (demand) regimes – falling into a macroeconomic vicious cycle is the abnormality of the distribution regime. Therefore, the most urgent task is to restore the distribution regime. The rule to determine money wage is derived from the aforementioned equation for labor share. That is, the rate increase in money wages = the rate of increase in labor productivity + the inflation target. From 1998 to 2007, the average annual rate of change for labor productivity was +1.47 percent. (Since short-term labor productivity fluctuates very much, it is desirable to use average data for the medium-term range.) If a modest inflation rate of, say, 2 percent is desirable, a wage increase of 3.47 percent is appropriate. Since the labor share declined, the wage increase could be even higher. If this is realized, the management will absorb 1.47 percent of the wage increase rate, and will transfer the remaining 2 percent representing the increase in ULC on the price. This means we can escape from deflation. In addition an increase in wages and salaries will increase household consumption, and thus macroeconomic conditions will be prepared for management to raise the upper limit permitted by the market. In such an environment, management has to construct corporate strategies to increase non-price competitiveness and to invoke the price-setting method that was established during the high-growth period. An increase in consumption will also recover the investment regime. Corporations will raise their forecasts for economic growth and increase fixed capital investment. Demand for capital goods targeting the domestic market will also recover. In line with the increase in capital stock and their operating rate, employment will also increase. If innovative investment increases, the growing trend in the vintage will level out, and the rate of productivity growth will be higher. Circular relations among the three regimes will be restored.

Money wages should be raised equally for the workers of all industrial sectors. Corporations with a higher-than-average rate of productivity increase can realize relatively high profits and use those internal funds to expand production capacity. Or, they can decrease their product prices and increase their sales. On the other hand, corporations with a lower-than-average rate of productivity will be urged to increase their productivity, and if they fail, they will be forced to exit from the market. If poorly managed corporations are allowed to depend on low-wage non-regular workers to avoid the increase in wage costs, it is nothing more than the payment of social subsidies to inefficient corporations who are supposed to exit from the market. Moreover, those bearing the cost of such subsidies are non-regular workers. The reinstated method of wage determination and dissemination is also the industrial policy that allocates funds to high-productivity sectors.

How can the above-stated method of wage determination be realized? What helped corporations to adopt the low-wage strategy was the socio-institutional framework of the employment regime, i.e. dualism and recent revisions of the worker dispatch law. Therefore, in addition to the raising of minimum wages, I have been advocating for labor law policies for unifying employment forms into regular employment (as well as for diversifying working patterns) (Haga 2013). Under such policies, management organizations and the national center of trade unions should reconstruct the *shunto* method on their own initiative.

One of the cornerstones of the *shunto* method was not to change the competition conditions for each corporation. This was enabled by setting the rate of wage increase for all industries. Thus, it was possible to avoid "co-ordination failure". Currently, the Federation of Economic Organizations is stating that "it is strongly urged that wages be judged solely in line with each corporation's ability to pay", and giving up the role to be taken by the employers' association (Japan Business Federation 2010, p. 68). Currently, "the capital" is certainly overwhelming "the labor", but in reality, "the capital" itself is fragmented and falling into the trap of "co-ordination failure". As long as the institutional framework for reducing wages – the existence of a large number of non-regular workers – is left intact, it is not possible to realize a wage-led and domestic-demand-led capital accumulation regime.[5] What is needed is a "solidaristic wage policy", prioritizing low-wage non-regular workers. Abenomics requests that large corporations raise wages. Even if such a request can be realized, the effects would be limited in eradicating low-wage work.

Unification of employment forms into regular work will stimulate employers to invest in the education and training of workers. Employers have been not only setting wages for regular workers in line with the latter's "employment criteria" in order to obtain their "consent", but also devising various systems for promotion and wage increase, thereby institutionalizing incentives for regular workers to spontaneously improve their skills. In Japan, since the 1970s, a personnel ranking system based on job skills and job experience has been widespread. Linking age and skills improvement, the age-wage curve for regular employees has economic rationality.

However, non-regular workers were not only faced with low wages, but also excluded from investments in education and training. Corporations' organizational capabilities have been deteriorating from the viewpoint of labor as well. According to the Japan Institute of Labour Policy and Training (2010), the top two reasons for "employing short-hour workers – defined as workers whose daily working hours or weekly working days are shorter than normal employees – (multiple answers)" were "relatively low labor costs" and "simple job contents" at 46.2 percent and 41.7 percent, respectively. However the latter reason, "simple job contents", does not mean that these job requirements are unchangeable. Gautie and Schimitt (eds.) (2010), in a joint research project on low-wage jobs in five European countries and the US, indicate that even within industries where the "low-road" employment strategy is prevalent (call centers, food processing, hospitals, hotels, and retail trade), there exist a few successful corporations that are taking "high-road" employment strategies (paying high wages, offering permanent contracts, and providing training) (Gautie and Schmitt [eds.] 2010, Chapter 1). Also, Ton conducted an empirical analysis of retail corporations in the US that are using the "high-road" employment strategy, paying appropriate wages and benefits as well as investing in training, and compared them with those using the "low-road" employment strategy (Ton 2012).

In Japan, businesses with a high share (and a large number) of non-regular workers belong to tertiary industries. As of 2007, while non-regular workers accounted for 35.6 percent (18.94 million persons) in all industries, their share was 52.1 percent (6.22 million) in "wholesale and retail trade, and eating and drinking services", followed by 41.7 percent (2.69 million) in "services not elsewhere classified", and 35.9 percent (1.99 million) in "medical, healthcare, and welfare", which are service industries. Non-regular workers employed in these three industries totaled 10.9 million persons, accounting for 58 percent of the total number of non-regular workers at 18.69 million persons (MHLW (d) 2013, p. 258). It is not true that service industries in the broad sense have limited room for physical productivity increase, and therefore are doomed to transfer wage increment to prices to increase value-added productivity. It is the current institutional framework for Japan's employment regime, not the nature of tertiary industries, which is allowing employers to choose "exit options," i.e. to pay low wages and poor benefits, to offer unstable employment forms, and to avoid investing in training. As demonstrated in European and US cases, the service industries in the broad sense have ample room for productivity increase.[6]

Construction of "inclusiveness"

While failing to act, the government has permitted corporations to adopt a low-wage strategy. This is why the capital accumulation regime is malfunctioning. However, as has been pointed out, it is Japan's welfare state system that has been preventing a situation reminiscent of the Great Depression in the US – a simultaneous spiral reduction in expenditure and production. Cash payments such as pensions and public assistance, and benefits in kind, such as medical services and education, are supporting domestic demand. General governments, including social security funds, are functioning as built-in-stabilizers, thus preventing social conflicts from becoming radicalized.

The above-stated reform in Japan's employment regime is, in fact, a part of the strategy to fulfill the welfare state. Unification of employment forms into regular employment and raising the minimum wage are regarded as not only an institutional transformation of the employment regime into the "inclusive" type, but also as a part of national strategy to enhance the welfare state system.

Conclusion

Triggered by the outbreak of the financial crisis in 1998, as well as its across-the-board influences, the malfunction of the capital accumulation regime is firmly in place. More fundamentally, the malfunction was caused by corporations that chose to adopt low-wage strategies to secure profits while enhancing their price-cutting strategies. Their selection of the "low-road strategy" was enabled by the old and new employment regimes. Abnormalities in the distribution regime due to low wages are causing the demand regime to stagnate, providing an environment for destructive price-cutting competition in macroeconomic aspects, and prompting deflation through reduction of unit labor costs in microeconomic aspects of corporation costs. Herein lays the reason why current deflation is characterized as "wage deflation". Further, abnormalities in the demand regime are causing sluggishness in the investment regime, and keeping the unemployment rate high. Characterized by deflation, the malfunctioning of the capital accumulation regime is the result of the confluence of the government failure and the market failure. The government implemented the employment regime reform that sent the economy in the opposite direction – replacing a stable (rigid) employment relationship with an unstable (flexible) one, and the market adopted the low-wage strategy with the aim of reducing short-term reduction of labor costs. In the midst of the malfunction, corporations are losing their organizational capabilities with respect to fixed capital, as well as labor. Moreover, the reason why fiscal and financial policies have a poor effect on the labor economy can be found in the malfunctioning of the capital accumulation regime. Even when government spending is increased, a multiplier effect is not likely to be realized under the current capital accumulation regime. If absolute values in compensation to employees and operating surplus decline, tax revenue would not increase, resulting only in the expansion of the number of outstanding government bonds. Financial policies of qualitative and quantitative easing are not promising at all, since fixed capital investment is sensitive to interest rates, and the increase in bank lending (and the resultant increase in money supply) is demand-led, not the other way around (Lavoie and Stockhammer [eds.] 2013). Further, as has been pointed out (note 3), prices are determined not through the money supply, but primarily through unit labor costs on the supply side. Therefore, exiting from deflation is impossible.

The malfunctioning of the accumulation regime not only denies macroeconomic policy effects, but is also eroding Japanese society. The number of persons who committed suicide leaped to 30,000-plus in 1998, the year this chapter considers the turning point, from 20,000-plus in previous years, and remained at that level until 2011 (Office for Policy of Suicide Prevention, Cabinet Office, Community Safety Planning Division and Community Safety Bureau, Metropolitan Police Department 2014). While it goes without saying that reasons for committing suicide are multiple, Sawada et al. point out that "results of statistical analysis show that suicide in Japan is linked with socio-economic factors" (Sawada, Ueda and Matsubayashi 2013, p. 61). The low birth rate in Japan is also attributable to multiple factors, but a compelling factor is the low wages for young people. In particular, the low wages are discouraging young workers from getting married, and the percentage of unmarried young people has been increasing. The marriage rate for males in their 20s and 30s whose annual income is less than 3 million yen is about 9 percent, but this figure jumps to about 26 percent for people of the same age group whose annual income is more than 3 million yen and less than 4 million (MHLW (c) 2014, p. 81). This difference in annual income is due to the ratio of non-regular employment among younger age groups. The "relative poverty rate (share of households below the poverty line)" has also been increasing, from 12.0 percent in 1985 to 14.6 percent in 1997, and to 16.9 percent in 2009. And more serious is the "relative poverty rate among children (17 years and younger)", which has been increasing from 10.9 percent to 13.4 percent, and 15.7 percent in respective years. This trend reflects the fact that non-regular work is predominant among female workers, especially female heads of households.

Being supported by the welfare state, Japan's capital accumulation regime is barely avoiding overall collapse of total demand. However, if left this way, it is destined to erode society and gradually decline by itself. We cannot limit the impetus for radical institutional reforms to the Great Depression (which brought about the New Deal policies) and the defeat in WWII (which brought about Japan's postwar reforms). Currently, we are in a transition period where the old social structure is losing its legitimacy and a new one is being sought. The process of seeking a new system will be activated by various social conflicts functioning as triggers. However, the built-in stabilizer of the welfare state is restraining radicalization of such social conflicts and curbing the increasing sense of impending social danger. But the tasks are clear. Through incremental institutional reforms, an "inclusive" employment regime should be realized. Through inducing managements to adopt a wage-increase strategy, we should be able to exit from the malfunction and transfer to a wage-led and domestic-demand-led capital accumulation regime. Such measures are urgently needed to prevent Japanese society from disintegrating.

Notes

1 See Chandler for firms' "organizational capabilities." What determines superiority in market competition on the surface are those organizational capabilities in the deeper layer.
2 Since the rapid economic growth period (1955–1973), Japanese corporations' destructive price competition was developed and maintained under a system of oligopolistic competition. Yasuo Maruyama analyzed and criticized this "excessive competition in the real sense of the term", namely "deficit-making competition as a form of price competition" (Maruyama 1968, p. 15). Such price competition was maintained during the bubble economy. The Bank of Japan Research and Statistics Department, while focusing on the tendential decline in operating income margin, pointed out that "despite various forms of rationalization to cope with the high yen after the Plaza Accord, and despite managerial efforts to produce high-value-added goods and small quantities of various goods, such efforts might not have resulted in increasing profitability in the core business." They attributed such results to the fact that "R&D and depreciation" increased and pushed up the "cost front" while "sales price has been kept rather low" in the "product price front." During the bubble economic period, "improvements in financial balance" were able to cover the "tendential decline of earning capacity (Bank of Japan 1992, pp. 58–59).
3 Herr states that "wages become the nominal anchor for the price level because unit-labour costs in a closed economy represent the most important factor in determining the price level" (Herr 2009, p. 949).
4 Chirinko, while investigating various neoclassical models of fixed capital investment spending and their empirical results, states that "output (or sales) is clearly the dominant determinant of investment spending" (Chirinko 1993, p. 1881).

5 For a large-scale economy such as Japan, a stable capital accumulation regime is wage-led and domestic-demand-led (Lavoie and Stockhammer 2013).
6 Regarding the increase in low-wage jobs in Europe and the US, there are two perspectives: skills mismatch and globalization. The former perspective asserts that, due to the development of information and telecommunication technology, demand for low-skilled jobs has decreased, causing the increase in low-wage jobs. The latter perspective attributes the increase in low-wage jobs to the increase in imports from low-wage developing countries, as well as the increase in overseas direct investments to those countries. However, as was discussed in detail by Gordon, both perspectives tend to understand that the increase in low-wage jobs is an unavoidable phenomenon, but neither of them is supported by empirical evidence (Gordon 1996). In Japan as well, low-wage jobs are increasing in domestic-demand-led service industries, a phenomenon that is due to the employment strategy adopted by management to avoid fostering worker skills.

References

In English

Bank of Japan Research and Statistics Department (August 2000), "Price-Setting Behavior of Japanese Companies – The Results of *Survey of Price-Setting Behavior of Japanese Companies* and Its Analysis" https://www.boj.or.jp/en/research/brp/ron_2000/ron0009b.htm/

Bewley, T. F. (1999) *Why Wages Don't Fall During a Recession* (Cambridge, MA: Harvard University Press).

Bowles, S. (2012) *The New Economics of Inequality and Redistribution* (New York: Cambridge University Press).

Burawoy, M. (1979) *Manufacturing Consent* (Chicago and London: The University of Chicago Press).

——— (2012) "Manufacturing Consent Revisited," La Nouvelle du travail, 1.

Chandler, A. D. (1992) "Organizational Capabilities and the Economic History of the Industrial Enterprise", *Journal of Economic Perspectives*, Vol. 6, No. 3, pp. 79–100.

Chirinko, R. S. (1993) "Business Fixed Investment Spending: Modeling Strategies, Empirical. Results, and Policy Implications", *Journal of Economic Literature*, Vol. XXXI, pp. 1875–1911.

ESRI (Economic and Social Research Institute, Cabinet Office) (a) (2003) *FY2002 Annual Survey of Corporate Behavior.*

——— (b) (2014) *FY2013 Annual Survey of Corporate Behavior.*

Fabiani, S., C. Loupias, F. Martins, and R. Sabbatini (eds.) (2007) *Pricing Decisions in the Euro Area: How Firms Set Prices and Why* (New York: Oxford University Press).

Gautie, J. and J. Schmitt (eds.) (2010) *Low Wage Work in the Wealth World* (New York: Russell Sage Foundation).

Gordon, D. (1996) *Fat and Mean* (New York: Free Press).

Hein, E. and M. Matthias (2012) *Financialization and the Requirements and Potential for Wage-Led Recovery – A review focusing on the G20*, Conditions of Work and Employment Series No. 37 (Geneva: ILO).

Herr, H. (2009) "The Labor Market in a Keynesian Economic Regime: Theoretical debate and empirical findings", *Cambridge Journal of Economics*, Vol. 33, pp. 949–965.

Lavoie, M. and E. Stockhammer (eds.) (2013) *Wage-led Growth: An Equitable Strategy for Economic Recovery* (New York: Palgrave Macmillan and International Labor Organization).

Marx, K. (1976) *Capital*, Volume 1, Pelican edition, p. 503 (London: Penguin Books in association with New Left Review).

Steindle, J. (1983) "J. M. Keynes: Society and the Economist" in F. Vicarelli (ed.) *Keynes's Relevance Today* (London: Macmillan Press) pp. 99–125.

Ton, Z. (2012) "Why 'Good Jobs' Are Good for Retailers", *Harvard Business Review*, January–February, Vol. 90, No.1–2, pp. 124–131.

In Japanese

Bank of Japan Research and Statistics Department (1992) "Keikichoseika Ni Okeru Kigyokoudou [Corporate management trends]" *Nihon Ginkou Geppou* [The Bank of Japan monthly bulletin], November, pp. 35–64.

Cabinet Office (each year) *White Paper on the Economy and Public Finance*.

Deposit Insurance Corporation of Japan 2007 *Heisei Kinyukiki Heno Taio – Yokin Hoken Ha Ikani Taio Shitaka* [Responses to Heisei Financial Crisis: How Deposit Insurance Functioned] Tokyo Kinyuzaiseijijou Kenkyukai.

Development Bank of Japan (each year) *Setsubitoushi Chosa* [Survey on Planned Capital Spending].

Director General for Economic and Fiscal Management, Cabinet Office (2013) *Japanese Economy 2013–14* http://www5.cao.go.jp/keizai3/2013/1225nk/pdf/n13_3_2a.pdf

ESRI (c) (each year) *Kigyoukoudou ni Kansuru Ankeito Chousahoukokusho* [Annual Survey of Corporate Behavior].

——— (d) (each year) *Kokumin Keizai Keisan Nenpou* [Annual Report of National Accounts].

——— (e) (each year) *Minkankigyou Shihon Sutokku Nenpou* [Annual Report on Gross Capital Stock of Private Enterprises].

Haga, K. (2013) "Tohshi to Kinyu – Shihon Chikuseki Rejimu" [Investment and Finance: Capital Accumulation Regime], *Jokyo*, Special issue on Thought and Theory, No. 2, pp. 12–40.

Japan Business Federation (2010) *Keiei Roudou Seisaku Iinkai Houkokusho* [Report of the Committee on Management and Labor Policy] (Tokyo: Keidanren Publishing).

Japan Institute of Labour Policy and Training (2010) *Tanjikan Rodosha Jittai Chosa* [Survey on Short-Hour Workers].

Koike, K. (2005) *Shigoto No Keizaigaku* [Job Economics] (Tokyo, Toyo Keizai, Inc.).

Maruyama, M. (1968) *Nihon No Katokyoso* [Excessive Competition in Japan] (Tokyo: Diamond, Inc.)

MHLW (Ministry of Health, Labour and Welfare) (a) (2012) *Chinginkouzou Kihonchousa (Zenkoku) Kekka no Gaikyou* [Basic Survey on Wage Structure (National): Summary of Report].

——— (b) (2011) *Heisei 22 Nen Kokuminseikatsu Kisochousa no Gaikyo* [Comprehensive Survey of Living Conditions: Summary].

——— (c) (2014) *Kousei Roudou Hakusho* [Annul Health, Welfare and Labour Report].

——— (d) (2013) *Rodou Keizai Hakusho* [White Paper on the Labour Economy].

Office for Policy of Suicide Prevention, Cabinet Office, and Community Safety Planning Division and Community Safety Bureau, Metropolitan Police Department (2014) Status of Suicide in 2013.

Sawada, Y., M. Ueda and T. Matsubayashi (2013) *Jisatsu No Nai Shakai He* [Toward Evidence-Based Suicide Prevention] (Tokyo: Yuhikaku Publishing).

Statistics Bureau, MIC (Ministry of Internal Affairs and Communication) (each year) *Labour Force Survey*, "Results: Detailed Tabulation".

14 Indian capitalism in the global context

Jayati Ghosh

Introduction: situating Asian capitalism

In the past two decades, some developing countries such as the BRICS have emerged as major exporters and importers, as well as new sources of foreign capital flows. This is widely perceived to have significant implications for existing trade structures and patterns, as well as for global power as expressed in other ways. In particular, it means that developing countries have alternative sources of capital inflows, alternative markets other than those in the North, and even alternative channels of migration compared to the past.

A premature celebration of this emergence may not be justified and for some countries could even be described as hubris. This is particularly so if growth expectations continue to rely on a development strategy that is unlikely to deliver sustained growth in the future. There are at least three reasons why the current growth strategy may face constraints: the *impact of financial liberalisation*; the *mercantilist obsession with export-oriented growth* with adverse distributive consequences; and the *inadequate attention to ecological imbalances* that result from the patterns of material expansion. Growth strategies need to change towards models that focus on the potential of domestic and regional markets, not just global markets. This means increasing employment and ensuring that wages increase with productivity, along with improving the viability and incomes of microenterprises and self-employed workers.

In this chapter, I consider the potentialities and limitations of Indian capitalism and the constraints and challenges facing its advancement in a global economy in which there are rapidly changing trajectories, shifts in global power and newly emerging fragilities, as well as new sources of economic dynamism. To begin with, I assess the position of India relative to China in the global economy, as well as the significant differences across the two economies. I note that it is a mistake to club together China and India – they are very different economies with completely varying degrees of both internal strength and external impact. However, currently they do face somewhat similar challenges, albeit of different degrees.

Despite recent economic growth and a contemporary situation in which the Indian economy is seen as potentially stronger and less vulnerable than other newly emerging markets such as Brazil, for example, it is clear that the trajectory of Indian capitalism has indeed rendered its development unbalanced and increasingly fragile. This is largely due to domestic political economy features, most significantly the inability of the state to control the large capitalist class and direct its investments in ways that are beneficial for society or even for capitalist expansion in the medium term. This is reflected in poor state resource mobilization; inadequate spending on infrastructure; excessive costs of development-induced displacement that have created strong social and political tensions and are being increasingly questioned by different institutions and processes within the country; a poor record of employment generation even during phases of rapid expansion of output; increases in asset and income inequality that have become both socially and economically dysfunctional; and very limited improvement in human development indicators.

Despite these limitations, there are still significant possibilities for more sustainable and equitable economic growth processes to emerge, although these require a fundamental shift in power relations and changing balance of class forces, to impose some discipline on the domestic (and global) capitalist class within the country and promote the development of small enterprises that still account for the vast bulk of employment. Paradoxically, the vibrant but chaotic democracy that is often seen as a complication in enabling rapid growth may become an important means of generating more sustainable economic growth based primarily on the home market and on generation of decent work. This makes the nature of Indian economic interaction with global capitalism one that is likely to change in various different ways in the coming decades. Past patterns cannot be assumed to continue, but internal changes will necessarily have a wider impact given the size of India's population and its economy.

China and India in the global economy

In the recent past, there has been much discussion of the possibility that, in the coming years, India's rate of growth of economic activity might actually be higher than that of China. It is not just that the extremely rapid growth of the giant Asian neighbour is slowing down substantially, but also that India's GDP growth is projected to be higher than before.[1] But as it happens, over the past two decades the differential performance of the two economies has been such that – even with the recent slowdown – China is still likely to account for a larger contribution to global GDP growth than India for some time to come, simply because of its much greater size. Figure 14.1 describes the share of China and India in global GDP (according to World Bank estimates). This shows that until the late 1970s, the Indian economy was actually larger in size and accounted for a slightly bigger share of world GDP (although it must be borne in mind that Chinese data for that period are notoriously unreliable).

It was only in 1979 – just after the agricultural reform in China that unleashed the productive forces of the peasantry in the context of a relatively egalitarian countryside – that China overtook India in terms of global income share.

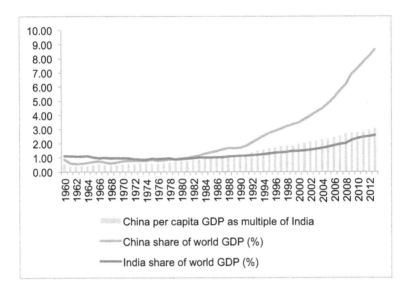

Figure 14.1 China overtook India in terms of share of world GDP at constant 2005 prices only from 1979 onwards

Source: World Bank WDI online, last accessed on 29 March 2015

Thereafter, and particularly in the 2000s, the gap grew by leaps and bounds, to the point that in 2013 the size of the Chinese economy was around 3.3 times that of the Indian economy when measured in terms of US dollars at 2005 prices. This means that, if India is even to equal the output contribution of China in the coming year, its growth rate must exceed three times the growth rate of the Chinese economy.

The difference in GDP growth is also obviously reflected in differences in per capita GDP. Taken once again in terms of 2005 US$ prices, per capita GDP in China was only around half that of India in 1960. China exceeded Indian in per capita GDP only in 1985, but thereafter the divergence was dramatic, because of the combination of faster aggregate output growth and lower population growth in China compared to India. In 2013 Chinese per capita GDP was more than three times that of India.

Clearly, it would be a mistake to group together China and India – they are very different economies with completely different degrees of both internal strength and external impact. It is true, of course, that in the past two or three decades they have both experienced relatively high and sustained rates of growth of aggregate and per capita national income without experiencing any major financial crises as well as substantial reductions in income poverty (much greater in China). Further, they are both seen as heralding a major shift in the international division of labour through changes in their own output and employment patterns: thus China is typically described as becoming the "workshop" or "factory" of the world through the expansion of manufacturing production, and India as becoming the "office" of the world, in particular because of its ability to take advantage of IT-enabled service sector offshoring.

Comparing the economies of China and India

The two economies are fundamentally dissimilar in some important ways. Although there are superficial attributes in common, such as large populations covering substantial geographical areas, regional diversity, relatively high rates of growth over the recent period and so on, the institutional conditions in the two economies remain very different. India was a traditional "mixed" developing economy with significant private sector participation (including a large private corporate sector) from its independence onwards, and even during the "dirigiste" regime the emphasis was mostly on the regulation of private capital. Indeed, one of the problems of the so-called "planned economy" in India was the inability of the state to make the private sector behave in ways that fitted in with the plan allocations of the state, leading to mismatches between production and private demand as well as periodic macroeconomic imbalances. The neo-liberal reforms undertaken in the phase of globalisation have further expanded the scope for private activity and reduced regulation. Essentially, in India, macroeconomic policies have occurred in contexts similar to those in other capitalist economies, where involuntary unemployment is rampant and fiscal and monetary measures have to be used to stimulate effective demand. The inability to undertake land reforms or other strategies that would have involved substantial redistribution of assets not only meant that wealth and income inequalities continued to be very high, but the ability of the Indian state to undertake economic policies that were perceived to go against the interests of the landed and other elites was also affected.

However, China, by contrast, has had a very different economic structure for most of this period, where the basic elements of a command economy have been much more in evidence. The most important difference to be noted here is that the Chinese state after the revolution of 1949 embarked on comprehensive and sweeping land reforms that dramatically altered asset distribution in the country and changed the political economic landscape that determined subsequent policies. While land relations have undergone numerous changes since then, from collectivisation to more dependence upon independent small holder peasantry, the dominance of landlordism was clearly eliminated and greater equality of access to land and other assets also affect the access to other forms of wealth and avenues for economic and social mobility. They also meant that economic policies had very different results from what they would have had in a more economically unequal context.

Even after the quite sweeping economic reforms that have taken place since 1979, state control over macroeconomic balances remains substantial. Furthermore, because of the significance of state-owned enterprises and the Town and

Village Enterprises (TVEs) in total production, the ability of the state to influence aggregate demand does not depend only upon fiscal policy in terms of purely budgetary measures, since many "off-budget" expenditures can be increased or reduced. Further, monetary policy as is generally understood in capitalist economies has very little meaning in China, where private financial activity is limited and state-owned banks still dominate in the provision of credit. Rather, macroeconomic adjustment has typically taken the form of "administrative measures", such as moving to slow down an overheating economy through a squeeze on credit issued to regional and provincial governments and public and private corporations ensured through administrative fiat, rather than the use of specific economic levers. It is true that the Chinese economy is currently in a phase of transition into one where more traditional "capitalist macroeconomics" is applicable. But the Chinese government is able to quickly ensure macroeconomic correction when it is required because that transition is still limited.

The control over the domestic economy in China has been most significant in terms of the financial sector. In India, the financial sector was typical of the "mixed economy", and even bank nationalisation did not lead to comprehensive government control over the financial system; in any case, financial liberalisation over the 1990s has involved a progressive deregulation and further loss of control over financial allocations by the state in India. But the financial system in China still remains heavily under the control of the state, despite recent liberalisation and sale of some shares to foreign investors. Four major public sector banks handle the bulk of the transactions in the economy, and over the past several decades the Chinese authorities have essentially used control over the consequent financial flows to regulate the volume of credit (and therefore mange the economic cycle), as well as to direct credit to priority sectors. Off-budget official finance (called "fund-raising" by firms) has accounted for more than half of capital formation in China even in recent years, and that together with direct budgetary appropriations have determined nearly two-thirds of the level of aggregate investment. The recent trends in expansion of shadow banking have certainly affected real estate investment and some other forms of economic activity, but the basic strength of the banking system and the ability of the Chinese state to rescue it in case of any serious difficulties should not be doubted.

Another difference between the countries has become less evident in recent years – the significantly higher rate of GDP growth in China compared to the more moderate expansion in India. The Chinese economy grew at an average annual rate of nearly 10 per cent for two and a half decades, while India's economy has grown at around 6–8 per cent per year over the same period. Chinese growth has been relatively volatile around this trend, reflecting stop-go cycles of state response to inflation through aggregate credit management. The Indian economy broke from its average post-independence annual rate of around 3 per cent growth to achieve annual rates of more than 5 per cent from the early 1980s. It is only in the most recent period that the Indian economy has apparently grown at rates in excess of 8 per cent per annum, coming close to the Chinese average. The recent slowdown has reduced the rate of expansion to around 6–7 per cent.

The higher output growth in China has essentially occurred because of the much higher rate of investment in China. The investment rate in China (investment as a share of GDP) has fluctuated between 35 and 48 per cent over the past 25 years, compared to 24 to 32 per cent in India (briefly touching higher rates of around 35 per cent). In fact, the aggregate incremental capital-output ratios (ICORs) have been around the same in both economies.[2] Within this, there is the critical role of infrastructure investment, which has averaged nearly 20 per cent of GDP in China compared to around 2 per cent in India from the early 1990s.[3] It is sometimes argued that China can afford to have such a high investment rate because it has attracted so much foreign direct investment (FDI) and is the second largest recipient of FDI in the world at present. But FDI has accounted for only 3–5 per cent of GDP in China since 1990, and at its peak was still only 8 per cent. In the period 2000–07, FDI accounted for only 6 per cent of domestic investment. In fact in recent times, the inflow of capital has not added to the domestic investment rate at all, macroeconomically speaking, but has essentially led to the further accumulation of international reserves, which have been increasing by more than $100 billion per year. Indeed, China's role as a major capital exporter is now well-established and has contributed in no small measure to the changing global balance of power.

In terms of economic diversification and structural change, China has followed what could be described as the classic industrialisation pattern, moving from primary to manufacturing activities in the past 25 years, with associated expansion of services. The manufacturing sector has doubled its share of workforce and tripled its share of output, which, given the size of the Chinese economy and population, has increasingly made China "the workshop of the world". In India, by contrast, the move has been mainly from agriculture to services in share of output, with no substantial increase in manufacturing, and the structure of employment has been stubbornly resistant to change. The share of the primary sector in national income has fallen from 60 per cent in the early 1950s to around 15 per cent in the early 2010s, but the share of the primary sector in employment continues to be well above half, indicating a worrying persistence of low productivity employment for most of the labour force. The higher rates of investment in India over the past two decades have not generated more expansion of industry in terms of share of GDP, but have instead been associated with an apparent explosion in services, that catch-all sector of varying components. The recent expansion of some services employment in India has been at both high and low value-added ends of the services sub-sectors, reflecting both some dynamism and some increase in "refuge" low productivity employment.

Another major difference relates to trade policy and trade patterns. Chinese export growth has been much more rapid, involving aggressive increases in world market shares. This export growth has largely been based on capital relocating to this destination to create global value chains, which has been attracted not only by cheap labour but also by excellent and heavily subsidised infrastructure resulting from the high rate of infrastructure investment. In addition, since the Chinese state has also been keen to provide basic goods in terms of housing, food and cheap transport facilities for registered urban dwellers, this has played an important role in reducing labour costs for employers. India has cheap labour because of low absolute wages, rather than due to public provision and the underwriting of labour costs, and infrastructure development has been minimal. So it is not surprising that it has not really been an attractive location for export-oriented investment, its rate of export growth has been much lower, and exports were not an engine of growth until relatively recently. This difference was also reflected in employment patterns: in China, until the late 1990s, the rapid export growth generated employment which was a net addition to domestic employment, because until WTO accession, China had undertaken much less trade liberalisation than most other developing countries. This is why manufacturing employment grew so rapidly in China – because it was not counterbalanced by major losses of employment through the effects of displacement of domestic industry due to import competition. This is unlike the case in India, where increases in export employment were outweighed by employment losses, especially in small enterprises, because of import competition.

In terms of inequality, in both economies, the recent pattern of growth has been inequitable. In China the spatial inequalities – across regions – have been the sharpest. In India, vertical inequalities and the rural–urban divide have become much more marked. In China, recently, as a response to this, there have been some top-down measures to reduce inequality, for example through changes in tax rates, greater public investment in western and interior regions and improved social security benefits. In India, it is political change through electoral decisions that has forced greater attention to redressing inequalities, though the process is still very incipient.

Despite these very substantial differences, the two economies do face somewhat similar challenges, albeit of different degrees, especially with respect to the sustainability of growth and the emerging inequalities. These concerns actually predate the current global financial crisis and the associated slowdown in many economies, which have obviously also affected growth prospects in China and India. In both countries, the strategy of development had delivered relatively high income growth without commensurate increases in employment, especially in the organised sector; and the bulk of new employment is in lower productivity activities under uncertain and often oppressive conditions. In both countries, the growth has been associated with sharp increases in spatial and vertical inequalities, evidence of greater fragility of incomes among marginalised groups and adverse shifts in certain human development indicators.

In terms of the future prospects, therefore, both economies end up with very similar issues despite their major differences. There are clear questions of sustainability of the current pattern of economic expansion in China, since it is based on a high export–high accumulation model which requires constantly increasing shares of world markets and very high investment rates. Similarly, the hope in some policy quarters in India that IT-enabled services can become the engine of growth for the entire economy is one which raises questions of sustainability, quite apart from questions about whether it will be enough to transform India's huge labour force into higher productivity activities. The issue of sustainability is particularly marked with respect to the impact on the environment – both economies suffer from severe problems of excessive resources extraction and degradation and environmental pollution, which are adversely affecting human welfare as well as the potential for future growth. The most important current problems in the two economies are also rather similar – concerns about financial fragility; imbalances across sectors and regions; growing problems in agriculture; insufficient employment generation compared to the needs of the population; and social tensions arising from popular resentments regarding corruption, concerns about land alienation and significantly increased inequality.

Understanding recent capitalist expansion in India

Until recently, the policy discussion on productive transformation in the BRICS has tended to focus on changes in per capita incomes and the structure of output, rather than on the level and composition of employment. This has been based on two assumptions: that rapid GDP growth will cause increases in aggregate employment; and that this growth will be associated with industrialisation that will cause shifts in the structure of the work force. However, neither of these assumptions can be easily accepted today, even in the more successful countries. Recent patterns of economic growth invalidate the assumption that high output growth automatically translates into rapid employment growth. This runs contrary to traditional theories that have argued that greater economic openness and integration will promote labour-intensive activities in countries with surplus labour. These theories do not take into account forces that affect growth in open economies and cause declining employment elasticities of output (the percentage change in employment associated with a 1 per cent change in output) in manufacturing and other sectors. In extreme cases, improvements in labour productivity can even reduce employment: thus, if the growth of output is slower than the growth of productivity, employment will decline. Across the developing world in the past two decades, employment elasticities of output growth have generally fallen (and in some cases even turned negative) during the years when they have opened their economies to trade and investment, even when they have had relatively rapid output growth.

Growth and structural change in India

Following Kuznets (1966), modern economic growth has generally been seen to be associated with a high rate of structural transformation in the economy, including a shift from agriculture to non-agriculture and subsequently from industry to services, as well as a shift from self-employment to wage employment in companies. Kaldor (1964, 1976) brought in structural change as not only a result of growth, but in effect a cause of it, with the causality running from manufacturing growth to GDP growth, and to growth of labour productivity. In terms of demand, this is because non-agriculture (manufacturing and services) has higher elasticity of demand for its products than agriculture. On the supply side, two processes cause manufacturing to play a special role, even relative to services. The first is Verdoorn's Law, whereby the growth rate of productivity in manufacturing industries rises with the growth rate of manufacturing output (but with a coefficient less than unity, so as to ensure continued employment growth in manufacturing). So productivity growth is higher in manufacturing than in services, and tends to have a greater impact on aggregate output and productivity. A corollary of this is that the growth of manufacturing is faster than that of aggregate output, and therefore the share of manufacturing in output increases. The second process is a Lewisian mechanism of employment growth in industry increasing the rate of productivity growth in other sectors.

Either way, growth and structural change (in terms of the composition of both output and employment) are closely intertwined. Indeed, this is the essential process of development, whereby industrialisation generates not only higher per capita incomes but also less inequality, as noted by Galbraith (2012). However, even a relatively "slow-acting process of structural change" has not always operated in traditional (or even augmented) Kuznets fashion. While the share of agriculture in output has generally tended to decline, this has not always been accompanied by a commensurate decline in employment in agriculture. It is possible to identify five types of economies with varying degrees of structural change and economic transformation, which in turn have implications for poverty reduction: cases where countries have successfully made the transition to manufacturing, such as the East Asian developmental states; cases of high but stalled levels of manufacturing that have produced dualist labour market regimes, as in some countries of Latin America and in South Asia; cases where services drive the current growth path; agrarian low-income economies; and mineral-rich economies. These differing processes can be illustrated with specific examples.

The experience of India is rather different from the more classic cases of industrialisation, such as in South Korea, or even more retarded industrialisation, such as in Mexico. For most of the post-independence period in India, increases in per capita GDP were significantly lower than in South Korea and even Mexico. Per capita income increased relatively slowly until the mid-1990s, and faster thereafter. The share of the primary sector in GDP declined from 55 per cent in 1960 to 21 per cent in 2004, although in a cyclical fashion that reiterated the continued dependence of Indian agriculture on the vagaries of the monsoon. However, employment in the primary sector continued to dominate total employment throughout this period. It hardly changed at all for the first two decades, and over the entire period it declined by only 10 percentage

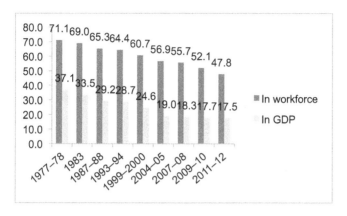

Figure 14.2 Share of agriculture

Source: National Sample Survey Organisation, various large sample rounds and Central Statistical Organisation, National Income Accounts, various issues

points, from 72 per cent in 1960 to 62 per cent in 2004. The share of manufacturing in GDP increased very slowly and was still below one-fifth at the end of the period, suggesting that the Kaldorian process of aggregate output dynamism being generated by this sector has not occurred in India. Further, the share of manufacturing in total employment has barely changed at all, going from 10 per cent to only 12 per cent over this entire period.

The share of agriculture and allied activities in GDP fell from around 55 per cent in 1960–61 to less than 18 per cent in 2011–12, but the share of employment it accounted for declined much more slowly over the entire period, from 72 per cent in 1960–61 to 48 per cent in 2011–12. Figure 14.2 indicates the changes in both of these indicators from 1977–78 onwards. In the past decade, an agrarian crisis across many parts of the country has adversely impacted the livelihood of both cultivators and rural workers, yet the generation of more productive employment outside this sector remains woefully inadequate. The issue of lack of structural change specifically in terms of employment may prove to be the most critical failure of all. The share of manufacturing has stagnated at low levels of both output and employment – in 2011–12 it accounted for only 14.4 per cent of GDP and 12.6 per cent of the work force.

This obviously means that the more recent period of faster growth in India is one that has been dominated by services, which have accounted for nearly 70 per cent of the incremental GDP between 1991 and 2004, and by 2004 employed around one quarter of the work force to produce more than half the GDP. The question of the extent to which this can be called service-led growth is still moot, however. The phenomenon of rapid expansion of the service sector, rather than manufacturing at relatively early stages of development, and the associated "premature de-industrialisation" has been much discussed. Singh and Dasgupta (2005) note that this need not always be a pathological sign, and that the service sector may also play a role as a positive engine of growth through the mechanism of raising productivity because of the rapid technological progress in the "new services". The IT industry in India is cited as an example in this context, as a contrast to the more pathological de-industrialisation that occurred in Latin America in the wake of the Washington Consensus policies that led to the abandonment of industrial policy.

However, Chandrasekhar provides a somewhat different interpretation. He accepts that that services growth, especially that of modern services such as communication services, financial services and IT and IT-enabled services, has not been accompanied by a proportionate growth in employment, reflecting an increase in labour productivity. This makes India's trajectory more acceptable from the productivity angle, even if not the most advantageous from the point of view of unemployed and underemployed workers in a labour-surplus economy. Moreover, technological changes and developments have made a number of services exportable through various modes of supply, including cross-border supply through digital transmission. Thus, in the case of IT and IT-enabled services in India, the expansion of output is driven by the expansion of exports, with positive balance-of-payments implications.

Despite rapid growth, the absolute size of the sector in India remains small, and India remains a small player in the global market. The contribution of the business services sector, which includes both software services and IT-enabled services and is the driver for export-led services growth in India, is even smaller, having risen from 2.6 to 3.3 per cent of GDP between 1985 and 1995, and then to 4.3 per cent in 2005. In fact, the share of business services in total value-added revenues in market-oriented services fell from close to 50 per cent in 1985 to 36 per cent in 2005. This does not suggest that the software and IT-enabled services boom has been the prime driver of growth in India. Rather, the vast mass of differentiated but largely low-productivity unorganized services still accounts for half the GDP and most of the employment in the services sector.

This makes the argument that services are reflective of a new dynamism in India less convincing. Instead, the more recent pattern of growth in India is apparently based on a newly emerging form of dualism. As the manufacturing sector experiences some degree of jobless growth (as companies shed workers to gain cost efficiencies, and automation of menial jobs drives down the need for more workers), IT and IT-enabled services companies are hiring and lever-aging technology to grab the worldwide outsourcing market. India's software thrust of the last decade was essentially export of lower-end software and IT-enabled services facilitated by the availability of cheap skilled labour. So it has been in large part a technology-aided extension of the earlier waves of migration by service-providers of different descriptions: doctors, nurses and blue-collar workers of various kinds. An expansion of that kind cannot be self-sustaining. Further, while this can continue to provide a source of employment for more skilled labour for some time, it still provides employment to less than 1 per cent of the work force, and therefore cannot be seen as any kind of solution to the basic problem of inadequate economic growth and employment in the aggregate. This suggests that genuine structural transformation of an economy still requires industrialisation, and this remains a necessary stage that cannot simply be bypassed.

In that context, clearly the emphasis of the Modi government in India on industrialization is relevant. However, it is in effect a continuation of the existing National Policy on Manufacturing proposed by the former UPA government, albeit publicised with more fanfare. The point is that such industrialization actually requires specific industrial policies, that are often sectorally directed, and cannot rely only on creating a generally "favourable environment" for investors to ensure industrialization. It also typically requires active state engagement with the creation and provision of basic infrastructure, which also cannot be left to market forces or the whims of private investors to be successful. Thus far, there is little evidence of systematic orientation of state policies in this manner.

Patterns of employment

What is particularly surprising in the recent Indian experience is that growth has not been associated with much employment generation, and in fact the employment elasticities of output growth have actually declined as the economy has become more exposed to global competition that was supposed to have favoured more labour-intensive activities. This increase in labour productivity in traded goods sectors is actually a typical feature in several developing countries that have been exposed to external competition, which tends to force or incentivise the adoption of the latest labour-saving technologies being developed in the advanced economies. In addition, a significant part of the increase in GDP has come from services that are not very employment-intensive, such as financial services and telecommunications.

The share of manufacturing in both output and employment has been stubbornly constant at relatively low levels. Low-productivity work continues to dominate in total employment, so in the aggregate there is little evidence of labour moving to higher-productivity activities. Interestingly, this is true across sectors, such that low-productivity employment coexists with some high value-added activities in all of the major sectors, and there are extremely wide variations in productivity across enterprises even within the same sub-sector. The expected formalisation of work and the concentration of workers into large-scale production units have not occurred – rather, there has been widespread persistence of informal employment and increase in self-employment in non-agricultural activities. Most striking of all is that the period of rapid GDP growth has been marked by low and declining work force participation rates for women, in a pattern that is unlike almost any other rapidly growing economy in any phase of history over the past two centuries. Remarkably, these features have persisted through different growth models and policy regimes in the post-independence period, whether Nehruvian mixed economy or open economy market-based strategies, and through varying periods of slow growth, stagnation and rapid growth. The specific concern for our purposes is with the more recent period, when the significantly accelerated expansion of economic activity over the past two decades could have been expected to generate more significant structural changes as well.

The period since the early 1990s has been marked by stagnation of formal employment growth despite accelerated output growth, and lower intensity of employment in the most dynamic manufacturing and services sub-sectors (Kannan and Raveendran 2009, Arora 2010). Even within sectors that are perceived as more dynamic, the majority of workers persist in low-productivity activities, with only a small minority in each sector involved in highly remunerated and high-productivity work (Bairagya 2010). The most rapidly expanding activities in terms of GDP share, such as finance, insurance and real estate (FIRE), IT-related services and telecommunications which together now account for nearly 20 per cent of the GDP, still employ less than 2 per cent of the work force. The persistence of the vast majority of workers in extremely low-productivity activities is therefore evident.

Informal work overwhelmingly dominates total employment. In 2004–05, informal workers were estimated by the National Sample Survey Organisation to account for 96 per cent of all workers, and there is little to suggest that the share of formal work would have increased greatly since then. This is in marked contrast to the experience of China, for example, where the period of rapid growth has been associated not only with industrialisation but particularly the emergence and preponderance of medium- and large-scale units that provide formal employment to workers. The persistence and continued domination of low-productivity work in all the major sectors despite several decades of rapid aggregate income growth suggests a particularly unusual growth pattern in India. The incidence of self-employment (most of it highly fragile and vulnerable) has actually increased as a proportion of non-agricultural work, and the only reason for its overall stagnation is the decline in agricultural employment, particularly in the number of women workers self-employed in agriculture. Meanwhile, the share of the informal sector in GDP has fallen quite sharply during this period of high growth. Indeed, the recent period of most rapid acceleration of national income (NNP) was also the period of sharpest fall in the share of unorganized incomes as shown in Figure 14.3. Thus, while the formal organised sector has substantially increased its share of national income, it has done so without drawing in more workers in the standard Lewisian trajectory that involves a shift of workers from informal to formal activities in the course of development.

Another remarkable feature of the recent economic growth process in India is that, unlike most other cases of rapid economic growth that have been observed historically, recognized work participation rates of women have not only not increased, but have actually declined. This is significant for several reasons. It is now generally accepted that most women work,

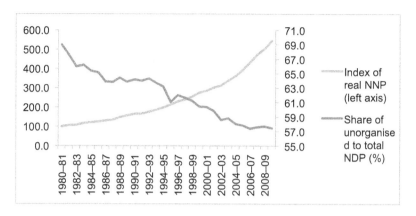

Figure 14.3 Unorganized sector in NDP

Source: Central Statistical Organisation, Government of India, Factor Incomes in India, 2009–10

even when they are not recorded as "workers" by official and other data gatherers. The tasks associated with social reproduction and the care economy are largely (though not solely) borne by women, but in many societies these are not counted among economic or productive activities. Similarly, many women are engaged in what is recognised otherwise as productive work, but as unpaid household helpers who are therefore only marginally seen as workers in their own right. The general invisibility of women's work is itself a mostly accurate reflection of their status in society: where women's official work participation is low, this is typically a sign of less freedom and mobility of women, lower status and lower empowerment. Indeed, where more women are active in the labour market and are employed (especially in formal activities), the share of unpaid work tends to decrease, and even the unpaid labour performed by women is more likely to be recognised and valued. This is why looking at the extent, coverage, conditions and remuneration of women's work is often a useful way of judging the extent to which their broader status in society has improved.

Female work participation rates (WPRs) in India have historically been significantly lower than male rates, and are among the lower rates to be observed even in the developing world (Ghosh 2009). What is more surprising is that despite three decades of relatively rapid GDP growth, these rates have not increased, but have actually fallen in recent times (Himanshu 2011, Srivastava and Srivastava 2010). The gap between male and female WPRs (for the 15+ age group) has grown, as male rates have remained stable and female rates have declined below their already very low levels (Figure 14.4). The decline is particularly sharp for rural women (Figure 14.5). The sharp decline in 2009–10 was dismissed as a statistical aberration when it first emerged in the NSS large

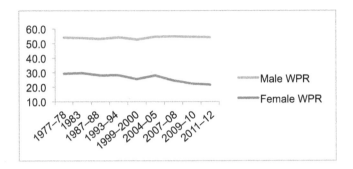

Figure 14.4 All India work participation rates

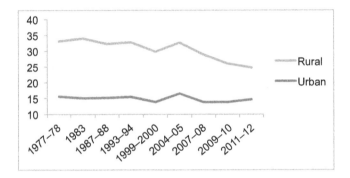

Figure 14.5 Female work participation rates

Source for Figures 14.4 and 14.5: NSSO Surveys of Employment and Unemployment

survey, but the subsequent large survey in 2011–12 has revealed a further decline, implying that there is a real tendency at work that has to be understood and explained. In urban areas, women work participation rates have been very volatile (possibly reflecting the vagaries of the sample survey) but nonetheless over a mildly declining trend.

It is widely believed that the decline in work participation rates is chiefly due to increasing participation in education, which is to be welcomed. It is certainly true that female participation in education has increased in both rural and urban areas, and especially so since 2007. However, this still does not explain fully the total decline in the female labour force, which has been significantly greater (relative to the increase in those engaged in education) in rural India and somewhat greater in urban India. Also, the decline is clearly evident even for the age group 25 to 59 years, where there is little indication of increasing involvement in education. It is worth noting that labour force participation rates (which include workers and those openly unemployed, who are searching for but not finding jobs) closely track the work participation rates, to the point that open unemployment rates of women have been falling because of declining labour force participation.

However, this also stems from the inadequate definition of work, which does not capture the significant amount of unpaid work performed (largely) by women, which is typically socially unrecognised and even invisible. The sample surveys capture some of this and suggest that more than four-fifths of women above the age of 15 years are regularly engaged in such activity, even though less than half of them are counted among "workers". While this both reflects and reinforces women's continued subordinate position in Indian society in general, it also points to another avenue through which Indian capitalism can exploit social conditions to achieve higher rates of surplus extraction.

The political economy of capitalism in India

Accumulation through extraction

These tendencies have been reinforced by the nature of the growth strategy adopted in India over the past two decades (Ghosh and Chandrasekhar 2009). The focus of the Indian state (and of most state forces at the regional level) has been on generating growth through various incentives designed to encourage the expansion of private capital. It is now obvious that this can very quickly become prey to corruption, crony capitalism and the like. But it is possibly less obvious that this strategy in itself generates incentives for such private players that effectively militate against a more broad-based and egalitarian economic expansion. So new forms of capital certainly do emerge and proliferate as a result of this strategy, but they do so in a wider context in which capitalist accumulation is based essentially on extraction: of land and other natural resources, of the labour of differentiated workers, of the products of peasant cultivators and small producers of goods and services. This has reduced the incentives to focus on productivity growth and innovation as routes to more rapid growth, since state-aided primitive accumulation and socially determined extra-economic relationships provide easier and more reliable means of generating private surpluses. All this has actually been reinforced under globalisation, rather than being diminished by external competition.

These transactions in land, labour and product markets are not simply voluntary exchanges between equivalent parties. Instead, the game is played with dice that are heavily loaded in favour of capital, especially large capital, through various means: social institutions that allow for discriminatory labour market practices; legal and regulatory institutions that can be and are mobilised to enhance the bargaining power of capital; and political forces that actively engage in supporting all of these. The process of capitalist accumulation in India has utilised the agency of the state to further the project of primitive accumulation through diverse means (including land use change as well as substantial fiscal transfers) and has also exploited specific sociocultural features, such as caste, community and gender differences, to enable greater labour exploitation and therefore higher surplus generation. These are in turn associated with various other more "purely economic" patterns that pile on the imbalances: financial institutions' input, product markets that do not provide reasonable credit access, and so on.

It has been argued (Harriss-White 2005) that the greater part of the modern Indian economy is implicitly regulated or determined by social institutions derived from "primordial identity" such as gender, caste and community. These interact with political forces, generating forms of patronage, control and clientelism that vary across regions. This makes the outcomes of government strategies, including those connected with liberalisation, privatisation and deregulation, different from those generally expected. Take the large bourgeoisie, for example, which is dominated by diversified joint family enterprises extending across different economic sectors. Even in the phase of globalisation, caste, region and linguistic community have been crucial in shaping these groups, determining their behaviour and influencing their interaction with each other as well as with global capital (Damodaran 2008). The very emergence of such capital has often reflected social forces: for example, there are no major business groups in the North and East that are not from "traditional" business communities, and nationally no Dalit (lowest or Scheduled Caste) business group of significance. Existing practices, such as gender discrimination in property ownership and control, have often been reinforced by corporate behaviour, such as the ability to utilise the existence of legal forms (such as the Hindu Undivided Family form of ownership) that deny any role to women (Das Gupta 2012). These obviously added to the weight of socially discriminatory practices – and they affected how business houses at large and medium levels dealt with more purely economic forces and their attitudes towards investment, employment and output.

Yet it could also be argued that these features of the Indian economic landscape are precisely what have been crucial in generating the recent phase of rapid growth, even as they have allowed the persistence of backwardness and accentuated inequalities in the course of that expansion. The complex nexus between politics and different levels of local, regional and national businesses has allowed for the appropriation of land and other natural resources that has been an integral part of the accumulation story and fed into the way that central and state governments have aided the process of private surplus extraction. More overt economic policies, such as patterns of public spending and taxation, are only one part of this – a substantial part relates to laws, regulations and their implementation (or lack of it) that provide the contours for the expansion of private capital.

These processes of direct and indirect underwriting of the costs of the corporate sector have been greatly assisted by the ability of employers in India to utilise social characteristics to ensure lower wages to certain categories of workers. Caste and other forms of social discrimination have a long tradition in India, and they have interacted with capitalist accumulation to generate peculiar forms of labour market segmentation that are unique to Indian society. Studies (such as Amit Thorat 2010) have found that social categories are strongly correlated with the incidence of poverty and that both occupation and wages differ dramatically across social categories. The National Sample Surveys reveal that the probability of being in a low-wage occupation is significantly higher for Scheduled Tribes (STs), Scheduled Castes (SCs), Muslims and Other Backward Castes (OBCs) in that order, compared to the general "caste Hindu" population. This is only partly because of differences in education and level of skill, which are also important and which in turn reflect the differential provision of education across social categories.

While in many cases class and caste do overlap, the latter always supersedes the former at least in socioeconomic factors. Caste is an extra-economic factor that acts in two forms, inequality of opportunity and inequality of outcome (Vanneman and Dubey 2011). Economic well-being cannot always overturn the inequalities of caste distinction, and that is reflected in the education levels, job opportunities, wage levels, access to social benefits and basic facilities, etc. Caste clearly affects family income, consumption and other parameters, such as education, health, etc. Such caste-based discrimination has operated in both urban and rural labour markets (Desai and Dubey 2010). One study of Delhi (e.g. Banerjee and Knight 1985) found that significant discrimination against Dalit workers operating predominantly through the mechanisms of recruitment and assignment to jobs led to Dalits largely entering poorly paid "dead-end" jobs that are essential but significantly lower-paying. Similarly, empirical studies of caste behaviour in rural India (Ghanshyam Shah et al. 2006, SK Thorat et al. 2009) have found that there are many ways in which caste practices operate to reduce the access of the lower castes to local resources as well as to income-earning opportunities, thereby forcing them to provide their labour at the cheapest possible rates to employers. In addition to the well-known lack of assets, a large number of social practices effectively restrict the economic activity of lower caste and Dalit groups and force them to supply very low-wage labour in harsh and usually precarious conditions. These practices in turn can be used to keep wages of Dalit workers (who are extremely constrained in their choice of occupation) low, even in period of otherwise rising wages. The persistence of such practices and their economic impact even during the period of the Indian economy's much-vaunted dynamic growth has been noted (Human Rights Watch 2007).

Gender-based differences in labour markets and the social attitudes to women's paid and unpaid work are also reflections of this broader tendency. The widespread perception that women's work forms an "addition" to household income, and therefore commands a much lower reservation wage, is common to both private and public employers. So for private employers, women workers within Dalit or other discriminated groups typically receive even lower wages for similar work. In public employment, the use of underpaid women workers receiving well below minimum wages as anganwadi workers (those who work in the crèches financed by the Integrated Child Development Services Scheme for pregnant and lactating mothers and children below three years) or Accredited Social Health Activists (ASHAs) has become institutionalised in the running of several major flagship programmes that are designed to deliver essential public services of health, nutrition, support for early child development and even education. Further, the role played by the unpaid labour of women in contributing not only to social reproduction but also to what would be recognised as productive economic activities in most other societies has been absolutely crucial in enabling this particular accumulation process.

So it may not be surprising that private producers find little value in accumulation strategies that are designed to enable structural transformation. Indeed, such transformation may even be to the detriment of their short term interests, if it reduces their bargaining power. The low tolerance levels of capitalists in India to anything that can even slightly improve the bargaining power of workers is evident in the growing impossibility of forming workers unions in most occupations controlled by the private sector. It is clearly indicated by the ferocious and orchestrated backlash against something as limited as the Mahatma Gandhi National Rural Employment Guarantee Act, which has provided some relief to rural workers who could at last begin to demand wages closer to the legal minimum.

The point to note here is not simply that such practices continue to exist, but that they have become the base on which the economic accumulation process rests. In other words, capitalism in India, especially in its most recent globally integrated variant, has used past and current modes of social discrimination and exclusion to its own benefit, to facilitate the extraction of surplus and ensure greater flexibility and bargaining to employers when dealing with workers (Bairagya 2010). So social categories are not "independent" of the accumulation process – rather, they allow for more surplus extraction, because they reinforce low-employment generating (and therefore persistently low-wage) tendencies of growth. The ability to benefit from socially segmented labour markets in turn has created incentives for absolute surplus value extraction on the basis of suppressing wages of some workers, rather than requiring a focus on relative surplus value extraction resulting from productivity increases. High-productivity enclaves have not generated sufficient demand for additional workers to force an extension of productivity improvement to other activities; instead, the accumulation process has relied indirectly on persistent low wages in supporting activities or on unpaid labour to underwrite the expansion of value added. So the particular (possibly unique) pattern of Indian inequality has led to a long-term growth process that generates further and continued inequality and does not deliver the expected structural change.

The implications of economic openness

The disappointing employment trend can be significantly attributed to the impact of trade liberalisation on the internal pattern of demand for goods and services.

Since the tastes of the elites and middle classes in the emerging world are influenced by the lifestyles in the developed countries, consumption becomes more import-intensive both directly and indirectly. Also, producers in developing countries find that the pressure of external competition in both the export and import sectors requires them to adopt the labour-saving technologies developed in the North advanced economies.

Further, competition in global markets creates pressures to reduce unit labour costs in tradable activities, which can be achieved by raising productivity without a proportionate increase in wages. When living standards do not keep pace with productivity improvements, the growth in output, relative to the growth in productivity, will fall. When an increasing share of output is being produced for export markets, this potential intensifies. Since the goal is not to produce for the domestic market, little is gained by insuring an adequate level of demand at home. If large numbers of countries pursue this strategy simultaneously, as is the case now, we see lacklustre levels of global demand.

Integration into global value chains may not solve the employment problem either, because the global technological trajectory is associated with significant increases in labour productivity and the emergence of global oligopolies earning high profit margins. So when poor countries open their borders to foreign capital and technology, despite their large unemployed reserve and low wages, the technology gap relative to the developed countries shrinks and labour productivity rises due to the use of capital-intensive production technologies. If production is also dominated by a few oligopolistic private producers (whether local or multinational), then one can expect high profit margins, low wages and poor working conditions, as illustrated by the spate of accidents in export-oriented garment industries in Bangladesh and Cambodia.

All global production chains are not the same; therefore, one cannot uncritically encourage integration into them. This is particularly important because of the "downsize and distribute" model that is driving more global production chain investment by multinational corporations (MNCs) to focus on shareholder value. When MNCs outsource to informal producers, there may be gains in price-competitiveness, but these can come at the cost of smaller average firm size and lower potential growth and productivity. In general, high rates of informality drive countries towards the lower, more vulnerable end of global production chains, which may not be desirable. Most crucially, demand matters, size matters – and therefore policy matters crucially, and cannot be unlinked from a broader plan for national development.

Many governments avoid taxing away the surplus profits of MNCs and other large businesses for fear of reducing production incentives. This diminishes the state's capacity to spend either on employment generating projects or on social security. As a result, success on the export front may not ensure employment growth. In the less successful exporters, markets for domestic producers do not grow fast enough to generate sufficient jobs, especially since products using more labour-intensive technologies have to compete with imports.

Consequently, greater economic openness is probably the primary cause of the growing divergence between output and employment growth. In addition, macroeconomic policies that have aimed at restricting domestic demand for stabilisation or adjustment purposes have also had adverse effects (despite the fact that conventional economists applaud the "macroeconomic prudence" of such measures). Local employment generation is inhibited by restrictive monetary policy regimes (e.g. those that target very low rates of inflation and reduce the credit access of small producers) and fiscal discipline through reduced government spending.

Regrettably, public expenditure contraction in the most recent phase of global austerity has been directed not only at the employment-intensive social sectors, such as health and education, but also at spending that directly impacts upon agriculture, which is typically a major source of livelihood.

Conclusion: policies for sustainable industrialisation

The central challenge of the economic development process is to shift the bulk of workers into higher productivity activities that also offer higher remuneration and better working conditions. This requires diversification of production and consumption within the economy. Yet it is detrimental to establish enclaves of high value creation (e.g. export processing zones) that lack strong linkages with the rest of the economy. So basing growth simply on mineral rents and other resource-based or extractive industries is not an optimal strategy. It may generate growth as long as global markets for these products continue to be buoyant, but there will not be significant positive multiplier effects domestically if the surpluses so generated are not ploughed back into investment and if the employment in these sectors does not expand fast enough. So industrialisation is essential, but that too cannot only rely on external markets, even for small economies: without generating synergies that rely on the interaction between domestic production and consumption, it is impossible to have virtuous cycles of expansion that also allow for continuous productivity increases.

Sustainable industrialisation requires industrial policies, supported by trade policies that recognise the specific circumstances and needs of individual countries. There is certainly no "one-size-fits-all" trade policy, and no single trade strategy is optimal for all developing countries over all periods. Trade policy choices depend on the level of development, the size of the domestic and potential external markets, and other factors. Also, trade and industrial policies have to be different from the industrial policies used by countries in the past.

They have to be oriented towards competitive strengths and allow for the development of synergies over time. Consider the case of a poor mineral-exporting country, in which one or a couple of commodity groups account for a very large share of merchandise exports. Depending on the commodities involved, this can increase vulnerability rather than provide the basis for economic diversification, as the country is prone to potentially large fluctuations in demand and prices for those commodities. It is important to avoid dangers such as early exhaustion of non-renewable resources; overvalued exchange rates that undermine the competitiveness of other tradable sectors; and damaging ecological consequences that impinge on the livelihoods of the rest of the population.

In the desired model, therefore, social ownership and the common property nature of resources need to be respected and the proceeds from export success used to strengthen the rest of the economy. Public ownership by a democratically accountable state and taxation of net revenues will finance investment in productivity enhancement and economic diversification and provide for adequate social expenditures. Investment will focus on sectors such as infrastructure, ancillary industries and downstream activities such as processing and development of services that could cater to the local demand generated by the primary activity. In addition, it is crucial to regulate finance to guard against financial fragility and failure and ensure that finance reaches important sectors that would otherwise be bypassed or neglected. The state needs to use the financial system to direct investment to sectors and technologies at appropriate scales of production. Equity investments and directed credit are important instruments in such state-led or state-influenced development trajectories. It is important to nurture and encourage co-operatives, since small and microenterprises are fundamentally unviable in a competitive environment if they cannot utilise technological and organisational economies of scale. In the developed world, recent evidence suggests that, in the current recession, there has been an increase in the numbers of cooperatives being formed. A systematic industrial policy may continue the agricultural development process, which remains important because any process of diversification is unlikely to reduce dependence on agriculture in the short run. Agricultural growth has to be stepped up considerably to make an immediate impact on poverty and unemployment; these problems cannot be rectified in the long run through the "trickle-down" effect of growth in the non-agricultural sectors. Further, the structural change that results from an increase in agricultural growth via an expansion of the domestic market is likely to be broad-based, resistant to external shocks, and employment-intensive in contrast to any structural change produced by an "outward-orientation" of an economy constrained by a limited domestic market. Agricultural growth holds the key to the provision of food security for the domestic population. In an economy with uncertain export prospects, ensuring adequate food availability for the entire population, a crucial objective in itself, necessitates an increase in agricultural production.

It should be immediately evident that such a strategy cannot be fulfilled within the market-oriented neoliberal framework currently adopted by global capitalism and its local variant in India. A major reorientation would be required within the domestic political economy to support such a changed approach, and in addition, global power balances would have to change significantly. Most importantly, the international community would have to support and enable greater national autonomy in various ways, through different international financial architecture and regulations, revised trade rules and investor-friendly economic partnership agreements and reversal of the global privatisation and concentration of knowledge.

Notes

1 Indeed, recent revisions to the National Income Accounts by the Central Statistical Organisation of India CSO's latest revisions to the GDP estimates suggest that the widely noted deceleration of GDP growth in the period 2012 to 2014 was less sharp than has been generally perceived, and that the economy apparently recovered by late 2013.
2 The latest estimates of GDP from the CSO suggest a recent improvement in ICORs for India, but these numbers are still being debated and are currently under review.
3 China Statistical Yearbooks, various years.

References

Arora, Anshika (2010) *"Economic dualism, openness and employment in manufacturing industry in India"*, M. Phil. Thesis, Jawaharlal Nehru University.

Bairagya, Indrajit (2010) "Liberalization, Informal Sector and Formal-Informal Sectors' Relationship: A Study of India", paper presented at *31st General Conference of The International Association for Research in Income and Wealth*, St. Gallen, Switzerland.

Banerjee, Biswajit and J. B. Knight (1985) "Caste-based discrimination in the urban labour market", *Journal of Development Economics* Vol 17, pp. 277–307.

Damodaran, Harish (2008) *India's New Capitalists: Caste, business and industry in a modern nation*, London: Palgrave Macmillan.

Damodaran, Sumangala (2010) "Global Production, Employment Conditions and Decent Work: Evidence from India's Informal sector", *ILO Working Paper.*

Das Gupta, Chirashree (2012) "Gender, property and the institutional basis of tax policy concessions: Investigating the Hindu undivided family", http://www.macroscan.net/index.php?view=search&kwds=Chirashree%20Das%20Gupta

Desai, Sonalde and Amaresh Dubey (2011) "Caste in the 21st Century India, Competing Narratives", *EPW*, Vol XLVI, No. 11, March 2011.

Galbraith, James (2012) *Inequality and Instability: A Study of the World Economy Just Before the Great Crisis*, Oxford: Oxford University Press.

Ghosh, Jayati (2009) *Never Done and Poorly Paid: Women's work in globalising India*, New Delhi: Women Unlimited.

Ghosh, Jayati and C. P. Chandraskhar (2009) "The costs of coupling: The global crisis and the Indian economy", in *Cambridge Journal of Economics* Symposium on the Financial Crisis July 2009, Vol 33, pp. 725–739, doi:10.1093/cje/bep034.

Harriss-White, Barbara (2005) *India's Market Economy*, Delhi: Three Essays Collective.

Himanshu (2011) "Employment trends in India: A re-examination", *Economic and Political Weekly*, Vol XLVI, No 37, September 10.

Human Rights Watch (2007) *India: Hidden Apartheid: Caste discrimination against India's "Untouchables"*, Shadow Report to the UN Committee on the Elimination of Racial Discrimination. http://www.chrgj.org/docs/IndiaCERDShadowReport.pdf

Kaldor, Nicholas (1964) Introduction, in Kaldor, N. *Essays on Economic Policy*, Vol II, London, Duckworth.

Kaldor, Nicholas (1976) "Inflation and Recession in the World Economy", *The Economic Journal*, December, pp. 703–714.

Kannan, K. P. and G Raveendran (2009) "Growth sans employment: A quarter century of jobless growth in Indian organised manufacturing", *Economic and Political Weekly*, 7 March.

Kumar, Anjani, Sant Kumar, Dhiraj K. Singh and Shivjee (2011) "Rural employment diversification in India: Trends, determinants and implications on poverty", *Agricultural Economics Research Review*, Conference Number, Vol. 24, pp. 361–372.

Kuznets, Simon, *Modern Economic Growth: Rate, Structure and Spread*. New Haven and London: Yale University Press, 1966. xvii + 529 pp.

Mukherjee, Avanti (2012) "Exploring inter-state variations of rural women's paid and unpaid work in India", *Indian Journal of Labour Economics*, Vol 55, No 3, July.

National Sample Survey Organisation (2006, 2011, 2013) *Report on Employment and Unemployment in India, 2004–05, 2009–10 and 2011–12*, CSO, Government of India.

Shah, Ghanshyam, Harsh Mander, Sukhdeo Thorat, Satish Deshpande and Amita Baviskar (2006) *Untouchability in Rural India*, New Delhi: Sage Publications.

Singh, Ajit and Sukti Dasgupta (2005) "Will services be the new engine of economic growth in India?" *ESRC Centre for Business Research Working Paper 310*, London: ESRC.

Srivastava, Nisha and Ravi Srivastava (2010) "Women, work and employment outcomes in rural India", *Economic & Political Weekly*, 10 July.

Thorat, Amit (2010) "Ethnicity, caste and religion: Implications for poverty outcomes", *Economic and Political Weekly*, Dec 18.

Thorat, Sukhdeo, Prashant Negi, Motilal Mahamallik and Chittaranjan Senapati (2009) *Dalits in India: Search for a common destiny*, New Delhi: Sage Publications.

Vaaneman, Reeve and Amaresh Dubey (2011) "Horizontal and Vertical Inequalities in India", *Indian Human Development Survey Working Paper No 16*.

15 China in the crash lane

Richard Westra

Introduction

The argument of this chapter is straightforward. In opposition to the neo-liberal-inspired view, codified in the landmark 1993 World Bank publication *The East Asian Miracle*, the meteoric rise in the global economy of East Asia in general, and China in particular, cannot be grasped in terms of a largely endogenous process of social change. That is due to the application of so-called common, market-friendly economic policies operating in what many consider an "appropriate" institutional environment. Nor does this chapter hold what has emerged as the mainstream response to the centrality of "the market" in East Asian development. That is the "statist-institutionalist" position which sees East Asia's rise in the heavy hand of coordinating institutional structures, "governing" the market to propel East Asia into the realm of economic miracles.

Rather, this chapter offers an alternative story line. It maintains that it is momentous exogenous transnational forces to which we must look for the prime explanatory variable in East Asia's "miraculous" development. This is particularly the case for China in its post 1978 "reform" era where neoliberals begin to tout China as the newest "emerging market" model. Moreover, it is argued that, in contrast to other East Asian "miracles" (South Korea and Taiwan), we should not be misled by the "miracle" growth rates posted by China over the past several decades. As will be explained, it is precisely the morphing of transnational forces to which China is most exposed during that time that enforced the decoupling of its growth from development as this has been understood from the inception of capitalism. Specifically, for East Asia, we have in mind here development in the sense of the full-scale industrialization achieved by South Korea and, to a somewhat lesser extent, Taiwan. China will never experience capitalist development along those lines, it is argued. The chapter concludes by showing why, given China's persistence in hitching its future to the destructive, transfigured exogenous transnational economic forces we detail, it finds itself, in fact, staring into the abyss as its economy veers from triumphant neoliberal passing lane into the crash lane.

Take-off on anticommunist steroids

It is worth summarizing earlier work on exogenous transnational forces in East Asian development prior to treating China's post-1978 trajectory (Westra 2006; 2012, chapter 2).

First, Japan is not simply an example of post–World War II (WWII) "miracle" economic growth. Of all the East Asian "miracles", Japan evolved an indigenous capitalist development. Its post-Meiji growth trajectory fits in many ways with the statist understanding of endogenous development which draws empirically upon the historical experience of "late" developers in Western Europe such as Germany. Japan also blazed the trail of Western European economies and the United States (US) in embarking on projects of imperialist territorial aggrandizement. Indeed, as instructed by the latter imperialist stalwarts Britain, France and the US at the apex, coveting imperialist territory at the dawn of the 20th century was accepted as the hallmark of modernity. Therefore, if the post–WWII US occupation of Japan had left it "pastoralized" as was the initial intention of the Supreme Command of Allied Powers (SCAP), Japan would have nevertheless remade itself as a developed capitalist economy, albeit not at the "miraculous" forefront of global market competition.

Second, the "miracle" story begins with US vehement anticommunist policy projections at the onset of the Cold War in Western Europe, coupled with Mao Zedong's peasant army's triumphant march into Beijing in 1949. From that juncture the US fostered the frenetic remaking of Germany and Japan, showering Western Europe with financial largesse, and Japan with cutting edge technologies gratis. The US intention was to create three poles of accumulation based on the newly emergent US consumer capitalist development model (predicated upon multinational corporate automobile and consumer durable production). These "economic nationalist" development projects in effect produced glittering capitalist showcase economies which were expected to promote regional capitalist growth: US itself in the Americas, Germany in Europe and Japan in Asia. As Barry Eichengreen explains, the Marshall Plan in Europe and "Dodge Plan" in Japan "solved the [eternal capitalist development] catch-22 of having to export in order to pay for imports but being unable to produce for export without first importing materials and machinery" (Eichengreen 2007, pp. 65ff).

The US three pole anticommunist showcase world was embedded in a US-brokered international monetary regime or global compact/contract, the Bretton Woods Monetary System (BWMS), which cemented the US dollar as global hub currency: And where the rest of the worlds' money was exchangeable with US dollars, the US kept itself honest by the tethering of the dollar to a fixed rate exchangeability with gold. The whole edifice was then supported with a matrix of ostensibly international institutions: the World Bank (WB), International Monetary Fund (IMF), General Agreement on Tariffs and Trade (GATT), and the United Nations (UN) intended to promote development, ensure monetary/balance-of-payments stability, free trade and world peace.

Third, the dubbing of this edifice "Pax Americana", of course, became one of the times' glaring misnomers. But first, the Korean War, then, shortly after, Vietnam, provided a bonanza of wealth, prosperity, growth and development for East Asia's anticommunist soon-to-be miracles. Inward flows of booty including massive doses of war procurement funds propelled Japan into a sustained boom, with industrial output virtually doubling during the Korean War years alone. With the Vietnam War, the Japanese economy was given a further accelerating boost, both directly and indirectly, as the war brought countries such as Singapore, Thailand, Hong Kong, Malaysia and, of course, South Korea and Taiwan into the East Asian anticommunist capitalist prosperity orbit, with Japan's "embrace" as capitalist-prosperity central. Already in 1949, US State Department policy planner George Kennan envisioned such a state of affairs, noting that the US needed to support Japan resurrecting its "empire to the south" (Wiley 1991, p. 491).

The difference between key Latin American states that foundered on the shoals of import-substitution industrialization (ISI) advance from "middle income trap" to full-scale industrialization and "high income" status is not so-called market-friendly policies. Rather, it is the fact that military and civilian assistance to South Korea alone (strengthened by injections from Japan) between 1946 and 1976 equaled *total* aid to *all* of Latin America and *all* of Africa during the same period (Westra 2006). In the 1960s, US military and civilian booty flooding into Taiwan reached around $345 per capita at a time when Taiwan's per capita GDP was a third of that. The role all this played in capital formation is what allowed South Korea and Taiwan to surmount Eichengreen's development catch-22. And when we add the opening of US and assorted allies' markets to East Asian exports, well, all miracles at bottom have less than miraculous explanations.

Fourth, the paradox of China's rise on the one hand is that only Mao Zedong's socialist revolution and China's subsequent exclusion from so-called comparative advantage–predicated international economic intercourse forestalled what was surely the fate of a country in its predicament. That is, with China's post–WWII abject poverty, legacy of imperialist exploitation, huge subsistence agrarian population, geographic and ethnic division, parasitic landlord/gentry ruling class which was the power base of the corrupt and inept authoritarian Nationalist Party, China would be another Bangladesh today. Instead, neoliberal tales of so-called market-friendly policies as the sole root of spectacular growth are belied by China's socialist experience. During the Mao years, 1952 to 1972, China achieved a decadal growth rate of 64 percent or 34 percent per capita. That is higher than the decadal growth rates of Germany and Japan's late-19th– early-20th–century formative growth spurts; and comparable to that of the Soviet Union during its 1928–58 growth heyday (Meisner 1986, pp. 436–439). On the other hand, as China turned outwards in the world at the outset of the Deng Xiaoping "reform" era, it did so with a healthy disciplined workforce, imbued with industrial skills, and a rate of literacy over two-thirds of its population. Such a literacy rate is extremely high for a low-income country such as

China (Naughton 2007, pp. 81–82). And most crucially, China turned outward in a region economically pumped up on anticommunist steroids, marked furthermore by an advanced network of trading and technology linkages, all of which were intended to contain it with a band of "miracle", showcase capitalist states.

Contagion

Instructively, China commenced its post-Mao transformation with industry value-added equal to 44 percent of GDP in 1980, one of the higher industry-to-GDP ratios in the world at that time (for example South Korea's in that year was 40 percent, India's 24 percent). China's opening to the world economy entailed flows of resources into less energy-intensive light manufactures that were largely low-tech. This bucks the trend of third world, catch-up (ISI) development where the movement of industrialization is from light labor-intensive to heavy capital-intensive industry, a process which across much of the third world beyond East Asia entailed drastically curtailed consumption and mountains of debt. China's "reform" era instead commenced with a rising share of industry in an economy led by expanding light mass production. This initiated a "consumption revolution" based on relatively egalitarian income distribution according to conventional GINI measurement, initially binding production and consumption, and industry and development, in a "virtuous circle" (Lo and Zhang 2011, pp. 43–44; Naughton 2007, pp. 330–333).

As post-Mao reforms gathered momentum, Deng Xiaoping supported the creation of special economic zones (SEZs) in China as "windows to the world" which would help garner foreign exchange that would be put toward purchasing technologies to modernize Chinese industry. The first step was the opening of four SEZs in China's southern coastal provinces of Guangdong and Fujian (setting out Hainan Island as its own province, made five SEZs). They were designed to take advantage of proximity to Hong Kong and, to a lesser extent, Taiwan, which had parlayed export production and opening of export production/processing zones into expansions as formidable trading *entrepôts*. At the outset, SEZs entailed changes in law to permit foreign invested joint ventures. With foreign investment flowing into China, lobbying led to opening a total of 14 coastal city regions (largely in erstwhile imperialist enclaves) to SEZs by 1984. A second phase commenced in 1986. With a further relaxation of restrictions on inward investment, which effectively permitted full foreign ownership, China became ever more attractive as a platform for international business to export to world markets (Breslin 2003).

It was during the second period of China's opening that the stage was set for the ongoing orgy of corruption by Chinese Communist Party (CCP) figures. As assets of the state-owned sector were being "stripped", a "dual-track" price system widely in force from 1985 enabled those with privileged backgrounds and well-oiled connections to the party-state apparatus to garner huge benefits from "buying low and selling high" in consumer and producer goods. And between 1987 and 1992, the same cohort coveted massive tracts of land across China at bargain prices. Asset stripping of the state sector was eagerly supported by military and CCP provincial and local elites. This in turn fostered a spending spree by the now politically *and* economically privileged, on everything from their children's education to travel and entertainment, as well as suburban monster homes and luxury automobiles. May Day celebrations would even been used to bestow medals for "model workers" on the new business barons who were battening on former state property (Hart-Landsberg and Burkett 2005, pp. 54–55, 67).

But even more dramatic transformations unfolded from the onset of the third phase of China's opening. By 1992, initiatives to boost pockets of economic activity centered on market pricing and international investment had exerted sufficient centripetal force across the state sector to largely obviate the socialist planning system. This was broadly accepted when Deng Xiaoping made his celebrated tour of southern China early in the year, visiting SEZs he had authorized a decade prior to proclaim that labeling policies "socialist" or "capitalist" did not matter as long as they promoted development. During the 14th Congress of the CCP held October in 1992, the existence in China of a "socialist market economy" was "officially" endorsed. The proclamation was followed in 1993 by a larger FDI flow into China than in all the preceding reform years (Breslin 2003).

Paradoxically, however, government recognition of "market" predominance in China was accompanied by ever greater central government macroeconomic control, though shorn of socialist planning pretentions (Naughton 2007, pp. 99–103). As a consequence, paralleling the inward FDI deluge was an ensuing spate of investment-led growth. In 1992 and 1993, fixed investment grew at a rate of over 30 percent of GDP (Westra 2012, pp. 153). The emphasis here was on producer goods in support of infrastructure and construction industries.

The fourth phase of China's "reform" development began in 2001. Fixed investment contributed 39.3 percent of GDP growth. Between 1998 and 2002, the value-added share of heavy industry within the industrial sector as a whole rose from 27 percent to 36 percent. The period also brought to a definitive end China's initial reform-induced virtuous circle of relatively egalitarian income distribution, rising household consumption and economic growth. GDP growth outstripped increases in household income, and the GINI coefficient which measures inequality jumped from 0.24 in 1984 to 0.41 in 2000. From there into the fourth phase of China's opening, the GINI worsened to 0.44 in 2003 and 0.46 by 2006 (Zhu and Kotz 2011, pp. 19–21; Lo and Zhang 2011, pp. 49–51).

In quantitative terms, the extent of FDI inflow into China is staggering: from China's opening to the late 1980s it hovered between approximately $1.2 billion to just over $2 billion per year. In 1992, the figure was around $10 billion, and in 1993 it jumped to almost $30 billion. In 1997, as the Asian Crisis struck, FDI inflow into China stood at over $42 billion. By 2003, China received upwards of $50 billion FDI (Dang 2008). In 2007, FDI into China rose to near $75 billion. Then, as the global meltdown commenced in 2008, FDI into China topped $92 billion. It fell slightly in 2009 to around $90 billion, but then through 2010 and 2011, FDI into China again spiked significantly to $105 billion and $116 billion, respectively (US-China Business Council 2012). China, thus, has been the largest recipient of FDI flows to the developing world since 1993 and has vied with the US as the single-most prevalent destination for the bulk of FDI the world over (*China Daily* October 29, 2012).

Of the two lures for FDI in China – investing for domestic market access and FDI directed toward export production – it is the latter which overwhelmingly predominates. When China opened its internal market to foreign capital it did so with an underdeveloped internal infrastructure relative to its geographic expanse, making it nearly impossible to produce in one part of China and sell in the country as a whole. On the other hand, in contrast to the situation holding in China's domestic market, all levels of government in China heavily subsidize the international export economy in core areas of transportation and communications, in particular.

Until 2007, manufacturing in China attracted the greatest share of total inward FDI. During the peak years of 2002–2004, manufacturing FDI accounted for approximately 70 percent of FDI (Economist Intelligence Unit 2012). Nowhere else in the world does FDI in such huge quantities flow into manufacturing. By 2007, then, 94.9 percent of China's export total was composed of manufactured goods. In 2004, close to 70 percent of total FDI went to all foreign-owned subsidiaries. From 1995 to 2004 foreign capital generated 30 percent of China's growth; with foreign capital contributing to a full 40 percent in 2003–2004. The share of China's total exports constituted by foreign invested enterprises (FIE) activities leaped from 1 percent in 1985 to 58 percent in 2005 (Westra 2012, pp. 154–156). One estimate has it that by 2004 foreign capital controlled a full 76.6 percent of Chinese industry as a whole (Cheng 2007). Disaggregating this number, foreign capital controlled the majority of assets in 21 out of 28 of China's leading economic sectors in 2006 (Hart-Landsberg 2011, p. 59).

In high-technology exports like computers, the share produced by all owned foreign businesses continues to grow, increasing from 55 percent in 2002 to 68 percent in 2009. The share of FIEs as a whole in production of high technology exports is approximately 85 percent. Such trends are important in contextualizing the fact of China's emergence in 2006 as the world's number one exporter of high-technology goods, coveting a 16.9 percent global market share (Hart-Landsberg 2013). It is instructive, hence, that during the period 2005–2007 China's export dependence hovered just below 40 percent of GDP, a significantly greater export dependency than South Korea, for example, at any point during its 1982–1996 growth spurt (World Bank 2013a). In addition, while the average share of GDP constituted by private consumption of East Asian miracle economies South Korea and Taiwan ranged between 50 to 60 percent over the course of their launch toward modern development, China's fell from around 50 percent in 1990 to a miserable just over 30 percent in 2004 (Hung 2009, pp. 8–9).

What are the domestic constituents of China's lure for FDI? The first draw, as touched on above, is that when China opened its windows to the world, in contrast with third world countries on the erstwhile US-rebuilt "Free World" membership roster (with comparably low GDP per capita), Maoist policies of primary and secondary education as well as good basic health care for China's vast peasantry offered up to foreign capital a literate and disciplined workforce, topped off by an authoritarian polity ensuring broad social stability.

The second draw was low wages. But it is *not* simply a matter of China's teeming populace and seemingly inexhaustible surplus labor force here: In the move away from agricultural collectivization at the close of the Mao era the state allotted arable farmland on a per capital basis to households through a "responsibility system". Beyond the quota of produce to be delivered to the state, households could utilize the land for their own purposes. Besides the massive boost this gave to agricultural productivity, releasing rural labor en masse from staples production at the outset of China's opening to foreign capital, the guarantee of land to rural households created a fallback subsistence option for off-farm laborers which lowered the cost of labor as it simultaneously rendered part-time and short-term employment contracts palatable to the burgeoning off-farm cohort (Nee and Opper 2012, pp. 161–163).

Superimposed on this arrangement is the *hukou* household registration system, still a feature of China's law to this day. It fosters a social divide in China between "legal" urban resident permit holders and those from registered rural households (somewhat akin to "illegal" migrants from Latin America flooding into US agriculture and meat packing). Rural residents swarming to China's urban centers are excluded from education, health care, housing and state entitlements. Nor can they sell their land or rural homes, ultimately anchoring their and any offspring's future in rural villages. This further represses real wages below subsistence levels and constitutes a de facto subsidy to foreign capital (Standing 2011, pp. 107–108). China's "floating population" was estimated at 211 million in 2009 and projected to grow to 350 million by 2050 if government policy remains unchanged (*China Daily* June 27, 2010). And, as floating migrant workers have no legal right to be in cities, at times of social unrest or economic downturn, they can be evicted at the crack of a whip.

The global take

Besides the anticommunist steroidal pumping up of the EA region, China's economy is a creature of momentous world economic changes from the 1980s which saw the US transubstantiate into what I have referred to as a *global economy* (Westra 2012): dependent upon the world for the array of consumer goods its populace demands and dependent upon the world for capital inflows to sustain its budget and trade deficits, all the while manifesting the world's largest national debt while national savings rates hover near zero. Yet, through the persisting role of the dollar as world money, it has remained as firmly in the global driver seat as it was when it was the world's workshop and creditor! Let us track the changes in the architecture of international production and finance that enable such a feat and look at the way China is ensnared in the web.

Internationalization of production and emergence of an actual international division of labour was an idiosyncratic feature of post-WWII capital accumulation and multinational corporate (MNC) profit strategy. Spearheaded by US MNCs, through the 1950s and '60s, production was internationalized by "tariff jumping" FDI, where MNCs strove to capture markets they might otherwise be excluded from. MNC activities as such supplemented domestic corporate investment and profit-making. By the mid-1970s, with the advanced economies (except Japan) caught in a protracted crisis, MNC international activity commenced a shift from tariff jumping to relocating production and assembly to "export platforms" which serviced global markets. This began a process of advanced economy corporate capital attrition against its unionized domestic labor force and ultimate replacement of domestic production by internationalized outsourcing.

As the 1970s drew to a close, trends in the US economy reached an impasse. US MNCs faced ever increasing competition in the domestic market for consumer durables from powerful MNCs of the core capitalist showcase economies – Germany and Japan. Further, the effects of social wealth thrown at its global military adventures came home to roost, engendering a spiralling inflation that, when paired with US growth travails, produced the phenomenon of *stagflation*. The confluence of the foregoing undermined confidence in the US dollar, which despite the demise of Bretton Woods a decade earlier, had maintained its global status as hub currency.

The crossroads arrived at demanded, in principle, that the US begin taking its domestic medicine to remake its industrial economy and face the mandate of "Free World" institutions World Bank and International Monetary Fund (IMF) to deal with potential alternatives to a "dirty floating" dollar as world money. However, the coming to power of Ronald Reagan signalled the US intention to seek a wholly new international orientation where the US would remain globally paramount notwithstanding abdication of its industrial economy. The key move here was the unilateral raising of interest rates by Federal Reserve (Fed) Chair Paul Volker in 1981 to upwards of 20 percent. Inflation was quashed. And, with the value of the US dollar measured against the value of other currencies exploding by over 50 percent, money streamed into US dollar–denominated assets; this cemented anew the attractiveness of the dollar, backed by Treasury (T-bill) IOUs, as global reserve currency. However, what remained of US civilian manufacturing production would henceforth be largely priced out of foreign markets.

Yet, this did not mean that in any way US MNCs intended to relinquish their commanding position in the US or global economy. Through the 1980s and into the 1990s, US MNCs moved from relocating production and assembly to export platforms toward the wholesale dissembling or *disarticulating* of global production into what has become known in business school circles as "value chains". What the latter concept captures is the fact that MNCs disintegrated and disinternalized production systems, scattering pieces of them across the globe. As a result, it has been estimated that 60 percent of global trade is now constituted by trade in sub-products or components, labelled "intermediate goods" (WTO 2010).

The disintegration of national production systems and disarticulating of manufacturing processes has further brought about a qualitative transformation of the MNC itself. MNCs were remade as "virtual" or "not-at-all-manufacturing" businesses; that is, MNCs became branded monopolists that simply no longer *made anything* (Westra 2009, pp. 138–9). Thus, business school celebrations of "flexibility", with the intimation that MNC deverticalization reinstated markets and invigorated competition, were spurious to say the least. The information and computer technology (ICT) revolution in MNC global *logistics* paralleling the shift to not-at-all-manufacturing ("logistics" being a term co-opted from the military) has empowered MNCs to exercise Stalinist-like centralized suzerainty over vast geospatially dispersed networks of suppliers. The lynchpin of this centralization is the *non-equity mode* (NEM) of MNC global control. NEM operates through the new coterie of aforementioned contract manufacturers, MNCs (most from advanced states) in their own right, that manage the global reassembling and international reverticalization of manufacturing, with the actual business of making things now relegated to suppliers under NEM thumbs. By 2010, NEM control–type businesses employed a global labor force of around 20 million. NEM contract manufacturing accounts for approximately 90 percent of production costs in toys and sporting goods, 80 percent in consumer electronics, and 50 to 60 percent of automotive components worldwide (Hart-Landsberg 2013).

As the scenario of MNC disinternalizing of manufacturing operations and global disarticulation of production played out, manufacturing activity exploded across the third world. By 2000, third world share of global manufacturing value-added rose to 24 percent of the world total. In 2001, the share of manufacturing exports in third world exports as a whole was 70 percent, with the total value of third world manufacturing exports increasing a full four times between 1980 and 2002 (Westra 2012, p. 92). It is no surprise to find developing East Asian economies front and center in the global sea change. The share of global GDP of these economies, including China, of course, rose from below 10 percent in 1980 to over 28 percent by 2010. East Asia's share of global exports also leaped from 8 percent in 1980 to near 26 percent by 2009. But the telling figures here are export dependency predicated upon intermediate goods trade. The region's export/GDP ratio jumped from approximately 15 percent in 1982 to a whopping 45 percent by 2006, significantly outpacing increases in trade by both low- and middle-income developing states in the world as a whole. More dramatically, sub-products comprise over 50 percent of total interregional import/export (figures for the EU 15 and North American Free Trade Area, which includes Mexico, are 22.1 percent and 36.3 percent, respectively).

Of China's imports of manufactures, the share of intermediate goods grew from under 24 percent in 1992–1993 to over 59 percent in 2006–2007 (Hart-Landsberg 2013).

The point to be made is that the current trajectory of manufacturing across the developing world entails a divergent dynamic from that propelling the ISI drive during the post-WWII period. At that time, developing states sought to build wholly integrated industrial structures in the direction of full-scale industrialization, according to the template offered by the advanced economies. This model involved moving "up the ladder" from light through heavy industry toward the consumer durable automobile society. The model is marked by the wholesale shift of populations out of agriculture into manufacturing which, as the production ladder was climbed, fed the virtuous capitalist circle of rising incomes and living standards for workers and the translation of industrialization into growth and the latter into development. However, the model is *only* consummated in the anticommunist capitalist showcases of South Korea, Taiwan (in part) and the anticommunist servicing *entrepôt* city states of Singapore and Hong Kong (in the latter, the daunting task of demoting landed ruling classes and the large-scale shifting of populations from agriculture is never confronted).

From the 1980s, the international dissembling of manufacturing processes along with their geospatial dispersal systematically decouples the foregoing. The figures on the diminution of manufacturing as a percent of total labor force employment among advanced capitalist states – from 37 percent to 50 percent in the 1950–1970 period to below 18 percent at the close of the 20th century, with the US level around 10 percent – are incontrovertible (Feinstein 1999).

In the world as a whole, according to the International Labor Organization (ILO), industrial employment as a percentage of total employment has remained constant at around 21percent since the waning years of the 20th century (ILO 2011). But let us not be fooled! First, this figure is buoyed considerably by ex-Soviet states, including Russia and Ukraine, maintaining industrial systems of a bygone era (which year by year are being increasingly dismantled). Second, among countries that constituted what was dubbed the third world following WWII, *only* in South Korea and Taiwan does the percent of the labor force employed in industry rise (combined with significant diminution of the workforce in agriculture below 10 percent), exhibiting a similar profile to that attained earlier by advanced capitalist states. In China, for example, employment in agriculture remained over 50 percent at the close of the 20th century. Industrial employment (figures include China's massive construction sector) rises from 24 percent at the beginning of the 21st century to a peak of around 28 percent (though as we will see, it is now falling without having reached even lower levels attained by advanced capitalist, anticommunist showcase or ex-Soviet states). However, with employment in agriculture still over 36 percent, and keeping in mind our discussion of the burgeoning floating population and *hukou* system, we already have a *prima facie* case for China representing something radically different from so-called catch-up industrial development (CIA, The World Factbook, various years).

In fact, from the early 21st century, the trend in the world as a whole is no longer a movement of populations from agriculture to industry which marked the capitalist era from its inception. Rather, it is from agriculture to the service sector. And the service sector, across the third world is the domain of exponential increases in so-called vulnerable, informal and contingent employment (Westra 2009, pp. 176–177). Further, the evidence shows that much of the developing world with historically scant levels of manufacturing employment and low per capita GDP is now in the throes of "premature deindustrialization" and will *never* taste capitalist wealth effects enjoyed historically by advanced states and the anticommunist third world showcases that climbed the economic development ladder (Dasgupta and Singh 2006).

Volker's unilateral interest rate hike is crucial here in shattering the third world ISI dream. Much of the dollar liquidity that flooded into the world's financial system through the 1970s was borrowed by ISI states at inflation driven below zero interest rates. Thus, starting with Mexico in the summer of 1982, crises would soon sweep across the developing world. The impact was devastating: as late as 1996 the cumulative output of the third world as a whole still had not recovered to the 1979 level (Duménil and Lévy 2004, pp. 86–88). Further, the structural adjustment programs (SAPs) imposed on an enlarging raft of debt that had besieged states by 1989 cleansed much of the developing world beyond East Asian anticommunist showcases of full scale industrialization pretentions. SAPs were designed to reverse allegedly wrongheaded institutional and policy biases toward industry and reset third world states back on the comparative advantage track as exporters of agricultural products and raw materials. SAPs' domestic "deregulationist" impact was then intensified by global imposition of neoliberal trade "liberalization" dictums. These smashed remaining buttresses that developing world states emplaced to contain global MNC incursions. Therefore, when manufacturing returned, it did so sliced and diced, firmly under MNC global "logistical" control and is preying upon a now permanently fragmented and dispersed global labor force (Westra 2009, pp. 172–173).

Further, the high US interest rates which quashed inflation on the global hub currency compelled other advanced states to follow with interest rate increases. An absurd situation was thus engendered across the advanced capitalist world, where not only were real interest rates over twice the rate of growth of respective national products, but they also exceeded returns on productive investment and rates of profit in the *real* economy. Such conditions then accelerated the transformation of global financial and credit markets. As Elmar Altvater and Kurt Hübner explain, it is not just a question here of bloating debts from the third world crisis or even mounting debt casualties among private and public borrowers in advanced states, all hit by higher interest rate rollovers. On the one hand, the very "dynamic" of debt changes: Credit used for investment in *real* economic activities is repaid out of profits which, if higher than interest rates, leads to debts being paid off. However, as credit is increasingly deployed in debt restructuring or private and government consumption, its avenues of financing are reduced to deductions from current private and government income and/or more debt. On the other hand, the direct exposure of US commercial banks along with other assorted financial intermediaries to third world and other debtors shocked the global financial system into a wholesale transformation of lending through *securitization* with its smorgasbord of new-fangled financial instruments. This places the debt onus squarely on the shoulders of debtors caught between the aforementioned rock of ever narrowing repayment possibilities and hard place of incurring ever more debt (Altvater and Hübner 1989, pp. 59–64).

The concatenation of high interest rates, meagre returns on productive investment and expanding "liberalized" global financial/credit markets, along with spreading "secondary" markets in debt securities, exacerbated tendencies of international capital flow towards short-term, speculative financial arbitrage and away from *real* economic activities. Wall Street, with its sophisticated entrenched financial infrastructure and intricate connection to global financial hubs, emerged as the vortex, drawing in global liquidity only to then dispatch it in casino games. In fact, Wall Street operations constituted a surreptitious industrial policy transforming non-financial MNCs (particularly in the US, where ideology anathema to "big government" policy reigns) into financial arbitragers in their own right. Wall Street created a hothouse for MNC divestiture of "risky" assets such as labor forces and factories, which were often transferred into the hands of NEM-controled contract arrangements. A new metric, so-called shareholder value (market capitalization of businesses calculated by multiplying the total number shares by their price as a ratio of the net worth of a company), was evolved to assess Wall Street "policy" results. It is not surprising that, by 2000, corporate equities in the US would be valued at 45 times that of underlying MNC earnings (Glyn 2007, pp. 56–57).

With commanding business in the US (and elsewhere across the globe under compulsions emanating from the US) no longer in the business of *real* economy profit making, international banking morphed away from the "relationship banking" model which crystallized at the dawn of the capitalist era. A perfect storm of receding *real* investment opportunities for bloating pools of footloose funds, swelling global debt and spreading securitization casino play, based upon financial disintermediation, conjured up a new "originate and distribute" model of banking. Here banks originate loans only to sell them off through securitization, garnering fat fees in the process. The socially redeeming facet of relationship banking is thus removed. Banks evince little interest in the creditworthiness of borrowers or to what end loans might be put as both principal and interest is paid to end buyers of securities, *not* banks. At the end of the day, banking under originate and distribute compulsions gravitates toward a new preferred customer base – the finance, insurance and real estate (FIRE) sector, which had surpassed manufacturing as the largest sector of the US economy by 1986 – and a new modus operandi, asset inflation through debt (Hudson 2012).

The US rode high on the waves of world economic change: The US current account deficit, which bloated through the 1990s into the 21st century as the US abdicated its industrial economy, accounted for around 50 percent of global aggregate current account deficits in 2006, with China instructively accounting for 22 percent of global aggregate current account surpluses (Hart-Landsberg 2013). By 2005, 70 percent of "liberalized" global capital flows was being used to finance the US deficit (Rajan 2005). The US dollar as world money has thus acted as an *auto-financing* mechanism. Countries gain access to dollars by way of externally orienting their economies. They are forced to sell more goods for dollars than they import, or borrow dollars through securitization.

With the dollar as global hub currency, the US budget deficit transmutes into an *auto-borrowing* mechanism. US government spending is increased in a fashion that does not "crowd out" private sector borrowing. Nor is a rise in interest rates compelled, even though US domestic savings hover near zero. Further, the central role of the dollar in international investment makes the dollar the key "traded" currency in "liberalized" world markets. Thus, not only do global foreign exchange reserves spike astronomically since the mid-1990s, but the dollar also consistently composes more than 65 percent of *official* reserves, as many people suspect that, were China's foreign exchange distribution reported and opacity of offshore financial centers factored in, US dollars may actually constitute an even larger proportion of swelling "unallocated" reserves (IMF 2012).

It is important to emphasize that so-called liberalization of finance is not an independent variable. The evidence displays a clear pattern: Wall Street is the main progenitor of the new-fangled securitization instruments and command center for the global financial casino. And whichever parts of the world originate global meltdowns, whether East Asia or the US itself, funds from across the globe flood into US dollar–denominated assets.

Let us bring China back into the mix: The trade deficit with China in 2007 was the biggest the US had with any country. It exploded from $11 billion in 1990 to $274 billion by 2007. In that year, China's share of the US total trade deficit was 32.1 percent. China's trade with the US increasingly shifted to ICT products. These composed 37.6 percent of total US manufactured imports from China in 2005–2006, giving the impression that China was moving up the high-tech ladder. Bilateral and country based figures, however, can be tremendously misleading. As China's share of the US trade deficit exploded, over the same period, Japan's share shrank from 21.1 percent to 10.2 percent and the share of East Asia as a whole (excluding Japan) plummeted 16 percent to 7.9 percent. Hence, while China's trade surplus with the US has bloated, China has been running a trade deficit with East Asia as a whole (Hart-Landsberg 2013).

For economist Richard Duncan, the slicing and dicing of global production along with the routing of global value chains through low-wage China has been central to dampening inflationary pressures in the US economy (and dollarized world economy). These pressures would have otherwise built up as they had in the 1970s, he maintains, due to commodity price inflation (as cost of energy and food affect the consumer price index indirectly) engendered by speculative Wall Street gambits (Duncan 2012). But even accounting for China's cheap labor furnishing of the "American way of life", with US multiple deficits and destruction of its well-paid unionized workforce since the 1980s, we are brought back to the question of the source of US consumption sufficient to foment China's meteorically high growth rates, not to mention much touted pre-meltdown growth in the US itself. The answer is debt. And the evidence is incontrovertible. Spiking from the close of the 1970s to 2007, total US credit market debt skyrocketed from 170 percent of US GDP to 360 percent. Increasing in tandem with the total credit market was US household net worth. Breakdowns of the household sector's assets during the above period show real estate composing 32 percent; equities 25 percent; deposits 9 percent; government and corporate bonds 5 percent; and miscellaneous holdings (pension and retirement funds, etc.). The expansion of credit increased the value of both major household sector assets (real estate and equities). The median price of a single family home in the US more than quadrupled between 1980 and 2007. The Dow Jones Industrial Average surged from 1,000 in 1982 to 14,000 by 2007. Rising asset values ramped up mortgage debt 10 times, in turn fuelling a household spending spree largely financed by using homes as ATMs. The latter phenomenon saw consumer credit increase six times. As US consumption as a proportion of GDP jumped to over 70 percent, US net household debt bloated to 98 percent of US GDP (Duncan 2012, pp. 37–40).

One final matter before we shift to China's current malaise – interest rates. Remember, the 1981 "unilateral" US dollar interest rate hike by then Fed Chair Paul Volker – an increase dubbed a "coup", given the role of the dollar as world money and the extreme nature of the rise – did the initial dirty work in cementing the new US global orientation (Duménil and Lévy 2004, p. 69). By accelerating the disarticulation of "national" production systems and fragmentation of the global labor force (re-concentrating it only under China's low-wage and unique labor market regime), it exorcized the demons of US dollar inflation. High interest rates further contributed to the drift of global finance toward short-term speculation and securitization casino play that ultimately entrenched originate and distribute banking. And the Volker coup drew global wealth into dollar denominated assets, which cemented the T-bill IOU standard of global reserves and reinvigorated the dollar's role as world money.

But, with the world economy dominated by FIRE headquartered on Wall Street, global growth–based asset inflation stimulated by seemingly limitless credit, high interest rates are anathema. Besides US Fed policy, the sheer extent of foreign holdings of US assets, particularly holdings of anticommunist stalwart Japan and ironic progeny China, constitute a major factor. We may note the 2008 positive net international investment position (NIIP) of Japan and China at $2.5 trillion and $1.5 trillion, respectively, is virtually a mirror image of US negative NIIP at minus $3.5 trillion (Deutsche Bank Research 2010). In this way, the dollar as world money allows a monstrous net debtor – the US – to foment an internal expansion unimaginable for any other economy, and Wall Street, which is heir to the global booty the dollar attracts, to impel an external expansion to its, and the US's, benefit. One estimate has the US–China nexus, which we have seen is actually the US–anticommunist showcase EA nexus, dressed in new garb, accounting for more than 60 percent of cumulative growth in global GDP in the period 2002–2007 (Ferguson and Schularick 2007).

Into the crash lane

As the impact of the 2008–2009 US-originated mortgage debt–fuelled bubble reverberated across the globe, advanced-economy governments where banking systems had been most closely bound to Wall Street casino play responded with a flood of liquidity. Running the gamut from "asset" purchases through deposit insurance payouts and debt "guarantees", the rapid money injection to prop up US, UK and EU banks by end of 2009, according to Bank of England's Andrew Haldane, totalled $14 trillion (Alessandri and Haldane 2009). In the US, as the private sector debt which rocket-fuelled US, China and global growth contracted by $3.4 trillion between the end of 2008 and mid-2011, US government debt exploded by $3.9 trillion (with a multiplier effect far exceeding this amount) in an attempt to stave off wholesale depression (Duncan 2012, p. 110). China, with an economy cushioned by a large current account surplus and swelling foreign exchange reserves, nevertheless pumped the equivalent of $570 billion at the end of 2008 into a spate of infrastructure projects, eliciting the refrain "China saved the world" (*Globe and Mail* September 24, 2011).

Why the refrain rings so very true is that behind the direct linkage of US debt–driven consumption serviced by MNC value chains in East Asia directing final assembly through China has been the instigation of a global raw material resource supply boom. This impacted advanced economies like Australia and Canada, as well as so-called developing economies across Latin America and sub-Saharan Africa. The injection into China's economy of an amount equal to 15 percent of its GDP, making it the largest relative economic stimulus of all the meltdown bailouts, was accompanied by government admonition to state banks to ramp up lending. Predictably, China recovered rapidly from the US-originated crisis. The recovery saw fixed investment in China jump to a whopping 46.2 percent of GDP by the end of 2010 (Foster and McChesney 2012). Investment-driven growth in China dampened adverse effects of the 2008–2009 meltdown. And as China's demand for key raw materials increased, even as demand for these elsewhere in the world contracted, it further maintained growth trajectories among resource exporters in Latin America and sub-Saharan Africa (Hart-Landsberg 2013). All told, it is estimated that China's growth contributed over 40 percent of global growth between 2008 and 2010 (Bloomberg View 2011).

This feat has given rise to three interlinked narratives on China's future which dominate mainstream commentary: The first is that of global "rebalancing". Second is "decoupling", where China is slated as the major component in a new engine of global growth built on so-called emerging market BRICS (Brazil, Russia, India and China, with South Africa sometimes added for good measure). The third and most recent is that of "reform". Each narrative harks back to the neoliberal view of endogenous change with which this article began. Let us take them up one by one.

Put starkly, the *rebalancing* narrative forecasts that with the right policy adjustments China will consume in a fashion which induces high domestic growth rates while pulling in US and other advanced-country exports in a fashion which engenders mutual prosperity and remedies the US external deficit. The problems with this view are many. They begin with the fact that China entered the 21st century with per capita GDP significantly below the position from which anticommunist showcases South Korea and Taiwan launched their rapid ascent in the world economy, and light years behind where Japan commenced its meteoric growth trajectory back in 1955 (Glyn 2007, p. 89).

China's much trumpeted current GDP ranks it the second biggest economy in the world. But GDP per capita in US dollars in 2011 was $5,445, placing China just above Jamaica and giving it a middle-income country ranking (World Bank 2013b). Calculated in terms of purchasing power parity (PPP) dollars (a measurement that I would better accept if global public and private debt was settled in PPP "currency"), China's estimated 2012 per capita GDP is $9,100, putting it below Timor-Leste (CIA, The World Factbook 2013). What is significant about GDP per capita is that in the medium term historically, growth in a country with China's profile remains resource-intensive for some time. Certainly, given China's giant global economic footprint along with the size of its recent stimulus, it is to be expected that its impact on global demand continues to be significant. However, even taking account of China's spending flow into services such as education and health care, there is little in the way of direct demand for particular goods and services exported by the US and high-income EU economies. China's total demand in 2008 was equivalent to less than 25 percent of total US and EU consumption (Kaplinski and Farooki 2010).

In fact, in the area of consumer goods, Chinese demand is hardly a replacement for the US. China's consumption by 2010 was but 12.5 percent of US consumption. And the import content of Chinese domestic consumption is but 8 percent, three times less than that of the US (Hart-Landsberg 2013). Further, the nature of that consumption will differ sharply for some time to come from that shaping global value chains. MNCs catering to US consumers structured value chains around things like brand recognition, product diversity, quality control and environmental/energy impacts of production. This fed advances in just-in-time-production, zero inventories, as well as chain and retail logistics. Consumption in China, where 270 million *households* were within the $1,000 to $5,000 total annual income bracket in 2007 and just under 50 million *households* in the $0 to $1,000 total annual income bracket, turns on low-cost, standardized goods and evinces scant concern with quality, pollution or energy intensity which factor into the division of labor constituted by MNCs and NEM contract networks (Kaplinski and Farooki 2010).

On the other hand, advanced-economy consumers cannot be counted on to abet their own recoveries, not to mention China's. Nor does a replacement exist for US consumption. In 2007 and 2008, US household annual consumption averaged around $10 trillion. Household consumption in Japan and Germany during the same period averaged only $2.5 trillion and less than $2 trillion respectively (Hart-Landsberg 2013). By mid-2011, US household debt as a percent of disposable income had only fallen from close to 130 percent to around 110 percent. And even if US households successfully deleverage over the next decade, their spending will be considerably reduced in the absence of the home-ATM connection (McKinsey Global Institute 2012b).

Taking 18 core economies of the OECD, total (gross) debt to GDP ratios jumped from 160 percent to 321 percent between 1980 and 2010. For the private sector and government to reduce debt requires a current account surplus. However, that means China and other developing economies would have to dramatically ramp up imports. That is not in the cards. To deleverage, OECD households must save, which depresses consumption. But it is simply not possible for 41 percent of the world economy to save and pay back debt at the same time. Reducing total debt to approximately 180 percent of GDP, which neoclassical economists see as sustainable for renewed growth (debatably of course), leaves an estimated debt overhang of $11 trillion for the US and €6 trillion for the EU (Boston Consulting Group 2012).

The argument for *decoupling* has two dimensions, one explicit, the other implicit. The explicit dimension treats the global financial flow side of the rebalancing narrative. Its signal question is replacement for the dollar as global hub currency and the T-bill IOU standard of global reserves. But the "dollarized" world economy is the obverse of the US transubstantiation into a *global economy* with its full-spectrum dependence upon the world, yet ability to foment historically unparalleled domestic and international expansions. There does not appear to be much change in the equation. By the end of 2007 China held 20.3 percent of US T-bill IOUs, Japan 24.7 percent. By the end of 2011, China held 23.1 percent, Japan 21.2 percent (Murray and Labonte 2012). By the end of 2012 China's holdings reached $1.155 trillion, Japan $1.131 trillion (*Wall Street Journal* November 16, 2012b). Further, from the end of 2007 through mid-2011, China expanded its foreign exchange reserves to the equivalent of $3.2 trillion (and given China's hefty trade surplus with the US and smaller one with the rest of the world, we can assume between 75 percent and 80 percent of this is dollars). Whatever direction US monetary policy takes, the notion that China could simply divest itself of dollar holdings at will is ludicrous. There is no other debt market as deep and liquid as that of the US. And what currency is available in international markets to purchase all China's dollars (Duncan 2012, pp. 31, 78)?

This story is not about "manipulating" currencies for export gain. Yes, at the outset, the "sterilizing" of dollar export earnings by Japan and later China by respective central bank "dropping" the equivalent in yen or yuan in exporters accounts while either holding the foreign exchange in a "special account" or outside the domestic banking system in dollar-denominated assets kept currency appreciation at bay, to the competitive benefit of Japan and China's exporters. But a new world economic die has now been cast with the US abdicating its industrial economy and transubstantiating into a *global economy* dependent upon the foreign capital inflow.

From when China began to expose the yuan to limited international currency trading in 2005, yuan value rose 33 percent by 2010. As China opened the yuan more to currency market forces in mid-2010, the value of the yuan increased another 10 percent (*Globe and Mail* November 2, 2012). However, China's wages are so much lower than those of other regional exporters like South Korea and Taiwan. It is estimated the yuan could still appreciate 30 percent and not compromise China's relative low wage profile (Hung 2009, p. 10).

With the implicit dimension of the decoupling argument, the intimation is that the rise of so-called BRIC economies led by China (Brazil, Russia, India and China) signals the gestating of a new orientation for the global economy away from the pattern we describe. This is nonsense. From the juncture of the Volker "coup" and onset of global securitization and Wall Street casino play, the world economy has been characterized by burgeoning capital flows into the US and US dollar–denominated assets. This trend was punctuated by brief episodes of capital outflow, such as that preceding the Asian Crisis, only to see monies stream back to the US as the bubbles the flows had fomented burst. What marks the period from the beginning of the 21st century when the acronym BRIC was coined is that, as capital inflow to the US and dollar-denominated assets spiked, a parallel sustained capital flow to developing, so-called emerging markets occurred. This flow entailed increased volumes of securitized "lending" to private borrowers (upon the shoulders of which the debt onus weighs) not only in resource-exporting Latin America but also in South and East Asia, with a surge in utilization of arcane derivative instruments. When the meltdown hit, the emerging market flow was temporarily halted, as money retreated to the "safety" of dollar holdings (Vasudevan 2009).

The global multiplier effect of China's massive investment spurt, as we have seen, reinvigorated the emerging-market fête as raw-material demand revamped. In 2009, China was the number one or number two trading partner for 78 countries representing 55 percent of global GDP (IMF 2011). As US "quantitative easing" liquidity injections kicked in under largely zero interest rate conditions, speculative flows into developing countries trailing the "real" investments spiked. So potentially destabilizing are these speculative flows that even the IMF inveighed against them while states like Brazil and Thailand enacted capital controls in the form of withholding taxes to forestall rapid outflow (Westra 2012, p. 168). And what about the infrastructure investment in China that sparked the global growth spurt? As put by economist Nouriel Roubini: "There is no rationale for a country at that level of economic development to have not just duplication but triplication of those infrastructure projects" (Reuters.com June 13, 2011).

But it gets worse. While China's capital account is largely closed, preventing the huge destabilizing financial deluge experienced by other emerging markets, it nevertheless is the largest single recipient of capital inflow among these economies (IMF 2011). China is also the major draw of global FDI as noted previously. What that money is doing is of global concern. The answer is real estate. By 2010 China was attracting 23 percent of FDI, as the proportion going to manufacturing continued to fall (Economist Intelligence Unit 2012). Further, the admonition for banks to ramp up lending which accompanied the post-meltdown central government capital injection saw local governments use banks like credit cards. Much of the credit-based largess was funnelled into real estate, as debt in that market leaped as a percent of bank portfolios. In 2010 real estate amounted to 20 percent of all fixed investment. Its demand in 2011 was believed to constitute around 50 percent of that of all the world's key traded commodities and raw materials. When positions of hedge funds and commodity futures traders are factored into the mix, a collapse will be catastrophic (Westra 2012, pp. 170–171).

There is not just the issue of oversupply now, with "China's cities ringed with empty suburbs and skylines littered with half-finished tower blocks" (*Wall Street Journal* November 16, 2012b). A recent estimate of local government debt in China puts it at $3.3 trillion. Total debt in China was calculated as 182 percent of GDP at the end of 2012 (*Wall Street Journal* September 17, 2013). As banks closed direct lending taps, a "shadow finance" sector estimated to be one-third the size of China's banking sector by 2012 spawned to fill the gap, though the evidence is that banks' market shadow finance arrangements, collecting fees along the way (*Wall Street Journal* November 26, 2012). The issue for China, however, is not the amount of debt per se that the above processes have generated. Total credit market debt in China is currently 200 percent of GDP. Rather, it's the *rate* of *private* debt increase. In China this trend is 12 percent over the previous decades' rate, a greater rate of increase than peak levels in the US and Spain in 2007 and 2008, respectively, before their crises hit. According to the IMF, the indication of danger for China is the rapid increase in the ratio of private credit to GDP of 50 percent from 2008, similar to what occurred in the US prior to the meltdown (*Wall Street Journal* February 25, 2013).

The *reform* argument largely recapitulates the previous narratives, suggesting policy remedies we show are at best limp given the dynamics of the world economy. Its most recent nuance runs something like this: China's growing middle class will compel economic and political change in line with historical experience of previous developers. The sad truth of the matter is that China is one of the most unequal societies on earth, in line with the usual suspects in sub-Saharan Africa. Most recent alternative data show inequality worsened considerably from the pre-meltdown period, giving China a GINI measurement not of .46 as we noted for 2006, but a GINI of .61 (*Wall Street Journal* December 10, 2012). China has the world's most billionaires. Recent estimates put their number at 408. US billionaires number *only* 317. China's potential middle class is wedged between the billionaires and 700 million peasants. The middle class is projected to grow from 13.7 million households as of 2010 to 167 million, or 40 percent of the population, by 2020 (*Wall Street Journal* March 7, 2013).

However, the income figures for what constitutes "middle class" mean little on their own when emblems of middle-class life like Starbuck's "grande latte" cost over a dollar more than in Hong Kong. Survey data show more than half of China's working professionals are depressed, suggesting it is Chinese middle-class unhappiness that is "the biggest risk in the world" (*Wall Street Journal* March 7, 2013). No doubt part of such "unhappiness" stems from ever-inflating real estate prices. Buying a condo in Beijing, for example, costs over 20 times an average annual salary as opposed to 8 times in expensive Tokyo (Westra 2012, p. 171).

Talk by China's political class of genuine reform is theater. Of China's 1,024 *über* rich identified by *Hurun's Rich List,* 160 – with a total net worth of $221 billion – have seats in the current CCP Congress and associated bodies. To compare, the combined wealth of *all* 535 members of the US Congress was estimated at *only* between $1.8 billion and $6.5 billion in 2010 (*Wall Street Journal* December 26, 2012). Transparency International ranks China's level of corruption at around that of other BRIC economies. Control by the state of major investment projects, land, and commanding-heights banks feeds corruption by China's elite (*Wall Street Journal* November 16, 2012b).

But what is hastening China's maneuver into the crash lane is the seething discontent throughout the vast expanse of the country. The annual number of mass incidents of protest and social unrest jumped from 50,000 in 2002 to around 80,000 in 2006. In 2010 the number surged to around 180,000 (*Wall Street Journal* November 16, 2012b). What is even more instructive than the number of these incidents is that the central government often tacitly accepts them, for unlike Tiananmen or extreme cases like Tibet and Xinjiang Uygur's, they are directed at local governments. We can suspect that they prove useful to the CCP to keep local and provincial power in check. Remember, less than a century ago, China's provinces were ruled by warlords. Given China's historic divisions this is the most likely scenario to follow its impending economic collapse.

References

Alessandri, Piergiorgio and Andrew Haldane (2009) "Banking on the State", accessed online March 18 2013, http://www.bankofengland.co.uk/publications/Documents/speeches/2009/speech409.pdf

Altvater, Elmar and Kurt Hübner (1989) "The End of the U.S. American Empire?" in Werner Vath (ed.) *Political Regulation in the Great Crisis* (Berlin: Sigma).

Bloomberg View (2011) "China's Fall, Not Rise, Is the Real Global Threat", October 4, http://www.bloomberg.com/news/2011–10–04/china-s-fall-not-its-rise-is-the-real-threat-to-the-global-economy-view.html

Boston Consulting Group (2012) "Collateral Damage: What Next? Where Next? What to Expect and How to Prepare", accessed online March 22 2013, https://www.bcgperspectives.com/Images/Collateral%20Damage_What_Next_Where_Next_Jan_2012_tcm80–94255.pdf

Breslin, Shaun (2003) "Foreign Direct Investment in China: What the Figures Don't Tell Us", paper presented at *Regional Governance: Greater China in the 21st Century,*

Asia-Link Conference, University of Durham, October 24–25, accessed online February 3 2013, http://www2.warwick.ac.uk/fac/soc/pais/people/breslin/research/fdi.pdf

Cheng, Eva (2007) "China: Foreign Capital Controls Three-Quarters of Industry", *Green Left*, accessed online January 21 2013, http://www.greenleft.org.au/node/37577

China Daily (June 27, 2010) "China's 'Floating Population' Exceeds 210m", http://www.chinadaily.com.cn/china/2010–06/27/content_10024861.htm

CIA, The World Factbook (2013) https://www.cia.gov/library/publications/the-world-factbook/

China Daily (October 29, 2012) "China Passes US as Top FDI Destination", http://www.chinadaily.com.cn/business/2012–10/29/content_15854372.htm

Dang, Xiaobao (2008) "Foreign Direct Investment in China", a Report submitted in partial fulfilment of the requirements for the degree Master of Arts, Department of Economics, College of Arts and Sciences, Kansas State University, Manhattan, Kansas.

Dasgupta, Sukti and Ajit Singh (2006) "Manufacturing, Services And Premature Deindustrialization In Developing Countries: A Kaldorian Analysis" 2006/049 (Helsinki: UNU-WIDER).

Deutsche Bank Research (2010) "BRICs as Emerging International Financial Powers", accessed online March 18 2013, http://www.dbresearch.com/PROD/DBR_INTERNET_EN-PROD/PROD0000000000253249.PDF

Duménil, Gérard and Dominique Lévy (2004) *Capital Resurgent: The Roots of the Neoliberal Revolution* (Cambridge, MA: Harvard University Press).

Duncan, Richard (2012) *The New Depression: The Breakdown of the Paper Money Economy* (Singapore: John Wiley & Sons).

Economist Intelligence Unit (2012) "Serve the People: The New Landscape of Foreign Investment in China", http://www.eiu.com/

Eichengreen, Barry (2007) *The European Economy since 1945: Coordinated Capitalism and Beyond* (Princeton, NJ: Princeton University Press).

Feinstein, Charles (1999) "Structural Change in the Developed Countries During the Twentieth Century", *Oxford Review of Economic Policy*, 15, 4.

Ferguson, Niall and Moritz Schularick (2007) "'Chimerica' and the Global Asset Market Boom", *International Finance*, 10, 3.

Foster, John Bellamy and Robert W. McChesney (2012) "The Global Stagnation and China", *Monthly Review*, 63, 9.

Globe and Mail (September 24, 2011) "Can China Save the World Again?" http://www.theglobeandmail.com/report-on-business/international-business/can-china-save-the-world-again/article557723/

Globe and Mail (November 2, 2012) "Romney's Belief Aside, China is No Currency Manipulator", http://www.theglobeandmail.com/globe-investor/markets/romneys-belief-aside-china-is-no-currency-manipulator/article4890904/

Glyn, Andrew (2007) *Capitalism Unleashed: Finance Globalization and Welfare* (Oxford: Oxford University Press).

Hart-Landsberg, Martin (2011) "The Chinese Reform Experience: A Critical Assessment", *Review of Radical Political Economics*, 43, 1.

Hart-Landsberg, Martin (2013) *Capitalist Globalization: Consequences, Resistance, and Alternatives* (New York: Monthly Review Press).

Hart-Landsberg, Martin and Paul Burkett (2005) *China and Socialism: Market Reforms and Class Struggle* (New York: Monthly Review Press).

Hudson, Michael (2012) "Banking Wasn't Meant to Be Like This", January 27, http://michael-hudson.com/2012/01/banking-wasnt-meant-to-be-like-this/

Hung, Ho-Fung (2009) "Introduction: The Three Transformations of Global Capitalism", in Ho-Fung Hung (ed.), *China and the Transformation of Global Capitalism* (Baltimore, MD: Johns Hopkins University Press).

ILO (2011) *Global Employment Trends 2011* (Geneva: International Labor Office).

IMF (2011) "People's Republic of China: Spillover Report for the 2011 Article IV Consultation and Selected Issues. IMF Country Report No. 11/193", accessed online March 24, 2013, http://www.imf.org/external/pubs/ft/scr/2011/cr11193.pdf

IMF (2012) "Currency Composition of Official Foreign Exchange Reserves (COFER)", http://www.imf.org/external/np/sta/cofer/eng/cofer.pdf

Lo, Dic and Yu Zhang (2011) "Making Sense of China's Economic Transformation", *Review of Radical Political Economics*, 43, 1.

Kaplinski, Raphael and Masuma Farooki (2010) "Global Value Chains, the Crisis, and the Shift of Markets from North to South", in Olivier Cattaneo, Gary Gereffi and Cornelia Staritz (eds.) *Global Value Chains in a Postcrisis World* (Washington, DC: International Bank for Reconstruction and Development/World Bank), http://elibrary.worldbank.org/content/book/9780821384992

McKinsey Global Institute (2012b) "Debt and Deleveraging: Uneven Progress on the Path to Growth", accessed online March 22 2013, http://www.mckinsey.com/insights/global_capital_markets/uneven_progress_on_the_path_to_growth

Meisner, Maurice (1986) *Mao's China and After: A History of the People's Republic* (New York: The Free Press).

Murray, Justin and Marc Labonte (2012) "Foreign Holdings of Federal Debt", Congressional Research Service, http://www.fas.org/sgp/crs/misc/RS22331.pdf

Naughton, Barry (2007) *The Chinese Economy: Transitions and Growth* (Cambridge: MIT Press).

Nee, Victor and Sonia Opper (2012). *Capitalism from Below: Markets and Institutional Change in China* (Cambridge, MA: Harvard University Press).

Rajan, Raghuram G. (2005) "Global Imbalances – An Assessment", http://www.imf.org/external/np/speeches/2005/102505.htm

Reuters.com (June 13, 2011) "'Meaningful Probability' of Hard Landing in China", http://www.reuters.com/article/2011/06/13/us-roubini-idUSTRE75C1OF201 10613

Standing, Guy (2011) *The Precariat: The New Dangerous Class* (New York: Bloomsbury Academic).

US-China Business Council (2012) "Foreign Direct Investment in China", accessed online December 10, https://www.uschina.org/statistics/fdi_cumulative.html

Vasudevan, Ramaa (2009) "Dollar Hegemony, Financialization, and the Credit Crisis", *Review of Radical Political Economics*, 41, 3.

Wall Street Journal (November 16, 2012b) "Charting China's Economy: 10 Years Under Hu", http://blogs.wsj.com/chinarealtime/2012/11/16/charting-chinas-economy-10-years-under-hu-jintao/

Wall Street Journal (November 26, 2012) "In China, Hidden Risk of 'Shadow Finance'", http://online.wsj.com/article/SB10001424127887324712504578133053914208788.html

Wall Street Journal (December 10, 2012) "Charting China's Family Value", http://blogs.wsj.com/chinarealtime/2012/12/10/perception-vs-reality-charting-chinas-family-value/

Wall Street Journal (December 29, 2012) "Defying Mao, Rich Chinese Crash the Communist Party", http://www.wsj.com/articles/SB10001424127887323723104578187360101389762

Wall Street Journal (February 25, 2013) "China Has Its Own Debt Bomb", http://online.wsj.com/article/SB10001424127887324338604578325962705788582.html

Wall Street Journal (March 7 2013) "An Unhappy Middle in the Middle Kingdom", http://www.wsj.com/articles/SB1000142412788732362880457834534220152496 4

Wall Street Journal (September 17, 2013) "Researcher Puts China's Local Government Debt at \$3.3 Trillion", http://www.wsj.com/articles/SB100014241278887324665604579080683134844374

Westra, Richard (2006) "The Capitalist Stage of Consumerism and South Korean Development", *Journal of Contemporary Asia*, 36, 1.

Westra, Richard (2009) *Political Economy and Globalization* [Frontiers of Political Economy Series] (London: Routledge).

Westra, Richard (2012) *The Evil Axis of Finance: The US-Japan-China Stranglehold on the Global Future* (Atlanta, GA: Clarity Press).

Wiley, Peter Booth (1991) *Yankees in the Land of the Gods: Commodore Perry and the Opening of Japan* (New York: Penguin Books).

World Bank (2013a) "Data: Exports of Goods and Services" (% of GDP), http://data.worldbank.org/indicator/NE.EXP.GNFS.ZS

World Bank (2013b) "Data: GDP per Capita" (current US\$), http://data.worldbank.org/indicator/NY.GDP.PCAP.CD

WTO (2010) "Timeliness and Contract Enforceability in Intermediate Goods Trade", Staff Working Paper ERSD-2010-14, https://www.wto.org/english/res_e/reser_e/ersd201014_e.pdf

Zhu, Andong and David M. Kotz (2011) "The Dependence of China's Economic Growth on Exports and Investment", *Review of Radical Political Economics*, 43, 1.

Index